HEILUNGKIANG

Amur

River

Harbin

MANCHURIA

LIAONING

KIRIN

Vladivostok

A

JEHOL

CHAHAR

Mukden

SUIYUAN

MONGOLIA

Kalgan

Peking

Tientsin

Dairen

Chefoo

HOPEI

Taiyuan

Tsinan

SHANSI

SHANTUNG

Tsingtao

River

Yellow

SHENSI

Kaifeng

KIANGSU

HONAN

Sian

Nanking

ANHWEI

Shanghai

AN

HUPEI

River

hsien

Ichang

Hankow

Kuling

Fengtu

CHEKIANG

Nanchang

KIANGSI

Wenchow

Changsha

CHOW

HUNAN

Foochow

weiyang

FUKIEN

Kweilin

Amoy

TAIWAN

KWANGSI

KWANGTUNG

Canton

Swatow

Hong Kong

Macao

Pacific   Ocean

RYUKYU ISLANDS

Haiphong

HAINAN

A

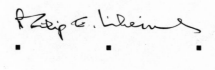

■   ■   ■

Book

The Philip E. Lilienthal imprint
honors special books
in commemoration of a man whose work
at the University of California Press from 1954 to 1979
was marked by dedication to young authors
and to high standards in the field of Asian Studies.
Friends, family, authors, and foundations have together
endowed the Lilienthal Fund, which enables the Press
to publish under this imprint selected books
in a way that reflects the taste and judgment
of a great and beloved editor.

GOLDEN INCHE*S*

The China Memoir
of Grace Service

EDITED BY JOHN S. SERVICE

一寸光陰一寸金

An inch of time is an inch
of gold.

CHINESE SAYING

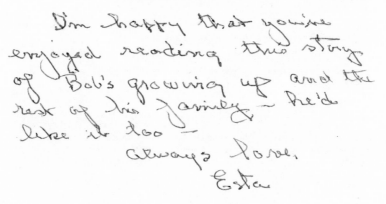

I'm happy that you've
enjoyed reading this story
of Bob's growing up and the
rest of his family — he'd
like it too —
Always love,
Esta

UNIVERSITY OF CALIFORNIA PRESS

Berkeley   Los Angeles   Oxford

Chinese Calligraphy by Robert C. M. Chin.

University of California Press
Berkeley and Los Angeles, California
University of California Press, Ltd.
Oxford, England
© 1989 by
The Regents of the University of California

Library of Congress Cataloging-in-Publication Data

Service, Grace, 1879–1954.
  Golden inches : the China memoir of Grace Service / edited by
John S. Service.
      p.   cm.
  ISBN 0-520-06656-1 (alk. paper)
  1. Service, Grace, 1879–1954.   2. Service, Robert R., 1879–
1935.   3. Missionaries—China—Biography.   4. Missionaries—
United States—Biography.   I. Service, John S., 1909–
II. Title.
BV3427.A1S48   1989
266'.0092'4—dc19
[B]   88-37141
                                                              CIP
Printed in the United States of America
9 8 7 6 5 4 3 2 1

The paper used in this publication meets the minimum
requirements of American National Standard for Information
Sciences—Permanence of Paper for Printed Library Materials,
ANSI Z39.48–1984. ♾

For Bob, my husband
and for Jack
*   for Bob*
*   for Dick, my three sons*

The pioneers do not always go . . . in lust of land; sometimes they go
to satisfy their souls.

William Allen White

In our missionary purpose there was never any thought of a harsh
dogmatism, of forcing our religion down the throats of an unwilling
people. We held no ideas of a narrow orthodoxy of "perishing
millions" who were eternally lost. This I never believed and never
preached at home or abroad. But we were swept into the mid-current
of enthusiasm in the great world crusade of that day. . . . We went not
to destroy but to fulfill, and sought to include each value from the past
in the new order. Just as East and West had inevitably come together
in the economic conditions of trade, we wished to share also the
deepest values of our civilization.

Sherwood Eddy

Memory is the end and the beginning; it outwears beauty and
splendor; it endures beyond sympathy and wit.

Stephen Vincent Benét

Contents

Illustrations

Note on Romanization

Place names are in the old, familiar Chinese Post Office spellings: for instance, Chungking. The traditional Wade-Giles would be Ch'ung-ch'ing; the new, official *pinyin* is Chongqing.

Personal names are in the form best known in each case: for instance, Sun Yat-sen and Chiang Kai-shek.

Chinese words that appear in the text are usually in *pinyin,* which is more phonetic than Wade-Giles: for instance, *bandeng* (bench), which is exactly how it is pronounced; in Wade-Giles it inexplicably becomes *panteng.*

Editor's Foreword

After Grace Service finished her *Golden Inches,* her three sons each received a typewritten copy. Over the years all of us and our wives probably read it more than once. Memories fade: there were always surprises in rereading this "narrative of our early years in China." But it was a family story.

In 1987 I happened to cross paths with John Rawlinson, whose family and mine had been close friends in Shanghai. John, a professor of Chinese history at Hofstra University, mentioned that he was working on a biography of his father, Frank Rawlinson, who had been a leader in the China missionary community and the longtime editor of the *Chinese Recorder* (and was killed by an accidentally dropped Chinese bomb at Shanghai on August 13, 1937). When John heard about *Golden Inches,* he asked to read it for material that might be relevant to his research. After he had read it, John suggested that there was enough history in it to make it of interest to more than just our family. So I discussed the idea, rather tentatively, with James Clark, director of the University of California Press, and he agreed. My first thanks must go to these two men.

Publication, though, presented some problems. Grace had not written with publication in mind. Writing for the family, she assumed a fairly broad knowledge of China and the events taking place there. Some details and anecdotes had interest and significance only to the family. Practical considerations also encouraged occasional abridgment. Chapter divisions were revised and titles added. My editing has, I hope, done no violence to Grace's language and been faithful to her intent. Her original manuscript is available at the Bancroft Library of the University of California.

For occasional details and clarification, I have fortunately been able to refer to the diaries that Grace kept from 1908. Material from the diaries appears in the notes. These diaries are also at the Bancroft Library. I wish to thank James D. Hart, director, and Bonnie Hardwicke, head of the Manuscripts Division at the Bancroft Library, for easing my access to them. At the University of California Press, Betsey Scheiner has been patiently helpful with editorial encouragement and advice, and Gladys Castor has provided the meticulous, considerate copyediting that a manuscript is fortunate to receive. I have also had much help from the rest of my family generation: my wife, Caroline; my brother Bob's widow, Esta; and my brother Dick and his wife, Helen.[1] They have remembered things that I had forgotten or never knew (from the age of eleven I was usually away from the family at boarding school or college). They have read and checked the manuscript and given valuable editorial suggestions. For the notes, I bear sole responsibility; and I apologize for the personal nature of so many of them.

Grace and Bob were both Californians, though both happened to be born while their parents were visiting their old homes "back east" (she in Iowa, he in Michigan). Grace's father was a banker in San Bernardino. Bob's was a rancher near Modesto in the San Joaquin Valley. They were both born in 1879, and both arrived at Berkeley in the fall of 1898 as freshman members of the class of 1902. Both were serious students, both joined fraternities (Kappa Alpha Theta and Psi Upsilon), and both were active in class and campus activities. In addition, Bob was a star track man (mile and half-mile). One activity that may have brought them together was the "Y," much more important on college campuses in those days than today. During their junior year, Grace was treasurer of the Young Women's Christian Association, and Bob president of the Young Men's Christian Association. However it happened, their romance became so well known that it received notice in the university annual, *Blue and Gold,* in both their junior and senior years. The university was of course much smaller then. They knew most of their classmates, and this connection with UC always meant a great deal to them.

Through the YMCA Bob came in contact with the Student Volunteer Movement. The organization was then at the height of its influence and popularity with college students. Perhaps it reflected an expansive, confident, optimistic spirit in America at that time.[2] Its best-known slogan was "The world for Christ in our time." Nondenominational, it recruited for the various mission boards. But the principal leaders of the Student Volunteer Movement—the dynamic, spell-binding John R. Mott and the more intellectual Sherwood Eddy—were also the leaders of the rapidly growing international work of the American YMCA. Not all Student Volunteers felt the call

1. At the back of this book, preceding the glossary, there is a brief identification of the members of the Service family who are prominently mentioned.

2. I think that the spirit of the Student Volunteers is well expressed by the quotation from Sherwood Eddy which Grace selected as one of her epigraphs. It is tempting to see the Student Volunteer Movement as having some benevolent relevance to "Manifest Destiny," an idea that was current at about the same time.

1   *The young man is recognizably Bob; Boggs was Grace's maiden name. (From the 1903* Blue and Gold.*)*

to preach; their goal was the social gospel: to do good and help others, to serve rather than to evangelize. Many of this inclination joined the YMCA; Bob was one of them.[3]

In recent years, there have been attempts to compare the Student Volunteers with our modern Peace Corps. There are obvious parallels: youth, enthusiasm, unselfishness, going to faraway, undeveloped countries, a desire to serve. But there is one very important difference: the Student Volunteers made a life commitment. I am sure that, to a man of his temperament, Bob's feelings of loyalty, obligation, and commitment were not substantially different from those of a man entering the ministry or priesthood.

The Young Men's Christian Association originated in England in about the middle of the nineteenth century. The rapid growth of commercial cities such as Liverpool attracted large numbers of young men from small towns and the countryside for employment as clerks and in other low-level, generally white-collar jobs. These young men usually had some education and came from Christian homes. They were adrift in a strange and not very friendly environment—with temptations too numerous to need description. Their first associations were self-help groups, formed for mutual aid and

3. Grace spoke of herself as also having been a member of the Student Volunteers.

benefit. Since they were already Christians, the emphasis was not on conversion but rather on encouraging continuation in the faith: this meant Bible study groups and prayer meetings. Advancement in employment often depended on training: education became a regular part of the Y program, with an emphasis on practical, vocational courses offered in evening or part-time classes. Wholesome recreation and good health were especially important in their new urban environment: the YMCA became well known for its varied recreational activities and for being a principal sponsor of athletics and physical education. Finally, to round out the complete man, there was the cultural side: the Y usually sponsored debating societies, lectures, musical groups of every kind, drama clubs, and many other activities.[4]

The first Associations in England were a success. The movement spread to the United States, where there was a similar need, and eventually to China and many other countries. The familiar triangle symbol stood for body, mind, and spirit. A common slogan was "service." It was the right spot for Bob, and his enthusiasm for it never flagged. This definition, found in one of his notebooks after his death, may express his ideal: "The Young Men's Christian Association is a fellowship of men and boys, united for mutual help in the development of Christian character, and for comradeship in Christian service."

Bob and Grace went to China at a propitious time for the YMCA in that country. The moribund Ching Empire was reeling from the harsh impact of Western imperialism. There had been a disastrous defeat by Japan in 1895. The country had been in grave peril from the imperialist drive for special rights and concessions in 1898. And the antiforeign folly of the Boxer Uprising in 1900 had brought terms that compromised Chinese sovereignty. The Court had finally conceded the need for change. There was to be an orderly transition to a constitutional monarchy. The old examination system, based on the memorization of the Confucian Classics, was to be replaced by a comprehensive educational system along Western lines. Similarly, many of China's intellectuals had come to realize that the rigid Confucian social order stood in the way of progress and could no longer be preserved unchanged.

There was basis, therefore, for the enthusiastic words of John R. Mott when he formally inducted Grace and Bob into the international work of the Y and told them that China was "on the threshold of vast changes."[5] But China was a huge country, shackled by an old, self-centered tradition, with a recent history of xenophobia and suspicion of everything not Chinese. This was especially true of the interior of the country. Modern changes had so far

---

4. For the history of the YMCA, I am much indebted to Shirley S. Garnett, *Social Reformers in Urban China: The Chinese Y.M.C.A., 1895–1926* (Cambridge: Harvard University Press, 1970).
5. See chapter 1.

begun to affect only the treaty ports along the coast. Chengtu, when Bob and Grace reached there in 1906, was little different in appearance, amenities, and life style from a thousand years before. There had been antiforeign agitation in Szechwan as recently as 1903.[6] To change China was going to be a slower and more difficult process—politically, socially, culturally, and economically—than Dr. Mott and most others anticipated. The travail of that change included the aborted republic, the anarchy and violence of the warlord years, civil war between Right and Left, and Japanese aggression. It was the background of Grace and Bob's life.

The Protestant missions had been in China for almost a hundred years. They hoped to lead this opening toward change in China. But the Chinese had proved remarkably resistant—almost impermeable—to religious conversion. The converts that the missionaries did make were most likely to come from groups low in social status. The new mood of the influential groups in China was for reform, not the radical solution—in fact, a revolution—that the missionaries offered. Some of the mission leaders had recognized the desirability of trying a more flexible, less dogmatic approach. Toward the end of the nineteenth century, several missions had organized local clubs modeled after the YMCA. When the first YMCA men reached China, most of the mission leaders welcomed them and offered cooperation.[7]

On the Chinese side, the YMCA was welcomed from the start. The first Y was established in Tientsin by Willard Lyon in 1895. Dr. Garrett, in her history of the YMCA in China, describes the initial impression:

> To the young Chinese of Tientsin, Lyon and the men who later joined him were like a breath of fresh air. They were well educated, but not scholarly academics like many of the missionaries. They were concerned with moral and spiritual values, but they were not theologians. . . . They were practical businessmen, but not interested in profit for itself. They were pragmatists rather than theoreticians. Their type is familiar in the United States: optimistic, versatile, motivated by a sense of obligation to serve. In our time their spiritual descendants often become members of the Peace Corps, and then, as now, their personal qualities appealed to other young people.[8]

The YMCA quickly adapted its program to Chinese needs and conditions. Foreign business was growing; government offices such as the post office,

---

6. Until we left Chengtu (in 1921) it was normal, whenever we passed through the streets and especially when we were traveling through villages, for Chinese children to come running with shouts of "foreign devil" (*yang guizi*). They were not, however, unfriendly; it was merely the only name for foreigners that they had learned from their elders.

7. When Bob arrived in Chengtu, a member of the English Friends' Mission had already been assigned to help him in opening the YMCA. Later, a member of the Canadian Methodist Mission (Bert Brace) was loaned to the Chengtu Y.

8. Garrett, *Social Reformers,* p. 56.

customs, and telegraphs were expanding; there was a great demand for English and business courses. There was much interest in science and in almost anything from the West. Local problems needed attention: opium smoking, foot binding, public health, illiteracy (Jimmy Yen's Mass Education Movement had its origin in the Y). One did not need to be a Christian to join and participate: all were welcome. From the start, the aim was to build an indigenous movement, with local community support and leadership.

In this favorable climate the YMCA prospered prodigiously. When Bob came on the field in 1905, there were Associations only in Tientsin and Shanghai. By 1922 there were thirty-six city Associations and two hundred student Associations. There were approximately one hundred foreign secretaries, who usually provided the initiating and guiding hand, but they were outnumbered more than four to one by Chinese secretaries. Modern universities were developing, but the student community was not yet very large. The YMCA reached a large proportion of this group. One activity that may have been particularly effective was YMCA work in Japan with the thousands of young Chinese students who flocked there to study. One result was that, from the 1911 Revolution through the Kuomintang years (1927–49), a large number of government officials and men of influence in China (except for military men) had had some association with the YMCA.[9] Ever since the arrival of the first Catholic missionaries in the sixteenth century, the great—but unrealized—missionary goal had been to win influence with China's most prestigious group, the literati. By its work with the students and intellectuals—China's new literati—the YMCA, in a sense, achieved this success.

Things went very well for the Y in China until about 1925. Then, the reorganization of Sun Yat-sen's Kuomintang with Russian help and advice, and the first United Front of Kuomintang and Communist parties, turned the country toward anti-imperialism and an active effort to regain the full sovereignty that had been infringed by the unequal treaties. Episodes like the May Thirtieth Incident, where Shanghai municipal police shot down unarmed demonstrators, fed the nationalistic fervor. The mood of the country shifted from reform to revolution. Many of the Y leaders were sympathetic to the nationalistic goals. But much of the Y's financial support came from the Chinese business community, many of whom abhorred radicalism and feared the Communist influence in the United Front. The Chinese Y temporized. It announced that it was not a political organization and tried to be neutral.

9. It was not only supporters of the Kuomintang who used the YMCA. When I went to Yenan in 1944 and first met Chen Yi, then head of the Communist New Fourth Army and later foreign minister, I was surprised to have him greet me enthusiastically as "the son of his old teacher." In his youth he had been a patron of the Y in Chengtu and taken some of the courses offered.

Attacked by the Left, it stayed in business, but its days of exuberant growth were over.

At about the same time, support from America began to diminish. Perhaps an aggressively nationalistic, antiforeign China was no longer so attractive to American donors. But even more important was the Great Depression. There were so many desperate needs for charity at home that little was left for foreign requests. The catastrophic reduction of its income forced the International Committee, over several years as the Depression deepened, to greatly reduce its staff in China.

Any narrative of thirty years cannot include everything; there has to be some selection. For instance, readers may note that Grace, though a missionary wife, says very little about religion in her personal life or that of the family. Grace used to concede that she was "not at all pious," and I think that her views became more liberal with the years (when she was alone in Berkeley for several months in 1933, her diary mentions several visits to the Unitarian church). In China, her diary shows a good deal of religious participation. Most missionary communities had weekly prayer meetings. Bob and Grace attended regularly, and were hosts in their turn. Though it may have been unusual, Grace even mentions leading one meeting. When they could attend church services in English, her diary usually gives an appraisal of the sermon (not always favorable).

There are many other details of her regular life that Grace mentioned in her diaries but did not consider of interest for her narrative. She listed books read and letters written.[10] From about sixty books a year in the early years there was a gradual increase to about one hundred and forty. Most were works of substance. Keeping herself supplied must have been a problem in Chengtu; in later years she did regular book reviewing for the *China Weekly Review* in Shanghai. From a check of several years, she seems to have written from six to seven hundred letters a year.

And, neither in *Golden Inches* nor in the diaries does Grace say much about what she and Bob were actually like. A son may not be the most objective observer, and each reader of this book will read between the lines and derive some conclusions of his own. But perhaps a few impressions can provide some background.

Bob and Grace were two very dissimilar people who remained very much in love and continued to be devoted to each other.

10. Grace always used *The Missionaries' Diary*, which was published in Shanghai. This had about one hundred pages in the back of the book to record the efforts of a model missionary: discourses delivered, candidates for baptism, enquirers examined, baptisms, communicants, and so forth. These were very useful for her lists of books read and letters received and sent.

Bob was friendly and outgoing, rather quiet but a good mixer. He was an eager and tireless competitor, whether at parlor games and cards, sports, or just trying to better his time over a familiar walk. He was an activist and organizer, but he was able to accomplish this without "taking charge." He had a keen but dry sense of humor and a fondness for banter and good-natured teasing. His tastes were not very intellectual: his favorite magazine was the *Saturday Evening Post,* and he loved Zane Grey's stories of the American west (such as *Riders of the Purple Sage*). He seemed to find it difficult to write letters, even to his own family, and his only concession was to write daily to Grace during their separations.

When it came to his work for the Y, Bob was a workaholic. On the administrative side, he had to carry most of the load of developing an organization, training a staff, and raising funds. The activities sponsored by the Y were many and various: boys' clubs, sports and physical education, educational classes, discussion groups, social and cultural programs. For practical considerations, many of these activities—whether for boys, young men, or the general public—had to be concentrated in the late afternoon and evening (after school and employment). Bob had a strong sense of responsibility and a firm insistence on doing his "share." I expect, also, that it was not easy for him to delegate. So he drove himself, worked extremely long hours, and skimped himself on weekends and vacations. All this was done with zest and enthusiasm: I never heard him say a word about being tired or overworked.

He was an optimist and a trusting person and usually assumed the best about the person he was dealing with. He liked working with people, always kept his temper, and excelled at conciliation and compromise. There was no trace of pomposity or pride, and he preferred easygoing informality. Most Chinese seemed to enjoy and like him, and I am confident that he had very few enemies of any nationality. He could, though, be stubborn. And on what he considered basic values and obligations, he found it impossible to be flexible.

Grace, in a pleasant, well-bred, and unpretentious way, was a lady. She may have seemed, on first meeting, to be a bit reserved—though not shy. But once the ice was broken, she was gracious and a lively conversationalist. Humor was not her forte, and she could be rather sharp—even acerbic. She was not so keen as Bob on games; but she enjoyed competition with herself, such as solitaire and Double-Crostics—at which she must have been in the champion class. She was more introspective than Bob and much more intellectual in her tastes. Her favorite magazines were the *New Republic, Century,* and the *Atlantic Monthly.* And her many favorite authors included Willa Cather and Joseph Conrad. She enjoyed writing letters and was an acute observer of things about her. She was also a sharp observer of people, interested in their lives and foibles, and less inclined than Bob to trust in appearances. She made many strong friends, but she probably intimidated some people. And I expect that she would lose to Bob in a popularity contest.

Within the family there were some habits and taboos. We boys were always treated, so far as possible, like responsible individuals. Our views were encouraged and listened to; we were never told to shut up. There was never any argument in front of us, and no discussion of things like family finances. In fact, I cannot remember that I ever heard either Bob or Grace raise their voices in anger or argument—though there sometimes were significant silences. Great importance was put on self-control and restraint. This was regarded as a sign of maturity and strength. As a sort of corollary to this there was little overt display of emotion or affection—or grief. Bob kissed Grace when he came home in the evening, and we boys kissed them when we said goodnight. But there was no cuddling and hugging.[11] Perhaps it was also consistent that praise was not lightly or lavishly bestowed.

As one reads Grace's story (and this is really her story much more than Bob's) it seems obvious that below this well-ordered surface there were powerful tensions and stresses. Of these, we boys were almost wholly unaware. In fact, I look back on a very loving, happy, exciting childhood. Probably my brothers felt the same way. They were great days!

One of Grace's disappointments was that she was not more successful as an author. She never stopped writing poems. A few of them and an occasional short story were published by writing clubs that she joined in Shanghai and Claremont. Even though it has taken a long time, I think she would be pleased by this publication of *Golden Inches.*

11. I still find it hard to get used to the excessive public displays of affection that now seem to be acceptable.

Author's Foreword

For a long time there had been in the back of my mind a thought of writing a narrative of our early years in China. It was not that they were extraordinary in any way; many others have passed through greater trials and dangers with less to cheer them, have had just as staunch friends and just as treasured experiences; but times are changing and conditions of thirty years ago are becoming forgotten today.[1] Our sons sometimes asked about some old happening or expressed interest to hear a tale of the past.

My husband wished that I would write something for them. Five years ago he told me I should begin. I looked over my diaries, all of which I have in uniformity since 1906. Some of the volumes have had baths in the Yangtze and have fallen apart. I collected the stray pages, browsed through their close writing, and tied them together in packages. In the winter of 1934–35 I was unable to be out much, and Bob kept asking why I didn't write. I promised him I would try, but told him that all I had in mind was a woman's story, a tale of the never-ceasing procession of small events that make up life anywhere. With him for so many years the Y had meant everything.[2] I said I did not plan to write an account of the Y in Szechwan, or even of his work; my story must be a more personal account.

In 1935 when Dick returned to China after graduating from Pomona,[3] he brought all the weekly letters I had written my mother from 1905 on. I began to go through them but had hardly started when the doctors told me that my strong, valiant husband could live only a few weeks. He was not to be told of the coming separation.

1. Grace was writing this in 1937.
2. By "the Y" Grace was of course referring to the Young Men's Christian Association, or YMCA.
3. Dick was her youngest son.

In those swiftly passing days, those long wakeful nights, the whole project took new shape in my mind. I realized the overwhelming change coming to my life and felt an urge to recall the past for the sake of Bob and the boys. Questions began to come into my mind; now and then when Bob was conscious, I asked him this or that about Y matters or events in our own family. He could never fully answer any of these queries, having already passed the point where the details of experience can be revived by memory. He always said, "I can't say just now, but perhaps tomorrow. . . ." Once he asked me to put him in the book. How could I write without having him in the tale! His life and mine had been inseparable. Life, everything, was *ours*. I told him this; and now I leave his name on the page of dedication as I jotted it down before I knew the tragedy of our separation.

Grace B. Service

PART ONE

GETTING THERE

1

Student Volunteers

(1905)

In March of 1905 we were living in a little apartment in West Lafayette, Indiana. Bob was general secretary of the Student Young Men's Christian Association at Purdue University. He had become keenly interested in the Y during his undergraduate days at Berkeley. After the Lake Geneva Student Y conference in 1902, he decided to put his life into the foreign work of the Y. He was asked to first go through a training period as secretary of a Student Y in America. Several attractive offers came his way, including the Y at Columbia University. He accepted what seemed the hardest and went to Purdue. He had started at Purdue in the fall of 1902, but I had not been able to join him there until after our marriage in the summer of 1904.[1]

About that time we asked the International Committee of the Y if there was a chance we would be sent abroad that year, or possibly the next. The committee thought there would be no opportunity before 1906. Suddenly one day there came a telegram from John R. Mott, the head man of the Y, appointing a time for seeing Bob in Chicago within the next few days. The message seemed to bode some change for us, but we hardly dared hope for anything definite so soon.

March was cold. I shivered when Bob left at 5:30 that morning on his way to Chicago. We both wondered what it might mean. Being alone, I got up

---

1. Grace's home was San Bernardino, California, but they were married in Independence, Iowa. Grace's father was adamantly opposed to her marriage, to the extent of disinheriting her and refusing to pay for or even attend a wedding. He disliked having the daughter of a banker (even a small-town one) "throwing herself away" on the son of a farmer; and he disagreed with her determination on a distant and probably dangerous life as a missionary wife. Grace had spent part of her high school years in Independence, Iowa, with her grandmother and a much-loved aunt. They offered the young couple a haven and support. Grace's father finally became reconciled, but only after many years.

2 *Grace, at about ten, with her mother, Virginia Boggs.*

later than usual. The morning chores were still unfinished when there was a telephone call. It was an old Berkeley friend. He had come east unexpectedly on business; finding that he could stop in Lafayette, he thought to surprise us. I told him how to reach us by streetcar and he was there in half an hour. Naturally, he was much disappointed not to find Roy.[2]

After a little visit, I started to show him around. We stopped at the Y, and one of the men there escorted him around the campus. Waiting in Bob's office for their return, I began to think. Obviously our friend would be with me for lunch and there was very little to eat. Delicatessens were few in those days and none was near us. On the way home we detoured by the grocery store where I traded and found a few ready eatables. I remember that the lunch included Saratoga chips and some of my own jelly.

We were still at lunch when I received another telephone call. This time it was Western Union, where someone realized that if I was to follow the telegram's instructions, I must receive its message at once. A woman's voice read

2. Bob was christened Robert Roy. His family preferred Roy, and so he was known through his college years. But Grace preferred Bob, and her wish prevailed with the friends made after their marriage. When we children heard someone say "Roy," we knew that the speaker was from away back.

the wire from Chicago: "Appointed foreign work. Will meet you here. Medical examination. Take one thirty train Big Four. Bob."

It was already nearly one and there was not a moment to lose. I hurried to our landlady next door and asked her to kindly gather up my silver and put away the food on the table. Hastily, I snatched up a few things and put them in a small valise. Fortunately, I was dressed for the street and did not have to change. We stopped at the useful corner grocery to get some money. In a few minutes, our friend and I were on the streetcar crossing the Wabash; a little later, we were on the train hastening north. He had decided to go to Chicago with me, as it would give him a chance to see Bob.

It was all tremendously thrilling. Bob met us; he was happy and excited. Very soon I was having my medical examination. The doctor would hardly

3   *Grace, between college and marriage, while she was teaching high school Latin in San Bernardino.*

believe that I was expecting a baby in the summer; I was still quite slender. As soon as I passed the doctor's examination, we were definitely accepted for the Y staff in the Orient; but we were not to sail until November.

That evening Mr. Mott talked to us both. I well remember his solemnity and some of his advice. He emphasized that this was a lifework; it was a lasting appointment, not like taking a position with a local Y in America. He repeated that we were set apart by our lifetime commitment. As we listened to his impressive words, we felt that we were making a solemn decision, full of privilege and responsibility. He reported China as on the threshold of vast changes. We would be there in a critical and important time, seeing changes of amazing extent and influence.

It was no wonder that we were too excited to sleep much that night. The only room available in the old Sherman House was for a family, with a huge double bed and two small ones for children. We tossed about in the big bed, rolling over for attempts at sleep and turning back to talk, until the bedding was all pulled loose at the foot. To think that we really were to go to the Orient! Mr. Mott had asked if I wanted to go to Canton where I had an uncle, but we had no preference as to location. China, though, was the land of our dreams.

We stayed on in Chicago for three days. As I was a student volunteer committed to foreign work, Mr. Mott asked me to talk to another wife. The husband was ready and eager for appointment to the Orient, but the wife blocked every offer by persistent objections. I talked, but to no effect; they remained in America. During our Chicago stay we visited Montgomery Ward's huge emporium, famous then for sending supplies to the ends of the earth.[3] We also took advantage of the opportunity for much talk with several experienced Y men who had served abroad.

Soon we were back alone in the little apartment in West Lafayette. We found everything spic-and-span. Our kind Hoosier landlady had cleared my table, put away the food, cleaned up, and taken my silver into her own safekeeping. The whole episode seemed a dream: the telegrams, Chicago, our appointment, our new plans for the coming months.

I was busy and happy that spring, making baby clothes, writing to relatives and friends about our sudden, all-absorbing plans. Bob was taking the track men out for cross-country running those fresh spring mornings. He was very blonde then, and the smooth muscles under his white skin made

3. This was the beginning of a long association. "Monkey Ward" gave a very useful discount to Y people and probably to other missionaries as well. Through our childhood, the more-or-less annual arrival of a shipment from Montgomery Ward was a joyously exciting event. And the fat, brightly illustrated catalogue was a vivid and sometimes perplexing view of a remote, vaguely known home.

4 *Bob, California's record holder for the half-mile.*

him look cleaner than the others as the pack ran past our house. I used to watch for them behind the curtains of our little living room and was always proud of his running style, just as I had been at track meets in Berkeley. I had never seen him lose a race.[4]

During these few months all our wedding gifts and other belongings had to be packed. Orders were carefully made out for Montgomery Ward. Finally, we broke up our first home and started our travels. Bob had agreed to

4. Bob could run the mile and half-mile well enough to beat Stanford and most other college rivals. But if Grace never saw him lose, it was because she was not able to watch them all. He was captain of the track team in his senior year and set a UC (and West Coast) record for the 880 that lasted for nine years after he graduated.

serve as registrar of the Student Y conference at Lake Geneva, Wisconsin. I went out to my grandmother's home in Iowa, where I had been born and where Bob and I were married the year before.

When the Geneva conference was over, Bob came and we soon left for California. My mother had just arrived for a visit but insisted that a pregnant woman, which by this time I certainly was, should not travel without feminine company. So she turned around and came right back with us. Knowing how little practical knowledge Mother had of such emergencies, I have always marveled that she made herself take this journey when she might have enjoyed a summer with her Iowa family and old friends.

We went through Colorado by the Royal Gorge and on by the old Union Pacific. At that time, this trip was considered a marvel. I stood the travel well but was tired when we reached Berkeley.

2

Virginia

(1905)

Bob and I spent July and August in Berkeley with Father and Mother Service in their big home on Oxford Street. We had the large north bedroom, so cleverly planned that it had no north window, but light, air, and views from both east and west. Everyone was lovely to me. Two of Bob's sisters were there at home, and the two younger brothers. Johnnie was thoughtful and pleasant, and Lawrence very kind to his new sister.

In August there was a family reunion. This was an eye-opener to me. My only sibling is a brother twelve years younger; in our family we had no large get-togethers. The Services had nine children; at this time five were married. Twenty-five people lived in the house for over a fortnight. At each meal the Japanese cook served two long tables in the large dining room. For breakfast there was fruit, porridge, huge platters of ham and eggs, coffee, milk, muffins, or perhaps hot cakes. Noon dinners brought the same big platters piled high with steak and onions, or roasts, or perhaps fried chicken. There were tureens of vegetables, mounds of bread, bowls of pickles and jelly, and a favorite dish of my father-in-law's: chopped tomatoes, cucumbers, and onions with a few chili peppers. He seemed to accept me as a member of the family when he found I liked raw onions. Dessert was often watermelon, or there was luscious, real home-made pie. It seemed to me that I had never tasted better food, or any more graciously served, than there in the old Oxford Street home. Now it is gone [burned in the Berkeley fire of 1923], its inhabitants of those days scattered or dead, and even its location lost in experiment gardens of the university.

In those days it was the custom that as soon as the Sunday midday dinner was done, all the Orientals who worked in the big homes had the rest of the day off. About four o'clock one would see a regular procession of sedate Chinese and Japanese cooks, mostly in blue serge, wending its way to the ferry trains for San Francisco. The Chinese wore clothes of their own style with short, full-cut upper garments and loose trousers; the Japanese preferred Western garments.

With no cook in the house, Sunday supper was prepared by each to his or her pleasure. I realized why my mother-in-law kept one pantry locked. Whole tins of sardines and shrimp would disappear. Jars of pickles would be emptied. Loaves of bread would vanish under the sandwich knife. Fruit was bought by the lug box. All supplies were on the generous scale of the ranch life to which the family had long been accustomed.[1]

The big house with its eight bedrooms and extra attic space held us all easily. The days were full of trips to the City, visits with friends here and there, and good times of many kinds. Evenings we played games, talked, or sang around the piano. They were all fond of music. There was little to attract us from home, for in those days there were no movies. Lulu had already broken the family circle with her recent marriage and departure for Germany; now and then we would think of our own coming separation.[2]

Needless to say, I stayed by the house and did not venture on city jaunts. During the reunion, it seemed once that the time had come and I went to the hospital. After a fruitless wait of several days, Bob came for me one evening. In a raincoat, with my two pigtails tucked inside, I went off on the Oxford streetcar. Home again, and no baby! It was discouraging.

A few days later, on August 26, there were sharp summons. Bob phoned the doctor. I was dressed and roaming about upstairs. I drifted into Irene's room, from whose window I could watch for the doctor's arrival. One of Irene's precious possessions was a china cabinet, a glass-doored case standing on what was really a bench. I thought the two were one solid piece of furniture; in fact, they were unattached. On the shelves were two or three dozen china teacups and saucers. She was "getting a collection," quite a fad for young women at that time. I sat down in a low rocker in front of the cabinet. I had seen the china frequently, but some new thing caught my eye and I opened one of the glass doors. Just then a sharp pain came; I involuntarily leaned back. The arm of the rocker pressed upward against the lower edge of the open cabinet door. This tilted the whole case backward. I was frightened and quickly leaned forward: the case pitched forward with a hid-

1. Bob's father (our grandfather) had come by wagon train to California in 1859. In 1868 he bought land near Ceres in the San Joaquin Valley and farmed there until he retired in Berkeley in 1899.

2. Lulu, eighteen months younger than Bob, was his closest sibling. In June 1905, just before the arrival of Grace and Bob from Iowa, she had married Fred Field Goodsell, a UC classmate and close friend of both Grace and Bob. The Goodsells had to leave at once for Germany, where he was to study theology. They later spent many years at Constantinople, where he was field secretary for the American Board. He ended a notable career as the executive head of the Congregational mission board (ABCFM). Fred Goodsell served with the YMCA in Europe and Russia during World War I, but the missionary paths of brother and sister never crossed.

5   *Grace with baby Virginia, in Berkeley before they sailed to China.*

eous sound of shattering china. Screaming, I pushed it level on its bench. But not before most of the china had crashed to the floor.

I called for Bob and rushed to our room. He arrived, and soon his mother, and I sobbed out the story. At this moment the doctor arrived and I left the house bathed in tears. Irene, still downstairs and all unconscious of the havoc in her room, came to the front hall to bid me good-bye. She was alarmed to see me in tears, thinking I must be suffering terribly. The doctor, in turn, inquired as we drove off, "Why so many tears? Could things already be so bad?" My husband's family was perfect in its understanding and forgiveness: never was this incident remembered against me.

The long-desired baby was born about two in the afternoon, without the doctor. He had gone out on calls in the forenoon, and his car broke down. Virginia arrived safely, however, with two nurses at hand. She was tiny, a blonde with large violet eyes. The hospital was the first "Alta Bates Sanatarium" on Dwight Way in Berkeley. She was one of the first five babies born there. Her picture was taken, along with the others, and [in 1937] hangs in the hall of the new building.

Bob was pleased that his child was the first granddaughter in the Service family. He left the day after her birth for a YMCA conference in New York, being already late by waiting for her arrival. Lawrence was the first of the Oxford Street folks to see the baby. He came slipping in when she was a couple of days old, telling me that he was giving her a gold ring. (This was later stolen in Chengtu.)

After I was able to be up and had spent about a fortnight at home, I traveled down to San Bernardino with the baby. I spent October there in my own home; then along came Bob, and partings began. Of course it was hard to say good-bye; but we were young and in love, and going together where we wanted to go. The separation was not as hard for us as for our parents. My father was still opposed to my marriage. I was sorry for Mother, who seemed lonely. It was a little different in Bob's case; his family was large and had a strong group feeling. We were soon back in Berkeley, doing the last packing.

Our appointment had first been for Seoul, Korea. This had now been changed to Chengtu, the capital of Szechwan Province in the far west of China. We were very thrilled: we wanted most to go to China and were excited to be going to a remote pioneer station in the far interior. We looked up Chengtu on the map and tried to visualize the long river journey. Hearing of some Methodist missionaries in Illinois who had been stationed in Chengtu, Bob had stopped to see them en route from New York. They gave him some information about travel, and the wife thoughtfully sent me a note to be sure to take lace curtains "for the home touch." I dislike lace curtains, save very fine ones, which I could not afford; so we purchased none and never regretted their lack. It is difficult to advise people who go to live in foreign places; essentials to one are not needed or desired by others!

In Chengtu, Bob was to be working with Dr. Henry T. Hodgkin of the Friends' Foreign Missionary Association. He had been prominent in the British student movement, and Mr. Mott had wanted him for the YMCA. However, Dr. Hodgkin was already committed to his own church's mission and could only agree to give some time and assistance to the Y. Bob was chosen as his associate because of his experience in American student work, at that time in the high tide of its popularity and influence. Chengtu was becoming a center in China of the new Western-style education. It was a logical place for the Y to establish an Association that emphasized work with students.

3

Shanghai

(1905)

Our ship was the *Mongolia* of the old Pacific Mail Line. A crowd went to San Francisco to see us off on November 16, 1905. There were relatives and college friends and a few Student Volunteers among the Y men. To us it was a thrilling, exciting day. We sailed at noon and it was warm in the sun. I was wearing a pongee blouse and a blue wool plaited skirt with a blue broadcloth-covered, dishy, pivot-on-the-corner-of-the-head hat, neat and stylish according to the dictates of the day, but impossible to keep steady in sea breezes. Standing on deck to catch last glimpses of the Seal Rocks as we passed out from the Golden Gate, I did not realize how chill the fresh wind was. The next morning I woke with a stiff neck and a cold which threatened croup. This kept me in the cabin, where there was also the small baby demanding my care. And I had a touch of seasickness. Bob had to turn in and care for the two-and-a-half-month-old baby, who was good as gold.

Traveling companions were the Leisers of Wisconsin, whom we had come to know and love in the summer of our honeymoon. They were going for the YMCA to Canton, but she was taken ill in Japan and had to stop there for medical treatment. Winnie Leiser helped Bob care for Virginia during the few days when I was laid low. But that was soon over, and when we began to appear on deck Virginia was a center of interest. She wore a white angora bonnet for the cool sea air of the winter trip.

At our long dining table a missionary gentleman sat beside me. He went down the menu every meal, never slighting a single course. At dinner there was usually an item called "punch." This was a frozen frappé, served after the entree. He saw me eating some one evening and asked what it was. I told him. "Has it any liquor in it?" "Not that I can tell." "Well, I must have some then. I'm sorry I've missed it." He ordered a serving at once and every night thereafter.

6 *The young family on shipboard, starting their trip to China. Grace's hat was
"neat and stylish, according to the dictates of the day, but impossible to keep
steady in sea breezes."*

Fifteen years later, going down the Yangtze in a time of warfare, this
gentleman boarded our steamer from a launch in the early hours of the
morning. He was escorting some Americans out of a fighting zone in Hunan.
He recognized me as soon as I stepped into the saloon for breakfast, and
began to ask questions about Szechwan. I, in turn, inquired about Hunan
and the dangers through which his party had just come. They had had a
narrow squeak to get through some opposing armies. He interrupted me.
"How about the food here? I've not traveled by this ship before. Are the hot
cakes good? What is their best breakfast dish?" I was thankful that he could
forget his narrow escape in a good meal. But not so the couple he had escorted. They had completely lost their nerve, and the husband made no
bones of saying that he would not return to Changsha for even a thousand

American dollars. I asked, "Well, what about Mr. —— who brought you out? He tells me that he is going back very shortly." "He speaks the language and is used to it all," was the reply.

During our stop in Japan there were great demonstrations celebrating naval victories in the war against Russia. I remember a huge floral arch to Admiral Togo near the station on our arrival in Tokyo. Bob attended a big reception in a Tokyo park. All men were to appear in frock coats and top hats; many queer outfits were seen, even quite nondescript nether garments with Japanese sandals. Japan was quaint, and the rickshas seemed agreeable, though my first ride, alone on a cool wet night when I felt none too sure that the runner would deliver me to the correct address, was not a pleasant experience. We spent a day or two with the Fishers of the Tokyo Y. We were horrified, of course, at Japanese men using the streets as public latrines. At Yokohama there were cordial letters from the Shanghai YMCA people. It seemed wonderfully pleasant to be expected and welcomed in anticipation. Several ladies wrote to me that they would be at the Shanghai jetty to meet us.

We arrived at Shanghai on December 18. There was no way of knowing beforehand that this was to be the day of the Mixed Court riots in Shanghai's International Settlement. These riots were caused by a disagreement about the place of detention for Chinese women prisoners while repairs were being made in the jail. Exception was taken to a decision by one of the foreign assessors [judges] at the court, and this started the trouble. Glass windows in several carriages had been smashed, and a few foreigners had been hustled on the streets. One of the men thus treated was Julean Arnold, then American assessor in the Mixed Court, who had intended to meet us.[1]

We arrived late in the forenoon and were surprised that the jetty was almost deserted. Remembering the letters received in Japan, I wondered a bit that nothing was to be seen of any ladies. Two American YMCA secretaries met us. Will Lockwood began talking to me while Robert E. Lewis asked Bob if I was apt to be nervous—because of the riots, no one knew just what to expect. Bob did not like women with nerves, so I soon heard all there was to tell. The ladies who had planned to meet us had been warned by their husbands to keep off the streets. Of course we agreed to fall in with whatever arrangements our friends were able to make.

1. Julean Arnold was another Berkeley friend and UC classmate (1902). He joined the U.S. State Department after graduation and was sent to Peking to study Chinese as the American government's first "student interpreter." After this Mixed Court assignment, he moved into economic and trade promotion work and spent most of a long and distinguished career as commercial attaché of the American legation in China. The Mixed Court, with Chinese and foreign judges sitting together, was a device to recognize the dual character of the International Settlement of Shanghai: foreign administration but Chinese sovereignty. It dispensed justice, however, only to Chinese: because of extraterritoriality, foreigners in China were subject only to their own laws and courts.

At this time the Shanghai YMCA was on Peking Road in a three-story brick building. At the jetty we were told that we could not risk sending baggage through the streets. How I wished I had known that when packing aboard ship! Thinking we would have all our things that night, I had been careless of where clothing was put; my chief thought had been to get everything in. However, I did have the baby's food and a few necessities in a basket which I had kept with me. Taking this in Mr. Lewis's closed ricksha, I was hurried off under escort.

When we arrived at the YMCA building, I was shown into a large upper room furnished with an extension table and matching chairs. It seemed to be a room used for board meetings. Mr. Lewis thought we might have to remain here several days. They promised to arrange everything for us as best they could. Poor men! I could see both our new friends were burdened by the unexpected difficulties attending our arrival. Whether there was a fireplace in our room of refuge, I do not recall; it seemed chill and bare. Bob went out of the room with the two men. My first thought was for the baby, and I opened her Japanese *koré* [a large rattan telescoping hamper] to arrange her little bed in its cover, as we had done on shipboard. Ere I had time to do more than this, in came the three men. Mr. Lewis said that a patrol of bluejackets from an American naval ship had just come down North Szechwan Road and reported it clear. Mr. Lewis still had his private ricksha standing by. He thought we should try to go to the Lyon home, where it had been planned that we would stay. The three men would walk with the ricksha, in which the baby and I would be hidden by its curtains. But we must hurry!

I snatched up the baby and we were off, the *koré* in front of me in the ricksha. We went straight to the Lyon house on North Szechwan Road. They then occupied a house belonging to the Barchet family, but well north of the Barchet Road corner where the old YMCA double residence was. It was quite by itself on what was then a country road. The Lewis and Brockman families lived in the Y residence, while the Lockwoods were in a terrace of houses belonging to Lord Li, farther out on North Szechwan Road Extension.

It was a little after noon when we arrived at the Lyons'. It seemed chilly in the high-ceilinged rooms. The small fire in the tiny grate of our bedroom made little impression on the atmosphere, but it was the best there was to offer, and the welcome could not have been warmer. What things I lacked for Virginia, Grace Lyon could supply from her own baby's belongings. Her Lawrence was then a year old. (He was killed by bandits in Los Angeles in the autumn of 1934 when a medical student.)

In midafternoon an armed American marine came around with a notification from the consulate advising American citizens, and particularly women and children, to go inside the International Settlement before dark that night.[2] Willard Lyon was away on Y affairs in Japan; his wife, Grace, was there in that somewhat isolated house with four young children and ourselves—new, green, and with a baby. The house stood in a garden with a brick wall on the Szechwan Road frontage. But a high woven-bamboo fence enclosed the other three sides and would have given no protection against marauders. Grace Lyon immediately hurried a coolie off with a note to ask Mrs. Parker if she could go to her in the Methodist compound, south of Range Road, the Settlement boundary. Will Lockwood agreed to look after us, and it was finally decided that, as the Lockwoods were living in property well known to belong to a Chinese, it would probably be unmolested, while a foreign house, standing alone as did the Lyon place, might be liable to attack by any villagers on mischief bent. The Lockwoods, therefore, planned to remain in their own house that night.

Grace Lyon, hurrying off with her children and some large bedding rolls, naturally did not like leaving her house alone with servants. So it was arranged that Bob would stay with her servants while I would go with the baby to the Lockwoods. In some ways this was a good plan, for there was no bed for us at the Lockwoods'. I could see it was reasonable, but I did hate to be separated from Bob on our first night in China—and under such circumstances. Will Lockwood spent the night, fully dressed I think, in the lower part of the house. I know I shared their double bed with his wife, Mary. We had never met before that day. Both of us were college girls, Kappa Alpha Thetas, she from De Pauw and I from the University of California. We both had babies. Her Edward was fifteen months old, Virginia not far from four months. One baby wakened and cried; this wakened the other. Soon we were up, then down, then up again. I was both cold and nervous. Finally, back in bed at last, trying to get some sleep while wondering what kind of night Bob was having, Mary softly whispered: "Do you know you are trembling so much that you shake the whole bed?" "Yes, I know it and I'm sorry, but I just can't help it," was my answer.

During most of the night Bob was sitting in the Lyon living room with a poker for a weapon. He was startled several times by unaccountable noises,

2. After the original, rather limited area of the International Settlement filled up by rapid growth, the Shanghai Municipal Council had begun a de facto but unauthorized expansion by building roads out into the surrounding Chinese countryside. The Settlement police assumed the right to patrol these roads (on the basis that they were Council property), but they had no jurisdiction over the large areas between them. In times of disturbance this could present problems for the residents. North Szechwan Road Extended, along which these YMCA houses stood, was one of the new roads into Chinese territory. The Lyon house was about a mile outside the Settlement boundary. Fifteen years later, in 1920, I was a boarder in the Shanghai American School just across the street from what had been the Lyons' house. By that time, all this semirural, "outside" area was entirely built up and in all practical ways fully incorporated into the International Settlement. North Szechwan Road was a bustling thoroughfare, with electric trams and reasonably adequate sidewalks.

but of course he did not know what noises to expect in China. Finally, finding that nothing came of them, he lay down on the sofa, covered himself with a rug, and dozed. The night passed safely so far as our neighborhood was concerned. The next night I again stayed with Mary Lockwood while Bob, armed with a revolver from the consulate, was a member of the foreign citizen patrol for this part of Hongkew where the Y folks lived. This is the only night in China that he was on armed guard, and there was no need for him to use his weapon. After these two days, the disturbances calmed down, and apprehension of trouble from lawless or ignorant Chinese ended.

We moved back to the Lyon house and within a few days obtained our luggage from the ship. Even after all seemed peaceful and quiet, I was bothered at night by a peculiar sharp rattle that we would hear at intervals through the night. Bob had no idea what it could be. From Grace Lyon we learned it was the watchman in a village across the fields to the west. In the Chinese way, he beat a certain cadence on a piece of bamboo to let householders know he was alert on his job and to notify marauders of his whereabouts!

After we got our luggage from the ship the baby had her carriage, and we acquired an amah for her. She was the wife of a coolie at the Brockman home. The amah was pleasant and the baby liked her at once. Of course, I could not talk to her but soon learned a few nouns and verbs—"hot water," "come," "not want"—and we got on. Christmas came and went. Willard Lyon was home by this time, and we had a pleasant, jolly celebration with new friends who made us feel entirely at home. There was a tree and a cobweb hunt for the children, and a few guests on Christmas afternoon.

Shanghai made very little impression on me at first. There were no high buildings in 1905. China looked drab, cold, and wet. The river [the Whangpoo] was not inspiring, and the land we saw scarcely more so. I do not recall any features that made the city attractive or unique. The streets were narrow and horse carriages abounded, each with its two uniformed men on the box. The driver wielded reins and whip, and his assistant the bell. Sidewalks were narrow and on some streets entirely lacking, so that I was often afraid of having my shoulder or hat nipped by a horse as I threaded my way along between foot traffic of the most motley variety.

We were bidden to tea by Dr. Hawks-Pott, then chairman of the National Committee of the YMCA in China. It was a long journey through the city by carriage to his home at St. John's University. Houses on Bubbling Well Road around where it meets Chengtu Road were then well out in the country. North of Range Road lay fields, save along North Szechwan Road where Chinese white-plastered tenements of the old style swarmed with inhabitants.

We attended Union Church; aside from it I do not recall that we entered a single public building of interest. We went to the American consulate and all

I remember of it is that the river nearby seemed very dirty and noisy. I attended a meeting of the American Women's Club there in the parlors of the consul general's wife. The club was a small circle of women, reading papers and doing the things usual to such groups in America.

As time went on we heard a good many rumors of possible trouble. New Year's Day, we were told, was to be a bad time for all foreigners. After that passed safely, Chinese New Year's Day, late in January, was to be a day of poisonings carried out by servants against their foreign employers. Through all this we went on with our plans to go west as soon as possible. For one thing, our salary would not commence until we reached our final destination; private funds, outfit allowances, and expense money could not last for ever. We were eager, too, to reach our new home and get to work on the language.

We had thought to travel with a bride and groom, both of whom had been in China previously and who expected to return from home leave at this time. They were Canadians, and the bride was well known for her medical work in Szechwan. But their group was delayed for some reason. We then decided to travel with Mr. J. W. Davey of the Christian Literature Society. He had been to the Coast to buy supplies and was returning alone to Szechwan. I was busy those days making warm short clothes for the baby, using white Japanese flannel, like albatross or heavy nun's veiling.

4

The Houseboat

(1906)

Despite rumors of evil, we left Shanghai for Hankow on the river steamer *Kinling* at midnight on January 17, 1906. Friends saw us off and presented us with many comforts and remembrances. We had many loving messages, and our hearts were firmly bound to the Y friends who had helped us in Shanghai.

Among our fellow passengers was a newly married English couple. She had just come out from England, while the groom came down from Szechwan to meet and wed her in Shanghai. Naturally, her luggage was still marked with her maiden name. The very proper Number One Boy of the ship failed to see why the baggage of Miss L should be placed in the cabin of Mr. S. The bride's panic over her lost trousseau, and the groom's distress as to its whereabouts, soon became apparent. After explanations to the Number One, happiness was restored, and the blushes of the bridal pair provided a pleasant interlude. We all, with the ship's officers, tried to give them a start on a happy honeymoon.

In Hankow we stayed with the Clintons, who were Y friends. Mildred Clinton's amah gave Virginia a pair of little red satin "tiger shoes," with the head, ears, eyes, and mouth, and even silk-thread whiskers, wrought on their toes. Bob and I were more delighted with them than the baby was, though she did take notice. On Chinese New Year's Day we boarded the old *Kiang Wo* for Ichang and the way west.

Pearl Buck has written of the Yangtze River steamers: "Their polyglot crews were headed by blasphemous, roaring, red-faced old English captains who had rampaged along the Chinese coasts for years and had retired into the comparative safety of the river trade. Not one of those captains but was full of tales of the pirates of Bias Bay and of bandits along the shores of the river, and they all had one love and one hate. They loved Scotch whisky and hated all missionaries." We saw some of this type but more often found appreciative and friendly hearts under the blue uniforms of the ship's service. Bob was a keen and enthusiastic player of games for sport's sake, and he was tolerant and kindly. He usually made his way to friendship with all he met as companions on journeys.

In command of the *Kiang Wo* was Captain Mutters, an "old China hand." He was said to be gruff and could talk violently if occasion demanded, but he also had a soft heart. After boarding his ship, I was sitting in the small saloon holding the baby while Bob attended to getting the baggage aboard. The captain saw me there. "Young woman, where are you going?" "Ichang, and then on to Chengtu." I told him. "Where's the young man who is undertaking this?" asked he. Later the captain won my heart by telling me that our baby "did very well." From him, this meant a good deal.

The river was falling rapidly, and we had to tie up almost every night between Hankow and Ichang. Bob played many games of chess with the officers and others, but the time passed slowly. Once we were hailed to help a stranded steamer off a sandbank. We put out a hawser, and the steam winch was set to work. They yelled to us that their ship was "coming all the time." Suddenly our position shifted, and we could plainly see men standing not more than knee-deep in the water on the other side of their stationary craft. Captain Mutters let out a string of the most virulent profanity and ordered the hawser cast off. We proceeded on our way, leaving the other ship for better luck with some other helper, or to settle on their sandbank for a few months of inactivity. A falling river augured well, we were told, for houseboat travel on the river above Ichang. On the last day of January we were in Ichang.

In Shanghai we had provided ourselves with Chinese *pugai* [thick cotton-wadded quilts, like comforters] and blankets. These were for houseboat travel on the upper river. We found, when we reached there, that these would also be needed at the China Inland Mission Home in Ichang. This guesthouse was efficiently and economically run; everything was clean and the food ample; but there was little to soften the austerities. In our bedroom we found a woven cane frame for a double bed set up on two long benches (*bandeng*). There was a small table for a lamp, and an unpainted wooden shelf for a washstand. It held a white enamel basin and water pitcher and a drinking-water bottle and glass. A pail below was for waste water. There were two straight cane-seated chairs. No heating arrangements were provided, and the February weather was raw.

Years later a young friend told with laughter of her first impression of her bedroom in this same Home. Her mission office had failed to inform her that she would need her own bedding in Ichang. So she felt particularly forlorn when she was ushered into a cold, whitewashed room on a bleak winter day to see only a hard, bare, cane bed-frame standing on "horses." Then she raised her eyes to the motto above to see "The Lord Will Provide."[1]

In spite of meager amenities, we were soon at home in our room and stayed there quite comfortably for seventeen days. Bob unpacked our portable kerosene heater, and I begged a low chair. Our hostess, Mrs. Row, saw my predicament: it was hard to bathe the baby from a high, stiff chair or from a suitcase dragged from under the bed. She kindly provided me with a low rattan chair. We bought our own kerosene, so could have its heat whenever we wished. Later, I found we were considered very extravagant "in an American way"; but we thought a baby needed warmth, and we sought a bit of comfort ourselves. Virginia was very good those days, playing with her rattle and becoming dearer and sweeter to us all the time.

We were delayed in Ichang because some of the paper and printing supplies in Mr. Davey's charge had failed to be loaded on our steamer when we left Hankow. We had to await their arrival before setting off on the houseboat trip. During this time we were the only American guests at the Home. Several British newcomers for both the China Inland Mission and the Church Missionary Society were there, and a number of them became our very good friends. Some were our own age, and among these at least two incipient courtships had begun. Bishop and Mrs. Cassels were also there. We greatly enjoyed meeting all these people whose lives and environments had been so different from our own. At table I was seated by the bishop and chattered happily away to him in my "carefree American fashion," never dreaming that one should be suitably reserved with gentlemen of such position and cloth. One of the elder single missionary ladies told me years later of how they marveled to see me "talking to the dear bishop just as I did to anyone else."

The interest of this stay in Ichang was enhanced for our newly arrived British friends by the necessity of changing into Chinese garb. A few, such as our groom of the lower river, had already made the change. In Ichang, however, the men all came out in new Chinese clothing. At that time this was thought to be more suitable for the climate, easier to obtain, and—perhaps most important—less conspicuous. It was picturesque but seemed awkward to me, and I was very thankful that we did not have to follow this rule. Especially did it seem peculiar and inconvenient for foreign men to be burdened

1. There were no foreign-style hotels beyond the coastal treaty port cities. Inland, one had the alternatives of medieval Chinese inns or the hospitality of local missionaries. But the missionary population and missionary travel were expanding rapidly. At focal points such as Ichang the volume of transient travel had outgrown the capacity of local hospitality. So a hostel (or "Home") was established, usually by the mission most active in the area. For Grace and Bob's introduction to these hostels, it happened that the operating agency in Ichang, the China Inland Mission, was perhaps the most austere and "hair-shirty" of the Protestant missions.

by wearing the queue. In Shanghai I had seen one such man with a long blonde braid, and the impression was decidedly unpleasant. The men had been foregoing haircuts for some time and looked forward, no doubt with mixed feelings, to the time when they could boast long dangling braids. The Chinese, to cover any hirsute deficiencies, were exceedingly adept in adding black silk threads to augment the thickness and length of their prized queues. With such skillful aids, even hair of shoulder-length could be made quite presentable.

Early in February a large party of British young people left by houseboat for Wanhsien. I recall that I had my first ride in a sedan chair when we went down to the river to see them aboard. It was the custom for houseboat travelers to go aboard and get settled and then make the start after daybreak the next morning. This party had two boats: one for the men and most of the freight, the other for the chaperons and the single ladies.

Ichang was a most unattractive city, low-lying, dirty, and seemingly full of vile and odorous black mud.[2] The pyramid-like hills across the river looked clean and pleasant, but the weather was gloomy and raw and did not make us feel like excursions. Just to look down one of those dingy, foul-smelling streets was enough for me. I wondered then, with a new concern, what Chengtu could possibly be like. Bishop Cassels assured me that it had wide streets well paved with stone slabs. Even doubts of the future did not tempt us to turn back. We felt committed to our new life. I sometimes think back to those Ichang days, a little happy time with our baby before the days of our great testing.

Mr. Davey's cargo arrived, and he now began strenuous efforts to hire suitable boats for our journey to Chungking. He had a considerable bulk of cargo, and we had no small amount of our own. It was decided that three boats were needed.

The first was what the Chinese call a *kuazi*. This was a four-room houseboat, about eighty feet long and fifteen feet wide. These boats had trim lines and a lean, shipshape look. The long hull, all curves and with a solid grace, was built of heavy timbers and stiffened by a compartmented hold. The draft was perhaps three-and-a-half feet and the deck about four feet above the water, so the space under the flooring was considerable. Sockets in the compartment bulkheads held slats which supported removable floor sections. The material of construction was pine [and cypress] of several kinds, but all were included by the Chinese in the all-embracing name *baimu*. Some of this

2. Today the city of Ichang is a vastly different place. It is the site of a mighty dam across the Yangtze, from which electrical power flows through 500,000-volt transmission lines as far as Shanghai. And through locks in the dam there is a steady flow of modern, machine-powered vessels. A wonderful source of information about the great river and the cities along it is Lyman P. Van Slyke, *Yangtze: Nature, History, and the River* (Stanford: Stanford Alumni Association, 1988).

← Bow

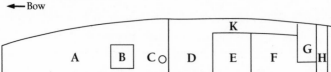

7   Grace's sketch plan of the houseboat.
A—open deck for crew, roofed at night by straw mats which were in daylight
pushed back over our permanently roofed portion
B—cockpit, where the food for the crew was prepared
C—mast, the wooden partition behind this was made of hinged door-like sections
D—living and dining room
E—Mr. Davey's room
F—our cabin
G—kitchen
H—Captain's bridge, a heavy plank raised about four feet above the deck
and extending across the boat
I—open deck
J—Captain's cabin
K—passage

wood is knotty and full of pitch; other kinds make better boards. The boats
were not painted; an overall finish with wood (*tung*) oil gave them the fresh,
attractive appearance of natural wood. They were stout craft, well adapted
for the perils and strong surges of the great river they served. But nowadays
they are seldom seen.[3]

Just aft of the foredeck were the living quarters reserved for our use [see
fig. 7]. These took up about thirty feet of the ship's length. Partitions fitted in
grooves could be changed to suit the wishes of those chartering the boat. Our
own rooms are D, E, F, and K on the sketch. The space marked G was for our
cook. Our trunks and valuable possessions were in the hold compartments
under our feet; they would be safe, and accessible if needed. There was an
inside passage, but the crew were required to go over the roof when passing
from front to rear—which, in practice, they seldom did. However, when
passing through rapids and difficult stretches, the whole boat had to be open
from front to back so the captain and pilot could see through. On each side
of the boat there were three tiny glass-paned windows with sliding wooden

3. *Kua* in the name of this type of boat means "to stride, bestraddle." The name seems apt in
giving a sense of power or aggressiveness. They had the high stern but otherwise were very
different from the more familiar cockleshell Chinese coastal junk. Low in the water, with a long,
flat foredeck, they had something of the efficient, purposeful look of a modern tanker. That they
were seldom seen when Grace wrote in 1937 was an indication of the extent to which they had
already been replaced in long-distance freight and passenger transport by modern ships, first
steam and then diesel. The Yangtze traveler of today still sees native junks engaged in local
traffic; but they are a far cry from the majestic craft of Grace's account.

shutters. Inside our flimsy wooden partitions we hung dark-blue "coolie cloth," the cheapest kind of native cotton material, to foil any prying eyes. The floor was oiled and well finished, and the whole interior neat and attractive.

The other two boats were smaller cargo craft without passenger accommodations. They were loaded high under their roofs with bales of paper, cases, and packages containing a great variety of things. Mr. Davey was taking goods for many friends in Szechwan as well as for himself and his work. Shanghai friends had urged us to buy some furniture there. We had iron beds, springs, and mattresses from America. To these we added a large English bureau, a "double" washstand, and a massive teak sideboard, all purchased at a Shanghai auction. We had also acquired a dozen dining room chairs. Mr. Davey had been a bit dismayed to hear of the three larger pieces, but seemed to think the chairs were a better buy. However, when he saw them he was anything but pleased. He assumed we had bought the common bentwood, or Vienna, type of chairs. These were much used on the China coast, perhaps because they could be imported from Europe knocked down and took little shipping space.

It happened that we had been fascinated by some wooden, cane-seated chairs of Chinese make and known as Ningpo chairs. Not only were they rigid and impossible to knock down, they could also in no way be nested. They proved a very bulky possession, but also a joy for many years. Every time we saw bentwood during our early years, we remembered the loading of those Ningpo chairs at Ichang and laughed.

At last all the things were loaded onto the three boats, which were to proceed up river under man power. Trackers were to haul them by long plaited-bamboo ropes, whose constant rubbing across rocks on many points of the shore had worn deep grooves in the limestone. A certain complement of trackers went with each boat; the captain [usually the owner] hired more to assist at rapids and places of peril or difficulty. This crew of trackers slept and ate in the front of the craft; the captain and his family and the pilot lived in the rear. Our rooms were clean and bare. In them we placed our own cots, baggage needed on the journey, and two or three locally made bamboo chairs—bought for a few cents. Dining table and chairs of the usual straight-backed Chinese style were supplied by the boat.

Mr. Davey's boy had gathered together some cooking gear, a charcoal brazier, and a tin oven.[4] Mr. Davey courteously inquired our preferences when laying in food for the journey. Being British, he was especially solicitous as to what kind of meat we liked. We told him we were not fussy; but I added that

4. This oven would have been made from the ubiquitous square kerosene tin. These tins were designed to transport "oil for the lamps of China," but they found a myriad other uses, some of them rather surprising.

Bob did not care for mutton. What he told his boy I do not know, or what the latter could buy; but he did get half of an old goat and there it was, hanging by the door of the kitchen when we went aboard. I can remember nothing now save boiled potatoes and strong-tasting mutton stew with chestnuts. The bread was also poor, but the cook had few resources and no conveniences.

5

Tragedy on the River
(1906)

We went on board our houseboat on February 16. The next morning, amid a great din of the crew, a cock was killed and held so that its blood ran down on the prow of the boat. Then, as soon as it was light enough to see, the boat cast off and we headed into the Ichang Gorge, just above the city.

Soon we fell into a regular boat routine, tending the baby, looking at the scenery, writing letters, and continually marveling at the handling of the boat, the vistas of the river, and the daily life of our Chinese companions.[1] The gorges of the Yangtze are magnificent; in a houseboat we found them much more impressive than on later steamer trips. A houseboat going up the river moves very slowly. One is so near the water that one senses vividly the power and sweep of the current. There is a greater distance to look up at the cliffs, and more time to note their varying shapes as one slowly changes position. A small boat may take hours to round a turn in the cliffs where for a long time there seemed to be no opening for the river. On a steamer this corner may be behind one in half an hour; its passing does not seem the achievement that it does under man power with the long lines of trackers pitting every ounce of their strength against the relentless force of the stream.

The river has carved its way through canyons of beauty and wonder. In some places there are no paths for the trackers, and they sit on the foredeck, whistling in an eerie way for the prevalent up-river wind to help their craft along. Or they row feverishly to gain on the current as their yells and cries resound from cliff tops lost in clouds. A strange hush often lies over the oily-looking water in places where no sounding has ever recorded its depth.

1. John Hersey's *A Single Pebble* (New York: Knopf, 1956) is a wonderfully vivid description of junk travel through the Yangtze Gorges and the life of the men whose humble strength pulled the boats upstream. Hersey is China-born: his father was also a YMCA secretary and, coincidentally, arrived in China with his young bride in the same year as Bob and Grace.

When we had almost reached the west end of the Gorges, a week out of Ichang, Virginia became ill. Steadily she grew worse. We had been giving her a standard brand of baby food, on which she seemed to thrive. I had not been able to nurse her since shortly after our arrival in Shanghai, where the unusual excitement of our first few days stopped the milk supply. Every day we took pains to clean the baby's bottles and prepare her things. All our drinking water had to come from the river; of necessity its preparation, aside from boiling, could not be as carefully done as one might wish. We lacked many facilities and could only do as all such travelers do: be as careful as circumstances permitted. We always used boiled water and boiled the baby's utensils. When she began to be ailing we changed her diet as best we could with the various infant foods we had with us. But nothing arrested her illness.

We now had most of the rapids to negotiate. Between Ichang and Chungking, the Yangtze has thirteen large and seventy-two smaller rapids. "Where hard limestone layers cross the river, and in other localities where torrential tributaries have built great alluvial fans, the valley bottom is no wider than the stream itself. At such places there are dangerous rapids."[2] At various times there have been attempts to reduce these dangers by blasting out rocks obstructing the channel; now, in 1937, the Nanking government has recently made another attempt to do this for the safety of navigation. It still presents many difficulties, perpetually changing as each rise or fall of the river produces different currents and whirlpools, all with varying hazards of rock and channel. The very sight of the worn and eroded rocks, laid bare when the river is low, makes one realize the stern task of the boat with nothing but human strength to pit against the force of the stream. Now steam is used, but in 1906 primitive methods prevailed on the Big River.[3]

We had expected to reach Chungking in about twenty-five days from Ichang. One boat with extra trackers had been known to do this trip at the same time of year in nineteen days, but we had three boats and it would take us longer. It is not easy to keep several craft together on such a journey. Apart from the varying ideas of each boat's captain, there is also the fact that at each rapid, boats take turns in passage up. A very small misadventure could make a boat lose its turn, and should such position be lost there might

---

2. George B. Cressey, *China's Geographic Foundations* (New York and London: McGraw-Hill, 1934).

3. China's new government has been able to do much more in clearing obstructions. Even more important has been a complete marking of the channel, mostly with lights on precisely anchored little rafts—whose positions must continually be checked and altered with the rise and fall of the river. Now the ships no longer tie up from dusk to dawn: powerful searchlights grope and mark each shore for the pilot. Today's traveler thus loses not only much of the old excitement of the rapids but also a chance to see some of the scenery. The final diminishment will come if the Chinese government builds a proposed high dam that will drown the rapids and make the river into a lake almost as far as Chungking.

be considerable delay. There were no doctors at any ports of call; foreigners were to be found at only one port, Wanhsien.

During the time of the baby's illness we were traversing that section of the river where the worst rapids occur. At many of these rapids, travelers went ashore and walked around the perilous places, carrying a few precious possessions with them. Now one can hardly imagine the scenes of those days at these danger spots: the roar and surge of the wild waters, often rising in huge waves at the crest of the rock barrier; the yells of the gang bosses, stimulating the trackers to greater efforts with voice and whip; the long lines of tracking men, fairly lying on the ground as they bent far forward and clutched rocks and earth to aid them; the ropes of such immense length that often the trackers were out of sight around rocky points, ropes laid out in ways found most efficient by the long-experienced local pilots hired by the captains to take command at these critical places; the signals of the drummers to trackers far ahead; the sight of the great boats as they came up to their crucial trial in surmounting the rise of water in front of them. The pilots were clever at taking advantage of every little eddy or back current, but to the spectator on his first voyage, who saw the boat containing all his worldly goods hanging on the crest of a treacherous wave as the fury of the river pounded against its wooden shell, the scene held more drama than one liked.

We were fortunate at the rapids, for I dread to think what might have taken place had we lost our houseboat at one of them. Such things have happened. If we had had to camp on the shore with what we could salvage from a wreck, it might have been still harder; or if we had been on the boat when it was swept down stream after the breaking of tow-ropes, the situation might have been worse. Only once did such a rope give way, and the danger was short-lived and did not result in disaster. Even now, all my memories of anxiety at Virginia's illness are forever blended with the sounds of rushing water, of the hiss of the crisp surge against the thin wooden side of our boat, of looking out when caring for the sick child and seeing into the heart of a whirlpool, of rocks half-disclosing their jagged points near the side of our craft, of a feeling of man's utter impotence and the irresistible power of wild water.

Perhaps it was just as well for us that we had no time to spend in worry for our safety during this time. We thought only of our baby and of caring for her. When the men burnt incense, laid out new ropes with much care and ceremony, undergirded the ship with heavy bamboo cables to give added strength to the hull, we gave these details but scant attention. As the boat crept up the rapids we put our valuables in safe places and waited to stir about until we were in calmer water. We lost fear for ourselves in our care for the precious baby.

Only once did we go ashore at a rapid and that was at the Yeh Tan (Wild

Rapid) where the captain of our boat asked us to do so. The baby was fretful there and looked pinched and ill in her basket as we carried her with us along the bank. We had hurried to Wanhsien, hoping to find there a new doctor for the American Methodist Mission in Szechwan. But he had left with China Inland Mission folks of Yunnan to help them with a sick child.

It is impossible to write much of those days of anxiety and anguish. Those who have lived in isolated places in our homelands well know the feelings of helplessness that come to parents. We knew these and more. The whole life purpose that had brought us on this journey was tested in our hearts as the days passed. We questioned ourselves over and over as to what we had done, or omitted to do, in our care of the baby. Mr. Davey had several children, but he had not been through such a crisis. He did all he could for us. When we found no doctor in Wanhsien, one of our British friends from the Ichang stay heard of our distress and came to the boat just before we started off. He wrung our hands with sympathy and offered a prayer for our little daughter. Now time was doubly precious. We made all haste to Chungking, engaging extra trackers and pushing on as fast as was humanly possible.

Still, our Virginia was never to see that city. On March 4, a Sunday evening, we knew the child lay dying. Suddenly it came over me that I would soon be in the presence of Death, whom at this time I had never met. I do not remember what or when I had eaten that day, but I was afraid that evening that I would faint or be ill and so would not be able to do the necessary things for my baby. I asked Mr. Davey to have the Boy make some cocoa, and when it came I drank it so hastily that I scalded my mouth badly.

Virginia died at eight in the evening. I washed and dressed her and we put her in her basket with lighted candles close by. Bob and I, exhausted by our strenuous week of nursing and anxiety, slept fitfully with tears on our faces. That night we were anchored below Fengtu, near a tall pagoda on the top of a high hill. The next day the boat captain went by land across a loop in the river and bought a little coffin for us at Fengtu town. I prepared the coffin, using one of the pretty "puffs" given Virginia for its lining. Mr. Davey insisted upon putting her in the coffin. A workman who came to the boat with the coffin then sealed the lid down with a lime preparation in the Chinese manner. We kept the coffin in our room the rest of the trip to Chungking.[4]

---

4. Emotions, for both Grace and Bob, were controlled. There was not much talk of Virginia in our family. But Grace always reminded us quietly on August 26 that "this would have been your sister's birthday." And on trips up or down the river, we boys knew the significance of the "tall pagoda on a high hill" at Fengtu. When Caroline and I made our first return trip up the river in 1975, I found myself looking for it: it is still there, lonely and unchanged.

Grace says, "There were no doctors." There were, however, Chinese practitioners of traditional medicine: unsanitary, unscientific, but with a centuries-long experience of healing, and a knowledge of herbal remedies well proven for many diseases. I am sure that neither Grace, as long as she lived, nor any of her missionary colleagues and contemporaries, would think it strange, or in any way worthy of note, that they never thought of these Chinese "doctors."

I suggest that neither school of healers, the unused Chinese or the unavailable Western, would have been of much help medically. Virginia had "bowel trouble," probably diarrhea or some form of dysentery. She was sick for about ten days: most likely it was dehydration and the loss of body salts that brought death. In 1906 there were no doctors who understood these factors and their quick and relatively simple remedy.

6

Illness in Chungking
(1906)

Mr. Davey had been very helpful to us all through these hard days. Now he urged us to get out of the boat: to walk, take photographs, fill our minds with other things. We did go ashore several times the day after Virginia's death. Cloudy and drizzly weather in the Gorges had prevented photography, but we took good pictures of the houseboat on this bright Monday.

That night as we were going to bed I happened to feel Bob's hand. It was terribly hot as it rested on the side of the bed. I told him he must have fever and he reluctantly agreed. Next morning Mr. Davey looked grave. We decided to give Bob nothing but light food, mostly condensed milk and crackers. Before we reached Chungking the crackers were exhausted and the milk was getting very low.

At first we gave him quinine, but Mr. Davey was sure it was typhoid. If so, quinine would not be good; so we stopped that. Then we gave almost no medicine but kept the patient quiet in bed. Neither Bob nor I had ever had a fever, nor had we seen anyone with a severe fever, so we knew nothing about treatment for such illnesses.

By this time Mr. Davey had seen the imperative need for reaching Chungking speedily. Still more trackers were hired, until they overcrowded the boat and slept even on its roof. We did everything humanly possible to hasten our journey. I lived in a daze. My husband, always so strong and athletic, lay ill on the bed; our baby in her coffin lay in the same little room. I cannot now recall that I ever felt Bob might be ill unto death; but I did wonder how one could live on day after day in this strange situation still carrying on the usual daily routine. To start this journey in health and high hopes was easy; to continue it to the end proved to be another thing. But there was nothing else to do; we could not turn back.

8   *"We took good pictures of the houseboat on this bright Monday"*
(the day after Virginia's death).

On the twenty-first day from Ichang we arrived in Chungking. The day before we expected to arrive, I asked Mr. Davey if it would be possible to send a messenger ahead. He said this could be done; we could get a man from a river-bank village to carry a letter. Mr. and Mrs. Warburton Davidson of the English Friends' Mission had written and invited us to stay in their home while we were in Chungking. However, I did not wish to take Bob there if he had typhoid. This would be too much to ask of strangers who were taking us in only because they had heard of us through Dr. Hodgkin. Also, I knew there was a doctor in the American Methodist Mission in Chungking. Mr. Davey told me this doctor, J. H. McCartney, had a hospital.

I wrote a letter to Mr. Davidson, who had not heard from us since we left Ichang. In this I told him of Virginia's death and of Bob's illness, suggesting that he reserve a room for my husband in the hospital and asking him also if he could have a grave dug and arrangements made for the baby's funeral. Mr. Davey had told me that a foreign cemetery lay outside Chungking. He also said that it was impossible to take a coffin containing a body inside any walled Chinese town, so immediate burial was what we must expect. The runner carrying this letter set off about noon on March 9. He reached Chungking that night after the city gates were locked, but he followed our instructions and had himself pulled up over the wall by ropes. He found the Davidson compound and handed in the message about eleven o'clock. It happened that the Davidsons had just returned from some social affair at the McCartneys'. It was an unusual occasion to be so late, a wedding anniversary or something similar. Mr. Davidson got back on his horse and immediately returned to see the doctor and show him my letter. They planned for the morrow and then separated for a few hours sleep.

On the morning of March 10 I was combing my long hair when I looked out of the tiny houseboat window and was surprised to see a *sampan* [a small rowboat] containing what looked like two foreign men. I grabbed up my glasses and saw they really were foreigners. They were, to my great relief, Dr. McCartney and Mr. Davidson. As we had been moving slowly upstream since earliest dawn, they had come swiftly downstream.

Dr. McCartney examined Bob at once and said that he did not have typhoid; his diagnosis was that it was probably malaria.[1] Mrs. McCartney had risen early that morning to have two rooms at the hospital prepared for us: one for Bob and an adjoining one for me so that I could be near him. Mr. Davidson, however, was urgent in his invitation for us to go to his home where his wife was expecting us. After such hard experiences and so much isolation, I longed for the warmth of a home. Also, our food and care would be a considerable burden for the McCartneys, as the hospital was set up for Chinese only and no provision was made for the needs of foreigners. Our food, for instance, would have to come from the McCartney kitchen. We were deeply grateful but decided to go the Davidsons'. A case of malaria in the home was not the same as a case of typhoid. Bob was helped to dress, and before noon we were in the Davidson home inside Chungking city.

After tiffin I went with Mrs. Davidson to an empty residence owned by their mission.[2] This stood outside the city walls, and Warburton had our little coffin brought here. We covered the casket with some black cloth and pinned large sprays of the most beautiful magnolias on its top. The casket had been rough and the varnish hastily applied; with the cloth and the flowers it looked less bleak. Mr. Davey was unavoidably occupied with the many affairs of our arrival and unloading, made more onerous for him by Bob's inability to help, and he was unable to attend the funeral services. These consisted simply of a scripture reading and short prayer at the grave side that afternoon in the small foreign cemetery on a hill near the Tsengkiayai Methodist boarding schools.[3]

1. Bob never succeeded in getting the malaria completely out of his system. He had recurring attacks every year or two (or so it seems in my memory). Often he managed to keep on his feet; I don't remember his ever going to a hospital, even when the fever was enough to make him delirious.
2. "Tiffin" is the Far Eastern word for the midday meal, luncheon. Grace and her teetotaler missionary friends may not have realized that it comes from an Anglo-Indian word for drinking.
3. When these events took place, in 1906, the American Methodist school compound and the nearby foreign cemetery were out in open country amid terraced rice fields and low, gravecovered hills, perhaps a mile beyond the city wall. Tsengkiayai (Tseng Family Cliff) was the name for the general area. In 1938 the Chinese government, driven out of Nanking and then Hankow, moved its capital to Chungking. Government departments, thousands of bureaucrats,

A few missionaries who had heard the news of our arrival were present to show their sympathy and concern. As the coffin was lowered by ropes into the grave, it did not lie straight. Dr. Freeman, whom we had tried to overtake in Wanhsien and who had arrived in Chungking a few days earlier, jumped down into the grave and straightened it. I had felt a terrible numbness for days since my first violent weeping and the beginning of Bob's illness. How could I constantly weep when he lay sick and my thought had to be for his welfare! But that friendly act by Dr. Freeman started my tears. I turned away from the grave as if looking for a friend, and one of the women stepped forward to comfort me.

The truth was that I had never before that day seen any of the people at that little service. It was a hard situation, but these new friends did all they could to soften it. I had little courage, but my endurance was sufficient for the day. Mrs. Myers made us take a cup of tea at her nearby home, and this gave me a chance to meet those who had stood by me at the grave. Their kindness brought them close to me that day. It is in these ways that people in foreign lands, isolated from their own blood, become welded together in ties of everlasting friendship.

But I was anxious to return to Bob, who had been sitting fully dressed by the fireplace in the Davidson home inside the city. He could not attend the laying away of his precious daughter; neither could he settle down in bed until it was done. When I came back and told him all was accomplished, he was content to be carried up to his room and get into bed to begin the struggle against his fever. Dr. McCartney was devoted in his attention. But the fever had taken strong hold in those days of untreated illness on the river and was slow to yield. We were obliged, accordingly, to spend some weeks in Chungking. During this sojourn Hetty and Warburton (we soon dropped formality) were like brother and sister to us. We will never forget their kindness.

---

and hundreds of thousands of refugees had to be accommodated. Tsengkiayai was the only direction the river-girt city could grow. By 1941, when I was assigned to the embassy in Chungking, the mission compound and foreign cemetery were little green islands lost in a maze of helter-skelter, flimsy, wartime construction. Not far south of the compound, and separated from the cemetery only by a brick wall, were the headquarters and one of the residences of Generalissimo Chiang Kai-shek. As could be expected, this became a favorite Japanese bombing target. The stone on Virginia's grave (to which Bob's ashes had been added by Grace in 1936) had been chipped and knocked askew by a Japanese near miss.

Being Methodists, as well as neighbors, the Generalissimo and his glamorous wife gave the mission great face by sometimes attending Sunday services at the school chapel. But the name Tsengkiayai is universally known in China today for a very different reason. Only a hundred yards or so to the north of the mission compound gate were the rented premises, down a narrow, crooked alley, which were the wartime office and residence of Chou En-lai and the Chinese Communist Party's delegation to the Nationalist Government.

When I returned to Chungking in 1971, the city had continued to grow, and the little foreign cemetery had disappeared.

Much later, we could laugh over some of the happenings. Trying to vary Bob's monotonous liquid diet, Hetty asked the doctor if he could take potato soup. The doctor inquired what it would contain and was told: milk, potato, and some onion. "All right," was the reply, "but no onion and no potato." As Bob had trouble sleeping, the doctor gave me a "sleeping mixture," telling me to give him a teaspoonful every night. I did and Bob slept like a log. One night a terrible fire broke out close to the Davidson compound. Flames lit the sky and showed red on our whitewashed bedroom walls. I was alarmed and talked to Warburton about possible danger. Their house was protected by a high brick wall, but other unprotected neighbors were in a wild state of terror. We could hear them yelling and dragging boxes in search of safety. Chungking is noted for these terrifying conflagrations.

Warburton suggested that I go with them to a platform on their roof to get a better view. Before going I tried to arouse Bob in case he might waken, see the fire, and be alarmed by my absence. But Bob lay like a dead man; try as I might, I could not wake him. Finally, I went aloft and let him sleep. The next morning I recounted this to the doctor. He asked how much of the sleeping medicine I had given. I showed him the spoon. "Goodness," said he, "no wonder he slept! I thought you would use a *British* teaspoon, which is a good deal smaller than this." My mother, years before, had given me a silver teaspoon for medicine and I had used it. After this Bob got smaller doses.

In April the weather grew hotter, and still Bob lay ill. One day the doctor assured me the fever was broken and our patient would soon be up. The next day his temperature reached a new high! Even the doctor was puzzled. We had to possess our hearts in patience and let time work in its own way.

In Shanghai we had been given Chinese names by Dr. Lyon in consultation with Chinese. In Szechwan the pronunciation differed so that the surname given us had the same sound as the word for "kill" (*sha*). Chungking friends said this would never do. We then asked them to pick a more suitable name. Our only stipulation was that it should *not* be the same as the Chinese name of Dr. and Mrs. C. W. Service of the Canadian Methodist Mission. Hsieh (gratitude) was chosen for us and we always liked it. Bob's given name was An-tao, which meant "peaceful way." Years later, Chinese friends in Chengtu picked a name for me: Yun-tao. This went well with his, and the same characters had been used by a noted woman writer of long ago whose full name was Hsieh Tao-yun. We later learned that the other Services had the same surname; actually, though we lived for years in the same city, there seemed to be little trouble caused by the name identity in both English and Chinese.

During this time in Chungking I was busy caring for Bob and writing the difficult letters home telling of Virginia's last days. It was good for me to keep occupied, and I tried to be as cheerful as possible for Bob's sake. The doctor wanted me to get out, so nearly every afternoon Warburton had trusty chair-bearers carry me through the only land gate of the city into the countryside. All the other gates opened toward the Yangtze or Kialing rivers. After a short excursion I would be brought home again. One day the men carried me into a dense crowd and finally set the chair down. It was a closed, or curtained, chair. I was soon glad for this protection when the bearers seemed to disappear and crowds pressed all too closely around me. When I told Warburton about this, he questioned the bearers and found they had set me down so they might better witness the execution of some criminals. We had stopped at the execution grounds.

Chungking occupies a high, rocky promontory between two rivers. There were then no wheeled vehicles inside the walls nor within sight of them. The city streets were narrow, crowded, dark, smoky, and full of jostling people. Pigs, dogs, and chickens scuttled and scrapped under foot; small horses climbed the steep stone steps like goats. All water for domestic and every other use had to be carried up from the two rivers by coolies using shoulder poles and larger wooden buckets. At each of the riverine city gates, long files of these water-men were always to be seen; some were privately hired servants, others sold their loads to a regular clientele or to the first buyer to come along. The hundreds of roughly paved sandstone steps were always wet from the slopping pails, and everywhere on the streets one saw signs of water carrying.

Many so-called streets were only slits between high walls; often a street was nothing more than a narrow flight of stone steps, many of them cut from the living rock. On these confined thoroughfares the open shop fronts displayed every sort of activity and occupation. Weaving, tailoring, brass working, blacksmithing, and a thousand other trades were carried on in public view. Innumerable food shops, and itinerant "tuck shops" carried about on shoulder poles, tempted the hungry. Their odors were often appetizing; but rancid grease, smoking oil, and burning peppers frequently put forth near-stifling pungency. Over all these mingled smells there was the inescapable odor from hundreds of open, unscreened latrines to be found on every street and byway. The content of these receptacles had commercial value: many sought a few cash by setting up such a public convenience.

I was invited to a reception being given for a new American consul. The doctor told me I ought to go. I wore one of my trousseau dresses, a heavy soft grey silk, woven of black and white threads. It had full sleeves, and was trimmed with heavy white lace. One British lady was entranced with this dress and asked, as a special favor, to be allowed to come to the house to examine the sleeves. She was the wife of a businessman and enjoyed the new styles more than most missionary ladies were able to. My clothes were of considerable interest in Chungking; though my trousseau was approaching two years old, it seemed novel and unusual to those who were years from home.

Finally, as Bob was not gaining in the city, we moved across the Yangtze to the newly completed residence of the Friends' Mission at their boys' school atop the hills. Warburton's brother, Alfred, and his wife, Carrie, were living there and made us welcome to their new home, which still smelled of fresh lumber and lime. In the little valleys between the two ranges of hills we saw the lovely blossoms of opium poppies which filled the small fields with their fragile grace. They gave the landscape beauty, but with a sinister threat to the public good.

7

To Chengtu

(1906)

Bob slowly began to walk about in the Davidsons' garden. We used to take a path around the hillside nearly every morning and sit at the cliff's edge to look down at Chungking, below and across the river, where it lay in a mantle of smoke and river fog. Slowly his convalescence progressed.

Our first letters from America brought the sad news of the death of my grandmother in Iowa. I had lived with her during eighth grade and the first three years of high school. We were married from her home and had started from there to California in the summer of 1905. She was always an inspiration; a staunch New Englander; quick and discerning in judgment and speech, with a clever turn at apt phrases; always hospitable and tolerant; clever with sewing and knitting. I remember her as she sat so often in her big rocker by the east window of the sitting room in her old home. Her work box was close at hand on a table, and near it lay the two weeklies, the Presbyterian *Interior* and the *Springfield Republican*, ready for reading. Grandma often read aloud and we loved to hear her. The most memorable articles were those accounts of Siberian political exiles as told by George Kennan in one of the magazines of the day.[1] The effect on me has never entirely disappeared, and long after I heard those readings I was sending postcards to Katherine Breshkovsky, then in Siberian exile. She could receive no letters, only postcards without messages.

After Virginia's death, followed so closely by the news of Grandma's passing (which actually came first but slow mails delayed our knowing it), life

---

1. The George Kennan that Grace refers to was a cousin of the grandfather of George F. Kennan, the famous diplomat, ambassador to Russia, and diplomatic historian. The first George Kennan traveled extensively in Siberia in the late 1880s. His reports, first published in magazine articles and then in the two-volume *Siberia and the Exile System,* were widely read and lastingly influential.

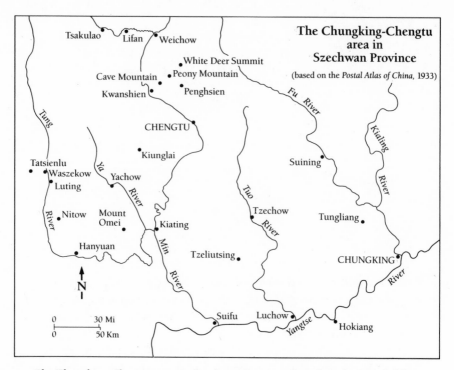

The following labels appear on the map:

The Chungking-Chengtu area in Szechwan Province
(based on the *Postal Atlas of China*, 1933)

Tsakulao · Lifan · Weichow
White Deer Summit
Cave Mountain · Peony Mountain
Kwanshien · Penghsien
Fu River
Tung
CHENGTU
Kiating
Kiunglai
Tatsienlu
Waszekow · Yachow
Luting
Ya River
Suining
River
Tuo River
River
Nitow · Mount Omei
Tzechow
Tungliang
Kiating
Hanyuan
Min River
Tzeliutsing
CHUNGKING
River
N

0 ——— 30 Mi
0 ——— 50 Km

Suifu · Luchow
Yangtse
Hokiang

The Chungking-Chengtu area in Szechwan Province (based on the Postal Atlas
of China, *1933)*

seemed very changed. I looked at my husband, recently a great California athlete. Now he was pale and weak. The scrubby beard and mustache, the hollow eyes and pallor gave him the appearance of the so-called "lungers" who in my childhood used to flock to California in search of health. Most of them came too late and were soon in their graves. One of my maternal uncles, not knowing the sturdiness of the Service family, had criticized Bob's appearance before our marriage, saying that he was "too blonde and looked like a consumptive." Sometimes life seemed difficult, but fortunately I was not of a dependent nature.

Soon Bob showed real improvement. The Warburton Davidsons were preparing to set out overland to Chengtu to attend a Friends' Meeting early in May. It would be a great opportunity for us, and it was decided that we could join them. They were to stop for a weekend in the small town of Tungliang, which would provide a rest for Bob. Warburton and Hetty were famous overland travelers and had a well-developed procedure which their servants followed with meticulous care. They arranged every detail so that the trip would be as easy as possible for us. We appreciated this at the time, but did not understand its full import until later when managing our own overland travels. As Tungliang carriers were considered especially good for long trips, Warburton sent there for men. They were excellent bearers.

Hetty, Bob, and I rode in comfortable four-man closed sedan chairs of the old style. At that time practically no one used the "open chair," which is little more than a simple rattan chair mounted unenclosed between two poles. The old Chinese closed chairs were somewhat bulky, but they were also easy

9   These are "four-man closed sedan chairs of the old style" similar to those in which Grace and Bob traveled from Chungking to Chengtu. The scene is the Service front gate in Chengtu.

10   *Later, foreigners came to prefer the less claustrophobic "open chair." These
are the Heldes on the road in 1918 (see chapter 30).*

for riding. They were made of bamboo and wood and had enveloping roof
and sides covered with blue cloth. Curtains of green oilcloth were provided
to keep out rain. There were also cloth curtains for privacy, and finely split
bamboo sun blinds. The seats were hard bamboo slats, but there were straw-
stuffed cushions for seat and back. In addition, one could fold a *pugai* to
cushion both seat and back. Bob had a *pugai* and also a large pillow for his
back. There was space under the seat for toilet articles: a wash basin, soap
and towel, and perhaps a candle. A few other things could be stuffed in as
well, perhaps some reading matter and a snack in a biscuit tin. Above, at the
front of the chair's roof, there was usually a small shelf with a retaining edge
which could hold some fruit or a book. Across the front of the chair, resting
on ledges under the side windows, was a removable cloth-covered lapboard
four to six inches wide on which one could rest a book or lean arms or
elbows for relaxation.

This was the daily routine. Early in the morning, the servants saw to it
that we had hot water betimes for face washing. Then the coolies came in
and soon were taking down beds and mosquito nets, packing bedding and

cots, and stowing things in load baskets and sedan chairs. After this came our breakfast, and a hurried packing by servants of food supplies, dishes, and everything in the commissary department. We then started off, and some seven or eight miles would be traveled before the bearers stopped for their breakfast. By the time this halt was over, our cook and food baskets would have pushed on ahead, and after our next lap of travel we would stop to find the tiffin table ready for our noon meal. Hot water would be available for washing, and we would walk about a bit to rest our limbs before we sat down to eat. Then up again and off for the afternoon's stretch, with several stops for the men to rest and smoke.

At the end of the day's stage we were welcomed by the cook, who had again forged ahead and found accommodation for us in what we fondly hoped was the best inn the town afforded. It might be a fairly new building or an old dilapidated place. In either case, dirt and smells were sure. Inn-keepers always kept swine and for some reason preferred to build their pens near the guest rooms. We chose the best rooms available; the coolies set up cot beds, hung nets, filled kerosene lanterns, and got everything ready for the night. Meantime, the cook was fully occupied with preparing a complete meal. He usually bought meat, prepared soup, a meat or fowl dish, vegetables, and probably served tinned fruit for dessert. He also baked in the evenings and cooked porridge to be quickly heated for the next morning's breakfast.

After our evening meal we wrote a hasty letter or made entries in diaries while waiting for hot water for good sponge baths. This affair of a bath might have to be accomplished behind one's bed net, or perhaps even in total darkness, for a constant crowd of onlookers stood closely around us to watch every movement. In 1906 foreigners were still a vast novelty to the inland Chinese. Many people pressed tightly around us every time our chairs were set down. At meal times the cook often could hardly serve us for the pressure of humanity. We would politely ask them to stand back, but in no time they would stand again at our elbows, watching each mouthful we ate, trying to smell our bread, and exhibiting the curiosity of overgrown children. People followed us to our bedrooms, scrutinizing every move through doors and windows; and when these were closed, damp fingers on soft paper windows easily produced apertures for many an unblinking eye to continue close study of the foreign devils.

After we went to bed we often heard the cook at work in the courtyard. The aroma of baking bread mingled with the stale flavors of the stuffy inn rooms. You will have noticed from this description of overland sedan chair travel in those days that the cook played an important part. He could not loaf on his job very much; a good one was well worthy of the Szechwanese title of *dashifu,* or "manager of important affairs." Usually, one gave the cook a two-man chair and made the food loads light so the kitchen could make quick time on the road.

Warburton, who was general of the expedition, rode a horse; this helped him keep close track of his caravan. At one time he would be in front, later riding by his wife's chair, then joking with Bob and pointing out some new sight to us. His care in rounding up straggling carriers made the journey go smoothly, for of course each night must see all our loads safely in the inn where we lodged.[2]

Our weekend stop in Tungliang was spent in the home of two fine English people of the Friends' Mission. Their house was a simple one, semi-Chinese, and with a rare and charming hospitality. Here in Tungliang we saw hundreds of Chinese gather for meetings addressed by the foreign missionaries, and we could feel something of the influence that our host and his wife were exerting.

As Bob had stood the trip well so far, we went on toward Chengtu. We broke the journey by stopping for a day at Tzechow, where we stayed in the home of the Manlys of the American Methodist Mission. They gave us a warm welcome, and plenty of freshly prepared food supplies for the remaining four days of our trip. The spring weather was delightful for most of our journey, though enough rain fell to show us the disadvantage of chair travel in a downpour. Rain in China often seems to attack from all directions and to descend with a force we never expect elsewhere. The early mornings were lovely in the pearly mists of the little valleys between the hills. We watched with interest the farmers go into their fields and plod about their work. On market days, the roads were long lines of blue-clad figures with shoulder poles, taking vegetables, fowls, or other farm produce to the village of that day's trade.

At last we crossed the Lungchuanyi hills. Spread before us was the Chengtu plain, the rich, verdant heart of Szechwan's great Red Basin. Soon we saw the massive walls of Chengtu rising beyond paddy fields. Then we were in the long, winding street of the suburb outside the East Gate.[3]

2. After a spartan introduction to missionary accommodations at Ichang, Grace had good luck on this stage. If my memory is correct, the Davidsons were in the small but fortunate minority of missionaries who were not wholly dependent on what their missions were able to provide. Certainly this overland travel seems a bit more "first class" than the usual Service family travel that I remember in later years. The general organization and daily routine were similar, but some things were different. For one thing, we usually ate Chinese food, prepared by our own cook, which we boys thought was great. Also, I don't recall the emphasis on the daily sponge bath. In fact, we considered overland travel to be a great lark.

3. The distance from Chungking to Chengtu by the road they traveled was about 250 miles. Normal travel time was ten days. With a weekend stop at Tungliang and a day at Tzechow, they probably took twelve or thirteen days.

PART TWO

SETTLED IN CHENGTU

8

Mount Omei Summer

(1906)

On May 10 we entered Chengtu and proceeded along the Great East Street, the city's chief thoroughfare. It was considerably more imposing than any street we had previously seen in a Chinese city. We had reached our goal. It was a momentous day, saddened only by the thoughts of our precious Virginia.

As the Friends were having a gathering of their mission, we were to be entertained temporarily in the home of Mr. and Mrs. Joseph Beech of the American Methodist Mission. However, we first went with Warburton and Hetty to the Friends' compound,[1] where we met Dr. and Mrs. Hodgkin and were welcomed by them and the elder Davidsons, "R. J." and "M. J." We stayed only a few minutes and then went on to the Methodist compound where we had another warm welcome from the Beeches. Their little Margaret was being carried by an amah with bound feet. I was stricken at the sight and felt this must be a frightful ordeal. I soon discovered that thousands, indeed millions, of women in China suffer this way all their lives. Now the custom is dying, but it still is not eradicated.

Dr. and Mrs. Canright lived in another house in the Methodist compound, and near by were the rising walls of the mission's new hospital. Mr. and Mrs. Openshaw of the American Baptist Mission in Yachow, four days travel to the west, were visiting in the Canright home. All these foreigners came in that evening to welcome us and hear of our travel. It was almost six months since we left California, and we had undergone a good deal in the way of experience.

Here at the Beech home we were in a foreign house built in a semi-Chinese manner. The upper rooms were low with slanting ceilings. A ve-

1. "Compound" is the term generally used for a walled enclosure within which foreigners live. It comes from a Malay word, *kampong*. In China one did not speak of a Chinese compound: it was always a place where foreigners lived—within walls.

11 "Within a few days Bob seated himself at a small bamboo table on a corner of this veranda. Opposite him was a Chinese teacher named Yeh. There began the long pull at language study."

randa surrounded the lower floor. Within a few days Bob seated himself at a small bamboo table on a corner of this veranda. Opposite him was a Chinese teacher named Yeh. There began the long pull at language study which has to pave the way for understanding and work in the land of Cathay. At that time there were no formal language schools. The trial and error system was largely used, and one had little help in grammar and in mastering the elusive tones. Our teacher spoke the Szechwan variety of Mandarin and we were thankful to make a start. I studied also, but very soon began to have attacks of sharp abdominal pain. These left me weak and with little ambition for anything.

After a fortnight we moved over to the Hodgkin residence, where we had an upper east bedroom with veranda. The two Friends families gave a large reception for us. Both Hodgkin and Davidson houses were open and we spent part of our time in each house. The weather was warm, the flower gardens were lovely, and most of Chengtu's foreign community of about fifty people turned out to meet us.

Bob continued his study on the Hodgkin veranda, and I continued having attacks of pain. Before June was far gone, three foreign doctors had a consultation regarding my problem. The pain, they decided, was neuralgia of the stomach, and I was given spirits of ether to allay it. Also, everyone agreed that we should get away for the summer.

Arrangements were made for us to travel to Mount Omei with Laura Hambley of the Canadian Methodist Mission and Helen Witte of the American Methodists. Miss Hambley had not been out [in China] long, but she knew enough of the language to manage the party. Miss Witte had arrived only a few months before us. The pleasure and profit of our first summer was largely due to these two fine friends, particularly to Laura Hambley whose kind thought had suggested that we accompany them and share living arrangements.

We had a small mat-roofed boat for the trip on the Min River to Kiating.[2] The ladies had another; the two boats were to keep together all the time. There were numerous vicissitudes on the journey. Mosquitoes were terrible in Kiating. There we left the river and took sedan chairs for a day and a half to Tawosze, a temple on the flank of the sacred mountain, Omei Shan. The mountain itself is over 11,000 feet in elevation, but the temple is at about 2,700 feet. After a miserable night in an inn at the foot of the mountain, we started up the lower slopes of the mountain to the temple.

Miss Witte was so sorry for her chair bearers on a steep grade of rough steps that she got out to walk. Her men then hustled along and soon had such a lead that they could not hear her calling them to wait for her. Of course, they knew that she now wished to ride; but preferring to carry an empty chair, they tarried for nothing. Finally, Bob had to push ahead and overtake them. By the time she got in, Miss Witte was so exhausted by the heat that she announced she would ride no matter how steep the road. Naturally, we were not accustomed to be carried up long, steep flights of rough-hewn steps; so we did have great sympathy for the bearers; and they played up to our compassion. After many similar trips we became used to such travel. We always did what we could to relieve the men. I was content to ride most of the time, but as I weighed only about one hundred pounds, I was not an excessive burden for three or four men. Bob did his climbing on his own feet.

At Tawosze we had two rooms at one side off one of the lower entrance courts. Everything was Chinese save our cots with bedding and mosquito nets. We also had two folding canvas armchairs made after a British army model. We used a square temple table for study and had some heavy wooden chairs that belonged with the rooms. Laura and Helen, our companions, had a larger suite of rooms on the opposite side of the same courtyard, and the four of us combined our eating arrangements. Laura had brought the cook, so she managed him for the first few days; then Helen took her turn; finally I, in my first few stumbling Mandarin words, tried to give directions for meals.

2. The Min River between Chengtu and Kiating is, by comparison with the Yangtze, a small and shallow stream. So the boat by which Bob and Grace traveled was much smaller and simpler than the stately houseboat of the Gorges. It was what the Chinese called a *wuban;* apart from its smaller size, it lacked the high stern of the Yangtze junk. The trip from Chengtu to Kiating probably took two or three days. Kiating is now known as Leshan.

The cook had never been much more than a table boy and knew little about cooking. Our fare was plain and simple. Helen had an amah, and we a coolie, so there was plenty of help.

All four of us were studying Chinese, but Bob kept at it more consistently than I. The climate seemed to make us sleepy, and we usually took naps after the noon meal. In the late afternoons there were hikes around the temple purlieus, or tennis in the upper stone-paved court in front of the main building. Some thirty-five foreigners were at Tawosze that season. We made many friends and had a jolly time, with picnics to the Flying Bridges and other scenic parts of the mountain, and tennis matches at the temple when there were not too many *hui*. This particular kind of *hui* is a gathering of friends or neighbors who visit the temple for collective worship toward some specific end. These groups would arrive in long processions with many banners, firecrackers, and incense. The whole place would be overrun with the worshippers, who were usually delighted with the unexpected extra benefit of seeing us, our rooms, and our peculiar ways.[3]

We became well acquainted with Dr. Florence O'Donnell at the temple that summer. She stayed with friends and occupied a room just above our sleeping room. As only rough floor boards separated us, we could hear her every step. When she took a bath, we frequently participated to the extent of a mild shower. Of course, in those temple rooms we had no conveniences and lived in camping style; but we did have portable galvanized bathtubs of oval shape into which the coolie would pour a bucket or two of water. We carried these to the mountain, and there in the temple they proved luxurious indeed.

3. Grace followed the usual habit of referring to any Chinese religious building as a temple, and those attached to them as priests. There were differences, in both faith and function. Tawosze, as indicated by the *sze* in its name, was a Buddhist monastery.

In these early days, the foreigners had not yet developed their own summer resorts. In their belief that it was essential for health reasons to get away from the oppressive heat and summer pestilences of the plains, mountain monasteries were a favorite choice. They were usually in a place of quiet isolation, purposely away from large towns. They were almost always in a situation of natural beauty. It was a beauty which their own presence and great age enhanced. One chief reason was that it was *only* in temple grounds, and on immediately adjacent temple property, that one could see groves of mature, majestic trees. Also, these monasteries were objects of pilgrimage and places where scholars and literati were fond of relaxing close to nature. So the monasteries often had extensive, if simple, accommodations for guests. The abbots in charge apparently had no objection to renting these to apostles of a rival faith.

Relations may have been economic, but faith could not be wholly ignored. Being a monastery, there was always a resident community of monks—whose numbers were governed by the size, prestige, and prosperity of the institution. And the monks, like monks everywhere, had their daily round of religious services. We boys were probably more interested in these than were our elders. The very early morning, soon after dawn, was a good time—as one lay in bed—to hear the deep, unintelligible chanting of the sutras, punctuated now and then by a low-voiced bell or a drum, or the hollow sound of the wooden fish. Of course, the missionaries had their own prayer meetings and religious services—on monastery premises—but these were more somber in nature.

During this summer I had the only attack of malaria that I had in China and was in bed for several days. Miss Wilkins, then of the Canadian Mission, was the trained nurse who helped me. How wonderfully she rubbed my aches and pains away! The Canadian ladies of Kiating had brought their own cows up onto the mountain and so were the only people who had fresh milk. They kindly sent me several cups each day while I was sick.

I wrote my mother about this friendly act. As she was always very ardent against cruelty to animals, she at once wrote back that she thought it terrible to take cows up to such places by roads which had flights of steps. In fact, she was thoroughly aroused by this innocent action of the missionary ladies. As we had seen plenty of horses scrambling with riders or heavy loads up the slippery, wet stone steps at Chungking's city gates, a leisurely mountain climb to Tawosze did not seem so bad to us. I wrote Mother how the Chinese outfitted cows and even pigs with straw sandals for such trips, to save their hoofs and prevent slipping on the steps. I also told her of the way pigs are often carried to market in slings made of bamboo slats, each piggy borne by two carriers. Of course, this was after the porker was fattened for sale and was intended to prevent the loss of a pound or two en route to the knife. Still, it gave the pig a ride and showed thought on the owner's part.

Mother was unimpressed. Her last remark in this months-long discussion was to the effect that I had already become hardened to ways that would shock and horrify in America. Five to six months was the normal time for an exchange of letters between Szechwan and California; one almost forgot the question before the reply came back. As to pigs, we have frequently seen them carried in odd ways. As recently as three years ago, riding on North Szechwan Road in a Shanghai ricksha, I suddenly found myself abreast of another ricksha in which rode two well-grown black pigs. One was on the seat, the other on the little foot platform.

An important event of the summer was a trip to Mount Omei's Golden Summit. We joined a party of friends. The intent was to travel simply, but of course we had to take beds and food. We went up the small road called "the ninety-nine turns" and returned to Tawosze by the "big road." The lower section of the small road above the Flying Bridges partly followed the bed of a stream, and the coolies carrying my chair often had to step from rock to rock with water rushing between them. Later the canyon became so narrow that there was no space for foot of man or beast. There we mounted a somewhat rickety "bridge" running lengthwise of the stream. Beams set in sockets cut into the rock walls supported a pathway of rough planks along one side of the gorge. Some of the ninety-nine turns were so sharp and steep that even my simple mountain chair with skillful mountain carriers could not negotiate them until Bob got in between the poles and lifted at the critical moments.

·12   This is the type of "mountain chair" that Grace used for her
mountaineering trips. (The actual occupant here is unknown.)

We spent a night at Nine Old Caves, staying in the excellent temple and
visiting the outer part of the caves. These were damp and slippery, and full of
bats swooping about us. We did not go far in, much preferring the beautiful
verdure of the mountainside. Here at this temple, a green-clad cliff hung with
ferns, creepers, orchids, and lovely wild begonias was a delectable sight.

Going on, we took in all the pleasures of a slow climb. Because Golden
Summit is slightly over 11,000 feet, the temperature change from Tawosze is
considerable. Vegetation runs riot all over the mountain. Ferns, rhododendrons, laurels, hydrangeas, and a myriad other species of shrub, flower,
and tree delight one's senses at every turn. In clear weather one gets a magnificent panorama from the Golden Summit; the mighty snow peaks of the
Tibetan border can be seen in all their glory. We were fortunate to have an
unbroken view of the whole line of peaks, a breathtaking sight.

As soon as we reached Golden Summit late one afternoon, our Boy urged
us to hurry to the platform at the edge of the great precipice. Here on one
side we saw the snow mountains; and on the other side, the setting sun being
low in the sky, we beheld our enlarged shadows, heads encircled with rain-
bow hues, thrown on the clouds below the cliff. A priest standing by assured
us that only the good saw this much-desired sight. The phenomenon is similar
to the Spectre of the Brocken, seen in the Harz Mountains; at Omei it is known
as *Foguang* (Buddha's glory). Buddhists claim it is light from the aureole of
Buddha and a sign of the holiness of the place. Pilgrims wrought up by reli-

gious zeal have thrown themselves over this three-thousand-foot precipice to meet the Buddha; to deter others, a railing is fixed at the cliff's edge.

On the trip down from Golden Summit the Big Road gave us new sights and more extended mountain vistas, as this road follows wider canyons. We also met many ascending pilgrims who choose the larger road because of its better steps and more gradual ascent. Among these were women, frequently with bound feet, who hired men to carry them up the mountain. Loads in these hilly areas are carried on V-shaped wooden back-frames. A passenger sits atop this frame on a couple of wooden slats. This puts him (her) facing in the same direction as the carrier, with knees just above his shoulders. The bearer is equipped with a sturdy crutch-stick like a third leg. When they stop to rest, they place the crutch-stick under the back-frame, lean back to ease themselves of the weight, and catch a brief respite from the heavy toil of the journey. At this time they expel their breath with a peculiar whistling sound. This apparently helps to revive their flagging spirits as well as their weary muscles. On the twisting road one often heard this whistle and knew that a loaded man was resting; sure enough, as one rounded the curve, he would come in view.

At Tawosze, Dr. C. W. Service had a little clinic. As he returned from a trip

13   The "Golden Summit" of Omei, the sacred mountain. Along the crest are pilgrimage temples. "Buddha's glory" appears, when conditions are right, on the cloudbank at the left below the great precipice.

14   *Back-frames for mountain travel. On Mount Omei about 1907.*

to Golden Summit, he heard that a young priest on the upper mountain had been badly mauled by a leopard. Because this was considered to be punishment for his sins, he was turned out of his temple. Nobody would help him, and he was lying helpless and abandoned in a rude bamboo hut. When Charlie [Dr. Service] saw his plight, he asked for him to be put on a *beizi* [carrying frame] and brought to his clinic. No one was willing to do even this, but Charlie finally persuaded a carrier to bring the wounded man down.

I heard about the affair and suddenly felt a great desire to see the doctor at work. The Chinese assistants had tried to clean up the man but he was a sad sight; dirty, worn with fatigue, and his body covered with itch. He wore only ragged pants, and some bloody scraps of old matting were tied around his body and arm. The wounds were chiefly around the left elbow. In the course of the doctor's cleaning the terrible-looking wounds some solution was used in a syringe. When I saw this liquid going in one opening above the elbow and coming out from two holes, one slightly above the elbow and another below it, I began to feel queerly. One of the Chinese assistants pointed to an open door. I went out and sat down on some steps rising from a small court. The next I knew, I was pushing a big bottle of ammonia from under my nose. The man recovered and became another medical triumph for the hard-working mission doctor, who found need on every side, even on his summer holidays.

Bob made another excursion to Golden Summit, this time with Mr. Manly, to do some exploring. They went to Nine Old Caves and around under the face of the great perpendicular cliff, hoping to be able to get up that way. They found no feasible route; but, scrambling up the side canyon, they finally came on a charcoal burner's trail and were able to ascend by it to the main ridge of the mountain. On the afternoon of their return after three days of strenuous climbing, Bob took a quick sponge-off and was soon on the tennis court, ready for a set. On his trip he had worn a blue woolen shirt from which the color ran; his white skin was dyed in streaks which did not come off for weeks. He began collecting butterflies this summer and found it an absorbing and interesting avocation.

The summer was not without its romance. Mr. Taylor of Yachow was frequently at our temple rooms for tea. And the tea, of course, was always in the suite of the Misses Hambley and Witte. Helen Witte was very coy, but we all saw how things were going. We jocularly referred to the courting gentleman as "Grey Legs" because of his favorite color in trousers, but this name was never applied to him in person. A mention of his nickname would make Helen blush. Bob and I left Tawosze the day before Laura and Helen. As I left the temple in my chair, I said good-bye to Helen, telling her to look well after Grey Legs, who would soon be lonesome in Yachow. She flushed deeply and burst out: "I'm so glad you know about us; we were wanting to tell you." So the cat was out of the bag! Alas, I was in a poor frame of mind to meet Dr. O'Donnell. She had told me she was sure the two were engaged; but I had said no, and that I'd eat my hat if they were. My only hat on the trip was a sun topee.

9

Our Own Home

(1907)

Back in Chengtu we were soon house hunting. The Friends were willing to let us have land for a house; but we had been told by the YMCA to rent, that there was no money to buy or build. It was difficult to find any suitable place, or one that we could rent if it were suitable. Chinese do not always care to rent to foreign tenants whose ideas of house arrangement and fitments were so different from their own. Mr. Beech finally came to our assistance. The [American] Methodist Episcopal Mission owned a property on a street named Wenmiaogai,[1] in the southwest part of the city, where it conducted a middle school for boys. It was expected that the school would grow and eventually need a larger place. To the west of the school was a temple.[2] To the east there was a Chinese residence property. This offered the only solution for the school's expansion. Mr. Beech proposed that the mission buy and lease it to the Y until needed by the school. The mission would have its room for growth, and a present income.

Mr. Beech took us both with him when he went to look at the property. The men insisted that I accompany them so I could penetrate into the women's quarters. Of all the places we had seen, this seemed the most satisfactory, though the rooms I saw were filthy and dark. Our vision looked into the future and saw fresh, clean walls, glass windows, and other foreign additions for comfort and convenience. After long talks and negotiations through a middleman, the purchase was at last complete. Next was a long interval until the owners could move. Then there had to be a mighty cleaning. Finally, we moved, bag and baggage, into the new premises.

---

1. *Gai* in the name means "street." It is the Szechwanese pronunciation of the character *jie*.
2. The temple was the local government's temple to Confucius. Its Chinese name was Wenmiao, "Temple of Learning." Because our street was the one on which the temple stood, the street was Temple of Learning Street. The temple helped to make it a good neighborhood and had some fine trees.

A rather imposing front gate opened into a forecourt. Crosswise in this court was a handsome spirit screen. At each side there was access to a small side court. These provided space for the gateman and his family, servants' living quarters, and a stable. Across the north side of the forecourt was an open structure, a sort of pavilion, or *tingzi*. This was convenient for sedan chairs. Passing through this pavilion, one entered a brick-paved upper court. There were rooms opening off each side and in the pavilion. Across the north side of this court was the main residence. This was a single-story building in the local Szechwan style and five *jian* long.[3]

We signed a lease for the property. The mission agreed to pay for lumber and materials for the needed alterations. The YMCA was to pay for the labor. We moved into the rooms on either side of the *tingzi*. The large room on the east was our living room; the corresponding room on the west was our bedroom. The windows were paper, the doors anything but tight. Luckily it was a record winter for warm, sunny days. Great was the excitement at opening boxes the contents of which we had never seen. Some of our household equipment had been ordered in the spring of 1905; it was now the fall of 1906.

The *Ladies' Home Journal* in those days had many pictures of house interiors. From them we gleaned many suggestions. Our front hall, with a landing halfway up the stairs and a door under this, was copied from such an illustration. The rooms at the two sides of the upper court were torn down and the material was used to expand the main residence. Both ends of the building were widened and a second story, for bedrooms, was added. What had been a long, single-story structure connected to the side buildings of a court now became an H-shaped, free-standing, two-storied, semiforeign house. Most rooms were Chinese lath and plaster, but there was a wooden wainscoting in the study, and the dining room was panelled in wood. The kitchen was at the back but within the main house. Most people had detached kitchens, so ours was considered a novelty. Of course it lacked any built-in cabinets. But we had plenty of cupboards made according to my plan. Table tops were finished in glistening black varnish with the tung oil base that is now so much in demand abroad.[4]

There was no one to manage the workmen but Bob; no one to show the masons how to construct a brick fireplace and chimney but Bob. He was kept busy all day, often finding his limitations of language most trying. What we did not know about house construction or domestic management we had to learn, and were glad of advice by those who had been through similar

---

3. A *jian*, often translated "room," is the standard space between pillars in Chinese residential construction. My memory guesses that it is about eleven or twelve feet.

4. Tung oil, or wood oil, comes from the kernel of a tree that is widely grown in East Szechwan. Before the day of synthetics it provided the base for the best varnishes and used to be a major Szechwan export.

experiences. To our youthful enthusiasm, everything moved at a snails' pace; still, there was progress. Early in 1907 we began to move into the house proper.

The sewing machine whirred hour after hour as I made curtains for every one of the new windows, which boasted so much glass that our Chinese friends were amazed. Next to the glass of our small casements in the big south bay of our living room hung little, ruffled, white dotted-swiss curtains looped back at the sides. Over-drapes were of a soft, rather heavy blue silk figured in a woven geometric design. (This material was later dyed and re-dyed until I finally gave it away in Tsingtao in 1934, still not in any way worn out.) On the floor of this room we put our tan and blue Tientsin carpet. How we danced about on this when it was unpacked and spread on the floor! On my birthday Bob gave me a cute little tea-table with a shelf. He had designed this himself and had it made by a carpenter on the place without my knowledge. What a joy it was to move into a clean, second-floor bedroom with nicely oiled floor, large casement windows, a clothes closet, and an adjoining bathroom with convenient backstairs for the carrying of bath water![5]

I was having attacks of severe abdominal pain every now and then. When a paroxysm hit I would hope I'd never live to experience another. Sometimes I seemed to lose my eyesight and could only feel for Bob's hand in my keen distress. We both tried to study as we could, and the teacher came regularly; but I was busy teaching absolutely green servants, and Bob had to be vigilant with the workmen. His neglect might mean a waste of time or material. But any negligence on my part might mean contamination of our food and consequent illness. I *had* to be on my job.

Looking back, I have seen many excellent servants to whom one can trust the details of foreign kitchens, but their care and method has been learned in the school of eternal vigilance during their training. To tell a Boy once to do a thing is never enough.[6] The perpetual daily alertness of the mistress, the repetition of instructions over many months is what finally produces care in the hygienic preparation of our food and the cleaning of our rooms. I have frequently heard women exclaim over stupid servants, saying that it is impossible to train them. There are *some* impossible to train, but *usually* it is the mistress who lacks the patience or will not take the time.

5. Our family lived in this house until 1920. All three of us boys were born there. Since I lived in it for the first eleven years of my life, and relatively short times in other places, I always thought of it as "home." When Caroline and I were invited to return to China in 1971, we visited Chengtu and I asked to visit the house. Where we had lived, there resided some twelve families. The whole place had deteriorated sadly. And it seemed much smaller than I had remembered it! By 1984 the whole compound had been torn down and the site covered with rather nondescript modern buildings. The Temple of Learning had disappeared long before.

6. When the word "Boy" is capitalized, it will refer to the servant, often of mature age and great dignity, who waits on the table and, depending on the household, fills the role of major-domo or butler. A lower-case "boy" is simply a young lad.

After our return from Mount Omei we had to assemble some servants. There were none to be had who could boast any foreign training, but we did try to find men about whom something was known. The cook was a young man known to the Davidsons. The table-boy was a chap who had been a Yangtze tracker. He was young for that hard life and had been brought to Chengtu by one of the Canadian missionaries. We took him, but he had no suitable clothes, and we agreed to buy the usual long cotton gowns. He was to purchase three, and we gave him the money to pay for them.

One day soon afterward there was a great commotion at our front gate. A man was crying to the gateman that we owed him money. Bob went out and discovered that it was the tailor who had made the Boy's three gowns. As we had already given the Boy this money, he was called and had to admit the debt to the tailor. However, he said he had no money. Bob could not have the tailor suffer for our servant's trickery, so he told the man that we would pay him but that the Boy would have to settle with us. This made the Boy exceedingly angry. Realizing that he had lost much face, he flew into a violent, black rage. In a trice, his face turned livid like that of a fury. He threw himself on Bob, yelling, muttering, spitting in his wrath. He seized Bob by the throat and pulled his necktie tight like a noose with his left hand while he struck out with his right in no gentle manner. Bob kept pulling at his collar, trying to loosen it, while he warded off blows. He did not attempt to strike back. Finally the man hit below the belt in a very menacing way.

I had run into the *tingzi* to find out what was going on. Bob called to me to stay well away; it was impossible to know what the man might do. The gateman had run for the policeman at our corner. This worthy came, but did nothing save look on. A large crowd soon collected at our gate, attracted by the Boy's loud cries that a foreigner was killing a Chinese. But all near enough to see could tell that Bob was not the aggressor. At last, the Boy was prevailed on to leave off his attack. He was then arrested and taken off by the policeman. I had to cut Bob's necktie off. The knot was so tight that it was impossible to untie even when cut free. The man stayed in jail for a week or two and then Bob sent his card to have him let out. Naturally, we did not want to have him working for us. But his old clothes had disappeared so we let him make his departure in one of the new gowns.

This is the only time Bob was ever attacked by any Chinese. By keeping cool and refraining from retaliation, he had all the spectators with him. They saw he had done nothing to warrant the attack. Some of our neighbors (Chinese, of course) spoke later to him and to our gateman about the affair, saying that the Boy had behaved in a very bad manner and that Bob had only defended himself as anyone would. His actions that day won him a place in our whole neighborhood.

Christmas we celebrated quietly at the Canright home on Christmas evening with the members of the Methodist Mission. We had nuts, fruits, and candy; and enjoyed old-fashioned pastimes such as "Spin-the-platter" and guessing contests. Mr. Joseph Taylor came over from Yachow that winter and married Miss Witte; we saw "Grey Legs" and Helen through the ceremony. This was the first wedding we attended in China. During that winter Archibald Bullock [UC 1906] arrived from California to teach in the government university only a short way down the street from us. He was from Berkeley and had been among the college crowd who saw us off for China. We saw him frequently and liked having him as a neighbor.

In the spring of 1907 I became friendly with the wife of the British consul and used to enjoy her visits. Sometimes she came in the forenoon and we had "elevenses"—cocoa or tea with a biscuit or sandwich. She even helped me hemstitch pongee curtains for the study. Florence O'Donnell was another good friend (we still keep up a correspondence though she left China in 1908). What fun we used to have at dinner parties in those days! Charades were greatly favored by the British. I shall never forget some of them trying to act out words such as "serviceability," "transportation," and "hospitality."

But through all this, our chief concern was to become acquainted with Chinese, particularly the university students who lived near us. One of our friends was Dr. T. Z. Koo, then a young instructor in the government university.[7] Students and other young men soon began to come around to call and to make friends. Sometimes, we realized, it was mainly to get some practice in English. Bob was constantly meeting new students and finally gathered a group for discussion. They delighted in choosing English names for themselves—such as Lincoln, Bismarck, or Solomon. Often they came to our house for games: tennis, quoits, checkers, and such amusements.

After we settled into our little Chinese house, the rest of 1907 was mostly given to language study. We had few foreign neighbors. The teachers at the government university (three or four were foreigners) were only half a block away; the American Methodists were fifteen minutes by chair. Though we had been told we would be too far away from other foreigners to see much of them, we found that friends came to see us in spite of distance. It was almost an hour's trip over to the Canadian corner of the city, so we could not go there very often.

In the spring of 1907, when I was at my wit's end with the everlasting noise of workmen in our small compound, Bob had sent me over to spend a fortnight with the Canadian ladies. On my return I missed several things

7. T. Z. Koo became head of student work for the YMCA in China and then became prominent in the international YMCA movement. That Chinese were able to become leaders of the organization in China and then move into a broader international role was one of the differences between the Y and the church-controlled missions.

around the house, the most important being a slender gold chain and a gold locket given by my mother to our baby. I should never have left them in a drawer; but evidently I did, and they were never seen again. There had been a few other thievings earlier, but nothing of moment. I was not well that spring; my severe pain came back; and finally I was upset by a more serious robbery.

We had no safe place to keep our money; of necessity, we had to use suitcases and trunks with foreign locks. We obtained silver dollars by selling Shanghai drafts, usually through the Post Office. There were fifty silver dollars in a roll; they usually came in packages of two rolls, or a hundred dollars. We had been locking these in our sturdiest leather suitcase which was kept in the closet off our bedroom. One May evening we were entertaining the British consul with his wife and some other friends at dinner. While our guests were in the house, we were with them on the ground floor. It must have been during this time that the robbery occurred. We had seen that the money was there during the day. The morning after the dinner, one of us unlocked the suitcase. The steel frame of the case had been forced so that a hand could be inserted. Nearly one hundred dollars were missing.

Such a robbery could not be allowed to go unnoticed. We had to call in the police. They marched all the house servants off—on a day when I had to go to bed ill and a hurry call was sent to the doctor. I lost my hopes of a baby expected for that autumn. I lay for three weeks flat on my back, not even a pillow under my head. Bob had everything to do: cooking, nursing, and all. I had fainting spells and needed to be watched, so he was tied to my bedside. The Methodist ladies took our laundry. They also sent us bread from time to time. The gateman could buy eggs and a few supplies near by; but since there were no other servants to tend the gate, he could not go far. I feel into a sad despondency and wept more than I had ever wept before. Bob was much distressed; the gateman offered sympathy, telling Bob that a woman would often cry a great deal after such a loss. The gateman knew life.

At this juncture, a young man appeared at the gate and offered to work for us. He had been with us for a while a year before but could not get along with the amah we then had. Now, with the amah and all our other servants gone, we gladly took him back. Gradually, other servants were found. The police could not identify our thief, and we did not want to keep the arrested servants in jail indefinitely. Bob finally asked for their release. We could not, however, reemploy them. So the work of training new helpers had to be started all over again.

10

Again to Omei

(1907)

I was still very weak after I got up. It was decided that we should go back to Mount Omei, to Tawosze temple again, for the summer. The first time I went outside the compound gate after my illness was when I rode my chair to our small river boat to start this trip. This time we traveled alone. In Kiating we had another terrific time with mosquitoes. We stayed in the empty house of the Canadian ladies. After we let down our net, these pests came up through a crack in the head of the bed. I doubt if we got half an hour's unbroken sleep that night.

As before, we left our boat at Kiating to proceed by chair to the mountain temple. The Ya River had to be crossed by a ferry. The river was badly swollen and the sky threatened more rain, so we were anxious to hurry on. Bob had to await some of our loads that had fallen behind. I got into the ferryboat with my sedan chair and bearers, the Boy, and a part of our baggage, leaving Bob to come across as soon as he could. Not until we were well out in the stream did I notice how high the waves were running. As we neared the farther bank and were unable to make the usual landing place, I began to see the distress of the boatmen. Our small boat tore along down stream at an alarming rate and they were not able to control it. We were past the gravelly landing and were threatened by large sections of the soft earth bank that were being undercut by the flood and falling into the water. I saw there was fear of our capsizing as the rising wind caught us broadside, so I got out of the sedan chair, freed myself from the boxes and carrying poles, and stood with my arms out of the sleeves of my raincoat. The Boy turned that ashy green which Chinese skin is apt to assume instead of our white pallor of fear. Just as things were looking worse than ever, and a crowd of people on the shore were yelling to us to put back, we saw a small cove where a tiny stream entered the river. Quickly the boatmen shoved with all their might on the oars and succeeded in pushing the nose of our boat into this haven. Men on shore seized ropes and held us secure. Bob crossed safely on the next trip.

Some days later I wrote an account of this trip in a letter to my parents. Bob asked if he might read it. When he had done so, he asked me as a favor not to send it. I had not thought of how it might strike my father and mother. Bob was always very careful of me, but this could look as though he had been careless of my safety. I changed the account before the letter was posted.

At Tawosze this summer we had a suite upstairs on the north side, on the same level as the tennis court. There was a large living room with a lot of exposed rafters overhead. The bedroom was smaller; and the kitchen scarce merited the name. It was merely a place where one could cook on a make-shift native stove. To it, a dark passage led from our living room. All windows had wooden shutters only, no glass. They were left open and we had plenty of air. If rain came from the north, the shutters on that side had to be closed. The south windows gave onto a veranda, so could always remain open. We hung a few curtains in one corner of the bedroom to make a little private nook for baths and dressing.

We had the same Boy who had come to us in Chengtu when I lay so ill. He acted as a general factotum and was devoted to us. There was also a cook—of a sort. He was the best we could find for the summer. Bob made me promise that I would not go into the kitchen, no matter *what* happened. I really kept the promise until some weeks after our arrival when we were preparing for another trip to Golden Summit. I happened to venture to the kitchen in search of something the cook could not locate. Our chef, I discovered, had been sweeping all rubbish, including empty food tins, under the rough kitchen table. That heap of refuse was an awful sight for a neat house-keeper! I was not very strong, but I made some metaphorical fur fly.

The Boy was fond of flowers and constantly went out on the mountain-side, bringing back hydrangeas, lilies, begonias in lovely profusion, and many other blooms. He also gathered ferns, roots and all, and fashioned hanging baskets so covered with moss and so filled with drooping ferns that one could not see their bamboo framework. We hung these verdant little baskets on our veranda and in our living room until our place was like a bower.

Bob had swung our big red-striped American hammock from the rafters of the living room, and I spent a great deal of time in it. He also kept two chair bearers for me, as I had no strength for walks or climbs. We used to go out on picnics often, alone or with others, carrying food and water bottles (of course we drank only boiled water, even on the mountain) in the bottom of my chair. The bearers would sit and watch us eat, filled with wonder at our strange ways. One could see that they had a feeling of commiseration for us as they sampled our queer, cold picnic food.

Keeping food at such a place as the temple was most primitive. We bought a live fowl and perhaps kept it a day or two. Then the cook had to take it outside the temple to kill it; Buddhists do not take life, and our doing so (even off the premises) was only by courtesy of the head priest. We often had a chicken killed Sunday morning and ate it for our noon meal. In the hot weather it would not be safe to eat meat that had been kept overnight, so we tried to finish up such food at the first meal after the killing.

There were some newly arrived missionaries at Tawosze that year. They objected to our having chickens killed on Sunday. The wife came to me and talked long and seriously about how wrong it was to have such work done on the Sabbath; chickens should be killed Saturday if they were for Sunday dinner. I was distressed, but not as much as she hoped. I knew plenty of missionaries had their servants kill fowl on Sunday, so I told her I could not believe my attitude had serious moral implications. It was not a moral issue of the observance of Sunday; it was a necessity for the preparation of wholesome food. An old missionary lady who heard of our conversation took me aside later and told me to pay no attention to such talk. "Tend your own kitchen and foods supplies, and don't mix morals and hygiene." I have always tried to follow her advice.

In the early part of the summer we had a letter from our Chengtu gateman telling us that our house had been entered. The second-floor bathroom window had been broken and entrance effected thereby. The large chest of drawers which stood there had been forced open, in spite of its foreign locks, and evidently things were missing. We wrote to some of the Methodist friends who were in Chengtu during the summer. They visited our compound and discovered that our table linen was the chief loss. We blamed the cook who had been put in jail in May after the dollar robbery. He alone knew where I kept this linen locked up, and certainly he would know that we had left the city. A small alley along the rear north wall of our compound made it possible for a night prowler to scale the wall, about ten feet high, and drop into our tiny backyard far from the gateman, who lived beside our front gate at the extreme south of the compound.

All during 1907, Chengtu foreigners were more or less taken up with plans for entertaining the West China Missionary Conference, scheduled to convene in Chengtu in January 1908. Each Chengtu family would have to keep as many guests in their house as could be managed. In view of this, we had ordered two long Irish tablecloths. These had arrived just before we left for Omei; still unused, they had been locked away for the summer. At this time the Chinese were commencing to fancy the use of tablecloths at feasts given by officials; our cloths probably became useful somewhere. I could never think of those cloths, and the other wedding linens that were lost, without keen regret.

On our Golden Summit trip that year we stayed an extra day at Nine Old Caves to take in more of the sights of the huge cliff under which the temple shelters. Early on the morning after our arrival, the face of this cliff was alive with monkeys, clambering about in the lush vegetation and chattering away at a great rate. This was a most arresting sight, and it was the only time we ever saw monkeys in their wild habitat in West China.

We took our teacher, Mr. Chu, for the stay on the mountain top. He enjoyed it, and Bob kept up his lessons. I had not the strength for study that summer and was forced to lie about, trying to win back my former vigor. I used to play chess with Mr. Chu, and we three took several rambles about the several summit temples. On any long trip I was carried in my chair. We had marvelous views of the incomparable snow mountains to the west.[1]

The priests remembered that on our arrival the year before we had immediately seen "Buddha's Glory," and they welcomed us with what seemed to be special regard. They gave us a pleasant suite of rooms. There was a good-sized guest room where Bob could study and where we had our meals, the Boy preparing them in our presence on a small charcoal brazier. Bedrooms opened off either side from this room; Mr. Chu had one, and we the opposite. It was so cool mornings and evenings that we were all glad of the brazier's heat. We spent more than a week at the summit; it was an interesting experience because through our teacher we learned more about the mountain and its temples than we had on our other visit.

On our return to Tawosze we had word from Chengtu that one of the teachers from the government university had been forced to move with his family into our empty house. There had been a big flood in Chengtu, and they had literally been driven out by the high water. This was truly a hard-luck family. The husband had given up a good teaching job in California for what seemed a very attractive offer: a good salary, house, servants, saddle horses, and other benefits such as free passes on the Szechwan railways. Prudently, he decided to proceed alone; his wife and four young children were to await his report before starting out to join him. Arrived in Chengtu, he found that not all was as promised. The housing was a couple of rooms on the campus, where no women were allowed; servants had to be trained; horses could be hired, for a price; and there was no vestige of a railway in Szechwan. But his first mail from America brought word that his family had grown impatient and were already on their way. This was in the spring when we were making over our own Chinese house. The husband anxiously tried

1. Capping the view would be the 25,000-foot sharp pyramid peak of Minyagonga.

to persuade us to rent a part of it to him. Bob felt sorry for the family and would have agreed. Though it seemed hardhearted, I was firmly against it. The place was simply too small to add a family of six; we needed some peace and quiet for study, and our home was important in the work we hoped to do.

Eventually, the university found a small Chinese house for the teacher and his family. It was close to the university, but on low ground. When the flood came, they had to escape. The husband carried his wife on his back; the oldest son carried the little girl. Our house was the only place to go. We were thankful to be able to provide a refuge.[2] By the time we returned to the city, they had moved back to their own place, leaving our house in good order. Only our student lamp did not work. I found that their servants had used native oil. After a grand boiling and cleaning and a new wick, it resumed normal functioning.

We became friendly that summer with the old head priest of Tawosze and found him a pleasant, kindly old man, albeit with a remarkable shrewdness and ability to read character. Rumor had it that he had been a man of the world whose desire for a son had never been realized although he took several wives. Finally he decided that he must have offended Heaven, and so sought a priestly life. He had risen to be the head of Tawosze and had made it prosperous.

One of his money-making ideas was the renting of rooms and apartments to foreigners. Once when we were looking at rooms which we thought we might take, we both exclaimed over their age-old dirt and the truly amazing array of spider webs hanging from the rafters. The old priest usually left such affairs to a subordinate, but that day he was with us. He turned to the windows, whose lattices he had caused to be propped open to reveal a mountain scene of great beauty, and remarked: "Do you not come to Omei for rest and a view? Here you have what you seek. These other things do not matter." We once saw his private room; it was an appalling medley of personal belongings, utensils, books, dried medicinal herbs, stores of all kinds, and piles of extra bedding needed for pilgrims. It looked as though there had never been a housecleaning since Creation.[3]

2. The family who took refuge in our home from the flood was named Larsen. Not long after this, they left Chengtu and passed out of our lives. By World War II the son, who had spent most of his life in China, became a non–Foreign Service employee of the State Department. I then met him for the first time. In the "Amerasia case" in 1945 he and I were among the six arrested. In the heyday of Senator McCarthy, guilt by association was elevated to new levels. An active group of Washington journalists developed the status of experts through the imaginative use of leaks and tips from persons with obvious access to FBI files. One of these triumphantly announced that Larsen and I had known each other and been associated since our boyhood in China. The association was two years before I was born.

3. The old abbot's friendship with Grace and Bob probably reflected Bob's developing proficiency in spoken Chinese; as the years passed, it became noteworthy. I have heard Chinese insist that hearing him behind a screen they would not guess that it was a foreigner speaking. But it

The other "business" of the temple was the cultivation and sale of white wax. This is used to harden other waxes and commercial glazes and is quite an important export from Szechwan. It is the product of an insect native to an area southwest of Mount Omei. The insects lay their eggs on the young branches of a certain tree. At the right time the branches are broken off and boiled; the wax rises and is taken off in clean cake form.

The final processing of the wax was at the end of the summer. A large balancing scale was hung outside the old priest's upper temple room so he could see the weighing of all the temple wax. One day I took hold of the large hook and hung my weight on it. I was just seventy catties,[4] and this was *after* my summer of recuperation when people were all telling me that I looked well again. I wonder how I looked when I came to the mountain.

A short time before we left Tawosze we had been over to join the first meal in the new cottage of the Beamans at Hsinkaisze. This is now quite a resort with a community of foreign bungalows. The Beaman cottage was the first built there; but only shortly after they moved in, Mr. Beaman was taken ill. They left the mountain, packed up their Kiating home, and had to leave West China. We bought a few pieces of furniture from them, the chief being a handsome desk which had been built to the specifications of a former member of their mission.

From the Beamans we also acquired two fine cows. We also took on Lao Yang, their cow coolie who had been well trained by Mr. Beaman. He proved a quaint old fellow and was a fixture in our household for many years. His wife, whose face was shriveled like a dried nut, also helped with the cows. They spoke a thick, blurred Kiating dialect which often puzzled our ears. Lao Yang liked a nip of hot wine in cold weather for a pain in one leg. A year or two after the old man came to us, our cook wanted a wife; this gay and gallant old cow man took the part of go-between in the transaction.

---

was pure colloquial Szechwanese, which could astonish and amuse Chinese from other regions. Having to start out by rebuilding a house certainly helped. Also, it seemed to be against his nature to be with a Chinese—any Chinese—without engaging him in friendly, interested conversation.

4. "Catty" is a Malay word. For reasons now forgotten, early foreign traders in China preferred it to the Chinese word *jin*. It was usually considered to be one and one-third pounds avoirdupois. Grace's seventy catties would thus be ninety-seven pounds. The imprecision is necessary because the Empire did not concern itself with mundane commercial matters. The merchant guilds in each major trading city established their own standard weights and measures. Furthermore, the *jin* (or catty) could vary according to the commodity to which it was applied: a catty of tea, for instance, could be less in weight than a catty of coal. This imprecision caused the *Encyclopedia Sinica* (Shanghai: Kelly and Walsh, 1917) to conclude: "It does not seem to be of much use therefore to give a Table of Weights and Measures" (p. 596). The Republic officially adopted the metric system but lacked the power to implement it. In the People's Republic the metric system is universal, "catty" is no longer heard, and a *jin* is one-half a kilogram (or 1.1 pounds).

We had so appreciated the beautiful flowers and shrubs on Mount Omei that we took back to Chengtu a number of roots and bulbs. Our Boy, devoted to plants, was the one who suggested the idea and he zealously did the collecting. Among the gains for our Chengtu garden were regal lilies, which grew marvelously for us, huge hydrangeas, and yellow-flowered terrestrial orchids.

11

Open House Days
(1907–8)

When we left Kiating that September we hired a cargo boat with a high *peng* (a rounded mat roof) and a good wooden floor. The Boy had gone with us as cook to Golden Summit and did so well that we now discharged the dirty cook at Kiating, giving him travel money. The hold of our boat was loaded with loose dried beans which looked to be a clean and non-odorous cargo. We put all our things on the floor level, and the boat was large enough to give plenty of room and, best of all, good head space. Our teacher was with us on the boat and we studied as we traveled. We could even sit at our new desk to study and write. The trip to Chengtu was expected to take about a week.

The floods that summer had caused damage along the river and we saw signs on every hand. Once, walking on the bank, we noticed tangled vines above our heads in tree branches. These were peanut vines that had been washed out of the fields and lodged in the trees. Even at Chengtu the river had covered the big stone bridge outside the South Gate. Close to this place, a big section of the city wall had been undermined (and took many months to repair). But, despite the summer flood, the river was now rather low for that time of the year—and our boat was large.

Life was very pleasant for the first two or three days, and we congratulated ourselves on the size and comfort of our craft. Then trouble began. At first we found only a few tiny white worms. In a few hours they had multiplied and were into everything: food boxes, beds, clothing, even into our ears when we took refuge tucked tightly inside a bed net. The little worms were everywhere. Complaints to the captain were useless; worms meant nothing to him. We then tried to hurry the boat, but its draft was considerable and the river seemed to be falling. We could only proceed by the main channel and frequently had to wait for other boats to negotiate narrow spots. After a couple of days of worms, we began to have a pest of little white moths. The worms were busying themselves in their life cycle under our very eyes. These tiny blundering creatures flew everywhere, and our tempers were decidedly on edge.

I began to feel that we would never reach Chengtu, and the eternal singsong of Bob repeating Chinese phrases after his teacher's intoned speech made me weary beyond words. To be honest, I was probably as much of a trial to live with as the worms and moths! Bob suggested that from a village about a hundred *li* from Chengtu,[1] I could reach the city in a day in my chair, the Boy escorting me. But when we reached the village that evening, it was impossible to find chair men. Next morning it was raining, which ruled out the possibility of making the trip in one day even if bearers could be found. So I settled down to sticking it out on the bean boat. We had still more trouble, having to lighten cargo at one place where the channel was shallow and the current swift. We did not reach Chengtu until the next Tuesday. Then there was a joyous farewell to that nice, clean boat full of its worms and moths with whom we had spent eleven unforgettable days.

We were delighted to reach our Chinese home again. A quick check showed that the robbers had taken practically all my table linen as well as some other things. Otherwise all was in good order. A few days of scrubbing, washing windows, hanging clean curtains, and changing shelf and drawer papers made us as clean and fresh as could be. I liked the new desk very much and had it set up in our living room, where it became my special possession and delight. Bob had a large Chinese desk of red bean wood in his study, so he did not need it. My new desk was of what was called "buried nanmu."[2] It had a large flat top. On each side above the table top were six small drawers. Between these stacks an open space was just right for a row of books. Below on either side were tiers of large drawers. Many and many a letter I wrote on that desk, and many that I received were stowed inside.

That fall we studied, and continued to widen our acquaintances among Chinese. Bob spent much time and thought making plans and establishing contacts with people. An advisory committee was formed as a preliminary step toward the organization of a full-fledged YMCA. Sunday afternoon meetings were held, sometimes at our house, sometimes at the Hodgkins'.

1. A *li* is generally considered to be approximately one-third of a mile. But when all travel was by foot, precise distance was not as important as a measure of time and effort. The rhythmic flexing of a shoulder pole with a load suspended from each end (or the bamboo poles of a sedan chair) produce a brisk, slightly bouncy stride. Traveling on the level, this standard pace would cover ten *li* in an hour (on the major roads, this would bring them to a teahouse). Hence the one-third of a mile approximation. But on hilly roads the *li* could be one-fourth of a mile, or even shorter. Quite consistently, the same distance could be twenty *li* if one was going uphill, and perhaps only ten *li* if one was going down.

2. Nanmu (*Machilus nanmu*) is native to West China and was considered to be one of most valuable and beautiful of Chinese timbers. The best trees were reserved for imperial use, often for pillars of the largest temples and palaces. It was also prized for the finest coffins.

15   Tennis teas were an important part of Chengtu social life. One man here
managed to play in a Chinese gown. (Probably in 1908.)

I was still miserable with my severe pain and suffered exceedingly with
backaches which wore me out. My cook could not make good bread, and
there were no bakeries whatsoever. The bread, rolls, cakes, and cookies all
had to come from my hands. For ourselves alone, this was not much; but we
entertained Chinese constantly, and they were all pleased to have foreign-
style refreshments. Late that year I finally got our new cook, who had been
our Boy at Omei, trained to make acceptable cookies and cupcakes. This was
a great help. Tea had always to be served to our guests. If they did not eat the
cakes served with it, these were gladly pocketed to be taken home to a small
brother or sister, to children, or even to a mother interested in sampling the
odd things served by the Westerners.

About that time we rented a piece of land at the rear of the Methodist
school adjacent to us on the west. It belonged to the mission but was then
not needed. It gave us space for two tennis courts with a tea pavilion west of
them in the shadow of a high wall. There was also some ground left over for
raising vegetables. Eventually we enjoyed many products of our own garden.

Our young friends among Chinese students began to ask if I would call on
their families or be at home to receive calls from them. Doors thus opened in
both directions, and we became deeply involved in our surroundings. I began to teach English to a few young men. At first my work was individual
instruction in conversation and composition. Our careful attention was given
to the young man who was later to become the first Chinese YMCA secretary

in Chengtu.[3] In 1907 I did not keep a careful record of the guests at special teas we had for Chinese students, but I know the total ran into 600 or 700. For 1908 I did keep a weekly record. It gives a total of 967 as counted. However, on numerous occasions we were not able to count late comers, so our figures would read "42 plus" and so on. Also these records showed only those who came to our regular, announced teas. Bob had many individual callers in both those years; in 1908 he doubtless entertained well over 1,200. These contacts were valuable to him and gave me considerable to oversee and manage.

When Chinese women called, I had to drop everything. They often came at inopportune times for us, as Chinese meal hours were not the same as ours, and they would stay and stay and stay. To come at ten in the forenoon, or even around noon, and then sit until three in the afternoon was asking a good deal of a hostess, but we had to conform to the habits of the country. A lady often brought a whole train of attendants: perhaps a sister or two, several grown daughters or younger children, and often four or five amahs. The guests sat down to visit, and the servants stood around gazing at everything and being what one might call movable fixtures in the room. It took me a long time to accustom myself to these calls. Gradually I learned the technique, and despite my lack of adequate language could carry them off with some sort of aplomb. I learned the polite phrases, and could fall back on the children and stock questions. Eventually, some of the women became my real friends, so that barriers no longer made such a chasm between us.

All women guests wanted to see our entire house. Most of them, if they expressed any opinion, thought we wasted too much time trying to be clean: clean kitchens and clean floors were no necessity to them. When I visited their homes, I was impressed by the dirty kitchens and their lack of any adequate attention to the floors. Their kitchens were in what we would call sheds. Most of their floors were dingy brick or grimy wood. Frequent expectoration, together with the habit of allowing babies to urinate freely on the floor anywhere and everywhere, made for unhygienic conditions and offensive odors. Cobwebs never seemed to bother Chinese; to this day I have to call servants' attention to them. Upper walls and ceiling spaces seem never to come within range of the Chinese eye; special orders must be given if you want to be sure that high corners will be cleaned. On the other hand, Chinese take great care in polishing the flat top and side surfaces of furniture such as cupboards and sideboards; and a Boy will carefully dust framed pictures every day, sometimes even dusting behind them.

3. The YMCA has always referred to its higher-level salaried personnel as secretaries. The term includes executives, administrators, and program directors. It is, therefore, quite different from the secretary who is an office or clerical employee. Bob, for instance, was always a secretary.

Another of my household duties at this time was my husband's collars. Men were still wearing stiff collars every day. It seemed impossible for the Chinese to get them stiff enough, or to keep from scorching them during the ironing. And there were no tailors in these early years who knew anything about "foreign-style" sewing. So what sewing I needed, I also did myself, by hand and machine. I sent for American patterns and made clothes as I could, studying the illustrations of magazines and inspecting the clothes of new arrivals from home. It was my boast that I could cut out a man's shirt one evening and have it finished, save buttonholes, by the next afternoon. I learned to stitch such pieces without any basting and thus could save time. I taught my amah to do buttonholes. Her first attempts were what my New England grandmother would have called "pigs' eyes," but Amah improved and became a fine buttonholer.

I was busy during these early Chengtu days. Often I rose at 6:30 in the morning to work down my bread. Then there was study, sewing, and general housekeeping. This could include a lot of mold prevention, and packing away all woolens and winter things at the approach of hot weather. Dry cleaners were unheard of, and laundry work demanded much attention and training of servants. It is quite a task to do up men's white summer suits, be they duck, silk, serge, or flannel. I found the Szechwanese to be good washers but poor rinsers. It was my rule to demand ample water for that use. By this means I kept our clothes from taking on that dull, muddy tinge which many housewives regard as one of the prices of living in the Orient.

Late in 1907 the West China Missionary Conference was impending, and I was determined to find a Boy who would be wide-awake and efficient. I interviewed several prospects without success. At last a young fellow named Liu Pei-yun appeared. I had never wanted a country boy, because it seemed to me that some education, however little, would hold more potential for training. This boy was the son of a buyer of silk yarn. He could read and write and was an apt pupil in learning the work expected from him. On arrival he knew nothing whatsoever of any foreign furnishings or usages. When I first showed him how to set the table, he asked what the forks were and how they were used! He became a trusted servant, was married in our home, and worked for us from the fall of 1907 until that of 1920. Bob then helped him set up a business for himself in Chengtu. In later years he visited us several times in Shanghai and has always kept up connection with our family.[4]

In January the long-planned conference was held. As all the out-of-town people had to pay their own travel expenses, we Chengtu residents were ex-

---

4. Liu Pei-yun's service to our family gradually went far beyond the role of cook. I remember him, for instance, far better than the amah who tried to look after me. The business venture, though, had an unhappy ending—but that comes much later.

16 The West China Missionary Conference at Chengtu in January 1908. The building was the just-completed hospital of the (American) Methodist Episcopal Mission. Though Chinese garb was popular, there appears to have been only two or three Chinese present—and their positions at the extreme peripheries, right and left, leads one to wonder about their status. Grace and Bob are at the upper right-hand corner: she with a rather large hat, Bob just behind her with only the top of his face showing.

pected to share by providing free accommodations. Bob and I moved into the ground-floor room behind our living room, giving our bedroom to Charlie and Robina Service of Kiating with their three little girls. Our other upstairs bedroom at the other end of the house was occupied by Dr. and Mrs. Tompkins of Suifu [now Yibin]. A room connecting with the dining room and kitchen, generally used as an ironing room and a place for drying clothes by charcoal heat (often necessary in our Szechwan drizzle), was transformed into a bedroom for two more visiting men.

Of course we did not have this many beds. We used camp cots ourselves. For the guests in the lower room we borrowed two slit-cane bed frames laid across benches. Heavy cotton *pugai* were quite satisfactory in lieu of mattresses. All the guests came with their road bedding, so there was an abundance to keep us all warm.

The conference was held in the newly completed Methodist hospital at the Shansigai compound.[5] As some of the attendants were too far from their lodgings to return for the noon meal, their hostesses had to send lunches to the conference building. Also, many were British and devoted to their afternoon tea in a way not always understood by Americans. This had also to be served daily, and made much work for many faithful Marthas, who had little time for the enjoyments of the Marys who could attend all the meetings.

Since our house was relatively near—less than fifteen minutes' walk from the Methodist compound—our guests returned for lunch. Often there were four or five extras. With these, our nine house guests, and ourselves, it made quite a gathering. It was a strenuous time for our kitchen staff and equipment. I had previously arranged with Robina Service that her efficient cook would do all the baking. He turned out bread, rolls, muffins, cookies, and cakes in abundance and took a great load off my shoulders. My cook had his hands full with the other items of our daily needs. We had laid in potatoes from Kiating (hard to get in those days) and had made mincemeat and pickles.

About two hundred and fifty people attended the conference, and it proved to be an interesting and worthwhile gathering. Among speakers from afar were Mr. Sloane of the China Inland Mission and Dr. Arthur H. Smith of Shantung. Mr. Pollard of Yunnan, though of our own West China region, had to travel for as long as any of these to attend. Dr. Shelton and Mr. Ogden came with their wives from Tatsienlu on the Tibetan border, where they had been studying Tibetan in preparation for their move to Batang—thirty days

5. The hospital where the conference was held was a very solid brick building of three or four stories. Its sturdy construction, and the fact that its surroundings were all low, led to its being used as a fortress by one of the armed Red Guard factions during the violent phase of Chengtu's Cultural Revolution in 1969. When I first returned to Chengtu in 1971, it was surprising to see this old mission landmark bearing heavy scars of rifle and artillery fire.

in toward Lhasa from Chengtu. All five of these leaders have now [1937] passed on.

It was a rare treat for us to see so many foreigners and to meet people of whom we had heard. To me the most inspiring talk was one by Mr. Pollard, who followed his address by presenting several Miao tribesmen who had accompanied him to Chengtu. These rather rough-looking fellows sang in their own tongue the hymn "Washed in the Blood of the Lamb," making a great impression by the evident longing and sincerity in their hearts.

On the last day of January there was much excitement over the visit of the viceroy, His Excellency Chao Erh-feng. The next day was the last of the conference, and Bishop Bashford gave the closing address in the afternoon. A group photograph was also taken that day. The same evening we entertained Dr. Arthur Smith and others for dinner. On the following Sunday, Bishop Bashford conducted a dedication for the new Methodist hospital, which had already been the conference site. This ceremony closed with the celebration of communion.

The next day guests began to leave. To the hostesses this meant providing each party with a cooked roast (beef or several fowls) and plenty of bread for their road boxes. The Charlie Services stayed on with us for their own mission conference. Their baby, Frances, was quite ill for a few days, and I helped her mother prepare whey for her diet. Winifred, the oldest child, had her fifth birthday during these days; we fixed a cake with candles and got up a small party with the Canright children as guests.

Our good friend Dr. Florence O'Donnell was now getting ready to leave China after a five-year term of service. She had become engaged to a man in her home, Nova Scotia. Great was the sorrow among her friends, both foreign and Chinese. For many years we were constantly asked about her welfare. One day before she left, a group of us, including the H. D. Robertsons and Mr. Fox (the British consul, later Sir Harry) took a ramble to some property outside the South Gate which had just been acquired as a site for the West China Union University. We sat on graves there and wondered what our surroundings would look like in a few years. Some one hundred and fifty acres are now the attractive campus of this thriving university. The buildings, trees, shrubbery, and grass have entirely changed the looks of those fields and grave mounds.[6]

The American community grew slowly. Late in 1907 another young Californian, C. W. Batdorf [UC 1906], had come to teach in the government uni-

6. During China's Resistance War (1937–45), the West China Union University gave refuge to several leading Christian universities from East China cities occupied by the Japanese. Thus it became, along with Kunming, where the principal government universities found refuge, one of the two leading intellectual and academic centers of China during those war years. Today it has become a much enlarged medical university and dental school. But the local people still refer to it by the old name, Huaxiba (West China campus).

versity near us. He and Mr. Bullock [also UC 1906] kept bachelor's hall together. We were always glad to help them when we could; I made curtains,
sheets, and such items for them. Early in 1908, Chee Soo Lowe, a California-
born Chinese who had graduated in mining from the University of California
[still another member of 1906], came to investigate the mineral resources of
Szechwan under employment by the viceroy. He was often in our home and
we greatly enjoyed him.

As the Chinese ladies became less bashful I began to have more callers.
Many of them besought me to start some sort of classes for them. They
wanted to "learn foreign ways," to knit, crochet, and even to bake the light
cakes which they ate in our homes. We were constantly invited to Chinese
feasts. Here the procedure is the reverse of our custom. Chinese socializing is
done before the meal, and the guests leave directly from the table. This
meant that we often sat talking while the very food we were to eat was in
preparation. We might hear the fowls squawking as they were chased and
killed to be served to us later. The men and women always ate in separate
rooms: the men in the main hall or some such public apartment, while we
women were relegated to women's bedrooms. I was teaching a few pupils and
kept busy in spite of not being well. I still had my attacks of severe pain now
and then and was forced to spend a good many days in bed.

12

Journey to the West
(1908)

My health was a problem; the doctor thought it might even necessitate my return to America. Such a prospect seemed terrible. I was devoted to our enterprise. I could see with what devotion Bob threw himself into work with young men; it was his very life. I felt I also had a share in it. And we had both learned to love China and the Chinese friends with whom we came in close contact in Chengtu. It was thought best for us to try a lengthy vacation in as different an environment as possible.

It seemed that this summer of 1908 would be our last chance to vacation at any considerable distance from Chengtu. In another year, we expected, the Chengtu YMCA would be organized and require Bob's attention; Mount Omei would be too far away. But for now, we had been to Omei the last two summers and were ready for something new. Furthermore, the elevation of 2,700 feet at Tawosze temple did not give much of a change from the 1,700 feet at Chengtu. Our eyes turned toward the Tibetan border. Here we could be among high mountains in a much cooler and more invigorating climate. Our Chengtu friends, the R. J. Davidsons, had gone in with a small party to Tatsienlu in the previous summer.[1] From them we learned about the trip and the equipment needed.

The spring was a time of preparations—in addition to our usual affairs. The Sheltons and Ogdens, whom we had met at the conference in January, were in Tatsienlu getting ready to move on to Batang, a big step forward into Tibet. Fortunately for us, the Ogdens stayed when the Sheltons moved on. The only other foreigners in this remote town were the Sorensons of the China Inland Mission and occasional game hunters and plant collectors who passed through on their wanderings.

1. Tatsienlu is now known as Kangding.

We wrote to the Ogdens for help in planning and could scarcely have arranged our camp without their friendly and thoughtful help. In Chengtu we had new folding camp cots made from a British army model (sewing the canvas tops was very difficult without heavy equipment). We also made new folding chairs, which added greatly to our comfort in camp. Bed nets had to be remade, and several butterfly nets were prepared. Bob had become keen on that hobby and wanted to see what new trophies he might find in higher altitudes. Our supplies were all carefully chosen. We had road boxes of galvanized-iron made. Even though the lids fitted tightly, they were—to our regret—not entirely watertight. Cuts had to be made in the metal sides to attach carrying rings; if a box fell on its side, water could enter. However, they were sturdy and served us well, many of them until we left Szechwan many years later.

Our party from Chengtu consisted of Harold and Vieva Robertson (young Canadians), Miss Collier (an American Methodist), and Bob and myself. We were to go first to Yachow, four or five days overland by sedan chair, and be joined there by Harry and Lona Openshaw (of the American Baptist Mission). The Openshaws were the mainstay of our party. Harry and Lona, along with Miss Collier, were "old-timers." We had been in China two and a half years; Harold and Vieva a little less than two years. Harry spoke Chinese with great fluency and had an outgoing personality that made him quickly popular with everyone around him. With him to manage for us, we felt sure that things would go easily.

One June Saturday, Bob took a language examination. On Monday Dr. Hodgkin started for England where he was to have an operation. That same day, in a mean drizzle, we were completing our packing. Tuesday morning, in a continuation of the same drizzle, we all started off separately from our homes in Chengtu. Our rendezvous was at the stopping place for the first night, eighty *li* from Chengtu. The inn was a terrible one. It was hot, smelly, and so airless that we felt as if we were suffocating. During the night Vieva and Harold seemingly fainted. One of them called to Bob, but by the time he got to their room both were recovering.

The next day was most trying. Rain fell continuously. The road had no paving of flat slabs, but was of nigger-head stones in a bed of clay. These rounded stones became superlatively slippery with the tread of feet on wet clay. The going was so bad that we could only manage sixty-five *li*. The load carriers were even slower than the sedan chairs. Late in the evening, when some of them came straggling in, we learned there had been a robbery. Miss Collier's two boxes had been rifled; one hundred dollars and most of her clothes had been taken. She was happy to discover that another hundred dollars remained. She had purposely separated her money. In one box, the

hundred dollars was at the bottom under a large Montgomery Ward catalogue, from which she intended to compile an order during the leisure of
camp. In the gathering darkness, the robber put his hand down and apparently thought the catalogue was the bottom of the box. We all acclaimed
"Monty's" good deed of that day!

Our inn that night was again about as bad as one can imagine. Wet filth,
pigs, awful odors, and a frightful stuffiness. The Robertsons' bedding-roll
had not arrived, and they were tired out after the preceding bad night, so we
shared with them. This meant one net for two cots. The floor was unspeak-
ably filthy earth, which sweeping could never make clean. (We believed attempts to clean such places only stirred up germs.) We finally put our two
cots on some rickety tables. Miss Collier had sent her servant back with the
load carrier to investigate. They returned at two the next morning, which
wakened all of us and started a frenzied chorus by the myriad dogs of the
village. After breakfast, Bob and Harold went back to the scene of the robbery (only about five *li*) while we three women went on to Kiunglai and the
Olsens of the China Inland Mission.

We certainly were thankful to get into the Olsens' clean home. Never can I
forget the impression her fresh curtains and spotless floors made after those
execrable inns. We had a good noon meal and the men soon joined us. They
went with Mr. Olsen to see the *hsien* (county) magistrate about the robbery.
(To complete the story of the robbery, when Miss Collier came back from
Tatsienlu on her return to Chengtu, she stopped at the Olsens' to see what
this official might have accomplished. He returned her money, and presented
her with the *skeletons* of the dresses she had lost. The flat pieces of dress
goods had been neatly cut out of skirt gores and waist sections so that, when
held up, each garment's seamy rib-work was all that was left.)

It was pleasant to linger, but we now felt an added urge to reach Yachow.
We had planned to spend the weekend there; now we knew we must help
Miss Collier to contrive a few garments. We had one more bad inn on the
road, and then Saturday saw us in Yachow before noon. We all hurried
through baths. Miss Collier was given some material by Lona Openshaw and
was able to buy more on the street. That very afternoon we cut two waists,
finished one, fitted the other, and had plans under way for Monday's sewing.
Miss Collier had sent a runner back from Kiunglai asking her associates at
the mission in Chengtu to send underwear and other clothing. We nearly
finished a dress for her on Monday, and that night the runner came from
Chengtu with a parcel of clothing. We were ready to move on. Our stay at
the Openshaw house had been most enjoyable, if busy. It was a mental, as
well as a physical, delight to be in clean surroundings. The food was good;
laughter and gay banter were sparked by Harry's jovial friendliness; and we
worked well, spurred by our eagerness to be off on our journey to the west.

We took the road again on Tuesday morning. We now had new carriers accustomed to mountain travel; and our loads were well packed and lightened. It seemed that bad luck was left behind us for the rest of the journey. Soon we were in mountain glens and canyons, following and crossing streams, rising day by day. The third night from Yachow was in a village just below a 9,500-foot pass. The flowers were lovely: tall lilies with up to sixteen blossoms on each stalk, yellow iris, clematis, and many others.

At Hanyuan we came down to the swift Tung River.² It is an interesting city situated on a point where two valleys meet. Steep banks and walls protect it on two sides; the third, landward side had a moat and a higher wall. One city gate was always locked: the wife of an official had used that exit when running away from her lord and master. The point of the city, looking south, rose high, almost like a mammoth ship. This city was a junction of age-old Asian trade routes. The southern road led to Tali in Yunnan, and thence to Bhamo in Burma. Our route, to the northwest, was the old highway to Tibet. Northeast was Chengtu and, at the end of the road, imperial Peking.

We stopped over on a Sunday at an inn in Nitow which Sir Alexander Hosie described as the best he had stayed at in China.³ It was good, but there was a pigsty close at hand. We all slept late that Sunday and had pancakes for breakfast. Harry led prayers for us. These were disturbed by an old hen who had evidently just laid an egg. She flapped about the room, cackling and telling the world of her achievement until laughter overcame us. Harry had two religious services for Chinese in the front part of the inn. We went for a leisurely walk in the afternoon while the servants washed linen, baked, and made ready for an early start in the morning. On Monday afternoon we crossed a pass whose altitude we found, by boiling our thermometer, to be 9,200 feet.

We then descended again into the valley of the Tung and followed up that wild stream for most of a day. At one very dangerous spot there had been a recent flood and landslide; we passed with haste and care. Boats cannot be used on this upper part of the river; people cross in buffalo-hide coracles, tub-shaped and fragile looking. At Luting there was no inn. One had burned, another had been undermined by a flood and fallen into the river. We were obliged to go to the official for help. He gave us rooms in his *yamen*,⁴ but

2. The Tung River is now known as the Dadu. It is a major tributary of the Min, a wild river that is nowhere navigable.
3. Hosie was a British consular official who visited Szechwan in 1883 and was British consul general at Chengtu in 1903–5. He was renowned for his exhaustive travels all over West China, some of which are recounted in Sir Alexander Hosie, *On the Trail of the Opium Poppy* (Boston: Small Maynard, 1915?).
4. A *yamen* was the residence, official and private, of a county magistrate or higher official of the Empire. The word continued to be used to refer generally to a government headquarters.

there was no place for the carriers and they had to fend for themselves. Besides our party of seven foreigners, Miss Collier had in her charge a Tibetan girl named Ossa, who had been attending the Methodist girls' school in Chengtu for several years. Ossa was a protégée of Mrs. Sorensen, who hoped for her help in teaching women and girls at Tatsienlu. Miss Collier had Ossa sleep in the same room with her.

Luting is the site of a famous bridge. It is an iron-chain suspension bridge swinging across the turbulent Tung River in a single span of 370 feet. The bridge was built in 1701 and has been repaired [rebuilt?] several times.[5] Thirteen chains support the floor and provide side rails, but one cannot help feeling that the bridge is sketchily built. The flooring is of irregular planking with many open spaces. The palings connecting the side chains are few. And there is an airiness about the whole structure hanging so jauntily over the wild and swirling water.

The bridge, though, is vital. One can visualize a thousand varied caravans which have passed over this old trade route. Travelers from India, Nepal, and High Asia have safely crossed the raging Tung by this tenuous cobweb of man's ingenuity. Hidden away in this obscure Chinese valley, it holds the glamor of mystery. Men are provided to escort animals across; mules and horses proceed with head and tail guides to keep them calmly in the straight and narrow path to safety. Because of the swaying of the bridge, most people walk across. Bob and I did so, but Miss Collier decided to ride. Midway across, the crosspiece at the front end of the chair-poles broke, letting the chair down with a great thump. She walked the rest of the way.

We left the Tung valley at Waszekow at about 5,000 feet and only sixty li from Tatsienlu. The next day we climbed more than 3,000 feet, following the roaring, foaming Lu River until we reached Tatsienlu at 8,300 feet. It was wild country; sometimes our path swung high above a stream, at other times it was at the very bottom of a canyon. Along the road there were many teahouses and resting spots for coolies, travelers, and the heavily burdened tea carriers.

These carriers transport brick tea for the Tibetan trade. Each long, narrow package is covered with plaited bamboo and weighs from thirteen to twenty catties: the usual weight is about sixteen pounds. The parcels are stacked crosswise on a wooden back-frame so that the load rises above the carrier's head and is distributed to his shoulders and hips. Mr. E. H. Wilson, the plant

5. The Luting bridge has become world famous. Its hairbreadth capture in May 1935 by the Red Army was one of the most heroic, and now legendary, exploits of Mao Tse-tung's epic "Long March." It is also interesting to note, in these days of frequent nonhistorical talk of Chinese "annexation" of Tibet in 1950, that the primary reason for this bridge's being built—almost three hundred years ago in the reign of the Kang-hsi emperor—was to facilitate military communications with Tibet, which was indubitably a part of the Ch'ing Empire.

explorer, records seeing a load containing twenty parcels of fourteen catties each.[6] The load thus weighed three hundred and seventy English pounds.

The coolies are unable to lift these loads from the ground by themselves, and each carries a crutch-stick to prop up his burden whenever he stops. As he rests he expels his breath with the same distinctive whistle of the *beizi* carriers on Mount Omei.[7] They can proceed only at a snail's pace; their average time from Yachow to Tatsienlu is twenty days. This is about one hundred and forty miles and is usually done by chair bearers in eight days. When one remembers the heavy loads, the steep roads and mountain passes, and the frequent storms of wind and rain, it is a wonder that they can do the trip in even three times that needed by sedan chairs.

In some places along the road a little cultivation was attempted, mostly of beans and corn. In tiny pockets of rock-bound earth, one would see three or four bean plants. The farmer had to take extreme care; a false step out of the little foothold for his plants (one could not call it a field or even a plot) might plunge him hundreds of feet into a raging torrent. Some of the hillsides were quite bare; others were partly covered by shrubby growth.

On Thursday, July 9, we had our noon meal fifteen *li* from Tatsienlu. In the afternoon we were met outside the city by Mr. Sorensen of the China Inland Mission and reached his home for afternoon tea.[8]

6. Mr. Wilson was one of the best-known of the many naturalists who combed West China for new and useful plants. See Ernest Henry Wilson, *A Naturalist in Western China* (London: Methuen, 1913). He was traveling in the Tatsienlu area during this summer of 1908 (see chapter 13 below).

7. If Grace had gone climbing with her eldest son, she would not have been mystified by the "distinctive whistle" of the load carriers. To some people it seems natural, when one gets winded, to take an extra deep breath. To these mountain men it seemed natural to facilitate the deep breathing by first clearing the lungs. What Grace heard was an explosive exhalation through open mouth and half-closed teeth. Until I read this account by Grace, I was unaware that I had picked up the habit on mountain trips as a boy, or that it was unusual.

8. Tatsienlu (or Kangding) is an important trade and administrative center in a border area that is ethnically Tibetan but politically within western Szechwan Province. The town itself has had a large Chinese element. For instance, the tea merchants, and also the carriers of those incredible loads of brick tea, would all have been Chinese, as would probably also the cultivators of those tiny patches of beans and corn that Grace describes. One of its chief attractions to foreigners, including Bob and Grace (and their sons), has been that it is considered to be a "gateway to Tibet." By World War II it was the terminus of a primitive, unpaved motor road. Dick had a chance, during 1945, to try to reach it by jeep from Chengtu but had to turn back because the road was blocked by landslides. Now the road is the main eastern route from China into Tibet and Lhasa. It has been greatly improved and paved; buses and truck convoys are frequent. I had a chance to go this way in 1984 when the Harrison Salisburys and I retraced the route of the Long March. But I, too, was thwarted. The alignment of the new highway passes by and leaves the city off on a short spur. We had a long day's trip ahead and there was no need to stop. I looked down on the fabled city from perhaps two miles away.

13

Tibetan Camp

(1908)

We stayed in Tatsienlu at the home of the Sorensens and found mail from America awaiting us. It was wonderful to be in clean rooms; we luxuriated in baths and clean garments. The Ogdens came over in the evening to visit and help us make plans. Miss Collier stayed with the Ogdens after turning Ossa, the Tibetan girl, over to Mrs. Sorensen.

The next morning our party assembled and was soon en route for the camp site, some thirty *li* beyond the town. Our road wound up the valley of the Lu River and crossed the bridge which is known as the "Gateway to Tibet." The site was beyond the summer palace of the King of Chala and near a small Tibetan village consisting of a few clustered houses. The sides of the narrow valley were covered with grass, flowers, and shrubs, with no large trees anywhere near. The general effect was like the high mountains in Colorado. Tibetan women walked off with our boxes on their heads or shoulders while their men looked on and nonchalantly rode their horses or gamboled about in a carefree manner. They did not have the curiosity that Chinese always show when any new person or thing enters their range of vision.

Mr. Ogden had rented Tibetan tents for us. Ours leaked: it was made habitable by the loan of a tent fly from the Ogdens. The sides of the tent were separate from the roof and could be raised or lowered to cool and ventilate the tent. Most of the tents were unlined, but ours, about ten by twelve feet, had a lining of figured Indian cotton. The design was printed in tans, browns, and soft reds on white; and the figures were Indian: turbaned, full-trousered people with leopards, elephants, and conventional flower forms. The camp had five sleeping tents and one with extending fly for kitchen and dining room. We four women took turns keeping house.

In the village we bought yak or *dzo* milk.[1] From the milk we made butter.

---

1. The *dzo* is a yak-cow hybrid which serves most of the functions of the yak in areas, like Tatsienlu, that are slightly below the high altitude favored by the yak.

Every few days we sent a servant to Tatsienlu. He went down late in the afternoon so as to be there for early morning market on the following day. He was given inn money and was not to go to the foreigners in Tatsienlu unless we sent letters or messages. Food supplies were simple but we could get excellent yak (*dzo?*) steaks, a limited variety of vegetables, and expensive eggs brought up from Waszekow. I am sorry to say that these were not always worth the care taken to get them a day's journey to Tatsienlu and then to us. Everyone insisted that hens would not thrive in Tatsienlu; hence the need to bring them up from down the road.

We named our camp "Chala" in honor of the district in which Tatsienlu is situated. Camp Chala was at an elevation of 10,500 feet and near the Lu River, from which we got our water. It was also not far from some hot sulphur springs.[2] One of the first days we were in camp our servants visited these springs and reported that the water was very hot and very cleansing. They evidently enjoyed a good soaking. Our men then had the coolies clean out the pool so it would be more attractive. We women ventured down there for baths, using a small pup tent as dressing room, and old clothes for bathing garments. The big thrill of our bathing was to follow the warm dip by a cold one in the nearby river. In these and similar hot springs, the Tibetans are reported to take an annual bath, getting in for a long soak and wearing their ordinary clothing. This takes the place of weekly ablutions and laundries for the whole year.

The steep sides of our valley blocked views of the snowy mountains on either side; but at the head of the valley there was a magnificent snow peak with a glacier on its flank. This glacier fed the Lu River, so it is no wonder that its water was like ice. In the clear mornings this peak was a fine sight and seemed very near. Also, in the early mornings there was often frost around our tents. The hardy wild flowers were not abashed by it and grew everywhere, even persisting inside our tents, where they stood under our cots and between the few planks which served in lieu of flooring.

We frequently went on rambles and picnics. The Tatsienlu friends came out to visit us now and then. And there were other occasional visitors. Among them were E. H. Wilson, the noted plant explorer; Mr. Zappey, a bird collector; Mr. Lowe, our Chinese-American mining engineer; and Captain Malcolm M'Neill, a big-game hunter. Once we met a French doctor and his wife who were evidently staying with the Catholics at their Tatsienlu mission. The men also spent a good deal of their time hunting. They shot pheasants and pigeons and kept us so well supplied with the latter that I vowed before the summer was over that I had eaten enough pigeon potpie to last a lifetime.

2. When I passed this way with the Harrison Salisburys on our 1984 Long March, I thought the motor highway might be close to the site of Camp Chala. So I inquired for hot springs. I found that there are several in the area.

17   Enjoying life at Camp Chala. Grace is in the center. Bob, with his new-grown beard, is on her left. On her right is Mrs. Sorenson from Tatsienlu, who was visiting the camp that day with her children (one in her lap, a second held by a Tibetan nurse at the far right).

The men made several excursions up to a glacial lake. They named it Lake Davidson in honor of E. J. Davidson of Chengtu, who had inspired our own trip by visiting the area the year before. On one occasion Bob and Harold Robertson had the coolies carry up a small tent and food. They spent the night at the lake and then climbed the next day to an elevation of 16,500 feet up the side of the high peak and onto the glacier. They arrived back at Camp Chala in the evening after their two-day trip just as a fierce storm struck us with rain, high wind, and a heavy fall of hail.[3]

3. Bob and Grace both loved the mountains and were fervent environmentalists long before being one became so popular. This Tibetan summer was an experience that they often reminisced about. Grace's feeling for nature was rather philosophical. She was a John Muir enthusiast and had most of his books. For Bob the lure was more physical: the excitement and challenge of climbing, and the pleasure of exploration.

For exploration was, indeed, an important and ever-present element. At that time, all the mountain areas of West China and the Tibetan borderland were little known and very sketchily mapped. It was the heyday of plant explorers bringing home wonderful new varieties of flowers such as rhododendrons and camellias. Hunters came for ordinary things like bear and leopard and, more seriously, for Himalayan exotica such as the goral and the serow (genera of goat antelopes); an even greater rarity, the giant panda, was sometimes thought to be a myth (the first live specimen was not collected until the 1930s). It was natural for travelers in these regions to feel a kind of obligation to collect useful information. Note, for instance, Grace and Bob's carrying a boiling-point thermometer (technically, a hypsometer) to determine elevations (relying on the fact that the boiling point of water falls as the elevation rises). Bob started collecting butterflies as a hobby, but he also hoped to find new species.

Housekeeping chores kept the women busy for a good part of the day with preparing meals, giving out supplies, doing laundry, making butter, and such items. In the evenings we played games and almost always went early to bed. The night air grew quickly cool, and our lanterns did not give much light for festivities. The men did get in a good many chess games; I remember going to sleep with two chaps huddled over the chessboard in our tent.

While we were there in camp, Bob received word from the International Committee of the YMCA in New York that we were to buy land and build a residence in Chengtu. This excited and pleased us, and we spent quite a bit of our time thinking and talking about house plans. The International Committee later decided not to build for the time being; so our excitement was all in vain.

We visited the large, barrel-shaped prayer wheels set in a small stream near our camp and turned by waterwheels. We went to see a captured leopard at the summer palace of the King of Chala. We crossed the river and climbed the mountainside to inspect a leopard trap. And we had our own leopard scare one evening at dinner when the servants were alarmed by suspicious noises near the cooking tent. We closed the tents at night, but they were flimsy shelters. We often heard the trampling of *dzos* as they grazed nearby, or their whoofs as they ambled off in the early morning. We woke early, for the sun on the roof of a tent was not conducive to lengthy sleep. Often there was Harry, still in his pyjamas and mounted on his horse (named Red), whooping us all up as he tore off for a dip in the hot spring. Jokes and friendly banter made camping jolly for all.[4]

Harry's *mafu* (horse coolie), named Lao Tsao, had some friends in Tatsienlu, presumably fellow horsemen. He liked a good time and complained that he was not getting enough money to give him appropriate "face." (The reason for his scarcity of money was that Harry was having a part of his wages paid to his wife and family back in Yachow.) One night there was a commotion among the servants; someone had come from the village, where the horse and his keeper were quartered, saying that Lao Tsao had tried to commit suicide. He first drank as much native wine as he could afford. He then tied his cloth turban around his neck as tightly as possible. (In Szechwan many men wear cloth turbans, especially horse coolies, load car-

4. The people who shared this trip remained close friends, especially the Services and the Openshaws, who, to us boys, were much-loved Uncle Harry and Aunt Lona, more "real" than those other aunts and uncles in faraway America. When I remember her, Lona had become a comfortably ample, very "motherly" woman. Harry remained spare and full of energy, never silent for long, full of yarns and stories. He and Bob would keep up a steady flow of banter, joshing, and good-humored teasing wit that could entertain both foreigners and Chinese. If there was anyone who understood how to interest and amuse a young boy, it was Uncle Harry. Fate was not kind, for they never had children.

18   *Harry and Lona Openshaw (about 1910). Yachow, where Harry worked,
was a small, frontier town. He wore Chinese clothes because he found them
practical and comfortable, but he did not follow the example of many of his
fellow missionaries in remote locations, who tried to reduce their visibility
with a queue.*

riers, and other outdoor workers.) Harry rushed off to the village to see what
could be done. Lao Tsao's throat stricture was removed, and he was revived
and admonished—with the aid of some cash to restore his face as a servant
of foreigners.

There were three high spots of the summer: a visit to the Dorje Drag
Lamasery, a mile outside Tatsienlu, where we witnessed a Devil's Dance; a
trip to Jedo Pass (for the men); and a picnic trip to the Moshimian Pass. We
also went down to the King of Chala's summer palace to see the barley har-
vesting. The reaping was carried out by whole families who gathered to make
the affair a regular festival. They erected booths to live in and seemingly had
a good time at their work.

For the Devil's Dance, our Tatsienlu friends had made plans. We had fine
seats on the veranda, or gallery, overlooking the courtyard where the dance

took place. The costumes were of rich materials in the brightest colors and in the most fantastic manner, with much gold and silver thread, tassels, and jingling metal. Each lama performer wore a large head mask fitted in such a way that his eyes looked out through the mask's mouth. Thus the height of each performer was increased, which added greatly to the effect.

The dancers came out in groups, often dressed in similar style, and performed to the music of drums and long and short trumpets, with now and then a blast from a conch shell. The musicians sat at one side and made a picturesque appearance. The long trumpets were the most intriguing of the instruments, being some eight feet in length and resting on props near their open ends. The dance movements were stately and resembled in some ways the dances of North American Indians. There were wizards and demons, goddesses and heroes, and kings with many attendants. Some wore human and some animal masks. Of the latter, the most important seemed to be a stag in imposing regalia.

The ignorance about the meaning and symbolism of this ceremony is surprising. It was hard for us to discover what was going on; even our Tibetan-speaking friends were not able to give us much help. Some years later I found an account of this same festival in this very lamasery. Those who are interested may read this fine description in *A Tibetan on Tibet* by G. A. Combe, a former British consul in China. Mr. Combe characterizes some of the climactic parts of the ceremony as "relics of the human sacrifices of pre-Buddhist days."

We were permitted to visit the shrines in the lamasery. In the main hall there was a considerable collection of brass butter lamps lit in honor of the festival. There were also butter images of some of their deities. We met Mr. Lowe, Captain M'Neill, and others at the Devil's Dance; as we had all brought food, we ate in picnic style together.

After the meal we met the King of Chala, then living in Tatsienlu and so shorn of any former power that he was chiefly tolerated as being useful in providing *ula* (a form of corvée to provide animal transport) for travel between Tatsienlu and Batang.[5] The king had two wives; as the first had not produced a child and the second had, he had elevated the latter to a position equal to that of Number One. The women of our party were taken to meet these two queens. Both were similarly dressed in long Manchu-like gowns of heavy dark-blue satin brocade, stiff with gold-thread Chinese characters, which looked like geometric figures on the rich background. Though their

5. This Tibetan borderland was divided into many small hereditary states, which were treated by the Chinese as tributaries. The heads of the smaller units were called *tusi*; chieftains of larger areas were given the Chinese title of *wang* (king). As Grace says, their power was much circumscribed (especially in a Chinese enclave such as the town of Tatsienlu); but the Chinese government had little direct contact with the rural Tibetans, finding it quite satisfactory to rule indirectly through these native princes.

garments looked Manchu, their heads were elaborately dressed in Tibetan style with braids and much silver, coral, and turquoise ornamentation.

We had not garbed ourselves for attendance on royalty. I was wearing a khaki suit with a Norfolk jacket and short skirt over riding trousers, high boots of tan leather (these always intrigued both Chinese and Tibetans!), and a soft white silk blouse fastened up the front with pearl buttons. The royal ladies had little conversation; the only thing I remember was a question directed to me by the Number One Queen. From the magnificence of her satin gown and heavily ornamented head, she inquired why I wore fish bones on my clothing. She had noticed that my buttons were of pearl ("fish bone") instead of precious metal.

In August, Harry, Harold, and Bob went off with Mr. Sorensen on a trip to Jedo Pass. This pass, some 15,000 feet in elevation, is several days "in" from Tatsienlu on the road to Litang, Batang, and finally Lhasa. The men were gone five days, and the Ogdens stayed with us women in Camp Chala while they were away.

On August 20 the Robertsons and Miss Collier left for Chengtu; the Openshaws and we had decided that we could stay on for another week. On one of our last days, we four went on a picnic to the Moshimian Pass. This was in the opposite direction from Jedo and gave onto the high levels of the Black Tent Tibetans. The altitude of this pass we found, by boiling our thermometer, to be 13,100 feet. Lona rode Harry's horse, and I went in my light mountain sedan chair carried by the men who had stayed with us all summer. It was hard for me to walk at 10,000 feet, and I had used a chair nearly every day. The day was fresh and bright, the air crystal clear, and we had transcendent views of the lofty snow peaks. Four big glaciers were all spread before us as though we could reach them in a short time. However, we knew the distances were deceptive.

We saw many rhododendron bushes and could look across the pass to forests below on the other side of the divide. There was a keen, chill wind, while the blazing sun burned us all and made our skins feel taut and fiery. During our return in the afternoon, the others had all gone ahead while my men were plugging slowly along with my chair. Suddenly there was a snort and a whoof as we were passing a marshy pond in a little meadow. Confronting us was a large, angry-looking *dzo* with lowered head and long, waving body hair like swinging skirts. The chair bearers began to falter, and the front man called out that they had better put down so all could run. That was the last thing I wanted, since the men could run and I would be left alone with the beast. So I told them not to set down. The old *dzo* came toward us in a threatening manner, but the men hustled as fast as they could and finally reached some bushes that took us out of the irate creature's sight. *Dzo* used to graze regularly around our camp; most of them were accustomed to people and never showed any hostility. The long petticoat-like hair on their lower body and flanks gives them a strange look and makes them appear larger than they really are.

Bob went out several times with Mr. Ogden to hunt bear, but they were never successful.[6] His largest trophies were pheasant, grouse, and rabbit. One afternoon I saw a bear as I returned in my chair from a trip along a river path above our camp. The animal was across the river, busily gathering berries from bushes close to the water. It stood up and stuffed these into its mouth. We had both wild blackberries and strawberries close to camp.

On Thursday, August 26, we rose early, and I made butter in preparation for the travel ahead of us. We had laundry done. In the afternoon we were in our tent with clean things folded and lying around us on the two cots as we packed our road boxes. There was regularly a stiff breeze in the late afternoon, but that day the wind suddenly turned into a gale. Our old tent blew up and crashed down upon us. It was a great mix-up, but we finally were able to emerge to begin chasing our garments, many of which had blown out as the tent went down. Some caught on bushes; others flew farther afield. Our packing was at last accomplished, and we set up our cots in Miss Collier's former tent for our last night in camp.

Next morning, the fiftieth of our days in Camp Chala, Messrs. Sorensen and Ogden and Captain M'Neill came out for noon dinner and to help us break camp. Lona Openshaw on Red (Harry's horse) and I in my chair set off for Tatsienlu, leaving the men to finish dismantling the camp.

6. Bob never lost his zest for hiking and climbing, but he must have lost interest in hunting. He kept his rifle and shotgun, but in the years that I can remember they were almost never used. And I cannot recall that the possibility of my learning to shoot was ever even mentioned.

14

Home from the Mountains

(1908)

In Tatsienlu we stayed with the Og-
dens, the Openshaws with the Sorensens. Our plan was to do some shopping
in Tatsienlu on Saturday, rest on Sunday, and make an early start for Yachow
on Monday. Friday evening, Captain M'Neill came for dinner at the Ogdens;
the talk was strictly of hunting, mostly of what might have been. The shopping on Saturday was chiefly of silver. Tibetan silver shops, at least those in
Tatsienlu, do not carry much stock, so most of what we wanted had been
made to order. One was a long silver chain, like those which Tibetan women
use to hold up their aprons. I used it as a muff chain during the winter of
1915–16 when we were on furlough in America. Many people have spoken
of it; even strangers have asked where they could buy one like it. Sunday
morning we heard Harry preach in Chinese, and in the evening went happily
to close the day with a sing at the Sorensen home. But bad news met us, and
it was not a happy evening.

The Tibetan girl, Ossa, who had traveled with us from Chengtu under the
watchful eye of Miss Collier, had had an intrigue with our cook, Fu. He had
seen her on the road and had been coming to her room in Tatsienlu when he
came into town to do our marketing. Of course, on all of these trips he had
been given inn money. He was also told not to go to the Sorensens' at all
unless specifically sent there with messages. The Sorensen home was built in
Tibetan style, so they lived on the second floor. This girl occupied a room
below the Sorensen bedroom. If she had called out or expressed any alarm at
any time, they would easily have heard her.

In true Chinese fashion, everyone in the whole town seemed to have all
the facts at his tongue's end. The wretched affair had come to light through
the Chinese adherents of the mission, who knew that Fu was about to leave
Tatsienlu with us. The girl claimed that entrance to her room had been
forced, but this excuse was flimsy; no noise had ever been heard, nor had she

made any complaint to the Sorensens or to anyone else. It seemed to us that the Sorensens were responsible for those who slept on their premises; we also thought the girl should have been sleeping with some older native woman. Naturally, we deplored our cook's conduct; but in camp ten miles away, and having given the man money for his lodgings, it was impossible for us to know where he slept when away from camp.

Fu was fired and haled to the *yamen*. Monday departure had to be given up as Bob tried to work out some plan for the cook. Despite his guilt, we had brought him on this long journey and could scarcely abandon him far from home. Mr. Sorensen, however, thought he should remain in jail. We had to go on, so departed the next day without him. We did leave some travel money so that when Fu got out of jail he would be able to return to Chengtu. Later he did come back, and his old parents appeared and prostrated themselves before us as they beseeched us to reemploy him. We felt we could not: he had caused us to lose much face.

We left Tatsienlu on September 1, and my diary reads: "Pleasant day. Glad to get off from Tatsienlu about 9. Friends came outside city with us. Made 40 *li* before lunch. At Waszekow about 4:30. Good chair men and all went well. River lovely. Read in *Marcus Aurelius*. Fresh tomatoes for supper.[1] Stayed in Mohammedan inn. Smelly, but better than the other."

At Luting we stayed again with Magistrate Pao. He and his wife entertained us at dinner and gave us gifts. The room at the *yamen* was excellent and we slept well. Next morning we were up early, as always for travel, but not as early as the magistrate. When we passed through the front courts of the *yamen,* we ran into a judicial show. The Da Laoye ("Great Old Father") sat on the high seat of his authority dispensing justice. A crier with strident tone gave forth a summons. A poor craven countryman tremblingly prostrated himself and knocked his head on the paved floor. The whole scene was like a tale from some book of ancient times: the bright sunrise tints reflected from the whitewashed walls; the vivid robes and hangings against the gray of stones; the court underlings with their inscrutable faces; the shrewd-faced official set over this sparse county. In a few moments we took in a hundred details of the official's prestige, the commoner's dependence. It is no wonder that a good, compassionate magistrate was called "father-mother official." Sometimes when he left a post, a grateful populace would hang a pair of his old boots outside the city gate, hoping he would come back to wear them.

We were told not to hurry; when we finally came to the outer gate, there

---

1. "Fresh tomatoes for supper" was worthy of note because they were unknown in the native markets of West China at that time. These tomatoes, therefore, had come from the garden of one of the foreign families in Tatsienlu. And that fact made possible the special treat of eating them fresh, for they had not been fertilized with what we foreigners politely referred to as night soil.

were both the magistrate and his wife to see us off with as friendly a spirit as though they had known us for years. We wished we had more adequate gifts to repay their kindness.

One of Lao Tsao's many friends (he was Harry's famous horse coolie who had attempted suicide) had given him a small monkey. It is thought, in China, to bring good luck to have such an animal around a horse. "Monk" was about the size of a large house cat; he was also cute and full of tricks. He sometimes rode on Red, the horse, or perched on Lao Tsao's shoulder. At this time all Chinese men wore queues. The monkey would sit on Lao Tsao's shoulder, holding the base of his queue. At Nitow, in the good inn, a tiny grey and white kitten was fascinated. She came tremulously out of hiding to see what kind of creature this might be. Monk sat rock-still until she was close, then gave a spring and would have nipped her had his chain been a little longer. The poor kitten jumped a foot straight in the air and fled like a streak. As we passed through the villages, the children ran along calling "Ba-ser, ba-ser," a name for any monkey, as we say "Towser" for a dog. Monk answered with gay capers for their benefit. Harry gave these children picture cards, so they considered our passing a double benefit (though they may have found the biblical scenes a bit perplexing).

On our trip toward Tatsienlu, seated one day at a roadside teashop while the men drank tea and rested, we had been told of a local wonder. A horse had been born without ears. When we expressed polite but mild interest, the horse was brought around for us to view his earless and somewhat dejected appearance. Our homeward journey brought us back to the same spot. It was rainy, the narrow road was a small river, and the men were tired. We sat down to tea with no recognition of where we were. At last, one of us asked. The proprietor's wife exclaimed in great amazement: "Why, you were through here a month or more ago. We showed you our wonderful earless horse and you have forgotten all about it. You don't even remember the name of the place!" We hastened to set ourselves right by assuring her we could never forget the earless horse. So here his memory is now preserved.

One of the agreements of this vacation trip was that husbands would not have to shave. Harry found it impossible to raise a decent beard, so he shaved now and then to avoid our laughter at his sparse hairs. Harold Robertson carried a fine dark bushy beard back to Chengtu, and Bob had a genteel Van Dyke of a sandy color. (In these younger years, his hair was light; as a child he had been a towhead.) The Chinese regard really light hair as white, for they know nothing of blondes save for a rare albino.

One day on our return trip we were sitting in a tea shop and an old woman was much taken with my appearance. My skin has never been white for I am a decided brunette, but she spoke of it as light and clear and admired my rosy cheeks. Finally, she asked if she might touch the flesh to feel if it were like that of the Chinese. This seemed to satisfy her for a while, but then she asked why a young *gu-niang* (unmarried girl) should have to make such arduous travels. Harry, acting as spokesman, told her that I was not a *gu-niang*. "She is married to that man with the beard sitting there on the bench," said he. To the Chinese, beards come only with age. When the poor old crone looked at Bob and saw that, to her, both hair and beard were white, she expressed great sorrow that I had to have such an old fellow for husband. "As for travel," said Harry, "she has already crossed a vast ocean and come many hundreds of miles up the mighty Yangtze River." "And where is America?" asked the ancient dame.

Another old woman, deformed by rheumatism and confined to her bed, we had also seen on our way in to Tatsienlu. Her son had a mountain teashop and had placed her ramshackle bed in the main passage to the inner court so she could open her curtains, hardly more than ragged shreds, and see the world go by. Travelers like us made a red-letter day for the old body. We had sat by the couch and heard her tell how kind her son and his family were. On our return trip, Lona and I stopped especially to see the cheerful old soul. We gave her a bar of soap (I doubt if she knew its use!), foreign [paraffin] candles, and a few small native towels—all we could muster in the way of gifts. She was as ecstatic in her thanks as any young bride and called upon everyone within range of her shrill, piping voice to see how foreigners came to call on her and give her wonderful gifts. She was the happiest old woman in the dirtiest old bed I've ever seen or imagined.

We had only a day and a half of rain, rested over Sunday, and arrived in Yachow on September 9. We were glad to see the city again, and the friends there gave us a hearty welcome. The Taylors ["Grey Legs" and his bride from Mount Omei] had us over for supper and a good visit. We saw Viceroy Chao Erh-feng and his large retinue enter the city. He was on a tour of inspection through his viceregency; and we were thrilled to see such a colorful traveling pageant.

The extra day of rest in Yachow gave our coolie a chance to do laundry, and for us to prepare for the next stage of our travel. This was to go from Yachow to Kiating by bamboo raft down the Ya River. It was a longer route to Chengtu. But the inns on the Kiating-Chengtu road were better than those on the direct Yachow road, which we had suffered in on our outward trip. Also, we wanted to see Dr. Service in Kiating; and we were eager for the rafting experience.

The rafts on the Ya are unique. They are made of heavy entire bamboo stalks laid parallel and lashed together. By heating the bamboos, the front of the raft is curved upward like the front of a toboggan. If passengers are carried, there is a platform of thin planking about a foot high. This is carpeted with matting, and over it is a *peng* (arched roof) of split-bamboo mats. The round bamboo poles are slippery with water that sloshes up between the poles. Walking, or even standing, tests one's balance—and means wet feet. Bob wore Chinese straw sandals. I tried to stay on the platform under the *peng*.

There is a surprising flexibility in the raft. One constantly feels a sinuous movement as it is borne over boulders by the rapid current. In shallow places where the water is swift, there is a curious hissing and crackling noise. This is due to the movement of stones and pebbles in the bed of the stream, with the hollow bamboo tubes acting as sounding boards. There are many dangerous rapids and whirlpools. Shooting these places can be very exciting. We felt at times as if we were riding a great sea serpent. At night we tied up at a small *matou* (landing place), and were off again at dawn. We left Yachow about ten one morning and landed in Kiating about noon the next day.

We stayed with the Services at Kiating and enjoyed meeting friends there. Charlie Service gave me a medical examination. I had a swelling in my left breast, but it gradually disappeared after some months. After this Tatsienlu summer I had very few attacks of my severe abdominal pain. Years later, at the Mayo Clinic in 1915, the doctors told me I had undoubtedly suffered from gall stones during these early years in Szechwan. When I told them of the trip, arduous and far from doctors and surgeons, which we had taken to benefit my health, they looked at each other and said I had been exceedingly lucky. My trouble had been chronic rather than acute, though each spell seemed acute enough at the time. They also said I might have a recurrence after I reached fifty. So far this has not happened. In any case, I certainly never regretted the Tatsienlu experience.

We traveled by sedan chair from Kiating to Chengtu and arrived there on September 18 [twenty-two days after leaving Camp Chala]. It was wonderfully good to find ourselves again in the house on Wenmiaogai. After tents and low inn rooms, our house seemed lofty and spacious. The grass and shrubs at Camp Chala had been green, but not with the lushness of our Chengtu compound. Little balsams and coral-stemmed begonias grew like weeds along the cement paths; our patch of watercress was thriving by the well; the cypress vines were lovely against the north wall; and the hydrangeas we had brought from Mount Omei were magnificent.

Cooked food had been sent in by friends for our first meals. We reveled in home mail and callers, all at once. We did not get to bed until late, for Bob felt he had to develop film before he slept. The next day was Sunday and we stayed home to rest. In the evening we began to read Fisher's *Church History* aloud. This should be repeated in blazing type. It was a form of discipline, I suppose. The book had been recommended as suitable for young people of our interests and work. We read for months, but it finally vanquished us; we never completed it. If drier reading exists, I do not know it. It was warranted to put Bob to sleep; and though I am fond of reading, I hated it with a thorough abhorrence. The book has even disappeared from our shelves.

Our first cook had been a Boy from Chungking whom we trained until he went to jail after the robbery in May 1907. Fu, who came to the gate offering to help us when we had no servant, had stayed with us as Boy that summer and later as cook. It was he who made the fern baskets at Tawosze in 1907 and dug up so many plants for us to take back to Chengtu. He was the cook we had taken to Tatsienlu, and left there in jail because of his trouble with the Tibetan girl. Our cooks, it seemed, were fated! Now, after more than two years in Chengtu and having spent many, many mornings in training two cooks, I found myself back where I had started.

This was not quite true, for I was now much more experienced. I had more language, knew what to expect and demand—and I was ready to try again. I decided that I would train Liu Pei-yun, who had been serving us as Boy. He had been working for some of our friends while we were away during the summer and now came back to us. He was young, willing, neat, quick, and clever. I started in making our bread, doing all the baking and teaching him as I worked.[2]

In one day after our return from Tatsienlu, Bob was taken on the street for an Austrian, a German, and a Frenchman. About mid-October he shaved his beard and appeared as himself again. Gradually we began to get back into our routine: language study, Chinese callers, and all the usual occupations. We tried to gather our friends together at informal suppers and tea parties where we could meet them easily. Many of the (then) young Chinese still recall these occasions though so many years have passed; certainly we have never forgotten them. Bob started some classes for English and Bible study. Plans for the starting of the YMCA were moving ahead. We continued our little Y prayer meetings: one Sunday afternoon at our house, the next at the Hodgkins'. Mr. and Mrs. J. P. Davies of Kiating visited us that October with their young John.[3]

2. Bob really believed that bread, and its many varieties, was the staff of life. Liu Pei-yun became remarkably adept at producing all of them: bread, cookies, cakes, and especially melt-in-the-mouth baking-powder biscuits that seemed to take no time at all to make. Sunday breakfast was a high point of the week because it meant waffles—consumed by us boys as a form of competition.

3. Grace mentions the visit of the Davies family from Kiating with their "young John." When she wrote this, she knew that John and I had been close boyhood friends and that it was his example that led me to think of the American Foreign Service. But she could not, unless she was clairvoyant, know the extent to which our lives would later be linked. During World War II we were both attached to the staff of General Joseph W. Stilwell, commanding American forces in the China-Burma-India Theater. As observers on the scene, we came to the conclusion that the Chinese Communists would win the coming struggle for power in China. This led, in the strange logic of the McCarthy days, to our being prominent in the list of those responsible for "the loss of China." And this led, finally, to our both being separated from the Foreign Service. Today when I meet people whose memories reach hazily back to the McCarthy days, the chances are about even that they think I am John Davies. I expect that John has the same experience.

On November 17 in the forenoon we heard of the death of the ill-fated young emperor, Kuang-hsu. Soon after tiffin, a Chinese friend stopped by to tell us that the empress dowager, Tz'u-hsi, often called the "Old Buddha," was also dead. It seemed a strange circumstance to our friend that the death of the old empress had been preceded only a few hours by that of the unfortunate emperor. No reforms could now be carried out under the emperor's patronage.[4] The friend thought there would be unrest, perhaps even war. He thought it would be wise for foreigners to leave China. We were interested, but not alarmed.

That year my birthday fell on Thanksgiving Day. The American community had a fine goose dinner at the Canrights'. Fourteen people were at the table, one being a Scot. We dug our potatoes in December and had 220 catties of fine ones.

4. In 1898, after China had lost a disastrous war to Japan and was facing new imperialist demands, the emperor Kuang-hsu instituted a drastic program of reforms. The xenophobic conservative forces of the Manchu regime, centered around the aging empress dowager, quickly staged a coup. The emperor was incarcerated in his palace and the empress dowager, ruling in his name, led China into the catastrophe of the Boxer Rebellion and further decline. Most of the country's scholars and concerned intellectuals sympathized with the plight of the emperor and saw his return to power as the best hope for reversing China's fortunes. The suspicion of Grace and Bob's Chinese friend about the "strange circumstances" of his death was well founded. It is accepted that the vengeful empress dowager, realizing that her own end was near, had the emperor murdered. It was just in time: she died the next day. The emperor's death was actually on November 14; in spite of there being a telegraph line, it was not publicly known in Chengtu until the seventeenth. The successor to Kuang-hsu, designated by the all-powerful empress dowager, was the three-year-old Pu Yi. For further details, see the motion picture *The Last Emperor*.

15

First Son

(1909–10)

As 1909 rolled around, our foreign community continued slowly to grow. Several new teachers for the government university were added to our neighborhood. At least three American professors (two of them geologists) extended their researches as far as Chengtu.

Our American-Chinese friend, the mining engineer, found himself in difficulties on the Tibetan border. The problem was that his investigation had not found gold in the amounts that the viceroy had hoped for. Since the viceroy was seeking substantial grants from Peking to develop gold production, he did not want to accept the engineer's disappointing report and let him return home. A busy exchange of telegrams over several months gave us plenty of excitement. Discretion dictated the use of a private code: the viceroy was "Jones." Local efforts were unsuccessful; intervention by the American legation in Peking was finally necessary.[1]

I now had a definite group of Chinese girls and young women who wanted me to start a class. "Just teach us anything," was their plea. Even our strange methods of knitting and crocheting looked attractive to them. They still liked best of all to come for long calls and go all over our house, looking at everything and speculating on all sorts of matters: the way we lived; the

---

1. Apart from not finding gold prospects large enough to please the hopeful viceroy, Mr. Lowe's problem was one of citizenship. He was born in the United States and hence was an American citizen; that was the only way a Chinese *could* become an American citizen in those Exclusion Law days. But Chinese law at that time regarded all persons of Chinese ancestry as continuing to be Chinese citizens—or, more correctly, subjects. It was not easy to convince the viceroy that the "Chinese" whose freedom of movement he was limiting was actually an American, protected by extraterritoriality.

Gold there certainly was in this part of Tibet—enough, for instance, for some temple roofs to be covered with sheets of hammered gold. But it is placer gold, widely scattered in the sands of river beds. The upper Yangtze, above the Red Basin of Szechwan, is known to the Chinese as the Gold Sand River (Jinshajiang). But these deposits have been depleted by centuries of panning. And neither the unfortunate Mr. Lowe nor anyone since has been able to discover any great Mother Lode.

real friendship which apparently existed between Bob and me; and the reason for our being in China.

Early in 1909 it was decided that the projected YMCA should be close to the government university so as to serve as a student center. The university was close to us, so our neighborhood was the logical location. No suitable building could be found. After long discussions, land at the rear of the Methodist school (next door to our residence) was leased. The International Committee of the YMCA loaned US$2,500, and a commodious and useful building was erected. This took up most of Bob's time during the summer and fall of 1909.

Because the building was situated behind the school and hence removed from the street, there was an access problem. It was agreed that there would be a separate entrance and an alleyway leading back to the Y. The planning of this was done by the Chinese secretary of the Y, who had already joined the organization. We were surprised by the size and ostentation of the gate produced under his direction.[2]

When the building was put up in 1909, the American dollar was worth about two Chinese silver dollars. In 1920, after the building had been used for more than ten years, the American dollar was worth only eighty cents in Chinese silver. As the Y was then moving to a new location, this building was sold. The price received made it possible to repay the debt, with a handsome profit.[3]

In May we had a two-story veranda built on the west side of our house. This helped protect the study and our bedroom from the afternoon sun. It also gave us a fine place for airing things, which was often needed because Chengtu's climate is very damp. Very soon the veranda seemed to have always been there. Vines quickly reached the eaves; the problem was to keep them from shutting out the air.

In the late spring we always had a big *peng* erected over the courtyard in front of our house.[4] One morning the workmen would arrive with great stacks of bamboo poles, large mats woven of split bamboo, and hemp twine. In no time, the pole framework was up and firmly lashed together. Mats were

2. Gates are important to Chinese because they are expected to indicate the status and importance of what they protect.
3. When the rate was two-to-one, US$2,500 brought Chinese $5,000. When the loan was repaid, the rate was US$1 = Chinese $0.80. The Chinese $5,000 could then be exchanged for US$6,500, or a profit of US$4,000. This reversal in the normal values of the American and Chinese dollars was one of the temporary effects of trade imbalances during World War I. The normal value was about US$1.00 = Chinese $2.00. The American dollar was usually referred to as the "gold dollar," and the Chinese dollar was either the "Mexican dollar" (which is where many of the coins in circulation had actually originated) or the "silver dollar." Very few foreigners used the Chinese word *yuan*. When Grace refers to "dollars" it should be understood, unless otherwise stated, that she means Chinese dollars.
4. A *peng* is a canopy or awning of bamboo or reed mats. On a vessel or raft it is the arch-roofed shelter; in this case it was a mat awning over the courtyard.

19   The Service house on Wenmiaogai. The view is from the back and shows
Grace's new veranda and its quickly growing vines. In the foreground to the right
is the vegetable garden; to the left is the tennis court. The picture was taken in
1910, and Jack is the small figure being held by Bob.

then sewed in place. Finally the roller sections were arranged, complete with
pulling ropes. These were like shutters that could be open or closed depending on the weather and time of day. The peng was very welcome because it
tempered the sun's heat and glare. It allowed us to take down the living room
curtains and keep everything open to catch any breeze there might be. In the
fall, the men came back and dismantled it. We paid a rent for its use.

For us the great affair of the year was the birth of our eldest son. We were
able to have the help of Miss Whittier, a most excellent nurse who was visiting in China and so had no obligation to a mission. The spring began early,
and the summer was long and hot. The doctor forbade chair riding; I could
not walk any distance, so I remained inside our compound for several
months. I had been none too well but was constantly busy with sewing and
doing what I could do at home with Chinese pupils and guests. By our count
the baby was expected on June 19, and Miss Whittier came that day to stay
with us. But the child did not come in June. The Robertsons' son was born
June 24; Vieva was much pleased to have her baby first.

All of July's hot, muggy days came and went. Still no baby. Bob had borrowed a bagatelle board from the Davidsons, and we had it on a table in a
small screened section of our west veranda. (We couldn't afford to screen the
whole house.) There we used to play when it got cooler in the evenings. The
only garb I could be comfortable in was a loose white silk dress. The doctor's
family went to the mountains and he was naturally anxious to be with them.

Every few days he would come to see me; I was only more hot, tired, and uncomfortable. Finally, one of the Methodist single ladies, who were neighbors of the doctor, asked me bluntly what was the trouble. "There must be something wrong, for the way the doctor is reading up in his medical books is a caution. He's at it every evening."

On Monday, August 2, the doctor came in the evening. He asked if I'd like to have one of the Canadian doctors called in. I said, "No, they've had several babies over on their side of the city this year and it's a pity if we Americans can't manage one." This cheered him a bit, and the next morning he arrived right after breakfast prepared to start things. I spent a rather uncomfortable day. John Stewart Service was born at 8:20 P.M. on August 3, 1909. He weighed eight pounds and had long fingernails and a nose that seemed somewhat smashed into his face.[5] We had to use bed nets, and they were a great nuisance in the hot, sticky weather when tending an infant. Kerosene lamps were hot, too. How I longed for one bit of ice in those stifling August nights! Still, we forgot all the discomforts in the joy of the child's safe arrival.

Bob had been delighted with his daughter; he was satisfied with his son. Up to his last weeks, Bob had an unfaltering faith that he would live to be an old man. He often spoke of how he would enjoy age, and hoped that he would not grow crabbed or intolerant with the years. Knowing his attitude regarding his own life, his first words to me about our son always remained in my mind. As we looked at the baby together, he said. "Here is your son at last; if anything happens to me, he will be your help."

All our friends sent good wishes. The workmen on the new YMCA building brought gifts: eggs, fowls and firecrackers, a pair of small "official" boots, and a marvelous gilt headdress with two long pheasant tail feathers. The boots and hat were to express the hope that the son would have the good fortune of becoming an official. In Chinese fashion, Bob gave a feast in return. Everyone was pleased that we had a son. Chinese friends were glad that they no longer needed to sympathize because we had no children.

After a few days the doctor went off to join his family at Kwanhsien, feeling sure that we were in good hands with Miss Whittier. On the eighteenth of August the baby weighed nine pounds, in spite of the heat. Chee Soo Lowe arrived at last from beyond Tatsienlu, and we were glad to have him with us. His son had been born since he left America, so he was much taken with our baby boy. He stayed a fortnight before leaving for the Coast, and California. Our flowers were beautiful that summer. The moonflowers on the new west veranda were especially prolific; their fragrant blossoms were lovely in the moonlight in late August.

5. My nose that was "somewhat smashed" made a notable recovery. Large noses are a distinguishing mark of the Service clan, and there is no need for me to take a back seat at family gatherings. In later years there was much banter about the reliability of Grace's long count.

We were tremendously happy over the baby that fall. I soon found myself busier than ever. There was a bout of making curtains for the new teachers at the government university. Then I had an urge to entertain all our friends: Chinese, foreign, everyone. This was a reaction after all those months I had spent in seclusion before the baby arrived. On Halloween we had a fancy dress party, with thirty-four for a buffet supper. We had prepared games, and Bob had marked out a maze on the tennis court. This we could not use because it rained.

In November I had a tea party for Chengtu's five foreign babies born that summer. The parents of three were in the Canadian Methodist Mission. The father of the fourth, Mr. Ritchie, was the local head of the Imperial Chinese Post Office. On my birthday we entertained twenty-four at dinner and had a lovely time. We entertained over one thousand students that year. And by its end, a student YMCA was organized and a building ready.

Our Christmas parcels were soaked in the "old river" [the Yangtze]. Baby shoes and all the cute things we had anticipated were reduced to moldy rags, repugnant to sight and smell. But nothing could depress us for long in those days. The small son was a never-failing source of happiness and always pleased our Chinese friends—though they were amazed at our methods of child care. At least they understood his food, for it was provided by nature.

Dr. Hodgkin, who had helped greatly with all the preliminary work of getting the YMCA started, was now asked to return to England as secretary of the Friends' Mission. This was a blow to the Chengtu Y, just at its beginning, and greatly added to Bob's responsibilities. The Hodgkins stayed with us while they were packing up, and left Chengtu in January 1910.

That same afternoon there arrived at our home a noted globe-trotter traveling in these far places to gather material for lecturing and writing. This gentleman kept us all in a whirl. One of his obsessions was that the only way to get on in the East was to hustle it. He illustrated this by telling how he found sedan chair travel in Kweichow Province to be easy, although he had been told it was difficult. He rode in his sedan chair with a loaded revolver in plain sight in his lap. When the chair men and load carriers were slow in eating their meal, he would simply tip over their table, throw their rice bowls on the ground, push them toward their loads, and yell at them to get started. He thought we all "stood too much laziness" from the Chinese.

Bob told him that, aside from questions of Christian ethics, he could never countenance such actions. They were entirely wrong for transients, but would be fatal for residents like ourselves who wished to win influence and friendship from the Chinese. In short, he did not like to hear such talk at our table. Our guest, we could see, thought we were all lacking in "American spirit." The subject was changed.

This visitor was a self-invited guest. He had heard of us as YMCA people and sent a telegram asking that arrangements be made for his stay. We presented no bill for board, lodgings, or any of the things we had done for him. And he asked for no accounting; but as he was leaving, after ten days that were hectic for us, he thanked me for his entertainment and handed me the case and works of a dismantled Ingersoll dollar watch. He thought we might find this useful or, if we did not need it now, we could save it for the baby. He also left me another keepsake. My good rubber hot-water bottle, which he had wanted for his bed, evidently met a sharp toenail. No one but a woman some six weeks from a supply of such necessities can appreciate how peeved I felt.[6]

Mention of our servants brings to mind a question which frequently arouses criticism from Westerners. How can people, especially those in Christian work, have so many servants? If you were living among coolies and working solely with people who had nothing, you might want to get along with little or no help, provided you could be efficient by so doing. If you want to live as a scholar or merchant lives in China, servants are needed. The Szechwan people do not make as adaptable servants as some other Chinese. They are very independent, and each man intends to do one thing and very little more. The cook will go out to buy (frequently hiring a man to carry his purchases) and he expects to do the cooking, but not the serving at table or afternoon tea. He usually turns up his nose at cleaning, but may clean the kitchen if this is required by his mistress. The Boy will do dusting, he will serve at table, he may iron clothes and do a few such things. The coolie cleans the floors and does all the heavier work (including carrying water if the supply is near). If the family is small, he may do the laundry work; otherwise a washerman will have to be employed. There is usually an amah for bedroom work and to help with the children. If one kept cows, a man was needed to tend them. And finally, there was a gateman; and he usually had a family, which was supposed to ensure that the gate would always be tended.

With no household conveniences, there was a great deal to be done. Public utilities were entirely lacking. The charges which in America go to water, light, gas, and telephone companies have to go in China to coolies for fetching water, cleaning lamps, tending fireplaces, and carrying chits around town.[7] All our water for cooking, bathing, laundry, and household use had to

6. For the uninvited guest's impressions of his visit to Chengtu, see William Edgar Geil, *Eighteen Capitals of China* (Philadelphia & London: Lippincott, 1911).

7. "Chit" is from a Hindi word *chitthi* and, as used by foreigners in China, had two meanings. In the interior, where there were no telephones, it was a note or message. An active lady could easily keep a chit coolie busy all day, especially if he had many places where he was instructed to wait for a reply. In the treaty ports, a chit was a bill for bar drinks, restaurant meals, or other charges that had been signed (or initialed) by the person incurring the charge. The chit holder hoped for a periodic settlement, perhaps monthly. This system was convenient and a vital part of the foreign life in the coast cities. Perhaps one reason that it worked was that there

be drawn from the well (there were no pumps) and carried to where it was to be used. Kerosene lamps had to be cleaned and filled each day. The cook had personally to attend to marketing (at many stalls and shops), make yeast, do all the baking and cooking, and perform other tasks, such as refining sugar and salt for kitchen use.[8] (We tried to have foreign sugar and salt for the table.) Then there was milk to scald daily, and butter to make.

One thing to be remembered is the time the servants use for cooking and eating their own meals. This is usually done in a leisurely way; but if there are guests or a special need, servants will toil on without stopping to think of their own affairs. Making good food and doing things that will please guests gives them—the servants—face! No mistress needs to apologize to the staff for guests; they are desired and appreciated. The cook knows there will be more buying; hence more commission in his pocket. The Boy knows he will serve and be close to the excitement of the occasion. Even the hard-working coolie, who likely enough has to wash every pot, pan, and dish, never utters a groan.

Consider, too, the extent to which the housewife is freed from worry. An unexpected visitor arrives shortly before mealtime; she tells the Boy to lay another place. It is up to the cook to supply the food; he always rises to the emergency. Perhaps he exchanges the noon dessert with the one prepared for dinner, or perhaps he works out a subtler plan. But he finds a way. And the hostess, confident there will be a meal worthy of her cook and her house, sits serene.

Chinese all love hot food. Indeed, much of the savor and zest of their dishes are lost when they are served lukewarm or cold. I have always tried to follow the advice given me soon after I set up housekeeping in China: never call a servant from his hot food to do any task. Sometimes it is unavoidable; but if I find they are at a meal, I usually tell them to finish and come back. Another large item in the servant problem is the slow pace at which a servant works. An ironing which we could do in one day takes the coolie three days, and thus it goes. Why should they hurry through one task when it just means something else to do? In the long run, one has to let the house go more or less at the pace of the workers.

Our Chinese friends could not understand the amount of work I used to

---

was no way to skip town except by ship, and a ship's sailing was a public and not very frequent event.

8. Native sugar in Szechwan was sold in dark brown cakes, salt in grey lumps. I remember that we "refined" them but am mystified about how it was done. But Grace by no means exhausts the list of kitchen accomplishments. About once a year we made and bottled a great batch of orange marmalade; Szechwan oranges are great and I still love marmalade. At the appropriate times, we preserved fruit; I think the local cherries and peaches were the best. In the fall there was a great making of mincemeat. And we even made soap for the laundry. We were by no means unusual; some families did even more—like smoking meat or making pickles.

do. They seemed to think it not proper. If one had servants, *they* should do the work. In Chinese eyes, for me to do my own mending was niggardly because it deprived some needy woman of work. Actually, wages in Szechwan were very low; even in 1935 a friend from there told me her staff of four servants cost less than a well-trained cook-boy.and helper in Shanghai.

One expense that I tried hard over the years to reduce was the fuel used in the kitchen. Most Americans would attend to baking and such matters in the morning and bank the fire in the afternoon. But a Chinese cook sees it differently. After the master and mistress have had their breakfast, he goes marketing. When he returns, there is his own meal to prepare and eat. (In Szechwan we always had a Chinese kitchen apart from our own for the servants' use.) After this meal the morning is well along and, as the cook expects to work all day anyway, he sees no need for haste in baking. Finally, I simply reduced my struggle for economy in kitchen fuel to a limitation of supply. I found a small range preferable to a large one; though the smaller would have seemed a handicap to me, no cook ever complained. I made tests until I found the approximate amount of fuel needed for a month. The cook was then held to this amount.

Another reason for having a constant fire is the frequent and unpredictable need for tea. Whenever a guest arrives, tea must be served. This is the Chinese manner of welcome. Hence, there must always be a fire, and water not too far off the boil. This is not easy where there is no gas or electricity.

The accounts for household expenditures went through my hands— except for coal and for fodder and similar costs when we had cows or horses. The fuel was soft coal which was delivered in sizable lumps. This had to be weighed, and one had to be alert to various tricks: stones in the bottom of the basket, too much wetness, or even a foot on a rope hanging from the basket being weighed. I was glad to turn this over to Bob. And, having grown up on a ranch before the day of tractors, he also knew about fodder.

I have mentioned the serving of tea. The Chinese, of course, serve tea to all visitors, day and night. When we set out for China, we had no tea equipment; we soon found it most essential. Staying with English Friends in Chungking and with the Hodgkins in Chengtu, we soon discovered all the requirements and ritual of the tea cult. The majority of the foreigners in Chengtu were British. To the British afternoon tea is no luxury; it is a necessity. It is served to all employees in British offices and shops in Hong Kong, Shanghai, and other ports. When waiting to be served by a sales clerk in a Shanghai shop, I have sometimes been asked to pardon a moment's delay: "My tea's getting a bit cold, I fear." British and Chinese can always get together on tea drinking, but I prefer the Chinese version. To my taste, their milder, more delicate teas, served clear, are much pleasanter than the common British brew, "strong enough to float a ship" and bitter with tannin.

16

Second Son

(1910–11)

After the heat of the long summer of 1909 in Chengtu we began to hope for a cool place to go in the hot weeks of coming summers. I lacked endurance, and the heat always prostrated me. Mount Omei, as I have said, was too far away for Bob's responsibility to the YMCA. Above Kwanhsien, a long day's travel northwest of Chengtu, there was a famous temple named Lingaisze that rented rooms to foreigners. But there was little privacy; everyone was crowded together in a way that hampered rest or relaxation. The verandas were narrow and in wet weather were usually draped with laundry. It seems to be a peculiarity of many missionaries in China that wet laundry hung conspicuously near their rooms never bothers them.

Missionaries had tried to lease land for bungalows near Lingaisze but had always been blocked by some of the Kwanhsien gentry—who feared that the presence of foreigners, even for a few weeks in the summer, might adversely affect the local *fengshui*.[1] Bob therefore went beyond Kwanhsien to another *hsien* (county). Near the small town of Shwangkow he found a suitable site. It was within two day's travel from Chengtu, and close enough to Lingaisze, where foreigners went, to make it possible to reach a doctor in an emergency. After much consideration, we and the Lindsays, of the Canadian Mission, decided to lease land and put up a couple of small bungalows of Chinese style. Later, the American teachers at the government university and the Robertsons also decided to join us. This would give us a group of four bungalows for the first summer.

1. *Fengshui*, literally, means "wind and water." Chinese traditional belief held that the dead are able to use the cosmic currents for the benefit of the living. It is to the interest of each family, therefore, to secure and preserve the most auspicious environment for the grave, the ancestral temple, and the home. Most important in these cosmic currents are the forms of the landscape and the directions of watercourses, which are the outcome of the molding influences of wind and water. The common reference to this as geomancy is incorrect. (See *Encyclopedia Sinica*.)

These houses were of the simplest Chinese construction so that they could be erected quickly and inexpensively: pole frame, wattle-and-mud white-washed walls, with glass windows and wooden shutters. Bob took several quick trips to the site that spring. Dr. Lindsay accompanied him on the first trip, and both were on horses—thus making twice the distance in a day that could be accomplished by sedan chair. Bob's pony was a stupid animal on the bridges; which in remoter Szechwan often leave much to be desired. They had to cross a bamboo-cable suspension bridge with a loosely laid footway of uneven boards. Bob, walking ahead, suddenly heard cries of distress from the *mafu* and looked back to see the wretched pony lying on its belly across a few planks, all four legs dangling helplessly in the air. It took a good deal of tugging and hauling by all hands to get the animal back on his feet on the uncertain flooring of the swinging bridge.

In April I took Jack with me one afternoon to call on the Methodist ladies. On our return, when we approached our street, we ran into a great jam of people. Finally, the chair men learned from one of our Chinese neighbors the cause of the excitement: part of our house had burned down. The crowd was so thick that my bearers said they would have to put the chair down, but I would not hear to that. So, by yelling and pushing through the crowd, the men at last reached our gate and entered over a mound of broken tile. Four of the servants' rooms at the west side of our outer court had been burned. We had been having the kitchen chimney cleaned, and the range thoroughly scraped and cleared of ashes. The coolie had carelessly thrown the ashes near the building wall, not thinking there might be a live coal among them.

Bishop Cassels and another man had just entered our compound to call on Bob when the fire was discovered. They hurried a man off to get Bob at the Y building next door, and he was quickly there. The police soon had the firefighters on the job. This chiefly consisted of tearing tiles off the adjacent roofs and throwing them down on the blaze to smother it [there was, of course, no piped water]. By the time I arrived, the real excitement was over.

Our friends the Neumanns had told us a great deal about Jim and Mabelle Yard who were coming to Chengtu in the Methodist Episcopal Mission. They arrived in June and I first met Mabelle on the eighth of that month at the Neumanns' home. This is a memorable date for me, as Mabelle has been a constant and treasured friend ever since.[2]

2. Mabelle Yard became Grace's closest friend. After they were separated (when our family left Chengtu in 1921), they kept up a constant, voluminous, and very intimate correspondence until Mabelle died in 1954, a few months before Grace. The friendship included the whole two families. Jim's liberal views, on politics but especially on subjects like giving Chinese Christians a larger role in the missionary enterprise, eventually led to his separation from the mission. There were four Yard girls; and we were three Service boys, sandwiched by age between them. They were our closest neighbors, so close comrades in play. The four all went to Swarthmore, and all married distinguished and interesting men. One husband is Louis Harris, the master of

As summer drew near, trouble appeared on the horizon. It concerned the little bungalows that were being built near Shwangkow. Bitter opposition to their presence was being expressed by some of the gentry in the vicinity. It is possible that they had been aroused by their brethren in Kwanhsien, whom we had hoped to avoid by moving to another county. After local efforts were unsuccessful, the trouble at last had to be reported to our consuls (the British in Chengtu and the American in Chungking). As our whole idea was to establish and maintain friendly contacts with the Chinese wherever we were, we could not push our desires after it became clear that nothing would suit the opposition save that we abandon the whole plan. The gentry finally offered to reimburse us for the money we had spent, so they acquired some nearly completed bungalows.[3] As we had the goodwill of the local people and artisans, we could console ourselves that racial prejudice was held by only a few. But by this time all the rooms at Lingaisze had been rented for the season.

Our old Berkeley classmate Julean Arnold, then a member of the American consulate staff at Canton, wired us in June, from Sian,[4] that he was coming overland with Professor E. A. Ross, the noted sociologist. They arrived on July 11. A note announcing their imminent arrival came only a few minutes before they appeared. It was a Sunday. Bob was at Shwangkow for the final settlement of the affair of the ill-fated bungalows, and I was entertaining a Canadian lady for the weekend. The cook had prepared a small duck for supper, but managed to piece out the menu—as Chinese cooks usually can.

Bob arrived home the next day, Monday. On Tuesday a telegram informed Julean that his wife was seriously ill in Canton. So our guests left on Thursday. Bob took the two men around the city and they had a glimpse of things, though most of the people we would have liked them to meet were away at the hills. As always, we enjoyed Julean; and we found Professor Ross to be a charming person. The night of his arrival he tiptoed in to see Jack asleep in his crib, told me of his own sons so far away, and assured me that my baby appeared to be a real American child.[5]

---

opinion polls. Molly, the third daughter, is currently (1988) head of the National Organization for Women (NOW).

3. The treaties then in effect, rightly called "unequal" by the Chinese, specified that missionaries should be able to purchase or lease land and buildings for their missionary work. Hence the referral to the British and American consuls. However, the problem of summer bungalows (as a part of missionary work) may have been an issue that the representatives of both governments were not anxious to confront at that time and place. It can be assumed that the offer by the gentry to make reimbursement was "encouraged" by higher authority.

4. Sian, the capital of Shensi Province, is now known as Xi'an, and has become recently famous as the site of the buried army of clay figures guarding the tomb of China's first emperor. The overland trip from Sian to Chengtu took these doughty travelers twenty-four days.

5. Professor Edward Alsworth Ross was a pioneer in the field of sociology in the United

Before he left, I asked the professor if there was any special home dish he would like. He expressed a desire for a good supply of hot baking-powder biscuits with butter, and syrup in a side dish. He had his biscuits and syrup and was duly grateful. He was tall, and it must have been hard for him to cramp his long limbs into a sedan chair. It was not surprising that the two men had walked much of the way, especially since Julean was a noted pedestrian. They left by small boat to descend the Min and Yangtze rivers and catch a steamer at Ichang.

That summer we had one of the heaviest rains I have ever seen. My diary (for July 27) says: "Cool. It poured torrents all day till after five in the afternoon. Dr. Lindsay came in after breakfast and he and Mr. McCampbell were caught here and stayed for lunch and afternoon tea. Dr. Lindsay spent the night." Bob was able to get over to the YMCA building, but there was no one there. The Chinese simply remained at home and, like Emily Dickinson in her acceptance of life, let it rain. No one tried to keep engagements. Our roof was of Chinese tile, and we had it carefully checked each year. But in this rain, the house leaked in many places, so we were hustling about, moving furniture and setting pails and pans. The Chinese compare summer rain to chopsticks; when one looked outside, the aptness was apparent. This rain fell in rods, not drops. It was as though the sky was a lake with a perforated bottom. The roar of the water on roofs and pavement was thunderous, and spray was everywhere. In *Hot Countries,* Alec Waugh tells of an Englishman who tries life in Europe but returns to Dominica in the Antilles, saying, "I must hear it rain again." After living in the Orient one can understand that man's feeling.

The last two weeks of August we spent at Lingaisze in rooms that had been vacated by one of the Canadians. It was hot and the mosquitoes were active, so we earned our vacation. Because of muddy roads, the trip took us two days; now there is a motor road, and people can whirl off and arrive in less than two hours. When we went there on this trip in 1910 we took our cow! It seems odd to have such a caravan. But Jack was taking milk and we had to have the supply with us.

That summer there was a sad death in our little foreign community. One of the American teachers at the government university, a neighbor of ours, started off alone for Kiating on his way to Mount Omei. Not far above Kiating his small boat was tied up for the night at a village *matou.* The boatmen went

---

States and spent most of his career at the University of Wisconsin. This trip resulted in *The Changing Chinese* (New York: Century, 1911). In it he speaks of Chengtu as the most progressive of pure Chinese cities—which he regards as "Western influence at its best" (p. 303). Grace's story of the learned professor giving the babe in his crib the accolade of being a real American boy was an old Service family joke.

ashore, leaving him barefoot on deck where he had been washing his feet in the river. It was dark; there was a bustle of activity among the boats moored close together. But no one heard any splash or cry for help. He evidently slipped on the wet deck and fell overboard, perhaps striking his head on his own boat or the one next to it. His possessions were found intact, and his body was recovered a few days later some distance downstream.

There was a new project for the Y in 1910. Dr. William Wilson of the China Inland Mission at Suining, eastern Szechwan, had created an unusual and impressive science museum. It was suggested that this exhibit merited a broader field of usefulness than was offered by the remote and rather small city of Suining. The location that naturally suggested itself was the provincial capital, Chengtu. Eventually it was settled that the museum would be moved to Chengtu and shown in a hall at the YMCA.

This meant more building. A hall about 60 by 90 feet was put up next to the YMCA building to house the museum. It was also necessary to house the Wilsons. Fortunately, the Methodist boys' school next to us on the west had just moved to the campus of the West China Union University. This made it possible to convert the upper part of the school (the rooms at the north end of the compound, which corresponded in our compound to the rooms we lived in) into a house for the Wilsons. This was quite a large dwelling, bigger than our own. All this construction was under Bob's supervision while carrying on his Y work and language study.

The Wilsons reached Chengtu in May and stayed with us until they could move into their house late in June. By the end of September, his exhibits were in place. They quickly met expectations in drawing Chinese visitors to the YMCA. People were fascinated by models of many contrivances which lighten labor, and gazed at small toy engines with interest and concern. Within a short time, thousands had visited the hall and viewed the exhibit. Many repeated their visits, bringing incredulous friends to see the wonders for themselves.

In January [1911] Dr. Wilson became ill with high blood pressure and other symptoms. It was decided that he should have a complete change, and rest for six months. The best way to achieve this was to return to Suining. They left in early February. In April Cameron Hayes arrived from America to join the YMCA staff. He had been long anticipated and received the heartiest kind of welcome. We prepared a suite of rooms for him on the Wilson compound (just next door to us), and he took his meals with us.

Soon after this Miss Whittier, fortunately again available, arrived for another stay with us. We had an Anglican friend visiting us and sat up quite late on the evening of Sunday, May 7, discussing the education of children. The next morning when the Anglican came down to breakfast, he was sur-

20 The science museum of the Chengtu YMCA in 1910. The director, Dr. William Watson, stands at left center; Bob is in the background at the right.

prised to see nothing of his host and hostess and a stranger alone in the dining room. This gentleman introduced himself as a doctor, and said that the Service family had a new son, born just before seven that morning. Our guest had not even heard the doctor arrive in the compound and was much astonished at the news. So were we, for we had expected to wait for some days longer.

We named this second son Robert Kennedy, after his father and J. L. Kennedy, a dear friend of both of us during college days at Berkeley.[6]

6. The new Robert was, naturally, also called Bob. Grace usually makes it clear which Bob she is referring to, but it should be borne in mind that henceforth there are two Bobs.

17

Peony Mountain

(1911)

Bob had been investigating possible places to go for the summer. We decided to rent some rooms in a temple at Danjingshan, about sixty *li* from Penghsien, north of Chengtu. Our departure was delayed, waiting for some vaccine. My diary describes the journey:

> July 5th. Cloudy. Got up at 4:30 and left the house about 7 o'clock. Little Bob was vaccinated at 6 by Dr. Freeman. Roads were fearful and mud the worst ever, so we could only reach Sinfan. Poor carriers. July 6th. Cloudy. Up early and off after delays. Men very slow. We reached Penghsien at 10 and had to wait there for dinner. Reached temple between 6 and 7 P.M., but beds and bedding did not arrive until 10:30 and then the cook stayed below with other loads. Put the children to bed on oil sheets spread on the *kang*.[1] Tired!!

Yes, we were tired that night. But oh, the moonlight and the charm of that old temple! We had never seen such glorious radiance from the moon. The soft night breeze and vagrant clouds, and the peculiar grey-green of the tangled verdure in the moonlight, placed a spell upon us. I remember how weary, and even cross, I was; but in spite of everything I was wrapt away into Faery. That temple was a perfect setting for a Midsummer Night's Dream.

The main temple building here at Danjingshan had been burned some years ago. A new one had been started, but never finished; only the massive columns and framework stood to tell of unfulfilled hopes. Still extant were various rooms of the lower levels of the old temple. And on both sides of a long court leading up to these there was a fine Buddhist Hell, a gallery of

---

1. This is not the flue-heated brick-platform bed of north China. It is a hard-seated couch or divan of wood that looks much like a very wide Chinese chair, wide enough for a person to recline (perhaps, in those days, to smoke opium). The two *kangs* are different characters, pronounced identically.

almost-life-sized clay figures, picturing all the torments of the damned in the most realistic manner. (When I wrote Mother about this Hell, she replied that nothing could prevail on her to stay in such surroundings. She thought it awful for us to take young children there; and that our actions were another proof of the way our sensibilities had become blunted. I wrote her we did not live *in* the Hell, but above it.)

This old court had in time past been a charming place; even now in an unkempt state it had much of beauty and repose. An ornamental bridge arched over a tiny watercourse. Guarding the lower approach were two old crêpe myrtle trees. They were gnarled but had attained old age gracefully; against the grey of their trunks, the fragile garments of their bright cerise blooms caused the catching of one's breath for very delight.

At the level of the unfinished upper temple, on a rocky ledge overlooking the large lower court, was a suite of guest rooms which had been used in times past by officials of Penghsien when they came to view the peonies from which this mountain temple derived its name, Peony Prospect Mountain. There was a large guest hall about forty-five by twenty feet, with a beautifully balustraded veranda along one side and overlooking the court below. The long opposite wall had a lengthy wooden *kang* beneath a row of windows opening onto terraces in the rear of the building.

These terraces were where the peonies grew. Their blossoms were gone before we arrived; but one could see that the plants were not in the best of condition. The old caretaker told us some of the roots had been kept for more than three hundred years. One can imagine the charm of this mountain-side flower show in the pride of its full glory being enjoyed by scholars and weary officials. No doubt many a poem had been written in that guest hall, and many a happy hour spent there.

At the south end of the long living room there were two small rooms. The first room had no door, but only a circular moon-door opening leading into it from the living room. We hung an oil sheet over this opening and used it as our bedroom. A wooden door led from this bedroom into a still smaller room which could be locked. This we used as dressing and bathroom. We put up curtains for privacy, nailed shut the lattice windows, and so had quite a useful retreat. Here we kept our traveling boxes and supplies under lock and key. At the north end of the living room were two more small rooms. One we kept for guests; our two serving women had the other. At this time I had a baby amah and a laundress.

There was only one old priest in residence. He seemed to act chiefly as caretaker, but a few times a day he would strike the big bell and a fish-head drum back in some obscure room. The huge Buddha who had occupied the place of honor in the old temple, and around whom the new structure was to have been built, still sat there mute and immovable, falling slowly into decay as the elements took advantage of his unprotected condition. He looked distressed at his own ruin.

On the night of July 11, all our table silver and the baby's diapers were stolen by a thief. He must have come right into our small bedroom and taken these things from very near while we slept. The silver was in a basket under our low bed. Luckily, our clothes were locked in the dressing room. Evidently the man woke the baby because little Bob cried at a time that was not routine. I got up to tend him and so discovered that the diapers were gone. Our silver was only cheap plate used for outings, but we did miss it sorely. Fortunately, the wash amah had put a few freshly laundered diapers in the locked room that night, so we had them to use until others could be obtained.

We sent a runner off to Chengtu to beg diapers for the baby. A friend who had lost her baby sent some to me. Another friend sent a few knives, forks, and spoons. The thief was never found; we suspected that it was the old temple caretaker or somebody under his tutelage. A few summers later, foreigners traveling through some of the villages nestling at the base of these hills saw small children running about in garments made of birdseye diapering. That nice white cloth was all used, we can be sure of that!

Cameron Hayes, our new YMCA associate, and two young American Baptist men were staying in some lower rooms of the temple. Cameron boarded with us; the other two men had their own cook. Evenings they came up to our big room to play games and visit. The men went on a good many hikes, but I stayed home with the children. Jack played about the big open living room and enjoyed a swing, hung from a rafter, with bars to hold him in. The baby slept most of the time and grew well, weighing twelve pounds at two months.

About the end of July, we began to get letters from one of the missionaries at Penghsien, telling us about antiforeign talk in that district and inquiring rather anxiously how long we planned to remain on the mountain. He reported a local jingle: *xian sha yang-zi; hou sha yang-ren* (First kill the sheep, then kill the foreigners).[2] We replied that we were all right (save for our robbery) and had seen nothing to alarm us.

---

2. There had been some history of antiforeign activity in Szechwan, generally aimed at missionaries and their converts, and particularly against the Catholics—who had become substantial landowners. This antipathy was strong among the uneducated and was often stimulated by some of the more conservative, traditionalist gentry, who saw the missionaries as subverting Confucian culture and customs. There had been extensive and serious antimissionaries riots in 1895, resulting in forced evacuations and much destruction of mission property. In 1898 there was agitation against Catholics. And in 1900–1903 there was considerable activity, chiefly in rural areas, related to the Boxer movement in north China. The jingle that Grace cites was undoubtedly one resurrected from the Boxer repertoire: "sheep" refers to Christian converts. It is also a good example of the Chinese fondness for puns: the *yang* for sheep and the *yang* for foreigners are different characters but, as in the note above, with the same sound.

On August 9 two Chengtu friends, the Misses Collier and Wellwood, arrived and were soon ensconced in our guest room. It had a wooden door instead of an open moon circle and was quite suitable for them; but the wooden walls were so old and dingy that there was no hope of scrubbing them clean. We finally solved the problem: the cook made a big pot of flour paste, and the Boy and coolie papered all the walls and ceiling with any kind of paper that we could lay hands on. There was, of course, no local shop where paper could be bought. It ended up that a good part of the walls were covered with pages from old issues of the *Saturday Evening Post* that we had brought with us to the hills. One of the guests later complained that she was unable to finish the story that she had started near the head of her bed.

One Sunday evening Amah set up a great screech that a prowler was on the peony terraces behind our rooms. All the men (seven foreigners and some Chinese friends and our servants) rushed out; but whoever it was had fled.

The next morning Bob rose early to go on an all-day tramp. The cook prepared him some breakfast and took the silver out from our bedroom in its basket so Bob could use a piece or two. After Bob left, I lay down again on the bed and fell into a doze. I heard some stirring about in the living room, but thought it was the cook clearing up after Bob's breakfast. Great was our dismay a short while later to find all our meager supply of table silver gone (again!) and also the tablecloth and a few garments which had been hung to dry at night at the end of our veranda. The servants raised an alarm, but no one was discovered around the temple building. The next day Bob had to go down the mountain to report our robbery to the headman of our village. It was probably already known there, but it was proper for us to report such trouble.

Bob had intended to return alone to Chengtu, but after he heard the various rumors and saw that we seemed to have been marked for robberies, he thought it best to stay on with us. In the years 1909 and 1910 we had had only one fortnight in the hills, so we felt justified in remaining until the weather would be better on the sultry plain.

Among Chinese friends who visited Danjingshan that summer was Mr. S. C. Yang [Yang Shao-chuan], the president of the Chengtu YMCA. One of the Chinese Y secretaries and his wife also spent a couple of weeks there. Bob took a number of trips of several days duration, roaming about where the mountains meet the plain, looking for a suitable spot for a summer resort. Danjingshan was not high enough, and other things made it far from ideal. And we had had these robberies. I was not afraid when Bob was gone, but it was good to have Cameron Hayes bring his cot into our living room at night.

On August 25 we had a letter from Mr. Yang in Chengtu. He reported that there was trouble in the city over railroad matters. The Szechwanese had previously raised a large sum of money, about $20,000,000, which the Peking government had promised would be used for the building of a railroad from Ichang to Chengtu. Recently, word had come that the railroad was to be built by giving a concession to a foreign company, calling for foreign officials and guards. This immediately aroused great resentment against the Imperial government, with a certain amount of antiforeign talk as a by-product. Also the whereabouts of the millions of dollars raised seemed to be in doubt—and has remained so to this day. In August 1911, the feeling rose to fever pitch in Chengtu; the government was accused of corruption, and matters were difficult for the local officials to handle. An organization that called itself the Association of Comrades to Protect the Railroad (Baolu Tongzhi Hui) headed the protests.[3]

Mr. Yang feared there might be a period of unrest and thought we would be wise to return to the city. We also received letters from foreign friends in Chengtu saying that the city gates were being kept locked. We had planned

3. There was also in Szechwan a quite different reaction to the impact of the West. It was a large, rich province with a long tendency of proud, semi-independent isolation. Expansion of trade in foreign imports and local exports, assisted paradoxically by the fact that in recent decades Szechwan had come to produce well over half of all the opium grown in China, was leading to the emergence of a new elite of gentry and businessmen. This group recognized the need for modernization but wanted to keep it in Chinese hands.

It may be helpful to recall the setting of the time. The much-weakened Manchu Empire had been ineffectively trying to stave off the demands for concessions by the imperialist Powers. Patriotic Chinese spoke of their country as a melon about to be sliced up. From the perspective of Szechwan, the French had made neighboring Yunnan a "sphere of influence" and were building a railway to Kunming, the provincial capital. There was much British talk that they considered the whole of the Yangtze valley (including Szechwan) to be within their sphere of influence. They also seemed to be threatening Tibet (under Szechwan's supervision) and were actively building railways in North Burma close to the Chinese border.

The Szechwanese answer was a version of what has been called "self-strengthening." Considerable progress toward modernization was being made in the first decade of the century. The new government university, which was a main reason for the Y's being in Chengtu, was the cap of a system of new-style middle and elementary schools. Some modern industry was beginning: an arsenal, a mint, small textile plants, by 1911 even a small electric light plant (but not for the public). Professor Ross, we have noted (chapter 16, note 5), commented on the progressive spirit in Chengtu.

The big problem of development for Szechwan was access. Because the Yangtze was still thought impossible for steam navigation, this meant building a railway to link Szechwan to the rest of China. All of China's railways up to this time had been built by foreigners: all on terms hardly fair to China, and many with conditions inconsistent with full sovereignty. Szechwan's new elite organized a corporation in 1903 to build a railway from Ichang to Chengtu. This went through some reorganization, collected a large sum of money, established a railway school, and did a little preliminary work. The government knew of and approved the corporation. In fact, the provincial government was a form of partner.

In May 1911 the Peking government suddenly announced that all railways would be nationalized, thus putting the Szechwan corporation out of business. A few days later it signed an agreement with a four-Power consortium to build the railway to Chengtu. The worst fears of the Szechwanese seemed about to be realized, inflicted on them by their own national government. Resentment unified all elements of Szechwan society. The Court, far away in Peking, refused the slightest compromise (even regarding the funds lost by the Szechwan investors). Tension grew through the summer. On August 24 (undoubtedly the day that Mr. Yang sent a special messenger with the letter that Grace mentions), there was a large mass meeting in Chengtu, which decided on a strike of businesses and schools. Trouble was clearly brewing.

to go down within a few days; now we hustled about, packed immediately, and left as soon as we could. On the day we left, we had lunch at the village below us and there found the village headman eager to befriend us. He thought we would be safer on the mountain than in Chengtu and assured us of a warm welcome if we would stay with him. He had plenty of rice stored away for any emergency and could protect us. Reason dictated that we decline; we pushed on and spent that night in Penghsien with Canadian friends.

From them we heard many more rumors of what might happen, but nothing definite. At such times we have noticed that many people are over-run with rumors and fears. Many of those tales are reported to the foreigner by servants or Chinese helpers who have found that the foreigner has a ready ear for wild and stirring reports. We never took stock in tales from servants, relying instead on Chinese friends of responsible position who always have more knowledge on which to base opinions and expectations. It has some-times been impossible to follow the advice our Chinese friends have given us, but we at least have known that it came from fuller knowledge and better reasoning than the tales told by servants, however loyal. At this time, we owed much to Mr. Yang and other friends.[4]

4. Grace is right to give credit to Mr. Yang. The YMCA operated in China quite differently from the "regular" missions. A YMCA could not be established in a city until there was a func-tioning board of directors, all Chinese, to assume leadership and financial responsibility. The International Committee of the YMCA in New York paid Bob's salary, but his role was to advise and assist the Chinese directors. When he first arrived in Chengtu, his first task (besides learn-ing Chinese) was to meet the appropriate type of community leaders and interest them in sup-porting the Y and perhaps becoming directors. This necessarily took a long time and is one reason for what may seem like a heavy social emphasis during the early years. S. C. Yang (Yang Shao-chuan) was a Christian and a member of a leading Chengtu family and was one of the first to support the formation of a YMCA there. He served for many years as the first president of the board of directors and was certainly influential in getting other community leaders to give their support. He was also active in the Comrades to Protect the Railroad and a member of the newly formed Provincial Assembly (which was also involved in the railway fight). It is Mr. Yang and the other directors of the Y, with all their connections among the local elites, that Grace refers to when she speaks of relying for information on "Chinese friends of responsible position."

PART THREE

DETOUR FOR REVOLUTION

18

Revolution

(1911)

We reached Chengtu on the evening of August 29. There was no trouble getting through the North Gate; but after we entered the city, we found barriers across the streets in several places. These were arranged so that one had to stoop to pass under them. Sedan chairs had to be set down, and riders were required to get out and walk under. The intent was to signify support of the Railroad Association.[1] We proceeded slowly. It had been a long, hot, rather nervous day. Miss Wellwood had carried the baby in her chair for an hour that afternoon, and that rested me. Bob was on horseback, and Jack in his own little chair. We were thankful to reach home about 7:00 o'clock, just as a thunderstorm was breaking.

The next two days were filled with rumor, speculation, and apprehension. Some thought we would all have to leave Szechwan for some place of safety down river. Others said they would not go, no matter what. Still others felt the women and children should leave at once.[2] I was really glad our house was rather isolated, for rumor and apprehension seem to grow where many are gathered together. Twenty soldiers came to guard the YMCA, then moved next door to the Wilson house. The directors of the YMCA, all Chinese, met on the thirty-first and agreed that it was safe for us to remain in Chengtu. The four American teachers at the government university came in several

1. This activity was part of the peaceful demonstrations by the Railroad Association, intended to mobilize mass support and reinforce the strike movement—which was spreading rapidly throughout the province.
2. To the consuls, concerned with the safety of their nationals, it must have seemed likely—given the rising resentment of the stubborn and self-righteous Szechwanese, and the uncompromising attitude dictated by Peking—that there was going to be violence. What could not be known was the scope and form of this violence. Any civil warfare could endanger foreign lives and property. Here there were added factors: a history of antiforeign activity; and the danger—because the railway contract had been taken from the Szechwanese and given to foreigners—that the mob, if it became involved, might turn its resentment against local foreigners. Hence, the general assumption that some evacuation might be necessary.

times a day to seek news. They were all young and unmarried, spoke little Chinese, and needed help.

On September 2, the office of the viceroy asked foreigners at the West China Union University, outside the South Gate, to move into the city for safety. That day an order arrived from Montgomery Ward. It seemed a bit foolish to be unpacking the boxes when most people expected that we would be on our way down river in a few days. We thought we might as well have the fun of *seeing* the things, even if we never used them. Boxes from home didn't come very often.

On the third we heard that Viceroy Chao Erh-feng had sent a thousand-character telegram to the Court in Peking, tendering his resignation. He was also said to have detained the leaders of the Railroad Association and to be holding them in his *yamen*.[3] The fourth was quiet. It was my regular tea day and we had many callers. We had a fine cake with coconut from our just-arrived stores. No need now to save our luxuries. Bob had an invariable rule for such situations: first use the things you like best. It's a good rule, within limits, for you are always eating your first choice.

On the afternoon of September 6 Bob and Cameron Hayes went to a meeting of American men at the Methodist Mission to discuss the situation. While he was away, a notice came from the British consul, Mr. Wilkinson, that we must all move at once to the Canadian hospital. Our own American consul was resident in Chungking, ten days away. He had instructed us to follow any directions which the British consul, on the spot, might send us. When I received this notice, I was walking on the tennis court, wheeling the baby in his carriage. Everything seemed peaceful, and we hated the thought of a sudden uprooting—perhaps losing all our possessions that we would have to leave behind. But we all had heard stories of early Szechwan riots.

3. Grace's dates may be a bit confused. On September 1 the Szechwanese leaders adopted a resolution to withhold taxes. On September 5 a meeting of the Railroad Association discussed a document asserting the right to act against "nation-selling" officials. This was intended to refer mainly to Sheng Hsuan-huai, the Peking cabinet minister popularly held responsible for the new railway policy and the concession for a foreign consortium to build the Hankow-Chengtu line. The viceroy promptly arrested the alleged author. The fuse was now lit. It was at this point (September 6) that the British consul, apparently in expectation of violence, suddenly ordered concentration of all British and Americans in the Canadian Mission compounds.

The next day (September 7) the viceroy, under heavy pressure from Peking, arrested ten of the principal leaders of the Railroad Association—who were also the leaders of the new Szechwan elite and of the Provincial Assembly. There was an immediate mass demonstration in front of the viceroy's *yamen*. The guards opened fire and there were casualties (estimates of the dead vary from eleven to forty). Scattered fighting now broke out between Imperial troops and militia and secret society units.

The conventional date for the beginning of the anti-Manchu Revolution is the uprising at Wuchang on October 10, 1911. Szechwanese like to claim that the Revolution really began with this outbreak of hostilities in Chengtu on September 7. But at the outset, the Szechwanese leaders had no idea of overthrowing the Empire; they were advocates of constitutional monarchy, who sought little more than the rectification of what they considered an unjust and disloyal policy. It was not until the rebellion in Wuchang had occurred and showed signs of succeeding that they fully embraced revolution.

The Canadian hospital was in the northeast corner of the city: we were in the southwest, almost an hour away. After supper we started to pack. Cameron went over to the hospital, taking several loads of our things. We stayed up until his carriers, who had to return to their shop near our house, brought word that he had arrived safely. The next morning we were all up early and left immediately after breakfast, amid sad expressions of the servants and a few Chinese friends who came hurrying in.

The outlook at the Canadian hospital was anything but cheerful. The building was not entirely completed; it was still surrounded by debris from the construction. The rooms were dusty, few windows were glazed, there were no stair railings, most doors were hung but lacked knobs and latches. Scores of foreigners were milling about, trying to decide what to do. It was noisy and disturbing. No naps for children were possible, so the plaints of many weary youngsters were added to the clamor echoing through the empty halls.

The Canadians quickly decided that they would all leave Chengtu the next day, September 8. Later in the day, word came from the provincial Office of Foreign Affairs that people would be safer in the city than on the river. A few did try to leave but found the city gates locked and guarded, so were unable to get out. Some others, who had left a day or two earlier, were robbed by roving bands of miscreants and had to return.

The hospital was a commodious building of three floors and a high basement. At first we had two rooms on the second floor. One we used as bedroom, the other as kitchen and dining room. We soon were able to move our bedroom to a larger room on the third floor where it was quieter and the children could have naps. The windows in this room were dormers and so high that we could see nothing but sky. At night, if shots were heard (and this happened often!), Bob would climb out onto the roof to try to see what was happening. With cots and mosquito nets, a couple of the cheapest coolie-style rattan chairs, and our road boxes to hold our clothing, we soon settled down to an odd life.

Our kitchen and dining room remained in the room on the second floor. It had a fireplace, and the cook was able to prepare meals over a coke fire in the grate. He slept on the floor to protect our possessions, for there was no way to fasten the door. Gradually, the servants brought more things from home: a small "wind cupboard,"[4] which we hung outside a window for milk and butter; our folding-legged table, large enough to seat six; and eventually a small cupboard for the cook. Cameron ate with us; and after a few days we were joined by Mr. Simkin, whose wife had left for the Coast in late August. His kitchen stove was smaller than ours, so he had it brought from his home.

---

4. A wind cupboard is what the Chinese call a mesh-sided box with shelves, to be placed or hung in a cool place. It was our substitute for a refrigerator.

21 *The not-yet-completed Canadian Mission hospital where the Anglo-Saxon community of Chengtu was concentrated for ten weeks, September–November 1911.*

We set it in front of the fireplace. Cooking was easier and safer, and we had a proper oven.

The community soon shook down into a semblance of order. Committees were organized; Bob was on the executive and regulations committees. It was decided to start a twenty-four-hour guard patrol of the hospital to be able to respond quickly to emergencies. One problem was the wood floors; there were cooking fires everywhere, and most of our cooks were used to cement kitchen floors. Schedules were made out, and all the men took their turn.

On Sunday, September 10, we had a church service in one of the large wards, most of us bringing chairs from our rooms. This became a weekly affair. Recreation was not ignored. The hospital was in a complex of five Canadian Methodist compounds; four of them had tennis courts. Tennis and chess tournaments were organized and provided much exercise and amusement.

All the Canadian residences were full. Counting those in the hospital, we had over 225 English-speaking foreigners collected in this corner of the city. We were near the East Parade Ground [a military barracks], which the officials thought would facilitate protection in case of antiforeign trouble. The French were concentrated at their medical center. The British and French consuls remained in their own compounds. The German and Japanese consuls gave refuge to their own, relatively few, nationals. We saw nothing of these other groups until we left the city.

There was always some excitement to color each day. On September 8 several foreigners from the university were trapped outside the city, and the officials refused to allow any city gate to be opened. Bob and two other Americans hauled them up over the city wall. Our old cow-man had been outside, but finally got in and started bringing us milk daily (it was almost an hour's trip each way). The Chinese Y secretary had the keys to our house, so we could send a servant to him for things we needed. One of the first items was the baby carriage; then tubs for laundry. The cook and two women lived at the hospital with us; the other servants went back and forth. Nearly every morning Lao Chen, our gardener, arrived with great bunches of flowers hanging from his bamboo carrying pole. Our chrysanthemums were never more prolific than that year. We had no vases, and no place to put vases if we had them. We gave away armfuls to anyone who would take them.

There were plenty of rumors. Here are a few from my diary:

Sept. 11 (1911). Fighting is reported from various places. Some say 1,000 or so were killed on the Tzechow road, only about 50 *li* from Chengtu.
Oct. 4. Lucy Belle's birthday. Cook made a dandy coconut cake and we Peony Mountain folks had tea together in the Assembly Room. Bob off to Y directors' meeting. In the evening I knit. Bob played chess. We heard 130 bags of mail have arrived. Situation no better.

Oct. 15. The British Consul sent word of some message from down river and no one will return home for some time.[5]

Nov. 4. We hear about 200 foreigners are to leave Chungking for down river on the 7th.

Nov. 16. It is reported that the Revolutionists hold Peking and that the Prince Regent has fled via Siberia.[6]

Eventually I had my sewing machine brought to the hospital and kept busy making warm clothes for the children. We inmates also worked out better living arrangements. The Yards and we brought over a few comfortable chairs and fixed a small living room where we women could sew while our children took naps in the bedrooms.

There were entertainments and a concert. And some of the ladies organized a scheme to make a mammoth cloth chute from strips of rice-sacking. This was to facilitate getting the women and children down from the city wall should we have to leave the city suddenly. Various women met regularly to sew on it. It seemed a crazy plan to me, and I declined to join them. One woman then accused me of being an influence in hindering the project. Years later we had a good laugh over it.

Life and death both visited our little concentration camp. There were three births; one child died; several people had severe illnesses; and one or two engagements came about. Some left the hospital with warmer feelings toward hitherto casual acquaintances; a few had broken friendships to sadden memories of our days together.

On the evening of November 17 we were informed we could leave the hospital for our own homes. Bob and I decided to lose no time. The next morning Bob was up early and did most of the packing. After lunch he and Jack left for Wenmiaogai. Bobbie and I followed after tea. Bob had the house well settled when I got there. It did seem lovely and *so* quiet. We had been at the hospital over ten weeks.

In 1908, when we reached our little Chinese house after the Tatsienlu trip, it seemed to me I had never been so happy in a home. In 1911, after our long enforced absence, we were doubly glad to be back at Wenmiaogai. I just walked from room to room, looking at our books, our pictures, our dishes, handling our belongings, and feeling thankful in every fibre of my being. Nothing was fine or elegant, but the things were our own; it was *home*. The

5. We can assume that the message received by the consul related to the outbreak of the revolution at Wuchang (across the river from Hankow). It is not surprising that the consul wanted a chance to observe local reactions before letting people go home, but it seems strange that the foreign community was given so little information.

6. Grace lists these items as rumors. This story about the fall of Peking and the flight of the prince regent certainly falls in that category. But the item for September 11 was basically true. Poorly armed and barely trained militia units marching on Chengtu to help liberate the imprisoned leaders of the Railroad Association were disastrously defeated by Imperial troops.

children were happy, too. And the foreign teachers at the government university, who had also returned to their quarters, came in to rejoice with us. The first few days were dark and drizzly, but we were not depressed.

We settled ourselves in our familiar rooms and took up duties, old and new. Some things seemed as ever; but there was a constant undercurrent of unrest. Our road boxes were not put away. However, our immediate task was to pack for two other families. The Wilsons had had to return to England from Suining. They wanted clothing, silver-ware, and many things to be packed for shipment at the first opportunity. And the Thompsons, who had occupied the Wilson house that spring, had gone to Mount Omei for the summer and been sent down river from there by the British consul's orders. They had only summer clothing with them when they left Chengtu, so had written in great urgency, hoping that some one would be able to bring their heavy clothing to Shanghai. Who would be able to take these things, we did not know. We tried to avoid the subject, but could not help knowing that many foreigners thought we would all have to leave the West. Rumors still filled the air. We lived from day to day.

On November 25 we heard that the new provincial government was to be inaugurated on the twenty-seventh in the Huangcheng, with the viceroy acquiescent.[7] Hearing that the Peking government had already fallen, or was doomed, he had no alternative. The twenty-sixth was my birthday and I had a chocolate cake and gifts. That day we heard the provincial treasurer had committed suicide rather than turn over his office to the revolutionaries. Many questions perplexed our Chinese friends, and they brought them to us frequently. Most personal of these was the cutting of their queues. Two Chinese Y secretaries cut theirs on the twenty-seventh and immediately came to show us. Having worn them since childhood, this was a big step to take; many hesitated, fearing that things might later swing back to the old regime—in which case the queueless would become conspicuous.

At about the same time, an old Manchu official named Tuan-fang had been sent by the Court in Peking to go to Szechwan to settle the unrest and disturbance over the railroad problem. He brought a contingent of troops and was still on the road from Chungking to Chengtu when his troops, hearing of Republican victories, decided to mutiny and join the revolution. They called on him to declare against the Manchus. Tuan-fang refused. They then

---

7. Although the viceroy had succeeded in restoring a semblance of order in Chengtu, his position was hopeless. Most of the Yangtze and southern provinces had declared for the Republic, the whole province of Szechwan was in revolt, and his vastly outnumbered military forces were demoralized and melting away (one reason was that they were heavily infiltrated by the all-pervasive Szechwan secret society, the Elder Brother Society, which was actively supporting the Railroad Association). By agreeing to a peaceful turnover of power, the old viceroy hoped to save his life. He was successful only briefly: Szechwan was the only province to kill its Imperial viceroy.

called an executioner and ordered Tuan-fang to bow his head for the sword of decapitation. Again he refused, and as he stood erect, his head was struck off. This occurred in Tzechow on November 27 and within a few days was being told around Chengtu streets. We knew little of Tuan-fang, but I have always remembered his courage in meeting death.[8]

Szechwan Province now declared itself for the new Republic. The head of the provincial government was Pu Tien-chün, who had been the president of the Provincial Assembly and leader of the Railroad Association. He and his associates were the cream of Szechwan's citizens, intellectually and in all ways. Every indication was that they had worthy plans and ambitions for the province. Their hopes, however, were doomed to be shattered by the instrument that might have made possible their realization. The military elements frustrated the success of the statesmen. What was really needed was a strong, popular military leader of vision, who could have swung the soldiers and people all in the same direction. This was lacking.

While we waited for developments, we tried to keep our daily life in the normal grooves. I made twelve quarts of mincemeat, in my usual manner for this time of year, using the hard Szechwan pears in lieu of apples, which we never had in the West. I put this up in quart Mason jars, ready for pies during the next few weeks. We never had many pies save at holiday seasons, and Bob was keen for our own mincemeat. Those were happy, busy days. It seemed that I had never more enjoyed getting ready for Thanksgiving. On the night before the festive day, I stuffed our fat goose and made fudge. A big foreign mail had come in that afternoon. After all the preparations for the morrow had been made, I lay down on the davenport in front of the fire to rest and read letters and magazines.

Our Thanksgiving Day dinner was a great success. The guests were the four foreign teachers from the government university, Cameron Hayes and Mr. Simkin, and Lucy Belle Wellwood. In the evening we played games and the men did stunts.

---

8. Tuan-fang was certainly brave, but he was also a crusty, uncompromising Manchu who exemplified some of the reasons why the Ch'ing dynasty was losing the "Mandate of Heaven." When Viceroy Chao Erh-feng proposed that some concessions had to be made to the irate Szechwanese, Tuan-fang was a leader at the Court in demanding a rigid, unyielding line. His impeachment of Chao Erh-feng on August 29 was certainly a factor in forcing the viceroy to try forceful action early in September. Because of his feeling so strongly on the subject, there was a kind of fitness in Tuan-fang's being sent to Szechwan to carry out his ideas.

Whether or not the Szechwan railway was the spark that ignited the Republican revolution, the Republic never got around to building it. After 1949 the Communist government made it a first priority; rails finally reached Chengtu a little more than forty years after the furor over who would lay them.

The story of the Revolution in Szechwan is sketchily told in most histories. I am much indebted to my friend Charles H. Hedtke for his dissertation, finished in Berkeley in 1968, entitled: "Reluctant Revolutionaries: Szechwan and the Ch'ing Collapse, 1898–1911."

19

Flight

(1911)

A large party of Canadians departed for home on December 2. We were sorry that our friends the Lindsays were among them; but we gained a piano which they left in our safekeeping. Later that same day we heard that the British consul was advising women and children to leave. The YMCA went ahead with its plan for a large meeting on December 6 to inaugurate a program of lectures and other activities. But discussion of the possible need for evacuation never stopped. On December 6 the American Methodists decided to go.

We felt very strongly that we ought to stay. There was then no antiforeign feeling, and we saw no reason to anticipate any. The Chinese leaders of the Y were sanguine about the situation. Admittedly, the government was not yet strongly established and there were many uncertainties. Still, the consensus among these community leaders was that the government would be successful in solving its difficulties and establishing order. We knew that the departure of all foreigners would be unsettling to the very people we most wanted to help. And we thought that the whole situation could be a great opportunity for the Y to prove itself.

Other councils, however, prevailed. On the next day, December 7, Bob decided that I should go to the Coast with the children. Only a few foreign men were to remain, and Bob had received permission to be one of them. I wanted to stay; but when we learned that even the French doctors were to go, I decided it would be unwise to keep the children there in Chengtu.[1] That night I cut out a blue serge Russian blouse suit for Jack and made the little trousers. There was some shooting during the night. The next morning we were up

---

1. The French consulates at Chengtu and other isolated cities had doctors, usually from the army medical service, attached to their staffs. Since the Catholic missions, generally under French protection, did not normally engage in medical work, these consular doctors probably also cared for the Catholic missionaries.

early. Trunks were brought out of the storage space under the roof and put in the guest room. I began to pack, sorting things out and piling articles on the bed and bureau. I was feeling badly about leaving Bob, but there was no time to repine. In the forenoon an English friend, Mrs. Hampson, came to talk about combining our travel plans.

Just before noon, Mr. Yang, one of the Chinese Y secretaries, came in to report that there was "an affair" on the street; the Ta Ching and some other banks had been robbed by men of the "Old Army" and they were continuing to loot pawnshops and such establishments.[2] He did not think it safe for Mrs. Hampson to cross the city to her home at the China Inland Mission. So we exchanged notes with her husband and she stayed on. Mr. Yang came in several times with "news." One of these was that revolutionaries from Hupeh had arrived; we never did learn what this signified. More immediate was the fact that the main business street was being looted. Everybody agreed that it would be best for Mrs. Hampson to stay the night.

As darkness came on we began to see fires. We heard that Pu and Chen, the heads of the government, had fled after an attempt on Pu's life at the East Parade Ground. Our coolie returned from carrying a note to the Canadian compound, and he certainly was a frightened fellow. His path took him through the center of the city; there he had seen merchants on their knees begging for their lives and property, while others were being pursued. He claimed to have heard people say that the mission compounds were to be looted that night, but we did not think this needed to be taken very seriously. While we were eating supper we saw more fires and heard that pawnshops were the targets. Fires continued all night; some people counted as many as thirteen burning at once. I wondered if it was wise to undress and go to bed, but we were tired and felt that the looters were out for the rich shops and were unlikely to come to our residential corner of the city.

I took our packing off the guest room bed so Mrs. Hampson could sleep there. After I had worked for a while on the little suit for Jack, we all went to bed. We had just fallen asleep, tired by a strenuous day, when we heard the gateman calling: "Get up, get up. Mr. Beech has come." Bob sprang up and pulled his trousers on over his pyjamas. (He wore them that way for two days.) I hustled into an eiderdown dressing gown. We heard the shuffle of many feet and went downstairs to find all the people from the American Methodist compound at Shansigai coming through our *tingzi* and on into the house.

2. These were men of the Imperial army. They had nominally surrendered when the Republican government had been established a few days before, on November 27. It can be assumed that they were dissatisfied with the terms offered them, or thought their future prospects very bleak. Nothing was as much to be feared in Chinese civil warfare as defeated or departing soldiery.

Our unexpected guests arrived at 12:45 A.M. It was not a dark night, though the moon was behind clouds, and I shall never forget how eerie it was to see our friends coming in on foot with a few glimmering lanterns and boxes carried by servants. Quickly, lamps were lit and fires, still smoldering in grates, revived. Children were taken upstairs and laid crosswise on the beds. Ten adults and seven children filled our rooms.

The Methodists had heard from various sources the same report that the missions would be looted that night. The shooting around them was rather alarming, so they did not go to bed at all and packed a few things in road baskets to be ready if they had to make a sudden departure. They had watchers on the street and high in their hospital tower.[3] When the rioters turned down their street, they decided to come to our place. We were in a quiet part of the city and close to the South Gate, which could be an advantage if we had to leave the city.

Our kitchen was soon running, and about 2:00 A.M. we served hot coffee and bread and butter. By this time I had dressed myself and taken Jack up and dressed him. Hastily, I collected our table silver, wrapped it in a small grey blanket, and gave it into the hands of Lao Chen, our trusty gardener. Where he hid it we never knew; only that later he placed it safely in our hands again. Clothes were next. If flight became necessary, we could expect to take no more than we ourselves could carry—and we had two small children. Road boxes would be too large. I filled two suitcases with essentials, changes of underwear for all four of us, flannels for the baby, and whatever I could get in that seemed best if one must run and leave all else behind. The irreducible need for each person was an extra suit of underwear. Several of the Methodist friends lacked even that, so we loaned them garments from our supply. It would be unwise to have all our money on our persons, so Bob distributed silver dollars to several of the servants for them to conceal and return to us later.

The two Chinese Y secretaries came in and out. They were having watch kept on the movements, and apparent intentions, of the rioters. It was a relief to learn, in the early morning hours, that the Methodist compound was unmolested. If the looters did come our way, we planned to take what we could carry and go out onto the athletic field back of the Y building. It could be reached easily from our compound by the little back gate that connected with the Y. (This was actually our old tennis court and vegetable garden, now taken over to provide a playing field for the members of the Y.) Nothing could be done to save our house or its contents if the rioters came. Bob spent a good part of the night outside, walking back and forth in the court, ready

3. The Methodist compound was not far from the central area of the city and a main shopping street. It is not surprising that the residents were nervous.

for any news from the front gate. I had the bedding from our beds rolled in oil sheets so as to be portable for flight, but I left wee Bob in his bed, for I thought we could simply roll him in his bedding and carry him that way.

After 4:00 A.M. the tension of the night relaxed. Some of the Methodist men went back to their compound to get things left behind in the midnight flight. They also wanted to do more packing so as to be able to leave that day. Mr. Beech was anxious not to spend another night in the city. Our cook did the best he could for breakfast, and we ate in relays as friends returned from the Methodist compound. Our bread had been exhausted for the 2:00 A.M. snack, but the cook made biscuits for nineteen. Luckily, he had set sponge the night before, so was able to do a big baking of bread that day.

Bob had sent Mr. Chen of the Y down to the river to hire boats; he came back shortly before noon, having engaged two. We did not feel strongly that we had to leave immediately; Mr. Beech did, so we let his party have these boats. They then decided to go to the river right after noon dinner. Our servants worked valiantly and got up another large meal. At that point, a certain Baptist gentleman arrived "to see what we were doing." No one was fooled: he had to consult his Methodist ladylove. I was amused, but the cook took it as no laughing matter. There could be no shopping on the street that day. But we drew on the storeroom and with plenty of potatoes made out a good dinner. When we were finished, the Methodists went to their two boats and were able to add a third. However, they had trouble getting enough carriers for their baggage, so our coolie and gardener went to carry things for them. As soon as the coolie returned, I set him to beating our rugs so that we could fold them away in tobacco and mothballs in their tin-lined boxes.

That morning Mrs. Hampson, escorted by one of the foreign men, had tried to cross the city to her home. They were stopped by crowds rushing from some center of disturbance and were forced to turn back. Late in the day her husband sent word that she had better stay another night with us. Miss Collier, who had stayed behind when the other Methodists went to the boats, was also with us that Saturday night. Mrs. Hampson was in the guest room, so Miss Collier slept in Bob's bed. Bob stayed downstairs on the davenport in the living room.

The president of the Y, Mr. S. C. Yang, had sent us a Chinese lantern inscribed with the large red character *ren*. This, he said, was a sign known to the revolutionaries as a signal that our place was not to be molested.[4] We had

4. The "revolutionaries" that Mr. Yang referred to were undoubtedly members of the Elder Brother Society (Gelaohui), the secret society that was very strong in Szechwan. It has been compared to both the Freemasons and the Mafia. Their members, mobilized into street patrols (the "some sort of native militia" on guard at our corner), could hardly keep off armed and determined military looters; but they could cope with private looters seeking to take advantage of the general chaos.

It was customary for these Chinese paper lanterns to carry a large red character for the name

it hung at the front gate as he directed. We also learned that some sort of native militia were on guard at the street corners, at least in our part of the city.

There was plenty of shooting during the night, though not as much as the night before. But there was more yelling, especially over in the Manchu City north of us.[5] Imagination pictured looting and killing. The persistent yelling kept me from getting to sleep. I finally became so nervous that I went downstairs and wakened Bob. He went out to the street corner and talked to the guards. They told him that much of the yelling was by the guards themselves. It helped, I suppose, to keep up courage. Orientals are prone to make their warfare vocal: it cheers the attackers and (they hope) frightens the enemy. Toward morning we got a bit of unbroken sleep.

Just as we were sitting down to breakfast, Mr. Beech arrived. Notes also came in telling us that Mr. Ritchie, the postal commissioner who had left for down river, had been robbed. The Canadians and the American Methodists had tied up at the Thunder God Temple, about six *li* below the city, to wait for a military escort. Mr. Beech and several other men went off to try to arrange this. They got the word that the officials did not want the foreigners to leave. All at once, things did not look favorable for departure. We began to think it would be better to suffer loss, if matters came to that, at home but near friends rather than on the river among strangers.

Our quandary was soon ended. About noon we received the following communication bearing the British consular seal as authority to require our obedience. "The consuls have just settled for all foreigners to go at once to the river bank. They are interviewing the government for an escort of sufficient men to take us down river. No one must remain and no one go alone." The die was cast.[6]

Now that we knew we *had* to go, we hastened to get ready. Miss Collier left us, going to the boats with Mr. Beech. Cameron Hayes hurried his final

---

of the owning establishment; the lantern given us would not, therefore, have been conspicuous. The character *ren* was probably the one meaning benevolence or charity. Mr. Yang obviously had good connections and was probably close to the center of government affairs.

5. In plan, Chengtu was a small Peking. In the center was the viceregal palace, the Huang-cheng (Yellow City), which corresponded to the Forbidden City. Around it was the Manchu City for the hereditary garrison of Manchu bannermen. Outside that there lived the great bulk of the population, the Chinese subjects. Many Chinese hated the Manchus as oppressors; in some cities there was a great deal of violence directed against them.

6. The new Republican government was unable at first to control and stabilize the province. There were problems in coordinating separate governments that set themselves up in Chungking and other main cities. The Republican military forces were weak and poorly led. New local military forces were continually forming and assuming control of territories for themselves. Remnant Imperial units refused to lay down their arms. Armies from the neighboring provinces of Yunnan and Kweichow invaded to fish in the troubled Szechwan waters. The warlord era had arrived, fully developed, almost overnight. In this chaotic kind of situation, it was normal for consuls in China to expect the worst and choose the cautious course. Actually, as it turned out, Bob and Grace's Chinese friends in the YMCA were right: the evacuation was not necessary.

packing in order to escort Mrs. Hampson to her home near the North Gate. He stayed there until they were packed and went to the boats with them. I ran over to the Yangs' (he was our first Y secretary) and found them weeping and feeling very much cast down. We told them we were ordered to leave and did not do so from choice, but it was an unhappy situation. At first, they wanted to go with us; then they realized that was not feasible. Finally, they determined to stay by things in Chengtu and do the best they could.

I had curtains taken down, folded, and put away in storage boxes. Our trunks were nearly finished, so they did not take long. Stores had been set out when I planned to go without Bob; now it was necessary only to add a few more. The kitchen I never went near—there was no time. I simply gave the cook some directions: do not forget yeast, bread-board, and portable oven; be sure to empty the filter, and leave no food in kitchen or pantry. By 4:30 in the afternoon we were ready, and the two Y secretaries were standing by to say good-bye and lock up for us. As I went out through the front hall, I saw my silk patchwork quilt, made by Grandmother, lying over the back of the hall seat. I remembered that Mrs. Yang had admired it, so I gave it to her as we parted. Jack was happy to be starting off in a sedan chair, so he was laughing and gay. The baby, too, was interested. But my heart was very heavy, and I knew that Bob was also much depressed. This was worse than going over to the Canadian compound in September. I looked around and wondered when and how I would see the place again. We were leaving furniture, dishes, books, and most of our treasures; many believed that, if once we had to leave the city, we would never see anything again.

The four American teachers at the government university had kept in close touch: they had actually been in our compound earlier that day when the evacuation order came. Bob had sent the gardener for boats and he had secured three. The Hampsons took one, the teachers another, and we had the third. Cameron planned to sleep on the Hampson boat, but eat with us. The teachers went out the South Gate with us that Sunday afternoon; the others were to join us later. All along the way the Chinese seemed friendly. While Bob superintended the loading of the boat, women on the bank talked to me, asking why we were leaving. One of them urged us to come to her house for the night. She was sure that her place was more comfortable, and that we could not get very far that night. How right she was! We did not leave until forty-eight hours later.

Monday was a long day. As soon as it looked as if we would not start that day, the men rushed back into the city. I suppose a few of the men must have stayed by the boats, but I do not remember any. I *do* know that every woman who had a husband wanted numerous things brought from their city homes. The people on the bank were most kindly, and we soon felt among friends. My two women servants came down to be with us as long as possible. They held the children or amused them, and sat about talking their heads off, as Chinese women love to do. They kept hoping we would give up the idea of leaving and come back into the city to stay. I certainly wished the same. Bob came back with some curios that he had decided he wanted to take. He also brought various useful things for the boat, and my jars of mincemeat. This seemed an odd thing to carry when we were supposed to be fleeing for our lives.

The university teachers were much perturbed because they had almost no money, the university being behind with their pay. The next morning, Tuesday, they went back into the city and fortunately were able to obtain their money. Word came from the British consul that we were to start not later than three that afternoon; we did, actually, get off around four o'clock. The date was December 12. Several boatloads of soldiers were our escort. We had our American flag (Jack's, given him on his first birthday) flying over our boat, so we sailed under our own colors. Jack continually asked for the amah; I kept thinking of her admonition to me: "You *will* take good care of these two boys, won't you?"

Our travel was slow. Some of the Canadians had taken houseboats. They were more comfortable than our smaller craft, whose rounded mat *peng* allowed one to stand erect only in the center; but the river was low, and the big houseboats were constantly scraping the riverbed. Frequently, the rest of us had to wait, and there was some wear on tempers. Our party consisted of forty-one boats with 148 foreigners, and we were under the charge of Dr. Mouillac of the French hospital in Chengtu.[7] He held military rank as surgeon in the French army, so seemed the natural person for the consuls to place in command. By nationality we were 64 British (which included the Canadians), 41 Japanese, 25 Americans, 13 French, and 4 Germans.

We moved down river slowly enough so that there was a lot of visiting back and forth, chances for walks along the bank, time to climb the cliff of the great Buddha at Kiating, and such things. The weather was pleasant, and the company good; in a different situation, we would have enjoyed the trip. However, some could never rest in peace. One gentleman, in particular, used to go from boat to boat each evening, warning us all of possible dangers at the very place where we were then tied up. His story was always the same, and we soon began to mimic it. "Now let me tell you, you must be careful here for this is the *worst place on the river;* all sorts of things can happen here; the people are a bad lot; it is well known to be the *very worst place on the river.*" In the end, the adjurations of this good gentleman merely served to

---

7. Soon after I arrived in Kunming in 1933, I met an elderly, militarily erect French doctor. He was in charge of the hospital serving the French community, and his name was Mouillac. The name meant nothing to me (I was two at the time of the river flight), but he was perplexed by mine. We finally found the connection.

amuse many of us who were young and refused to be horrified by tales of impending disaster. Still, some of our elders had been through riots in 1895 and 1902 and had learned that there could be perilous times in Szechwan. One of our boats, becoming separated from the party, *was* held up; but no harm was done as soon as it was discovered that they were foreigners. We also heard that a Japanese from Kiating, who had left ahead of our group, had been robbed of $1,200.

There was plenty of time for stories of the last days in Chengtu. One man told of the alarm in their compound one afternoon when there had been a great deal of shooting near by. Suddenly, there were new and louder reports. The Chinese who had taken refuge in their compound threw themselves on the ground, expecting a hail of bullets. Finally, a little old Chinese woman was discovered breaking her way through a dry bamboo fence at the rear of the compound. The "shots" were the snapping of the breaking bamboos. Another man had made a sad discovery. The baptistry of his church was full of loot, and more was in the chapel itself. It appeared that one of his trusted servants either was working in concert with the looters or had turned looter himself. Bullets had fallen on most compounds; and one of the pupils at the Methodist girls' school had been shot in the head. It was a wonder that no foreigner had been struck.

We all wondered how Mr. Simkin of the Friends' Mission was getting on. He had had to leave his compound on Friday night and stay with Chinese neighbors. He had come to our house on Sunday and had told us of his plans as he ate noon dinner with us—our last meal before starting to our boat. He had decided that he could not go with our party because we were to have military escort. So he went off alone, walking, heading for a small town on the Kialing River where he hoped to join Friends who would pass through on their way to Chungking. He was robbed, we heard later; but some silver dollars baked into a few biscuits saw him through.

The chief thrill of our trip came at Hokiang, a small town on the south bank of the Yangtze, about 360 *li* above Chungking. Some troops of the now-fallen empire had been brought to bay there and were firing on all passing boats. The British consul at Chungking had ordered a gunboat up to protect us.

On Sunday, about ten in the morning, we came to the gunboat a few *li* above Hokiang. The order was to pass on; we did so, assuming the gunboat would come along to protect us if we were fired on. And we *were* fired upon. It took about twenty minutes for our drifting boats to get beyond the range of their guns, but it seemed far longer. The gunboat, however, remained passively behind until we had all passed out of range of the firing, and then steamed proudly past the city and ourselves, having given us absolutely no protection at all.

I, for one, was tremendously angry; I hope I shall never feel so angry again. It seemed incredible that the gunboat, whose duty it was to protect us, had done nothing. A few people got into the holds of their boats; but that would have given little protection, so we stayed above. The baby was sleeping and just lay there with nothing but a mat roof to protect him. Bob went to the front of the boat to encourage the rowers, who would have much preferred to jump into the water or just lie flat on the deck. Jack and I walked in and out of the roofed part of the boat, while I got madder and madder.

The wretched gunboat did not even stop to ask if any of us was injured. As it was, there were a number of narrow escapes. One mother picked up her baby, and the next minute a bullet buried itself in the pillow on which the child had been lying. A bullet went clean through a boat next to us. As far as we know, only one person in our fleet was struck. This was a Chinese on one of the Canadian boats who was wounded in his jaw. We heard plenty of bullets sing close to us, and saw several drop in the water between our boat and the next.[8]

The gunboat's non-action remained a mystery. If it had anchored in front of Hokiang with guns trained on the city until our fleet had passed, it seemed probable that not a shot would have been fired. Perhaps the gunboat commander thought we were "just a crowd of missionaries." But he also knew that we had a French army officer and the Japanese consul from Chengtu. We eventually got over the excitement, but it gave us a lot of talk for days. Most excited of all were the British, whose navy seemed so derelict in duty.

But that night was Christmas Eve. We were safe on our boats and tried to be calm and happy, thankful that we had escaped the wild shooting at Hokiang. Our baby, little Bob, cut his first tooth that day in spite of (or because of?) the excitement about him. After we were tied up for the night, Bob and I slipped from boat to boat with a few gifts for friends. Our presents mostly were jars of mincemeat; I was suddenly thankful that we had this to make our Christmas seem more festive.

Christmas Day passed quietly as we moved on down river. Our dinner was roast chicken with dressing, onions, tinned asparagus and corn, and of course mincemeat pie. The next day, at 3:30 in the afternoon, we tied up on the city side of the river at Chungking. It was December 26; we had left Chengtu on the twelfth.

8. Grace mentioned earlier that our boat sailed under an American flag. There was a small tear in the upper right-hand corner, which Grace always insisted was made by a Chinese bullet on this day. The flag, considered mine but long since lost, had forty-six stars.

20

Nanking Interlude
(1912)

The next morning before breakfast, Bob and Cameron headed into the city to find Warburton Davidson and the American consul. Warburton and Hetty had been living for some time in a houseboat tied up across the river, but just then they were back at their home in the city. Hetty came down to our boat to see me, and not long afterward Bob arrived with welcome news: our consul had given permission for us to go into the city to stay two nights with the Davidsons, no longer. It is hard to express how good this was. Our boat had not been so bad—I have been on worse—but the mat roof was barely high enough to allow one to stand upright in the center. The wooden roof supports, of course, had to be lower. In caring for the children I had bumped against these arches until the whole top of my head was sore. And we had been taking care of two babies for seventeen days in very cramped quarters with a continual clutter around us.

Other friends, discovering what we were doing, began to want the same privilege. However, there were no other houses open in the city, and we were the only travelers allowed in. Still, I felt rather selfish as we started off. Hetty had a lovely warm room with a cozy fire awaiting us. The children were delighted. Hetty's servants were eager to help us. Bath water was heated at once, and plenty more for laundry use. My Boy started washing clothes at once and kept at it for hours on end; we left the house with some clothing still warm from the iron.

The next day we had tiffin with the American consul, who was from Alameda, California, and had been in the university at Berkeley in our senior year.[1] On the second day we went out to the cemetery in the morning to visit

---

1. The American consul was E. Carlton Baker, UC 1905. Foreigners were prone to say that it was hard to get things done by Chinese officialdom without *guanxi* ("connections"). As the Ser-

Virginia's grave. In the afternoon we went down to our new boat, a comfortable houseboat which we had engaged for the trip to Ichang. It was impossible for us to stay in Chungking, so we had no option but to go on down river. There were only two American women still in Szechwan when I left; neither had children, and they stayed until we all returned. One was physically unable to travel; the other decided to defy the consular order and remain with her husband.[2]

The Hampsons and Cameron Hayes joined forces with us on this boat, and the four men from the government university decided to accompany us on another boat. After we had gone aboard, there was plenty of time to get settled: the boats did not get away for another two full days. Just before we did leave, on the last day of 1911, the American consul came down to say good-bye. As he waved from the bank the sun came out for a brief moment. It seemed a good omen; but we were sorry to be leaving Szechwan, which had become our home in China.

The trip down the river from Chungking to Ichang was not remarkable in any way. What had taken us twenty-one desperate days to cover going upstream in 1906 was now done in a relaxed ten. There were breathtaking swirls now and then in whirlpools. Once a rower was thrown overboard when the front sweep broke loose in a rapid. Luckily, the man was able to swim and kept afloat until Cameron could throw him a rope and the crew could drag him aboard. A red boat accompanied us part of the way through the gorges; Bob found it convenient for shooting ducks—which we found good eating.[3] We saw the university teachers each night because our boats tied up together. Also, our cook was baking bread for them.

At Ichang the China Inland Mission Home was filled with refugees; we

---

vice family went off alone to the city, the envious foreigners left behind on their crowded boats probably thought that *guanxi* could also be useful among Americans.

2. The defiant woman was their good friend Lona Openshaw, which meant that her husband, Harry, was also defying the consular edict and staying in Szechwan. Grace and Bob certainly considered the matter very seriously. For Grace, after the loss of Virginia, the fact that there would be no doctors must (as she indicates) have been decisive. But I think that Bob's nature would have made it very difficult for him to defy "lawful authority." During his subsequent years in a continually unsettled China, Bob had more tangles with consular caution and became less in awe of the consuls' knowledge of local conditions.

When I told Bob in 1932 that I had decided to try the examinations for entry into the American Foreign Service, his first reaction was mild: an honorable, useful career of "service" (he had long given up any hope that I would follow him in Christian work and probably would have been disappointed if I had sought a business job such as Standard Oil). But he surprised me by going on, very seriously, that he "just hoped that I would not be like most of the consuls he had known, always unnecessarily telling people to leave, or not to go to places where their work was."

3. The red boats were a government service of small, "seaworthy," and very fast boats—powered, of course, only by men rowing—which performed the functions of river police and life saving. They could not, unfortunately, be omnipresent.

did the only thing possible and stayed on our houseboat until we could board a steamer for the onward trip. Here in Ichang we first saw the new five-barred flag of the Republic of China. After a wait of six days, we were able to move onto the *Tungting* and sailed for Hankow on January 16 [1912]. Most of the Szechwan people had crowded onto earlier boats, so we traveled in comfort. The Hampsons stayed in Ichang (in order to get back to Szechwan more easily when return would be permitted), but Cameron was with us, bound for Shanghai.

We also said good-bye to the four American university teachers. They had decided to stay at Ichang and live on their houseboat until they could get consular permission to go back to their work in Chengtu. Expecting quite a long stay, they converted their quarters on the boat into one large living room. Their cots became divans in the day. Rugs were found for the floor. Rattan easy chairs, cushions, and some leopard skins made the place attractive. We heard much later what happened to them.

Some time in March they must have received approval to return to Szechwan. Their boat tied up one night at a small landing place near the west end of the Wushan Gorge. In the dead of night, river pirates crept aboard, cowed the crew, and entered the main room where the teachers were all sleeping. Their first action was to throw kerosene on the beds and ignite the bedding. Suddenly awakened to find themselves in an inferno, the men launched themselves at the intruders. The struggle was fierce while it lasted. Mr. Sheldon received over a hundred sword cuts below his waist from a bandit who stood above his bed and chopped away. Mr. Hoffman had many cuts and a bad wound on his neck. Mr. Knight had many but less serious wounds.

When the melée first started, Mr. Hicks, the youngest of the four, had gotten out of his bed and knelt to pull his revolver from a small valise. His friends saw him there, but in the frenzy of their struggle there was no time to ask why he did not rise to help them. It was not until the pirates suddenly left and the fires were beaten down, that they had a chance to go to their comrade. He was dead, stabbed in the back as he bent over his valise. The attackers must have realized that they had killed him; this may have been the chief reason for their precipitate departure, without any loot. The three survivors had to return to Ichang for medical help, and it was quite some time before they could resume their journey. Mr. Hicks's body was sent back to America.

Back now to our own travel by steamer. In Hankow we saw the black ruins of the great fires that had swept a large part of the Chinese city. Both above and below Hankow there were numerous earthworks and riverside defenses where cannon could be seen. A Swiss gentleman from the Hanyang Iron Works described his house after it had been occupied by Imperial troops: "It looked as if feefty tousand tevils had made deir residence dere for two veeks."[4]

We reached Shanghai on January 22, slightly more than six years from our first arrival, and again in stirring times. It was exciting to be in a modern city, and it was a great relief that we had accomplished the long journey in winter with two babies and no illness. We were guests in the Brockman house; there were many Y friends in Shanghai; and we enjoyed being invited about. One evening we were invited to a Victrola party by some friends who had just received the machine from America. Refreshments were served; when I saw my piece of cake slipping about on my plate, I thought I must be dizzy and was getting ill. More careful investigation revealed that the piece of cake was actually a slice of ice cream. We had not seen anything like it for six years.

There is a definite complex that may be noticed in a woman who is normally interested in her wardrobe. When she has been isolated as we were in Szechwan for several years, she begins to think overly much about how her clothing looks, how it will impress those who meet her, and what she should do to remedy its old-fashioned condition. It is useless to tell her that she looks all right. On every hand she sees women, smart in new styles, with things she has not yet even seen pictured in women's magazines. Clothes that previously seemed wearable suddenly look frumpy and passé. Thus in early 1912 I found my seven-and-a-half-year-old trousseau garments decidedly out; I needed new clothes. With silk from Szechwan and some materials I had had sent from America, goods were on hand. Several new dresses were soon made and ready to wear. I began to feel more like myself and to lose the worry that my clothes made me conspicuous.

It was our normal time for furlough, and passage to America had already been engaged for us. Complications began to arise. It had been planned that Cameron Hayes would return to Chengtu so as to provide continuity while Bob was in America. Cameron was awaiting the arrival of his fiancée from America. Word now came that her health would require that she live near sea level. This ruled out Chengtu: the city itself was not too high, but it was necessary to go to the mountains in the summer. Cameron, therefore, would have to be assigned to work in some seaport city. And that meant, if Bob went on his furlough, that some secretary who had never been in Szechwan would have to go there to pick up the threads of his interrupted work. Bob felt that this would mean the loss of much that he had put into the Y in

4. The initial revolutionary uprising at Wuchang (one of the three Wuhan cities) on October 10 had the advantage of surprise, so won easy local victories. The Empire mustered some of its best armies and counterattacked in late October. After very heavy fighting, they recaptured Hanyang but were unable to take Wuchang, which was the Republic's temporary capital.

Chengtu; he begged to return. But returning to Szechwan was not possible for anyone for the time being; our furlough was to go ahead, and we were scheduled to sail about the middle of February.

On February 11 it was suggested that we go to Nanking for a few months, postponing our furlough until the summer. The Y wanted Bob for some special work in Nanking as a representative of the National Committee of the YMCA.[5] We traveled to Nanking by steamer and arrived on a cold, dark February morning. We rose at 5:30, had a snack of cocoa and toast, and debarked at the port, several miles from the city. Everything was damp and depressing. Even the old carriage in which we set out for town was anything but promising. It was an exceedingly ancient vehicle of the surrey type, patched with raw boards from a Standard Oil box, with a curtain made from a Sperry flour sack flapping in the rear. String held the harness together in many places. We looked like a moving advertisement for oil and flour; but apparently we were the only ones to notice.

There was a large YMCA house in Nanking, down a main thoroughfare from the Drum Tower. It was actually a double house: one half for residence, the other half for Y activities. We were to share the residence. It was the only time during our years in China that we lived in a YMCA house; and, as it turned out, we only camped in it for a few months. Basic furniture belonging to the previous occupant was still in the house. We had brought some rattan furniture and added various extras to make the rooms more homelike.

Newton Hayes of the Y was living in the house. Staying with him was a teacher in the government normal college. This man, Percy Grant, was an old friend of ours and a University of California graduate [1900], who had taught in the Far East for many years. He is a fine man to have around a house, being very good company and the best of candy makers. We had brought our Chengtu cook [Liu Pei-yun] down river from Ichang to help with baggage and children (servants traveled free in those days), so he was with us in Nanking and proved most useful. We established ourselves in the vacant bedroom designated for us and had a heating stove set up in the adjoining room which was to be a nursery. In no time at all we were snug and comfortable. We already knew some of the missionaries in Nanking, and the community welcomed us cordially. Bob, however, spent practically all his time with Chinese, so I was obliged to go about alone, even to places like church.

5. Bob's assignment to Nanking was probably related to the fact that, on January 1, 1912, it had become the capital of the Republic. But on February 12, the day after Bob's assignment, a deal was made for the abdication of the Manchu dynasty. The man who arranged this was Yuan Shih-kai, who commanded the principal military forces of the fading Empire. Part of the deal was that Sun Yat-sen would give up the presidency to Yuan. Yuan promised that the capital would remain at Nanking, but his base of power was in north China, and it soon became obvious that he had no intention of leaving there. On March 10 he insisted on being inaugurated as president in Peking; and by April 4 he had forced the Republic officially to move its capital there. Nanking's day in the sun was thus only a brief interlude.

During the summer of 1911 there had been a serious famine in the northern parts of Anhwei and Kiangsu. That fall thousands of refugees came south in search of food, and Nanking had a large number of these unfortunates. Directly opposite our gate were many mat huts of these people; every time we went out, either afoot or in rickshas, crowds of them would run after us to beg. It was an experience that we had never had before. Also, there had been heavy fighting in the city not long before; when we rode down from the Drum Tower on our arrival in Nanking, there were heads hanging in all the trees along that road.

A new national government had been set up in Nanking and was just beginning to function. Many of the people holding high position were returned students from America, and many had also had some connection with the YMCA. We knew some of these men and soon met many others. One of them, Dr. C. T. Wang, actually lived with us for part of the time we were in Nanking. It was an interesting time to be in the new capital.[6]

One result was that we had a continual string of visitors from Shanghai and other places. Late one night we received a special delivery letter telling us that a party from Ohio, accompanied by a Y man from Shanghai, would be arriving the next day. When we had come, there was not a curtain in the whole house. I had been slowly putting up curtains here and there to relieve the bareness and improve privacy. Percy had just left for home leave and now I needed his curtainless room for the two ladies of the Ohio party. I spent that morning sewing on cotton crepe curtains. They were cheap but pretty, and we got them hung a few minutes before the guests arrived. It was arranged that the Y man would share Newton Hayes's bedroom. To our surprise, there was another man in the party: a somewhat corpulent cousin of one of the ladies. We had no other bedroom, and a camp cot in an odd corner would never do for his bulk. A double bed was clearly indicated. We

6. Dr. C. T. Wang (Wang Cheng-t'ing) was typical of these returned students who supported Sun Yat-sen and his revolutionary party, the Tungmenghui, and suddenly found great opportunities for their services when the Republic was being established. In 1911 he was a secretary in the YMCA at Shanghai; soon after the revolution began, he was in Wuchang; he followed the new government to Nanking—and eventually to Peking. When he was staying with Bob and Grace, he was twenty-nine, an acting cabinet minister, and vice-chairman of the Senate. He spent most of his active life in various government positions, including several periods as minister of foreign affairs and one brief spell (1936–38) as the Chinese ambassador in Washington.

During World War II Dr. Wang was semiretired and living in Chungking. When a new American ambassador (C. E. Gauss) arrived in Chungking in 1941, Dr. Wang seemed, with his foreign affairs background and perfect command of English, to be a good guest to include at dinners welcoming the new ambassador. Chinese official dinners involve a good deal of emptying of glasses, in toasts and drinking games. The guest of honor can expect to be the focus of attention. Ambassador Gauss was experienced and cautious in these matters. He knew that he could fall back on a sensible Chinese custom of naming a *daibiao* (representative) to drink for him. The natural *daibiao* was the junior third secretary of embassy. So it was that I found myself lifting several glasses with Dr. Wang who, after a life of politics, had acquired an enviable reputation for holding his liquor. We had both, one might say, strayed from our YMCA beginnings.

22   The guests at a dinner at the Nanking YMCA in April 1912. President Sun
Yat-sen is fourth from the left in the front row; Premier Tang Shao-yi is on his
right. The other guests include cabinet ministers and "high officials." Newton
Hayes stands in front of the pillar on the right; Bob is barely visible in the
doorway at the back.

gave him our bedroom with its large British-style iron bed, while we slept on
the floor of the nursery.

One of the ladies wanted to visit the National Senate, which was in session. We turned to C. T. Wang and he was able to get admission tickets for
us. He later told us that we were the first women to visit this legislative body.
This was on March 22. The leader of the Ohio group, a Mrs. Tracy, was so
interested in what we told her of Szechwan that she insisted she would return to China in a couple of years and certainly travel there to see us. We
gave her a cordial invitation, but scarcely expected it to become a reality.
Distance, time, and the long houseboat trip through the gorges were enough
to discourage most travelers. The Chengtu Y noted keenly that it had never
yet been visited by any member of the National committee in Shanghai.

The YMCA frequently entertained Chinese at teas and dinners at our
house. Sun Yat-sen and Tang Shao-yi were among the guests at these functions.[7] On such occasions I did not appear, but I was responsible for the

7. Sun Yat-sen was the veteran revolutionary, head of the Tungmenghui, and president of
the Republic from January to March 1912. Tang Shao-yi had been a high official of the Empire,
generally associated with Yuan Shih-kai. During the Revolution, he came south, joined the
Tungmenghui, and helped to negotiate the settlement that put Yuan in power. Tang was premier
of Yuan's first government—but they soon had a falling-out.

food. On the evening of April 11 there was one of these YMCA dinners. I made sure of the arrangements, then ate early and went to spend the rest of the evening with some American friends. I stayed later than I had intended and had no servant with me, our household staff being busy with the dinner party at our house. My friends offered to send a coolie with me, but I saw no need to rouse one of their men to escort me. They got a ricksha and I went off alone. As we passed in front of the Drum Tower, we were stopped by soldiers who came out from under the big arch. They inquired who I was and where I was going. Hearing from the puller that I was a foreigner, a young officer came close to see if this was true. He was satisfied and let us pass.

Less than two hours later, about one o'clock on the morning of April 12, we were wakened by gun fire. It seemed to be coming from several directions, and some of it was not far away. We hastily got up and pulled our mattress onto the floor. The house was of brick, but the windows were low and our bed unusually high. The firing became worse, so we thought we had better dress. We did this in the dark, groping about, keeping away from the windows, and not wanting to turn on any lights (this house had electricity). Dr. Wang was also in the house that night and, though we did not know it at this time, was nervous because he had several thousand dollars in his care. When daylight came, we could see dim forms flitting about, and some shots were too near to be pleasant. I can never forget the sinister look of some armed men in the grey of dawn as they slunk around our compound wall—while I was peeking out of a nursery window.

Things quieted during the late morning. It developed that some Kiangsi troops had started the trouble (it was some of these men who had stopped

23 *Loyal forces at Nanking after suppressing a mutiny by Kiangsi troops in April 1912.*

24 The "loyal looters" carrying off the spoils. Grace speaks of seeing a stuffed leopard: it appears that there was also a tiger.

me at the Drum Tower). Loyal government forces had quickly overcome them and were then "allowed" (seemingly as a reward!) to loot some of the buildings at the former Exhibition Grounds. Bob and our current house guest later went over to the military headquarters and saw dead Kiangsi men lying about, some shot and some beheaded. The "loyal looters" carried all sorts of things past our gate that morning, and the procession was a comical one. Among the trophies we noted a stuffed leopard, mounted birds, and other items of dubious value to soldiers. Those who secured the baggage of the defeated Kiangsi men must have fared better as to spoils. Several bullets had struck our house, and the Chinese residence on the other side of our compound wall had been looted. As soon as he could, Dr. Wang set out to try to get a train for Shanghai. When we saw him several days later, he was very thankful that he had not lost that money in his care.

Early in the afternoon there was another sharp skirmish. A group of "rebels" had been hiding and were found by loyal troops. Some of our foreign friends were out in their vegetable garden when the firing began so suddenly that they had no choice but to lie down among the cabbages, seeking safety in the shallow furrows between the growing plants. I was upstairs on our front balcony, and Newton Hayes's Boy came rushing up to tell me to go inside the house. He and the amah kept close watch all day on the two children.

During this excitement, two foreign men from the YMCA National Committee arrived on the morning train from Shanghai. The city gates were shut and they had to get passes to enter. Eventually they reached our house, heard about the night's alarms, and then experienced the afternoon's excitement. They quickly decided that the city was too disturbed for their visit to accomplish anything; and one of them told me he would not *think* of spending the night in Nanking when it was in such an uproar. So they flew about, had a carriage called, and took off to catch the next train back to Shanghai. We were happy that they were off in safety. In a few days the flurry over the military revolt had passed. We heard that there had been some 150 to 200 executions, but soon the whole episode was merely an incident in the course of daily life.[8] The next week after this Nanking affair there came the news of the sinking of the *Titanic*.

We were beset during our Nanking days by curio dealers who came to our compound offering all sorts of things: beads, embroideries, vases, paintings, robes, almost anything one could think of. At the time of the Revolution, only a few months before, many of the homes of officials and the wealthy had been pillaged and sacked. What we were seeing must have been part of the loot. We bought some amber and quartz beads, and I secured a beautiful string of hollow ivory beads.

Early in May, Bob and Newton Hayes went to a Y conference in Shanghai. This left me alone with the two babies. The house, in the usual style, had detached servants' quarters, so I had Newton's trusty Boy sleep in one of the Y rooms under the nursery, and the amah was upstairs and close at hand.

When Bob returned to Nanking, he brought news that he was to return to Szechwan in June, while the children and I would go to Kuling for the summer.

---

8. Grace is quite right that the whole unexplained episode became merely an incident of daily life: it is not even mentioned in the standard histories of modern China. It is hard to think of a more apt reflection of the troubled times.

25 *The family in Shanghai, May 1912. Young Bob is one year old;
Jack is almost three.*

21

Alone at Kuling

(1912)

Bob's wish to see the Chengtu YMCA well launched had been heeded, and he was content to be going back to the work. It would have been difficult for some new secretary to go there; and it would also have been hard for the Chinese in the Chengtu Y to get used to a new associate before their work was firmly established. But some of our friends told us we were crazy to start west: we should be on our way to America.[1] We left Nanking at the end of May and proceeded to Shanghai by train, quite a novelty to us after six years without the sight of one. We did some preparation for the West, and gave up all thoughts of America for a few more years.

For the first stage of our journey up river, we traveled by the *Tuckwo* of Jardine's, and the trip was not without its thrill. At Nanking we picked up our cook and our heavy luggage. Between Wuhu and Anking, the ship caught fire about 8 o'clock one evening. The panic of those first few moments was terrifying. Thick black smoke poured from one of the hatches, and the situation looked serious for a short time. Eventually, the fire was put out with no great danger to vessel or passengers.

That year huge hats were the style. I had one, but it was packed. We were escorting a new Y couple because they spoke no Chinese. She had a tremendous black hat and a baby. When the cry of fire sounded through the ship, she rushed to her cabin and first of all put on her enormous hat. When she

---

1. Bob and Grace never argued in front of their children, but we knew, much later, that there had been disagreement over this return to Szechwan. Grace may have forgiven, but in this case she never forgot. The usual practice, in the YMCA and most missions, was six years in the field and one year at home. Bob's volunteering—indeed, seeking—to go back to Szechwan in 1912 postponed their furlough. As things worked out, it would be a postponement for more than three years. Grace's account makes it clear that the decision was reached when Bob went to Shanghai, without her being present or consulted. She felt that Bob put loyalty to the Y ahead of his consideration for the family.

stooped to put things in suitcase or valise, she would hit the hat brim on the edge of the berth, or a chair, or anything nearby. She then ran to do something else, always meeting the same difficulty. Fortunately the scare was soon over; otherwise I cannot imagine how she would ever have gotten her things together for a real emergency!

To get to Kuling in those days, one left the steamer at Kiukiang and then had a day's travel by sedan chair to climb the mountain. We were used to overland travel in Szechwan, where we always had to take beds and bedding with us. But we had been told of the rest house on the way to Kuling and that it provided beds. It was hot, so we supposed sheets and bed nets would be all the bedding we needed. We reached Kiukiang in midafternoon and started off at once for the foot of the mountain. Arriving at the rest house, we found iron beds, but nothing at all provided for mattresses. Our makeshifts were fairly poor, and we rose the next morning pockmarked from head to foot by marks of the bedsprings. Later we heard we should have spent the night at the small hotel in Kiukiang. We had forgotten that there were hotels for such as we!

The third of June we were in Kuling, settling into a friend's cottage which we had rented for the season. Bob was thirty-three on the fourth of June, and we celebrated with strawberries and cream and a cake. On the thirteenth we told Bob good-bye, and he started on the long trek back to Chengtu. I felt lonely on the side of the Kuling hill with two babies.[2] I had two single ladies with me for some time during the summer, but was mostly alone.

In Nanking that spring we had been hearing of the Braces of the Canadian Mission, who had just arrived in China and were to be loaned to the YMCA in Szechwan. Bob had met Mr. Brace in Shanghai at the Y conference in May. We rejoiced that they were to join us. They also spent that summer at Kuling, so I quickly became acquainted with Bert and Blanche. They had two sons, and a third was born there that summer.

Our good cook, Liu Pei-yun, returned to Szechwan with Bob, and I had a Shanghai man, recommended by friends there. He proved to be a sophisticated fellow who wanted to run my bills up as high as possible. The coolie stole kerosene and had a cache of it in an old tin under his bed, the cook conniving with him against me. My only comfort was the fine amah, who had

2. Kuling was the largest missionary summer resort in inland China. It had been started in the 1890s, was about 3,500 feet in elevation, and (only a few years after Grace's sojourn) had 350 houses, with a church and other community buildings. It was a foreign preserve until the Generalissimo and Madame Chiang Kai-shek started using it in the 1930s. It was conveniently close, perhaps, to Chiang's military headquarters at Nanchang, Kiangsi, for the almost yearly "mopping up" campaigns against Mao Tse-tung's small soviet republic in south Kiangsi. The next person to make it famous was Mao Tse-tung himself. At a historic meeting of the Communist leaders here in 1959, Mao bitterly rejected criticism of his (eventually disastrous) Great Leap economic policies and broke with one of China's great military leaders, Peng Dehuai. There are no foreigners in Kuling today; most of their homes, I expect, are sanatoria.

come from Nanking with me. The servants' quarters were terribly cramped and entirely miserable, so I was glad to have Amah sleep in the children's room, adjoining mine. There was a Japanese bath in the cottage, and when I became used to the idea of a fire under me while I bathed, I enjoyed it. At first I could hardly bear to get into such a contraption.

There were a number of Szechwan refugees on the hill that year, but most of them lived at considerable distance from our cottage. Chair carriers could be hired, but were expensive and impudent. In order to prevent excessive charges, there was a chit system by which they got their payment at the Estate Office. I imagine my cook demanded a large squeeze from men who carried me, because I *always* had trouble. One day when I had signed the chit for the proper amount, including the customary cumshaw, the men flew into a towering rage.[3] I had sent the chit out to them by the cook. They ran around the cottage and up onto the veranda outside my bedroom windows. There they screamed at me and were very insolent, demanding no chit but money in their hands. They told me that no woman could talk to them: they *would* have money, and if it was not forthcoming, they would come right into the room and take the string of beads off my neck.

While this tirade was going on, I told Amah to run out the door from the children's room on the other side of the house and go for my opposite neighbor, Mr. Adams. He happened to be at home and promptly arrived with plenty of vigorous Chinese language to clear the men off my veranda and grounds. After this I had less trouble, but the cook was a great trial. He considered me a newcomer and constantly told me I did not understand "the custom for cooks." I understood it, and had no idea of letting things go his way, my resources being insufficient for spending money in the way he thought necessary.

It was a very wet summer, and we could see the Yangtze, down below us, overflowing its banks and bringing ruin to many a farmstead. Mold constantly formed on floors and clothing. After wearing a white piqué jacket for just an hour, I hung it in the closet only to find it ruined by red mold the next time I needed it. At times when it rained, I had to keep oil heaters and lamps burning all day to counteract the dampness.

Jack became ill with a bowel trouble in August and had a most critical time. Of course I had a doctor, but Jack grew steadily worse. Late in August Dr. Logan of Changteh, Hunan, was called in consultation, and from then on the child began to improve, though slowly. For days he had asked for food; then he became too weak to speak much and was sadly changed from the fat, sturdy lad of three who had tramped around the hill with his father in June.

---

3. "Cumshaw" is a gift, gratuity, or tip. It is derived from the Cantonese pronunciation of *gan xie* (sincere thanks) and is a common word in the lingua franca of the Orient.

The baby, small Bob, was also slightly ill at the same time; and the amah was laid up for several days. I kept up and my friends were loyal in their devotion to us. Mary Smith, a Canadian nurse of the Szechwan Mission, gave up her language studies for over a week to help me through the worst period.

When I had to hire an extra amah for washing, she would not stay. I found the cook was at the bottom of the difficulty, having demanded a fat squeeze from her wages.[4] I had hoped to keep the cook on, not because I liked him, but because it would be so hard to get another. This affair, however, was too much. I came to an issue with the dictator, telling him he had caused me no end of bother and ought to be ashamed of himself when we had severe illness in the house. I paid him liberally and had witnesses to see that he received a good cumshaw and everything that was his due, and told him that he was to get off the hill and never come near us again. He left just as Jack began to show a little improvement.

I knew the child had been dangerously ill, but I did not know until later that my friends expected him to die. The only time I gave way at all was one evening when he was a trifle stronger and he suddenly put up his hands and said his little prayer, "Now I lay me down to sleep. . . ." I began to tremble and told Miss Smith I felt sure he would die. She assured me he was improving.[5] Dr. Logan would take no fee for his attention, but we sent a gift to his hospital. I never saw the doctor again after that summer, but thought of him always as a friend. I was saddened, years later, by his tragic death from the shot of one of his patients, a crazed soldier.

It was well into September before Jack could have any solid food. We all rejoiced when he ate his first bit of toast: he liked it so much. I had had a hard time alone and never knew how I could miss Bob until those days. And I began to dread the long houseboat trip up the river again, with thoughts of illness for the children to haunt me. By this time, all our nearer neighbors had gone down the hill, so that our cottage was rather isolated. Therefore, in September, the children and I moved to two rooms in the cottage of friends at the other end of the valley. The new living arrangement did not work out. When the Brockmans of the Y in Shanghai found how things were, they insisted that I return there and stay with them until the Yangtze would be suitable for houseboat travel and we could start up the river.[6]

---

4. "Squeeze" may be universal, but the use of the word in this sense originated in Asia. Webster (Unabridged) defines it as a commission charged by an oriental servant. Within limits, it was acceptable, and practised by all servants with some clout in the household (either the cook or the Boy). For instance, if a curio dealer brought his wares to one's house, it would be assumed that he gave the Boy a small percentage on any sales made. In this case, Grace's cook was clearly out of line in trying to force the amah to give him a part of her wages.

5. My first memory is of my bedroom at Kuling.

6. The reason that Bob returned alone to Szechwan in June was that the consuls were still refusing to permit the return of families. Grace does not mention the date, but apparently in

The trip down the mountain was much easier than going up, for we stayed at the small foreign hotel at Kiukiang. It happened to be the Eighth Moon Feast, and the evening we spent in Kiukiang was lovely, with myriads of tiny lights set afloat on the water of the river. We went out in a rowboat and it was like a fairyland. Jack was still too weak to do much. He had even usurped the place of the baby in the folding go-cart. And on the steamer he was unable to raise his feet over the thresholds of the cabin and saloon. In fact, he had to be taught to walk again after this illness, and Amah and I had two real babies to tend. Before his sickness Jack had been able to look out for himself quite a bit. My good amah had family problems and had to leave us at Nanking as our steamer passed there. In Shanghai, Mary Brockman's amah helped me with the children and we got on easily. She was a large, pleasant woman with a calmness and self-reliance that made one have confidence in her. How good she was to me!

I spent a busy month in Shanghai and visited with Y friends and all the Szechwan refugees. Mary and Fletcher left me with their two younger sons while they took a trip to visit some friends. I had a severe attack of tonsilitis, but was able to get off for the West at the end of October. Mary insisted that her amah go with us to Ichang. This was a most fortunate thing for me; if it had not been for her, I do not know how I could have gotten along. A crowd of friends came to the steamer to see me off, and I certainly was happy to be going back to Szechwan. Arrangements had been made that we were to meet the Hampsons in Ichang, and our two families would share a houseboat to Chungking. And Bob promised to meet us in that city.

September this ban was removed. Grace did not start up river at once, because of my recent illness and because junk travel from Ichang to Chungking was easier and safer when the river was lower.

22

Up the River Again

(1912)

Everything went well on the trip to Hankow. Our heavy luggage from Kuling had been left at the hotel in Kiu-kiang, and we picked it up there when our boat stopped. On November 3 we found ourselves in the home of the Hugh Morans of the Hankow Y. I had known Hugh's brothers in college, but had only an acquaintance with his wife. But there was Hugh at the dock with a cordial invitation, to which I succumbed. Hankow was again cold, and their apartment seemed very cozy and full of cheer. We expected a wait of several days before we could take a steamer on to the West. But almost immediately, I was taken ill with rheumatic fever. As things turned out, we were not able to leave for three weeks.

Naturally, I did not want to remain, sick, in the home of friends who had been kind enough to take us in for a few days. I tried to make arrangements to go to a hospital. That would be easy for me, but I would have to leave the two children in the Moran home. I could not burden them with the responsibility of my two babies, especially as they had a small infant of their own. Then I thought of the China Inland Mission, which ran a home for transients similar to the one in Ichang. That would have been all right if the children had been older and I not so ill; they, as well as I, needed the amah at night, and the rules of the mission establishment forbade the servants of guests sleeping on the premises. The matter was finally resolved by our staying on with the Morans. They were wonderful to us; and I could oversee Amah's care of the children, which saved me a lot of worry.

The English doctor came every day, listened to my heart, and stuffed aspirin down me to the tune of forty grains a day. The weather grew raw, with snowstorms and plenty of sleet. Szechwan friends began to swarm up from Shanghai, bound for the West, while I lay under my woolen blankets, restless and in pain, longing for Bob and wondering when I should ever be ready for the journey again. The doctor wanted me snug in a warm place, and I knew I could not think of that sort of a life during the weeks ahead. Bob had sent Liu Pei-yun, our Chengtu cook, to meet us. I was pleased to welcome him in Hankow, and he was of great help there. He could take the two children out on the Bund for the air while Amah had a chance to wash, bathe me, and do various things in my room.[1] No trained nurse was available, so Amah was obliged to do everything. When the children came back, I tried to keep them in my room so as not to disturb the house. Fortunately, our room was huge, and we had a constant grate fire. The bathroom, too, was large; and there faithful Amah slept, ready to wait on us at any time.

The doctor's idea was to keep me in bed for some time longer; but finally I got up and went to a Japanese shipping office to take passage for Ichang. I engaged an entire cabin, as I knew I would need the two bunks for myself and the two children, while Amah would have to spread her *pugai* on the floor between us. We were to take the ship at night; at noon of that day, as agreed on, I went in to pay for my tickets. There I found that one of the berths in my cabin had just been sold to a more than good-sized Canadian lady. Some talk ensued; the Japanese clerk sucked his teeth, drew in breath, and expelled it audibly several times before he got my meaning. I had the order for the whole cabin in my hand. He was "so sorry," and wrung his hands. When I told him I would give up the whole reservation, he could not believe it, and even insisted that it could not be done. I told him it could be done, and he learned one thing about Americans that day.

We waited for a British ship, on which I luckily found some old friends. The doctor was still talking, but I felt that further delay was not to be considered. The upper river was now low enough for houseboat travel, and I was keeping the Hampsons waiting in Ichang. I had hoped to be in Chengtu for Christmas. This was no longer likely after my long delay, but I did want to join Bob in Chungking before the holiday season.

I had been out very little in Hankow, but one visit I always remember. A new Y family was to move there soon, and the husband had come ahead to prepare a place for them to live. He took me to see the flat he had rented. When I exclaimed over the nice kitchen, in which a brand new sink was being installed, he told me in a very complacent manner that he loved his wife too much to expect her to live where she could not have running water and such conveniences. I laughed, and asked him if he thought my husband did not love me! Often since, I have laughed again as I recall this man's look

1. Despite the usual American TV pronunciation, the Bund that Grace refers to has no German origin. It comes from a Hindustani word and is an artificial causeway or embankment. In most of the treaty ports along the Yangtze, as in Shanghai, the Bund was the broad street along the riverfront, serving as both boat landing and park-promenade. Because these were river ports, with seasonally changing water levels, steamers actually tied up to large floating pontoons (called hulks) that lay just off the Bund and were reached by floating bridges. The slant of the bridge was a ready gauge of how high (or low) the river was.

when he stood there talking about his kitchen sink and his affection for his wife.

Down-river people often seem to lack understanding about the life of those who live in the interior. I have even heard remarks about the compounds of these dwellers in interior cities, and surprise expressed that they should have gardens. When one lives directly over the wall from where there may be an open cesspool or drain, and any sort of filth or disease, a little open space is all to the good as a preventative of infection, and one can appreciate a bit of garden around one's house. I suppose our kitchen door in Chengtu was less than fifteen feet from the compound wall, and we never knew what might be found on the other side of that mud barrier. Our kitchen was screened, but the efficacy of this sanitary measure was won only after the most strenuous work on the part of the housewife.[2]

The trip to Ichang was accomplished in due time. Once our ship stuck on a sand bar for ten hours, but managed to get off without assistance. These days were not easy. I was not yet able to dress myself; my shoulders were so painful that tears would run down my face when Amah pulled my dress over my head; and my heart also thumped a good deal and I had to stay in bed most of the time. I felt I could really keep warmer there: no doubt I should have been there all the time. I certainly could not have gotten on if I had not had a cabin for the children, Amah, and myself. Between Amah and the cook, the children were well cared for, and I did not have to worry about them.

In Ichang the Hampsons greeted us. We remained on shipboard until we could move directly to the houseboat. The cook tended to the whole bother of luggage and was a lifesaver to me in these matters. The houseboat was commodious and comfortable, and we left Ichang at about noon on November 26, my birthday. Amah parted from us there, and started back to Shanghai by the same ship on which we had arrived. She was liberally paid, and took a huge basket of Szechwan oranges for gifts to family and friends. I certainly was sorry to see her go, after all her goodness. She was more like a friend than a servant, and had done everything possible for me in my need.

We were soon settled on the houseboat and found it well appointed, with excellent captain and crew. My cook was our only servant, and he managed well and was able to help me with the children. They were both lively now, and we had to keep close watch over them. I had a rattan crib with sides for

2. The "strenuous work" by the housewife was getting the servants to keep the screen doors and windows closed. It could be very hot in Chengtu. As it lay in a basin, there was usually little wind. There was no electricity, for even a fan. In the kitchen, as Grace has already told us, there was always a fire in a coal-burning stove. And it was obvious that screens reduced the air circulation and made things even more uncomfortable. In those days, it might be added, there were many flies in China, and most Chinese thought little of them. Today, it is not quite true that "there are no flies in China," but they are very few. Grace could hardly have imagined the wonders that have been achieved in education about public health and sanitation.

small Bob. He used to stand in it to look out the window; he also used it as a playpen. I kept the sliding glass window closed, or open merely a crack, so no accident could happen. Soon I began to miss playthings that vigilant search could not discover. At last one morning when I was dressing, Bob wanted to play with the hairbrush. I let him take it. A moment later I turned toward him just in time to see him slipping it through the window crack down into the turbid Yangtze waters! I scolded, but he met everything with a smile, being too young to know better, and always imperturbable in his good humor.

As we neared the Wushan Gorge, we mentioned the tragic piracy of the government university teachers from Chengtu, which had happened at the west end of this gorge in March. It was dark and dismal on the day we passed through the gorge, and we all seemed to feel silent and depressed. The captain was pushing the men to get up to the next mooring place; but twilight came early after the gloomy day, and we were obliged to tie up for the night in the very place where the piracy had occurred. The Hampsons kept quiet about it, thinking that I did not know. I knew, but did not want them to suspect my knowledge. The cook said nothing to any of us. The next morning he brought me hot water after the boat had started and, looking at me in a meaningful way, asked if I knew where we had spent the night. I told him I did. "Were you able to sleep?" he inquired. "Yes, after a time," I replied. He then told me how sorry the captain had been that he was obliged to stop there, but he could not avoid it.

The days passed with this and that sight to see, and the usual thrills of this boat journey. Nowadays, danger is so ironed out of the trip that tourists are blasé, thinking the river quite tame and peaceful. That year it was never tame a moment. The gorges were magnificent, and at times the light effects on the cliffs were startling. Once we caught one of our towing ropes on another boat just above a rapid and had to let go, losing in a second's time a long distance we had laboriously gained from the raging stream. We had a chance to know what it felt like to plunge wildly toward rocks. Our captain handled the boat cleverly and there was no damage. At the Descending Horse Rapid, which was exceedingly bad that year, we got off the boat. After we had passed the danger spot, a leak was discovered in the compartment under my bedroom. The floor had to come up; boxes had to be shifted; and the men worked like beavers getting it mended.

At Kweifu we met one of the Chengtu Y secretaries on his way to Peking. I had taught him for several years and we were glad to see each other. Here also I received seventeen letters from Bob (not notes, but real letters!) and the day was a happy one. The next day we saw three bad wrecks. Goods were spread on the bank to dry, and a desolate business it looked to try to salvage soaked things. The rapids were murderous that year, and each one seemed a little worse than we had expected. Every day we saw wrecks. We got off the boat at the New Dragon Rapid, and the men all said it was the hardest yet.

At last the big rapids were all behind us and we reached Wanhsien in safety. Again I had seventeen letters from Bob, for his mail to me had been piling up during my illness in Hankow. I sent telegrams from Wanhsien to him, and also to Warburton Davidson in Chungking. I was addressing Christmas cards and counting the days to Chungking and Bob, who was to meet us there. The children became excited with talk of "Daddy," and used to call his name hopefully out of the window every day. I still took aspirin daily and had a good deal of pain, but we were on our way.

The day before we reached Chungking I was not feeling at all well, and so did not bother to do much packing, thinking that Bob would be there to attend to getting us off the boat. On December 16, in the early afternoon, we arrived in due course at the Chungking landing. I looked in vain for Bob; instead there was a coolie with chairs and a note. We were to go to the Davidsons' at once. Bob had not yet arrived from Chengtu. My heart just seemed to turn right over, and disappointment, rather than actual suffering, made me feel like lying down on the whole thing. For a few minutes I thought I *couldn't* move off that boat. I almost forgot those thirty-four letters I had had from Bob during the trip from Ichang. But one cannot stop at such a time. The children had to be looked after, and the cook was already negotiating with men to get our stuff off the boat. I roused myself and managed to get things together so that we reached Hetty's comfortable home without much delay. There I soon received a wire from Bob and felt revived.

No matter how carefully one tries to avoid strain, there was always anxiety on such trips up a river like the Yangtze. And after our hard experience on the same journey in 1906, it is no wonder that I felt exhausted when we reached Chungking. Every night on the boat I looked at the two children and was thankful for one more day and no illness. After Virginia's death I had thought I would never again make that long houseboat trip with young children and no doctor; but here I *had* done it again, without even Bob, always my dependence and help.[3]

But I still bear the marks of my Hankow illness. The rheumatic fever left a damaged heart to bother me later. As I look back now, I think my devotion to Bob was what drew me west at that time. It was not devotion to the Y work, much as it interested me. I just could not think of life away from Bob, and I knew he needed his home and my help in it.

In Chungking I had to go the doctor. He cautioned me to be careful; my heart was still far from normal; I needed rest and relief from strain. There

---

3. In 1906, with every effort at speed, the trip had taken twenty-one days; this time, with no pressure to hurry, it was also accomplished in twenty-one days. The difference probably was that they had one boat instead of three, an expert captain and crew, and no heavy cargo.

was still the overland trip to Chengtu before I could expect much rest. Bob did not arrive until late on the afternoon of the twenty-first, and then he came rushing in, wearing his old varsity sweater, the one that he used to put on after running on Field Days. Affairs pertaining to YMCA property in Chengtu had delayed him, but he had made a record journey overland from Chengtu in less than six days. It seemed the happiest day of my life when I saw him again and knew the six long months of our separation were at an end. Illness and separation—two hard words—I had experienced both. Now I felt better at once; it seemed I could stand anything if only Bob were at hand.

We had a happy Christmas with our good friends Warburton and Hetty and set off on the sedan chair trip to Chengtu on the morning of December 26. It was a year to the day from our arrival in Chungking on our way down river in 1911.

PART FOUR

ACHIEVEMENT IN CHENGTU

23

Back Home in Chengtu

(1913)

Liu Pei-yun was by this time an adept at managing travel, and he was able to care for us very well on this journey. Our party was the four in our family and two young Canadian ladies who needed an escort to Chengtu. We were glad to have them, but I wonder what they thought of me. I knew fairly well what they thought of Bob, as everything fell on his shoulders, though the cook relieved him of some details. I was not able to use my hands to amount to anything and rode along day after day with my painful wrists laid on a hot-water bottle in my lap. Some evenings I was too tired too eat, every noise in the inn would bother me, and I was about at the end of my string.

The children had a clever and unusual sedan chair that I had had made by a rattan shop in Shanghai. It had two seats, facing each other, with a table-like shelf between them. A heavy blanket covering seats and the entire bottom of the chair, put in before the children were seated, together with traveling rugs and cushions, made them as cozy as could be. They could even lie back and doze when the mood pleased.[1] However, there are many other details to be thought of when traveling with young children. Getting them in and out of the chair is always a skirmish. And when their chair is put down during teashop rests, there must be a vigilant warding off of gifts of food pressed on them by friendly Chinese. Also, of course, Bob had the responsi-

1. The only problem with the double sedan chair was that the children were not always in the mood for dozing. Two small boys, closely facing each other all day with their feet occupying the same space between them, would find it difficult—even if they were good little boys—not to get restless and combative before the day was done. Rhythm is very important in sedan chair carrying (as also in carrying loads with a shoulder pole). In chair carrying, the trick is that the carriers in front and back must always be perfectly *out* of step (if they keep *in* step the occupant of the chair is apt to get seasick). Sudden movements and shifts of weight in the chair make it hard for the carriers. I regret that we often heard the earnest exhortation "*bu tiao*" (don't jump about).

bilities for the carriers and our progress. At the same time he had a somewhat fault-finding wife, who was far from her usual form and who wanted more attention than any man in such a position could find time to give her.

Still, there were pleasures, real and doubtful, on the way. I see by my diary that on one of the last days of the year we had "a lovely, bright frosty morning with some thin ice in the rice fields. We saw strawberries amid white-frosted foliage as the sun came out. It warmed us after a chilly two hours. We spent the night at Hwangkioshu and slept next the piggies."

This journey ended as so many have done for us in Szechwan. The little house on Wenmiaogai stood ready for us. Though I had not seen it for over a year, and had been in many nicer places, it looked just like home to me. Bob had been getting along any old way, without curtains up or rugs down. Everything needed attention at once. We arrived home on January 5 [1913], and in ten days the whole house was clean and running about as usual. I tried to rest, but a thousand things were needing my supervision. We had several things done on the second floor: renovations in our bedroom, a more convenient door cut into the children's room, and a new closet built.

One day not long after our return I had a brisk fire burning in our bedroom fireplace while I was unpacking boxes and trunks. I was puzzled by a constant smell of smoke. Going to the fireplace, I stood beside it and happened to put my hand on the wall. I gave a jump, for the plaster was as hot as my hand could bear. I rushed to one of the glass doors onto the veranda and called to the servants that the house was on fire. One of them ran to the Y for Bob while the others began to fetch water. It took some time to get enough water poured on to quench the fire in the beams close to the chimney and in the lathwork. While repairs were made, we moved to the guest room.

In January we heard that a new man and his wife were to come to the Chengtu YMCA. Of course, this was welcome and exciting news and we were eager to know more about them. Many letters and telegrams were exchanged before their arrival in April. Mr. Richardson was a science man and came to help utilize the Science Hall as planned and set up by Dr. Wilson. They lived with us for some weeks and then settled into the residence next door where the Wilsons had been.

Bob became busy this year with plans for a central YMCA. As a result of official changes, a former public building was not being used. The YMCA was able to secure this as a gift. The Chinese-style buildings were repaired and thus became the site of the city YMCA.[2]

About this time there was a craze among Chinese students for the study of

2. The already existing YMCA, next door to us and close to the government university, now became a branch of the main, city YMCA, devoted to serving students. It would be interesting to know more about how a Chinese government (municipal or provincial?) was persuaded to donate a building to a private, Christian organization. It probably reflects Bob's success in recruit-

Esperanto. Several of them came to us and wanted to study it. We finally took it up to please them. Eventually, both of us were teaching Esperanto classes. I had almost forgotten this, but recall now how eagerly we conned the few textbooks available to us and how much enthusiasm there was in the study. I was also teaching in a Chinese school to please an old pupil of mine who liked "my English." I was also working away at Chinese and sewing, so there was little time to waste.

There was no chance to get away to the hills that summer, but along in July Mabelle Yard and I felt we needed a little change. We put our heads together and decided to go to Lingaisze, the fine temple at Kwanhsien, for a short stay. Miss Collier, our friend of the Tatsienlu trip in 1908, joined us and we had a wonderful time. Miss Collier stayed with some of the Methodist ladies. Mabelle and I had written ahead, and rooms had been secured for us. These were two tiny rooms off an upper court. Both faced onto the court, but access to the better room was through the other. We had our cots set up in the inner room, and my old amah, who had accompanied us, slept in the other.

At first, Mabelle and I arranged to board with some friends. However, we soon found that the unusual nature of our adventure made this unnecessary. We slept late and rustled up our own breakfast of crackers and cocoa, with the help of an alcohol stove, tinned milk, and an extra bottle of drinking water. For the noon meal we were almost sure to have an invitation. And for the evening meal we were in great demand. Indeed, sometimes we had more than one invitation; and we actually did not have time to make the entire round. Our friends entered into the spirit of our frolic in fine style; but the thought that two women with husbands and young children could, and would, leave them to go off on such an excursion filled their minds with blank amazement.

We had left well-managed households; competent amahs were with our children; and our husbands had promised to devote time to their homes. We reveled for ten days in the joy of not having to get up at any special time, and in being able to throw off all responsibility. My old gardener had come with us, and he carried plenty of bath water for our tub. We lay in our beds, under our nets, waited on by Amah and feeling like two schoolgirls off on a lark. We rose when we pleased, dressed as cooly as we could, and sallied forth to visit or to be entertained. We went to dine with some English people and were explaining our holiday to them. I told the husband, a Cambridge man, that we just wanted to forget the trammels of our daily existence in stuffy city

---

ing influential leaders of the local community to serve as sponsors and members of the Y's board of directors. One may assume that it also indicates that the original Y was proving popular and was seen as performing a useful function in China's modernizing society.

compounds, taking a brief interlude to enjoy things we desired but could not get. He was so worked up by this recital of longings that he rushed about and tore open a new box of stores to provide some especially fine cheese wherewith to grace their dinner table for us.

While we were having this carefree existence, it appeared that our husbands in Chengtu were the recipients of much attention from the ladies, both married and single. It got about the foreign community in no time that Mrs. S and Mrs. Y, such a heartless pair as you never heard of, had gone to the hills, leaving their husbands and children in the city heat. Poor men, and poor children! "We must have them over for tea," said this one and that. The men were invited out to evening dinners and picnic suppers, and something was "on" all the time. It was well for the digestion of our spouses that Mabelle and I did not stay away any longer.

That trip did us both much good, but when I got home to find my two offspring a sight to behold with prickly heat (meantime the large bottle clearly marked "Prickly Heat Lotion" standing untouched in plain sight on a shelf in the bathroom), I began to wonder how the minds of fathers work in the summertime. Strenuous attention on my part, together with plenty of cool baths, cured the children in a few days' time. And I was glad to be home, where I could also sense the appreciation of the other members of the family. This summer outing of ours was never understood by some. Even a year or more later I had a letter from an English friend in another part of the province saying she had heard of this trip without my husband and children. She wondered if it *could* be true, and was eager to "hear the truth" from me. I wrote her the facts and we are still friends.

Aside from an upset among provincial officials, there was little excitement that fall. Everyone was busy, and we kept on in the usual way, seeing more and more of Chinese friends and having excellent contacts with them. And it was good having the Richardsons as neighbors in the house next door.

The new year of 1914 began with a gathering of a good number of Americans for a progressive breakfast at the Methodist compounds. We started the children to eating their entire meal at the Canright house. Then the grownups had fruit at a nearby house; ham and eggs at another; hot waffles and maple syrup at a third; ending with coffee and doughnuts at the last place. We were all keen for such frolics at this time and thoroughly enjoyed the affair. So we launched 1914!

24

Third Son

(1914)

The new, main YMCA, which had to be Bob's chief concern, was near the middle of the city. The Science Hall and student branch were more or less in the hands of Mr. Richardson. This meant that Bob was away from home a great deal more. Occasionally, he came home for lunch (he kept a horse and could get about more rapidly than by foot or chair). But he usually remained away all day, eating Chinese food at noon in some restaurant.[1] It became more and more lonely for the children and myself. Bob's getting home in the evening depended on the activities at the Y. Several nights a week, he had classes, and these could keep him out until 10:30. A few classes still met in our house, and I was teaching a number of pupils.

Early in the year, I began to have definite trouble with my stomach. After some queer symptoms and a hemorrhage, the doctor pronounced it to be ulceration of the stomach. He thought it came from eating the native flour, which was ground by millstones made of sandstone. The grit in it was often noticeable. For weeks and weeks I lived on nothing but small amounts of milk sipped at frequent intervals. I did not remain in bed, because the doctor wanted me to keep up and around, thinking I would not lose so much strength that way. We had bought a huge upholstered chair from some British friends who left China shortly before this, and I almost lived in that chair. I would come downstairs and sit in it all morning; take a nap in the nursery after tiffin; and then sit in the chair again until bedtime. By the first of April I was supposed to be over this ailment; but I had little strength, and every

1. A few years later, I—and eventually my brothers—went every Saturday to have lunch with "Dad." Some of the Y staff often ate with us. The people in whatever restaurant we patronized knew Bob well and knew what he liked to eat—most of all, *baozi* (steamed meat dumplings that are a Szechwan specialty). For some reason, these were father-and-son affairs: Grace probably regarded them as a welcome respite. They were certainly a big weekly event for her sons.

evening found me simply worn out with the day's affairs. We were expecting a daughter in May.

On the twentieth of April Bob left about noon to go to Penghsien. He was hunting a place for the summer and planned to go to Cave Mountain to see if we could rent rooms there. He rode his horse and expected to be gone only a few days. He had not been away twenty-four hours when I knew there was something in the air. I sent for the cook and told him plainly that he would have to attend to the many affairs of the household; keep a fire, if it meant all night; and do whatever he was told by the doctor and whoever came to help.

The first thing was to send for Dr. Canright. Very soon he and his wife, Marguerite Irwin (a nurse), and Mabelle Yard were all there. I had a bad time and spent longer in bed than with all three of the previous children. Every time I attempted to aid in the work of Nature I would feel that I was fainting. They then gave me whiskey, and I know not what, to keep me going.[2] At last, when the doctor was downstairs having a cup of coffee, they called him; he thought I must have collapsed and rushed upstairs to find the baby born. This was at 10:00 p.m. on April 21, 1914.

All these months I had wanted a daughter so much, and the doctor had kept telling me he thought it was to be a girl. Whether he did this from guesswork, knowledge of occult signs, or for the pure psychology of suggestion, I do not know. But when the child was born, I was not conscious. The first words I heard were, "Oh, she's all right now." I supposed they referred to the baby. Such a glow of satisfaction and joy as swept over me! I can remember it to this day. Then suddenly, when I had opened my eyes, Margaret Canright said, "Don't you want to see the baby? He's a lovely little fellow." I was struck dumb and shook my head. Finally I murmured, "And I've gone through all this for a boy!" I had never seen the other children until they were bathed and dressed and fixed in the usual baby way, brought in by the nurse; but this time Margaret insisted that I should see the child at once. She held him close to me so that I could look at him, rolled in his receiving blanket. He was moving his tiny face and blinked at me knowingly; suddenly I felt a great bond between us. He had an understanding eye. I felt reconciled to the possession of a third son. They asked me his name and I said, "Richard Montgomery."

At daylight, unknown to me, the doctor sent a runner for Bob. This man overtook him on the hills the following morning, twenty-four hours later. When Bob read the note, he turned in his saddle, called to his traveling companions, and turned his horse's head toward Chengtu. Late that afternoon he

2. The grocery storeroom, always kept locked, was an attractively mysterious place. One of the mysteries to us boys was a never-touched bottle of whiskey. Our queries brought only a vague reply: medicinal purposes. Until I read Grace's account, I never knew that any of it had been "used."

came creeping in his stocking-feet up the stairs at home, having left his muddy riding boots outside the front door.

I had had a terrific chill on the afternoon of the twenty-second, and the doctor had given me some strong medicine, so strong that while it eventually brought me out of the chill, it also brought out on me some atrocious water blisters. When Bob arrived the next afternoon, he was amazed to find me a sight with these miserable blisters on my face, hands, hair, and all about. But we had the baby, even if he had arrived a fortnight ahead of time, and we were together; so what did blisters matter. And they were gone in a few days.

Bob asked what I thought we had better name the child. I said he was already named! We had earlier agreed on "Richard," should it be a boy. Bob had suggested "Colton" for the middle name. I did not much like the sound of the initials "R.C.S." and also wanted to name the child for an old college friend whose surname was Montgomery. So when the baby's father was not at hand at the birth, I took the occasion to give my choice of a name. Bob was somewhat surprised.

Bob had secured a small temple at Cave Mountain and took us there about the middle of June.[3] The mountain gets its name from the fact that there are a number of caves in small peaks that rise from the main ridge. Most of these hills had temples on them, so that, instead of one or two large temples, there were numerous small ones. The one we had was called Fairy Cave. Below our peak there was a fine spring in the Thunder God Cave. During the summer Bob rigged a windlass on the point of the hill, above and behind our temple, so that the servants could draw up water and save carrying it by bucket and shoulder pole up the steep side of the cliff. Of course, a coolie had to be at the bottom to fill the buckets, as the spring was inside the cave. But the plan was workable; Bob was always one for such improvements.

Our temple was unique. A long flight of stone steps led straight up the hillside to it. Inside, at the level of the main door, there was a large room at the left and, adjoining it, a small room. We took these for bedroom and bathroom. Carpenters soon fixed the bedroom so that it could be securely locked. Just outside the bathroom was a steep wooden stairway leading down to a little room below. It was given to the two amahs, who could thus be within hearing of my voice at night: only my floor boards were between us. To the right of the front entrance was a frightfully dirty room which we had whitewashed for a kitchen. There were rooms behind it for the servant. From the tiny stone courtyard inside the main entrance, a flight of stone steps mounted to the main room of the temple. This was enclosed only on

3. Cave Mountain, Peony Mountain, Kwanhsien, and one more important place still to come into this story, lay in an arc in the foothills along the north edge of the Chengtu plain. They were about forty to fifty miles north to northwest of Chengtu. Behind them were real mountains, up to 13,000 feet, and even higher in the west toward Tibet.

three sides, with the front entirely open. Here we hung our hammock in front of the idols in their high glass case. With a few canvas and cane chairs and a folding table for meals, the place soon looked like a summer sitting room.

On both sides and above the court were pavilions built in the same three-sided manner, but without any of the gods that filled the rear of the main hall. Above, up more stairs and through several passages, one came to the Fairy Cave. It was not extensive, was dry and cool, and we could keep food there if we wished. I have rarely seen a nicer cave. Still higher up there was a clever little pagoda-like pergola which was a sort of topknot to the whole temple complex. I thought I'd climb up there every day, but of course I did not. There were really too many steps for me, and with youngsters I was always afraid they might slip. There was a fine view from the little eyrie, but from where we were we could see no other abode of man.

Bob got us fixed in this place and went back to the city, leaving me a revolver (which I could shoot!), and telling the servants to be vigilant.[4] No one could get into our place at night unless he climbed the hill above and dropped down from the crags onto our roof. The lattice windows which opened from my bedroom were nailed shut, and those in the outer wall of the temple (unusual in such a wall and only there because they were high above the ground) had wooden bars across them. There was no priest in our temple. We rented it from the local township headmen and had entire possession.

After a few weeks a young Canadian came to sleep in one of the half-open side rooms on the living room level. He was studying Chinese and took his meals with a family who lived nearby, but they had no bedroom for him. An oil sheet hung up for a front to his room gave all the privacy needed. Soon after he came I was awakened at night by queer sounds. I thought someone must be crying out in a bad dream. It went on night after night, and my sleep was greatly disturbed.

Alone as we were on that mountainside, I felt somewhat apprehensive. I asked the servants about it and they told me it was our guest. They insisted that it was he, praying aloud to his God in the middle of the night! That very night I heard it again and, slipping from my bed, crept to the window toward the court and listened. His room was on the opposite side of the court and above the level of my room. I could see a dim light there behind his oil sheet. Sure enough, the young man was praying in a most highfalutin and emotional manner. He would cry out in a loud voice, asking the attention of the Deity, then mumble off a long string of petitions. Soon his voice would rise again in a high-pitched screech calling on God to look upon him, a miserable

4. Grace's diary for 1908 mentions that she practiced shooting a revolver while at their mountain camp near Tatsienlu.

sinner; and the gamut of petitions would again be uttered with variations of tone and intensity of feeling. On and on he prayed, haranguing the Almighty, with an ebb and flow in his passion like that of waves on the seashore.

I did not know what to do, but a few days later a solution came. When the gentleman was having tea with me one afternoon, I began to talk very seriously to the cook as he served us. I got off quite a stream of Chinese and the gentleman, seeing that I was much in earnest about something, asked me what I had been saying. I said I had been speaking about talking and yelling late at night; that I thought it must come from the servants and wanted it stopped. He said nothing, but after this did his praying so that we did not participate in its emotions. He did not, incidentally, stay long in the Mission.

The small level patches between our hills were all under cultivation, mostly of corn, and the farmers were much concerned to keep wild pigs from their precious harvest.[5] By the time that night praying stopped, the corn was ripened and we had new shouting and yelling to enliven the hours of darkness. Their yodels and cries made the night vocal. I used to look down on them from my high windows as they prowled among the cornstalks. Now and then the report of a blunderbuss would waken one from sound slumber.

Amid these surroundings, we heard of the beginning of the World War in August. The news was brought us by some Canadian friends who came to call on the evening of the fifth. They were sure it would be finished in six weeks, or three months at the longest, but I remarked, "You may be surprised, for the Germans may give you a run for your money." This somewhat thoughtless remark was taken to indicate that I was a German sympathizer, and was quoted months and even years later, though it never held any such significance to me. We soon had to watch our tongues. All the British, no matter how friendly they had been earlier, immediately became "subjects of a nation at War." They were war conscious in a way that, it seems to me, we Americans never were, even after the States entered the conflict.

We spent most of the summer without Bob, but he came now and then for weekends or short stays. Once while Bob was with us, word came from Kwanhsien that Mr. Richardson, our Y associate, was ill with typhoid fever and needed a nurse. We had two on Cave Mountain, and Marguerite Irwin offered to go. Bob started off on a rainy day to take her across country, along the flanks of the mountains. She had a chair, and Bob his horse. It was a terrible trip, most of it in pouring rain. One never knows how long these storms will last; and the longer the wait, the more difficult travel becomes. At

5. These mountain farmers in Szechwan depend heavily on corn: it seems to be as important in their lives as corn is in Mexico. Yet the books all say that corn is native to the Americas. I have never found an account of how it got to the far west of China; but Spanish Catholic missionaries reached Szechwan in the seventeenth century.

one place, crossing a flooded river, he had to carry her on his back some distance from a boat to the shore. She was a large, heavy, nervous woman, and he had many experiences with her before they reached Kwanhsien. It was highly diverting to hear the horse coolie tell of their adventures by land and water. Bob had also a tale to tell, and Marguerite a longer one.

We had terrific storms that year. One night there was an especially violent one with sheets of rain, blinding flashes of lightning, and thunder that seemed to shake the very foundations of our temple. Over our heads was nothing except rafters and tiles laid on wooden stringers. In the midst of this cataclysm of the elements some of the roof tiles directly over my bed were lifted by the gale. A regular spout of water, filthy from the uprooting of the tile, poured down and soaked my net and bedding; then the tile fell back into place again. It was a thoroughly cross young woman who had to get out of her bed, wet and dirty, seeking dry quarters and finding none. The whole room seemed to leak that night, and I was deadly sick of temple living. But the next day, when the sun shone and everything sparkled with freshness, the whole situation was altered; I looked out of my high windows and was glad to be alive and in the mountains. We put everything out to sun and were happy as grigs—the children, servants, and all.

Mabelle was ill that summer and I used to go over to their temple to help care for her. We had no doctor on our mountain, and it stormed too badly for a messenger to go for one. However, she began to improve with the weather, and all went well.

25

Furlough at Last

(1915)

At last the summer was over and we were back in Chengtu, glad as ever to be inside the walls of the little Chinese compound again. Everything in the whole house was moldy and had to be cleaned and sunned. The servants and I were busy as beavers for days.

I had had the Montessori equipment sent out from America and began to use it to teach the two older boys. Jack thus unconsciously learned his alphabet and started to read. He took to it like a duck to water and enjoyed everything from the first.[1] Bob, being younger, needed more encouragement. He was the imaginative one, always ready to visualize a situation for play or a story. I created "Pop-eyed Pig" and "Mr. Tumble-toes" for his amusement, and tales of these two odd companions were heard in our nursery for several years. "Our Bob," as he was usually called to distinguish him from his father, asked me one day to look at his "white gloves," and although they did not look so white to me, he proudly announced that they were "real skin."

I tried to keep the children out of the kitchen save when they saw me there, but it was a treat for them to help with some special dish now and then. The making of mincemeat was one such occasion. Small Bob, drying himself on the hearthrug after his bath one evening that fall, announced in a prideful manner: "Of course, I am just a yittle boy and can have only a tiniest taste of a piece of mince pie, but I can help mama make all them pies' insides!" The phrase, "tiniest taste," came from me, and I doubt if he fully sensed its meaning. They did help with the mincemeat, and in a few such activities I tried to keep alive the desire to do something for the home at holiday time, which is so hard to cultivate in children brought up among the many servants of the East.[2]

---

1. Grace is right that the learning was "unconscious." To this day, I cannot remember anything at all about this Montessori experience.
2. We boys may all have helped Grace in the kitchen, but Bob was the only one to derive

26 At a meeting with the governor in Chengtu (about 1915). The tall man in the center is Harry Openshaw; young Bob and Jack are in the foreground.

During this year I read sixty-four books and longed for more. I wrote four hundred and five letters, a good many more than I received. I taught less than in any year since our arrival in China, but I now had three young children as my first care. I had good help, but never allowed the amah to have responsibility for the children. Their food was my immediate concern, and I always attended to that myself with the cook's aid.

Ties that bind friends often make the world very small. Early in 1915 we learned through friends that Mrs. Tracy, who had visited us in Nanking in 1912, was in India. As soon as I heard this, I told Bob that she and her party would be in China that spring. She had told us in Nanking that she would make the trip west to visit us. Before the end of March we had a telegram saying that she and her cousin would come to Szechwan, bringing Will Lockwood of the Shanghai Y with them. Mr. Harvey of the National Committee of the YMCA was already planning to visit us at this time, so we had a party of four to entertain. Soon we were exchanging telegrams; when Bob was away on a short trip, I had to decipher and reply to several long code messages.[3]

---

much lasting benefit. He became in later years a quite competent cook. And Grace is wrong in thinking that we kept out of the kitchen save when she was there.

3. The coded messages that Grace refers to were not for security but to save money. It was the general practice to use commercial codes in which five-letter code groups stood for common

These last messages were because of trouble in the Tracy party's travel. They had taken a small steamer at Ichang. This was wrecked, and they spent a week in various small craft: police boat, sampan, and junk. Finally, they reached Wanhsien and were able to telegraph us. From Wanhsien it was possible to go across country by chair and reach Chengtu in fourteen days. The normal alternative would require at least ten days by houseboat to Chungking and then ten days by sedan chair to Chengtu. The problem was safety. Fortunately, Bob got back from his trip and was able to ask the opinion of his friend, the governor, about travel in the Wanhsien district. He was assured that all would be safe, and thus the party came.[4]

Bob's trips to the hills that year had been in connection with securing land for bungalows. He had found a mountain named White Deer Summit (Bailuding), which was not far from Peony Mountain (where we had gone in 1911) and Cave Mountain (where we were in 1914). At the end of March in 1915, Bob finally was able to sign a 99-year lease for the whole mountaintop, which was a *zhaizi* and enclosed by a rough stone wall.[5]

Our furlough, which I had hoped would materialize in 1913, had been deferred until 1914. Then I was ill, and the birth of our third son would have made travel very difficult. Now it was the spring of 1915 and still nothing was definite, though we hoped to go that fall. I was beginning to feel the strain very keenly. Our clothes were worn out, and we had not ordered foreign food supplies. Now, in the midst of this uncertainty, we were to have guests from afar, ones we would wish to entertain as nicely as we could. When Chengtu friends learned of our problem, they were lovely. Several offered me anything in their storerooms.

Mrs. Tracy's party stayed eight days, and they saw a spring fair and the places of interest in the city. At a new theater run by a friend of ours, they were vastly entertained by a performance of *The Prodigal Son*. Some of the realism was startling. A half-grown pig appeared on the stage, and the prodigal attempted to eat from his food basin. We knew the actor taking the lead, so it was doubly interesting. Our friends were also struck by the layout of Chinese theaters, the freedom of conversation, and the incessant and interminable eating and drinking throughout the performance. Waiters were constantly passing in and out, running about with tea, kettles of boiling

---

statements or whole phrases. Incidentally, it seems noteworthy that the general secretary of the Shanghai Y (Mr. Lockwood) escorted Mrs. Tracy on this long trip (she had also had a Y escort on her 1912 trip to Nanking). She, or her fairly recently deceased husband, must have supported the YMCA very generously.

4. It may be noted that Bob did *not* ask the advice or permission of any consul, either the British in Chengtu or the American in Chungking, for this travel. And the governor, having promised safety, may have had an interest in assuring it.

5. A *zhaizi* was a stronghold or stockade, usually built on a mountaintop, to serve as a place of refuge from banditry or civil war.

water, and various things to eat. Every so often an attendant would appear at one side of the hall with a large container of hot Turkish towels, just wrung out from boiling water. Someone in the audience would raise a hand, and in a trice the attendant would toss him a steaming towel.

We enjoyed Mrs. Tracy's visit and were sorry to see her go. But the important news was that Mr. Harvey had told us that we were to go on home leave at once. For the time being, preparations for that had to blot out everything else.

It is inevitable that plans made in one country to be worked out in another country cannot be perfect. When we went to Szechwan under the Y, we well knew its distance and isolation. But the man in America told us there would be compensations: Bob would go to the Coast every year for a conference of Y workers; I would have all expenses paid to accompany him every second year. Once on the ground, we soon saw the futility of such promises. We had now been in China nine and a half years and had gone only once to the Coast, and that by consular order. In all this time, we were just having our first visit by a member of the National Committee of the YMCA in China. Our isolation precluded much of the give-and-take and pleasant cooperation enjoyed by the other YMCAs in China.

Packing and more packing was the order of the day, and social events crowded upon one another. Officials and friends on every side wished to entertain Bob. We were both honored at a large reception given by the American Methodists. They were our nearest neighbors, and we belonged to their Chinese church. At one Chinese men's dinner, so many speeches were made that Mr. Harvey later teased Bob about things said there by Chinese who hated to see Hsieh An-tao leave. (This was Bob's Chinese name.) There was little time for sleep. Indeed, Bob never got to bed on the last night before our departure.

We remained in our own home until the last. Calls continued up to the moment of departure. May 20 was a pleasant day and we were up early. The governor of the province and several other officials came to wish us well. Three University of California men, just arrived in the city on a scientific trip, came by for a brief meeting.[6] We ate tiffin with the Richardsons and were off at two in the afternoon.

Numerous friends were waiting out beyond the East Gate to see us off. On account of the low water in the river, our two boats awaited us thirty *li* below the city. Bert Brace accompanied us to them and remained for the night to

6. The UC scientists were led by Dr. George D. Louderback, professor of Mineralogy and Geology at Berkeley. He was accompanied by Messrs. Eaton and Taliaferro. To the Chinese (and perhaps some envious foreigners), the farewell call by the governor meant considerable "face" for Bob and the YMCA.

have a last long talk with Bob about Y matters.[7] After midnight Bert caught a few winks of sleep and was up and away at 4:00 in the morning when the boatmen roused to activity.

At last we cast off and were afloat on the Min River, starting the long water route to San Francisco. We lay about, lazy and thankful to rest. Even the discovery that we had forgotten the silver money arranged for by Bob did not worry us. On the first day we stopped long enough for Bob to call on the local missionaries and buy a few dollars. At Kiating, where we stopped for two days, we bought more, and all was well. Mr. Harvey had one boat and we the other. Jack slept with Mr. Harvey, and they both ate with us. We soon fell into a routine: meals, naps, short walks at stops, baths, and bed. I began now to be thankful that the two elder lads were not entirely dependent on an amah and could do a few things for themselves.

The usual things happened: Jack, on a walk with his father, fell into a small creek; the cook burned a whole batch of biscuits; I had trouble with the baby about his bottle. He was then over a year old, and I had never dreamed to travel with a bottle. He drank water from a cup, but no power on earth could force him to take milk that way. We had tried for weeks on end, and he only set his teeth the harder. Finally, the doctor said he was losing weight and we would *have* to give him the bottle. How happy and sweet he was as soon as he saw it! What a nuisance for a big baby with teeth and taking eggs and such things. But boat life was pleasant, and our food was good. On the evening of May 28 we tied up at Chungking.

Here we spent five sweltering days. At first it looked as though we would have to go to Ichang by houseboat, but at last we left on a small Chinese steamer, the *Ta Chuan*. We went aboard one evening and spent an awful night. The decks were too narrow to lie on, and loading went on all night with yells and raucous sounds to keep things in a turmoil. About daylight there came a terrific thunderstorm, and as soon as it abated our ship started. A breeze then swept over us, and we ran for clothes, more and more of them, until we were in sweaters fairly hugging ourselves to keep warm!

In another week we were in Shanghai. It was wonderful to be in a foreign-style city again. Everyone lived so luxuriously. There was ice; Bob and I realized how greatly we had missed it. We visited hard with our friends, and the days passed quickly. Our ship sailed on the twenty-sixth of June. We had a perfect day in Honolulu, going to bathe at Waikiki with friends. We docked at San Francisco on July 20. My mother was there with the Service relatives from Berkeley to meet us.

7. We had encountered the Braces at Kuling in the summer of 1912 while they were await-ing permission to travel to Szechwan. Bert Brace was actually a member of the Canadian Meth-odist Mission who was loaned by that mission to serve as a secretary in the Chengtu YMCA. He would now be the senior foreign secretary during Bob's absence.

In Berkeley, we hired a nursemaid to come from noon till the children were in bed. That slice of her time cost us as much as our whole full-time corps of Chengtu servants. She made it possible for me to go with Bob to visit the Panama-Pacific Exposition in San Francisco and also to call on friends.[8] We made a short visit to San Bernardino. (My father had not attended our wedding and had not seen Bob since 1903.) We went on east in September and stopped in Cleveland, Ohio, to leave the children in capable trained-nurse hands, where they had the oversight of Mr. and Mrs. Robert E. Lewis, our friends from the landing in Shanghai in 1905.

Next was New York and a Y conference at Atlantic City. The good fellowship was a joy; we loved seeing the Hurreys, Coltons, and other old friends we had not seen since before we went to China. Of course we met many new secretaries and members of the International Committee.

One lady has remained forever in my memory. She was the wife of a Committee member and graciously invited me to ride with her on the Boardwalk one evening. I remember her clothes, fussy and ornate, just as she was puffy and impressive. It soon became clear why she chose me for a ride: she wanted to do me good! She had heard me say that I was an only daughter; she knew then that she should tell me what a wrong thing I was doing by going to China; I ought to think of my mother and remain in America. I laughed. My mother was full of zeal for missions, I told her, but felt that I had almost too good a time. It was true that she did not want me to return to Szechwan (chiefly because of the distance and difficulties of travel), but she was glad to have me in the Orient.

The plump lady looked at me and shook her head, at first slowly and ponderously, then briskly and even alarmingly. "Now, why do you talk so to me? I know a *mother's heart* and I know how your mother feels. You are doing a wrong thing in going to China. I have a daughter and I would not *think* of having her go to such a place to live. Travel is all right, but *living* is another thing entirely. And you have stayed away ten years. It is all wrong." She regarded me as a brand, not plucked from the burning, but ready even to jump back into the fire. The next day someone tried to introduce us, but she forestalled it with emphasis, "I *already know* Mrs. Service."

Someone also wanted to introduce a Y secretary named George Helde to us. He put them off, saying that he didn't care to meet folks who were stupid enough to stay ten years in the far reaches of China without any return to America. George came to China that year, and two years later became Bob's associate in Chengtu.

8. Grace seems to have forgotten, but I also went to the Exposition. I remember it vividly: I saw my first airplane (doing loops in the sky) and a live American Indian (standing around in feathers and war paint and looking bored).

Back in Cleveland, we moved into a furnished house in East Cleveland. Bob was to work in the Central Cleveland Y under Mr. Lewis, who was then the Metropolitan general secretary. We found an excellent colored maid, and Jack was happy attending first grade in a nearby public school.

In November we went to the Mayo Clinic. Bob was found to be in perfect condition. They found my blood very poor; were sure I had had gallstones in China; and were concerned about the stomach ulcers. They did not remove my tonsils, though I told them I had had much "rheumatic sore throat" in China. They agreed with my Cleveland doctor and wanted me to have plenty of rest and quiet, free from all responsibility. This was a hard thing to plan when one maid was all that the budget could carry. I was lucky to have her for the work in the house while I played nursemaid.

Mrs. Tracy, our visitor in Nanking and Chengtu, now proposed a delightful plan for six weeks in early 1916. We hired a nurse-housekeeper, and I went to Florida as Mrs. Tracy's guest. It was all like a dream come true. As the train left Cleveland on a day in late February, I let my household cares slip off my shoulders. A suite at the Ormond Beach Hotel awaited us. There were delightful motor trips around the vicinity, a longer one of several days to the central lake district, a jaunt to Key West by the East Coast Railway, a weekend at Miami, and twenty-four hours at Palm Beach where we stayed at the Royal Poinciana and followed the gay round of the pleasure seekers through a day's cycle. Finally, we motored to Jacksonville and there separated. I came north by way of Chattanooga to visit relatives. After all this gayety, I reached Cleveland to find measles.

Late in the spring I had another treat when I was allowed to accompany Bob on an eastern trip. This took us to a Y conference in New Jersey, and then on a tour of various important cities from Washington to Montreal and Toronto. Bob was to observe city Y methods that might be helpful in developing the work in Chengtu. In New Hampshire we had a weekend at Mrs. Tracy's farm. In Boston we visited Bob Feustel, an old Purdue friend. From his home I moved to a boarding house to be with our old friend from West China, Dr. Florence O'Donnell, who was now Florence Piers of Halifax. We had not met since she left Chengtu in 1908. Now she had three children, including a young daughter, Virginia, named for our first baby. How we visited and talked Chinese and laughed and enjoyed ourselves!

Soon we were back in Cleveland, packing for California and the ocean trip. We visited in Michigan[9] and Iowa, had a few days in my home at San

9. Bob's grandfather (John Service) took up land in 1840 near what is now Weston, Michigan. It was from here that Bob's father (also John Service) started off across the plains to California in 1859. And it was here that Bob was born in 1879 while his parents were back visiting the old home.

Bernardino, and then ten days with my parents at Long Beach, which the boys loved. Back in Berkeley, we enjoyed Father Service's first motor car, a Chandler. We were to have had a month there, and then sail from Vancouver on September 7. Because a railroad strike was threatened for September 1, we had suddenly to hurry our departure by several days. Bob always regretted this and the short time he had with his parents on this furlough. He should have asked for more time with them, but he never asked for any favors for himself. He never saw either parent again, for both died before our return to America eight years later.

26

Return to China

(1916)

Our ship from Vancouver was the *Empress of Russia*. We found more than sixty friends on board and had such a good time with them that we did not meet many new people. In Tokyo we visited Cameron Hayes, our old associate from Chengtu, who was now married and involved in YMCA work for the Chinese students in Japan. After Japan we spent two days in a typhoon. The air was stifling because every door and porthole had to be kept fast closed.[1] The ship rolled so badly that I slept for part of the time on the floor. I had an elaborate method of pinning sheets to hold Dick [age two] in his berth. Because of the storm we spent a night beating up and down off the bar at the mouth of the Yangtze. With daylight and a falling wind, we were able to cross and arrived safely at last in Shanghai.

As soon as I reached China, I began to have tonsil trouble. It was decided that I must have an operation while we were still in Shanghai. They worked on me for two and a half hours and still could not remove all of the tonsils, which were "imbedded." I had ether, and it was necessary to give me oxygen twice during the operation. What a time! Bob had been told that it would take half an hour, so he was dreadfully alarmed at the delay (of which I was totally unconscious). I felt like à rag after this ordeal and, though I was better, suffered for eight years longer with tonsil problems before I could get them all out and my throat clean.

1. The air on shipboard was stifling because air conditioning had not yet arrived. If the weather was reasonably good, fresh air was brought into one's cabin by an air scoop projecting outside an open porthole. The ships of that day still burned coal. Our ship took on coal at Nagasaki, and Grace omits what most impressed this seven-year-old: long lines of little Japanese women, scantily clad because of the heat, working through the night under bright floodlights, passing baskets of coal from hand to hand up long ladders from the coal barges up the side of the great ship and in to the bunkers. Like mechanical toys, their brisk pace never changed or slackened, and their sound was like a great flock of sparrows. Soon they all became black with coal dust.

The river trip was pleasant. We made the last section (Ichang to Chung-king) by the *Shu-hun* with the famous Captain Plant in command. The ship was not large, and its engines of 2,400 horsepower made the whole vessel vibrate; but they had the power to negotiate the rapids and gave us a feeling of safety.[2] The bridge was low, as Captain Plant wanted to be close enough to shout to his crew above the thundering din of the rushing waters in the rapids. The front of the top deck was thus available for the passengers. We had brought some rattan easy chairs so that we could sit there to enjoy the beauties of gorge and river. Nowadays such chairs are provided. We had a fine view of the dangerous Goose Tail Rock just above the west end of the Windbox Gorge. It stands some eighty feet above low water, and when the river is high its top may be forty feet under water. Junk pilots, Captain Plant told us, regard this place as the most dangerous in all China. Indeed, at certain flood levels they will not take boats either up or down.

In Chungking we learned that the overland road to Chengtu was unsafe.[3] Nonessential baggage was left in Chungking, and we had to travel with a military escort. The things left behind were to be forwarded by river when that was possible. We spent a day at Tzechow in order not to arrive in Chengtu on Sunday, so we actually arrived on November 20. Bert Brace and Newton Hayes met us outside the city. The Richardsons had left China for good during our absence, and Newton Hayes had arrived to join the Y staff. He was China-born, unmarried, clever, and pleasant; and we knew him well from Nanking days in 1912.

Friends began to call as soon as we were inside our gate. How jolly it was to be at home again. Mabelle Yard had four of our former servants there awaiting us, so the usual routine could quickly be established. Books, furniture, and various things which had been loaned to friends had all been returned and put in place. The house was clean and windows were washed, and plenty of cooked food was sent by friends, so that we ate tiffin soon after arrival.

2. The legendary Captain S. Cornell Plant devoted most of his life to proving that steam navigation of the Yangtze above Ichang was feasible. He learned the river so well that he could match the Chinese pilots. With this knowledge, he designed, owned, and commanded the first successful ships to pass the gorges and reach Chungking. These upper-Yangtze craft needed great power and maneuverability and were quite special for their day: shallow draft, twin engines, and four rudders. The current in some rapids could be about fifteen knots. Sometimes the ships would literally have to pull themselves upstream by putting a cable ashore and using the capstan to gain more power. On these occasions the coal stokers did their utmost. Stories of red-hot funnels were often heard; personally, I cannot attest to more than scorched paint.

3. "Unsafe" in these circumstances meant that bandits were active. This was a perennial problem of warlord China. They could be local hoodlums taking advantage of the breakdown of effective government; or they might be defeated, "disbanded," or simply unpaid soldiery. The hoodlums, if caught, might lose their heads (to be exhibited in some public place such as the nearest city gate). The soldier-bandits had a fair chance of instant redemption by being absorbed into one of the many competing warlord armies.

December was busy with unpacking and settling, and with teas, dinners, and receptions. We had no kitchen stove (the new one had been left with the heavy baggage in Chungking); a temporary, but not very satisfactory, expedient was to build a coke-burning Chinese stove in a corner of the outdoor laundry. The most satisfying thing about our return was the warm welcome from the Chinese. They made us feel that they were sincerely glad to see us back again.

The International Committee of the YMCA (in New York) had decided in 1916 to buy land and build us a residence. Bob had talked plans in Shanghai. As soon as we reached Chengtu, a land agent was put to work. In June 1917, after much correspondence, we were told to buy land near the university. But the money was not immediately available and matters were delayed. In April 1918 word came to buy at once. This was done; but no house was built until after we left Chengtu in 1921.

There was more result on another building project. Bob, it will be recalled, had signed a lease in March 1915 for White Deer Summit. We and several other families had quickly started building bungalows. When ours was planned, we did not know that we would be leaving that spring. And when the furlough news came, Bob had no chance to make trips to supervise the construction. The bungalow had been completed and had been rented for the summers of 1915 and 1916. But the head carpenter had turned the plan half around: our east living room faced north, and the mountain panorama could best be enjoyed from the kitchen!

Bob's personal life always settled about a house: he wanted more than anything else of a personal nature to own homes of his own. Our mountain, White Deer Summit, actually had a fairly flat top (which made it good both as a place of refuge and as a summer resort). The highest knob was called Big Round Top (Da Yuan-bao) by the Chinese. Bob had originally asked that he, as finder, have first chance at this site. Now he decided to build another bungalow—on Round Top. All that winter we were tremendously happy, making plans for a Y residence in Chengtu and for our own bungalow on the mountain. We sold the "old" bungalow, completed the plans in February [1917], and started building in the spring.

When we started our return from America I had thought to send the children to the recently established school for foreign children run by the Canadian Methodist Mission in Chengtu. But when we reached Shanghai in the fall of 1916, I learned there was already a rumpus at the school. Some criticized the teacher; others valiantly upheld her. It seemed to me that it would be impossible, as a parent, to avoid getting involved. I immediately decided to teach the children myself and ordered supplies from the Calvert School of Baltimore.

Jack had been through the first grade in Ohio and the teacher had told me to have him skip the second grade. I taught him first from books I had, and when the Calvert supplies arrived, he went into the third grade. Small Bob had been a kindergarten pupil for half a year in Ohio, and he now began the first grade of Calvert. To shorten a long story of teaching: I prepared Jack for high school, Bob for the sixth grade, and Dick for the fourth, except for some outside teaching which the latter had when small. We used every grade prepared by the Calvert School, including the kindergarten work which I gave Dick. I liked the excellently planned sheets sent for daily lesson use, and found the textbooks all that could be desired.

We usually had school from 8:30 to 12:30 every school day morning, taking a half-hour recess and perhaps a run or two around the house in between a couple of lessons. I found this schedule hard to keep and was obliged to cut down on Chinese calls, both receiving and replying. Many Chinese friends liked to visit about eleven in the forenoon and could not understand how I could be occupied at such an hour. I had to give household orders the night before, do accounts then also, and arrange everything to free my time for teaching. It sounds easy, it writes even easier, but it takes more mental resolution than one would imagine. Any classes I taught at the Y (and I always had some there) were held in the early afternoon when the children had naps.

Some American friends wanted me to form a class and teach their children along with mine. I had no inclination for this and knew it would make trouble with the Canadians, who already felt somewhat touchy because I did not send the boys to their school. Two or three of their ladies had long talks with me concerning these matters. I felt then, and still feel, that I was wise in giving our sons American teaching in our own home. They had companionship, and always at weekends I made a point of having them meet other children for good playtimes, so that they did not suffer from being alone.[4]

January 1917 was damp and penetratingly cold, with plenty of drizzle and much slipperiness under foot. We were talking, talking, talking of war matters, becoming more and more exercised over reports from the British and French. The few Germans in the city tried to maintain friendship with us Americans, but this became increasingly difficult. There was a sharp earthquake in Chengtu, and the Chinese took it to be a portent of evil.

On one of the bleakest nights of this dark period, Bob and I were invited to dine with the new governor. The evening turned out to be spectacular. We

4. We had good times, but the number of places to play was limited. Inside the city, there were the American Methodist and Canadian Methodist compounds. Outside the city, there were the American and Canadian parts of the West China Union University campus. In about 1916 the Davies family moved to Chengtu, and we had a new, and popular, alternative: the American Baptist compound.

entered through the beautiful main entrance of the Huangcheng (the grand, walled seat of government).[5] Everything was dripping wet as we proceeded in our closed sedan chairs down the long line through four huge gates hung with flags used like curtains drawn aside. The way to the official residence was marked by big red-banded lanterns on poles set in sockets in the stone pavement. I counted a hundred lanterns, and there were many more not in this direct line. The dancing reflections on the broad expanse of wet stone pavement enchantingly offset the dark, low, horizontal lines of buildings and roofs. Darkness in sky and wet stones, flame in the lanterns and red pillars, a warmth of pageantry against the night: we had all of the Orient in our slow progress to the upper rooms and our reception there.

It was an innovation for such an official to entertain ladies with the gentlemen. We thought that both sexes might eat together. It turned out to be entirely "proper": the ladies ate in the women's apartments. The only new-style thing was that the governor, himself, brought the married men after the meal to get their wives. Thus I had an opportunity to meet His Excellency.

Bob wore evening clothes, and I a blue silk dress with long georgette sleeves and a slightly low neck. We were both well wadded inside, not knowing what to expect in the way of temperature. I was wearing my riding tights and a thick "Spenser." However, there were charcoal braziers and even a foreign stove in our dining room, so we were comfortable.

The meal served was a foreign-style one, thought to be the height of style at the time in Chengtu, and we had everything from pheasant to hare. I tried to talk to the governor's wife, who was a pleasant person from near Shanghai. We were the only American couple there, and we never did figure out just how we were included. Until that evening, Bob and this governor had never met. Bob had sent his card at New Year as a matter of etiquette; a few days later the invitation arrived.[6]

The Yards had their fourth daughter in late January and almost immediately had to depart on furlough. We joined with the American Methodists in giving a farewell reception for Jim and Mabelle. It was a gay occasion and there were several felicitous speeches. For his part, Bob prepared a letter supposedly written to Jim by one of his Chinese students of English. In reality this letter was a skillful mosaic of sentences taken from a few of the many letters Bob and I had been receiving from our young students: only a few words had been altered to fit the circumstances. It caused much mirth, but there is space here for only a snippet:

5. The Huangcheng (see note 5 to chapter 19) was built in the Ming dynasty (fourteenth century) and was like a scaled-down Forbidden City.

6. At this official banquet the governor's principal foreign guests undoubtedly were the foreign consuls: British, French, and Japanese. But there was no American consul, and so Bob was invited. This story will be continued.

Please recept my sincere and respectful congratulations for your fourth noble and fair child was born. How pity it is not a son! Do you not think? Referring to that bad chance, I am filled with deep sympathy, and hoping all are renewed now.

In that same month of February, America broke relations with Germany, and by April we were in the war. At home, we were reading aloud *Mr. Britling Sees It Through.*[7]

7. *Mr. Britling Sees It Through* (1916) was a novel by H. G. Wells that described "the effects of the first two years of World War I on the emotional and intellectual life of Mr. Britling, an English writer who loses a son and a German friend on different sides in the war. He is finally able to build an optimistic philosophy for the future" (*The Reader's Encyclopedia,* p. 692).

27

White Deer Summit

(1917)

In June we went to White Deer Summit where we were to have the Yard bungalow for a month while our new place was being completed. We arrived on the mountain in a rain and all of us were wet. I had ridden Bob's horse most of the way up, letting him take his own time. We reached the summit and, unexpectedly, found that the road descended toward the Yard bungalow. I neglected to have the saddle girth checked, and the result was a tumble. The mud was terrible where I fell and I was a sight. Worse, my glasses fell off and it was getting dark. After much search they were found in thick shrubbery.

Our former bungalow was the only one occupied (the season was just starting), and the occupants were expecting us for supper. We finally arrived at 7:45, only to find that they had decided the weather was impossible for travel and so had gone to bed at 7:30! They were amazed to have five wet, draggled, and muddy folk arrive, all desirous of hot baths and food. By now a heavy mist had enveloped the mountain; it became clammy and cold, and we shivered after the heat of the plain.

Bob had to return to Chengtu after a few days. I went to Round Top every day to watch the progress on our new bungalow. Also, I had to answer a great many questions. The living room was L-shaped. It had windows in all four directions, two outside doors opening onto two verandas, and two interior doors to a hall and guest room. This room with its nine windows and four doors was considered very odd [see fig. 27]. Some British friends insisted (in spite of having seen the plan) that such a room could not be! They felt that I must be putting something over on Bob during his absence.

As we were not going to stay, we did not try to settle in the Yard house. The roof leaked badly, so it was a time of continual removal; boxes, beds, and

187

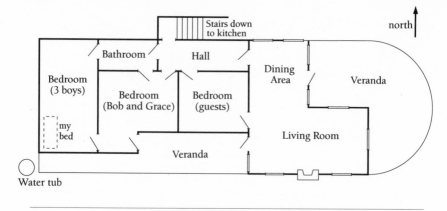

27   A plan, from Jack's memory, of the bungalow at Round Top. The bungalow was built during the summer of 1917; the semicircular veranda extension was added a year later.

belongings seemed to need shifting for every rain, and these came daily. At night, the cook (Liu Pei-yun) put his *pugai* on the floor outside my bedroom door. Several times we heard sneak thieves, but we had the heavy lattice windows nailed shut so they could not be opened. As there were no curtains, I undressed in the dark, and in the morning dressed behind my bed net.

One night there was a low, tense yelling. The wild, threatening note was alarming. I got up in the pitch dark and found Liu sitting on the floor, alert and listening. Through the crack of my door we whispered back and forth, debating what it might be. Finally he announced it must be Amah having a nightmare. We then boldly lit a lantern and Liu went through my bedroom to the little back hall and called up to Amah, who slept in the attic. Eventually he was obliged to climb halfway up the ladder. At last, with a final wild screech, she came to consciousness and our worry was ended.

During that spring, the military leaders of the three western provinces— Yunnan, Kweichow, and Szechwan—had been at odds. Yunnan troops had been in Chengtu for a long time; they were eased out at the end of April, and we were glad to see them go. Unrest continued, however.[1] In early July

1. At the end of 1915, President Yuan Shih-kai announced that he was changing his title to emperor. The first to say no was a Yunnanese general, and his first move was to invade Szechwan, where the local commander had decided to stick with Yuan rather than the Republic. The next-door province of Kweichow quickly joined the Republicans and also invaded Szechwan. Yuan fell, but the Yunnan and Kweichow armies remained. Szechwan had obvious attractions: it was many times richer and more populous than their own provinces, and control of even a part of Szechwan's opium trade was a prize worth fighting for. First, a Yunnan general was top man in Chengtu. By the spring of 1917 he apparently decided that his position was a bit exposed: he withdrew to the southwest of the province (where he could still control the Min and Yangtze rivers). The Kweichow commander then aspired to control Chengtu. Szechwanese forces disagreed, hence the heavy fighting during the summer of 1917. (Kweichow lost this fight, but was not finished.)

stories of general warfare and indiscriminate burning of houses began to reach our mountaintop. As our carpenters and masons were all from the city, they became exceedingly nervous and kept wanting to return home.

When Bob left us on June 27, he had planned to return in a fortnight to check the construction and to bring money. He also expected to send some money by friends who would be coming ahead of him. Time went on and no money came—though plenty of rumors reached us every day. I borrowed all I could in order to pay the workmen and try to hold them. But no foreigner on the mountain had much silver, and things soon became desperate.

One Britisher arrived and reported that the city was in complete turmoil. Life there had become too dangerous for him; he knew that Bob would soon be coming to the hill. My reaction was the opposite. I knew Bob's only thought at such times was to help: to serve those in trouble. When there were dangers, his impulse was to go to the scene so he could help the weak to places of safety and try to prevent pillaging and burning. Our neighbors on Wenmiaogai said he was a "strong helper," and this pleased him greatly, though he never would repeat it outside his most intimate circle.

Later, I found that the *North China Herald* of Shanghai had carried a news item about Chengtu dated July 19, 1917:

> The sights in many of the burnt quarters of the city are truly heart-rending. Reuter's correspondent has not yet found any one who blames General Liu Tsun-hou for what has occurred. After General Tai Kan's exit the citizens raised flags in honor of Liu Tsun-hou. The French Consulate has suffered severe damage and is uninhabitable from shells and bricks crashing through the roof. Mr. Hibbard of the Canadian Mission saved the missionary girls' school; Mr. Cook of the Church Missionary Society put out a fire near his mission; and Mr. R. R. Service of the Y.M.C.A. saved the American Methodist Hospital and also put out a fire threatening the block of buildings which contains the offices of the American Bible Society and the Foreign Office.

This last mentioned block also contained the post office, and Bob received the warm thanks of the postal commissioner. The *Herald's* correspondent did not know that Bob was also sheltering some schoolgirls in our house. The American Methodist girls' school had closed for the summer vacation, but it had been impossible to send home some of the boarding pupils. With the city in such chaos and full of roving soldiery, the teacher in charge did not dare to leave them in the school building, so she brought them to our quiet home. Bob turned over the place, and the girls settled in the downstairs rooms, leaving him the study. Where Bob slept was determined by the fighting; it was cooler upstairs, but bullets came through now and then. The girls were in the house for several weeks. When they left, the Hoffmans, who lived near the university and the south parade ground, came and occupied our house for a while. Many bodies of men killed in the fighting lay unburied for a long time on the parade ground; the Hoffmans were anxious to get away from the vicinity.

In the meantime, I had given my last dollar to the cook on July 12. Things were at an impasse. There was no choice but to send a runner for Bob. This is the only time in our married life when we were separated that I sent for my husband, and he understood that it was not because of my own fear or of my own will. I was responsible for our workmen and had to have assistance, being at the end of my resources.

On the night of July 16 we were having what the Irish term a "tempest." Torrents of rain were falling, and our house shook with the heavy reverberations of thunder, seemingly beneath our very feet. There had been no word from Bob and I was disappointed. The cook and I figured that the messenger should be back; we had begun to fear that he had been frightened by the fighting or perhaps seized by soldiery and impressed as a load carrier. I had almost fallen asleep when, soon after ten, I heard Bob's whistle. By the time I had roused the cook, Bob was fumbling at the door. We hastily lit candles and lanterns. What a sight met our eyes!

Bob had come on his horse. He reached the foothills late in the day and had to cross a torrent by a plank bridge. The horse slipped off with Bob on his back. They both rolled together in the raging water among the boulders, Bob weighed down by his money pouch full of silver dollars. They were fortunate to get out with only a few cuts and bruises, for there had been tragedies at that crossing.

The pony was left at the temple at the base of our mountain, and the priests insisted on giving Bob some hot tea and rice and a small native oil lantern. He came up the mountain by a very steep path that we called The Devil's Stairway. Soon the lantern fell and broke. He struggled on "by feeling" and by the fitful illumination of the lightning. Every stitch was soaked. Blood ran down in a trickle by one ear. His hat had been lost in the stream. He looked haggard and worn. But he was there and he assured me that all was well.

That was one time when I cried. When I saw Bob, I just sat down and wept; and even the cook knew why. He went out to the kitchen, blew up the coals of the coke fire, scrambled eggs and heated up some chicken, and told Bob that I had not eaten much for two days and he thought I had been worried. Of course Bob said that he did not want any trouble taken to prepare food at that hour. But, always the athlete and mindful of his physique, he tore off his wet garments and gave himself a brisk rubdown. Finally, after I had taken care of his cuts, he sat in pyjamas and wrapped in a blanket while we both ate our late snack together.

My troubles were over. Bob reassured the men, paid out money, and reported that other men were on their way (for some had already left because I lacked money to pay them). His presence and plenty of dollars worked wonders for the construction. In a week we were moved into the new bungalow. And Bob was off to the city, where things were still far from calm.

I was happy on the hill fixing up Round Top, and every letter from Bob told of his delight. *A home of our own!* It harked back to days before our marriage when he often used to hope for such a place. Those who had wondered about its plan now came to see; they agreed that the house was not only possible but that it was also pleasant and indeed all that one might wish for on our site. I sewed curtains and fixed wall lamps made of little Standard Oil tin lamps in Chinese glass cases. We did everything we could to make the place look like a home.[2] When Bob came for a few days in August, we had a gloriously happy time. A big chicken supper for all the adults on the hill was one event: twenty were present.

One September night when the lads and I were there alone we had a terrific storm. The thunder rolled with its most alarming resonance, and it seemed, as Grandmother used to say during Iowa tornadoes, that we could "taste brimstone." The next morning we discovered that the big wooden tub for catching rain water that stood under the eaves at the southwest corner of the house had been hit by lightning. Several wooden staves had been twisted and torn as though they had been cloth. We were lucky that the lightning struck so near water. That day it rained eight inches in a few hours.[3]

When we returned from furlough the year before, we had brought a

2. Our family spent five summers (1917–21) in this house on White Deer Summit. For us boys they were happy times. Many things must have contributed. One obvious plus was that, compared with life in the city, we were free. No compound walls; no traveling by sedan chair to other distant compounds; no need to arrange and schedule play. Soon there were about twenty bungalows (each a family) scattered about the almost undeveloped top of a mountain. For the children it was something like an idyllic and extended version of a city block in small-town America. But this freedom was possible, in a sense, only because our stockaded mountaintop was itself a super-compound. Except for our servants, no Chinese lived on the mountain: we were our own little world. Proof of the distance from unhygienic China was the fact that on the mountain, and only on the mountain, we were permitted to go barefoot or—usually preferable on account of wear and tear—to don Chinese straw sandals.

When travel to China became possible for Americans, White Deer Summit was one of the places I wanted to return to. On my first visits to Chengtu, none of my guides had ever heard of the mountain. By the third visit, in 1980, I had done some research. I hired a car, rode to the base of the mountain, and walked up (via the Devil's Stairway, in a miserable drizzle). It was easy to find our site: Round Top was the highest knob. But nothing remained except the rough, squared, sandstone blocks that had been the bases for the posts. After the last foreigners had left (about 1950), the farmers from below had regarded the houses as abandoned. Gradually the houses were dismantled to salvage the building materials. Today the mountaintop has become a plantation of medicinal herbs; and the small crew who work there have built a much simpler hut.

3. I always had somewhat of a proprietary attitude about this lightning strike. My bed was in the corner nearest to the tub, so my head may have been only about six feet away. Perhaps, since our house was the highest point of the mountain, without even large trees around it, it is surprising that we were not hit more often. One feature of living on a mountaintop was that we were completely dependent on rainfall for our water supply. Fortunately, summer was the rainy season; and we had plenty of rain-catching tubs.

portable Columbia "Grafonola." We enjoyed it all year, but it was at the mountain that we got the acme of pleasure from it. As we passed through the villages people used to ask whether we had brought the talking box. Women on tiny bound feet, old men and maidens, little urchins, countrymen, babies on backs, all climbed the long steep path to our hilltop and sat or stood entranced to hear what came forth from that box. I was often weary of cranking it, but the children were glad to relieve me. We served many cups of tea to these listeners and talked to them as well as we could (their mountain dialect was very different from what we were used to in the city). Sometimes they brought their corn pones and sat quietly outside as music was played in our living room. They especially liked songs by Harry Lauder: they said he sounded happy even though they could not understand the words.

That year we suffered greatly from the censoring of our letters. Some of them reached us as mere lacework. And for some mysterious reason the American postal authorities sent our letters via the Atlantic and Burma! It would appear that they expected the Burma-China border to be equipped with railway service, whereas nothing of this sort is in existence even today. We constantly wrote our relatives to mark our letters "Via Seattle" or "Via San Francisco." But it did no good: the letters were still sent by Burma and took four months to reach us instead of the usual two by the Pacific. Furthermore, many letters sent the long way were lost and never reached us.

28

Shadows of a Distant War
(1917–18)

There were certain foreigners in Chengtu who felt that "missionaries" should not have contacts with any Chinese officials. During that summer a peculiarly subtle and insinuating letter was published in the *North China Herald*.[1] It hinted that "activities" and friendships between certain missionaries and officials in Szechwan were endangering the lives and well-being of all the foreigners in the province. It was signed "From the Cave of Abdullam." We knew who had instigated it, but for a time the authorship was a mystery. The community was interested to discover his identity, as Bob was not the only man mentioned. It finally came out that the writer was a British teacher in one of the government schools. He had often come to our house and had as often been treated in a friendly manner. Feeling against him became very strong, and he lost all the contacts he had enjoyed among the missionary group.

Bob was an American Y secretary, loaned to the Chinese YMCA movement. He was responsible to the China National Committee of the Y; and it was his business to cultivate and know Chinese students, gentry, and officials. In all his relations, he took the most scrupulous care to maintain an even balance between all the military and civilian factions among the Chinese community. He was able to make these men feel that he was not partisan, and sought the welfare of all, the peace of the city, and the good of every one.

He had been amused to hear that he had been reported to be "an enemy of General X." When General X left town he had sent a special messenger with a particularly fine gift as a token of his regard, thanking Bob for all his kindness to himself and his troops, who had been entertained at the Y's science hall. Bob sent word that he could not accept: a donation to the YMCA would be better. Another official sent a military decoration. Still another presented

1. The letter appeared in the *Herald* of July 21, 1917.

many rolls of Kweichow pongee, excellent for men's suits. Bob did not accept any gifts that had been offered because of his position in the Y.

We heard through Chinese and others that a certain man had said he would force Bob out of the province, that he had collected information on his friendship with officials, and would use it "at the proper time." One of the generals told Bob he had been informed that we were people without social standing of any kind and should not be received by officials. The general laughingly said that whether or not Bob had social standing elsewhere, he certainly did have it in Chengtu, and that he was glad to have him as a friend![2]

The American consul of our district [resident in Chungking] knew of our work and friendships in Chengtu and never criticized them at all. It could be said that the criticisms were an indication of Bob's success in making contacts. He refused to let these rancorous statements bother him and carried on in his normal way. He always took pleasure in his social contacts with Chinese. In the good fellowship around the table at feasts he seemed to expand, become a raconteur, and surprised those who knew him as a quiet man at gatherings of his own nationals.[3]

Personally I suffered greatly that year. It started with rheumatism in January and then proceeded into neuritis. It seemed that pain lived with me, and I wondered how it would be to feel free from that bondage. I sought to fill my days so that I would have little time to think of my own limitations.

We Americans had an American Association, partly to keep up our feeling of being separate from the British, and partly to facilitate contacts with our consul in Chungking. I happened to be the secretary. Our group had been raising money for the Red Cross. That spring we decided to give a large benefit for the French Red Cross. To supplement the local activities, I circularized every American in Szechwan, asking for contributions to our fund.

There were still a few Germans in Chengtu, and one of them had been to Chungking. When he returned, he brought a few cases of groceries for a couple of young Americans. The road had been blocked for travel, and anyone was glad to find some way to get his goods transported. (Our own trunks, which had to be left in Chungking when we returned from furlough

---

2. Bob's social contacts with Chengtu's officialdom do seem to have been unusual. Grace's diary indicates at least seven personal meetings with the governor of Szechwan in 1914 and six in 1915. My experience as a consular officer in China was limited, but I can understand how a local consul could, in one of Grace's favorite expressions, "have his nose out of joint." A part of the basis for Bob's cordial official relations was certainly the fact that he was representing an organization with a Chinese board of directors who were leaders in the local community.

3. Bob's conviviality at the feast table seems all the more noteworthy because he would normally be the only person present who was a teetotaler. Grace is right: there was a kind of instant rapport between Bob and most Chinese, which showed itself in a vivacious and lighthearted side of his personality.

in 1916, still sat there—filled with clothes for the children and many other things we needed.) Some of our British friends, more violent in their outlook at this time than the French, heard of this kindness done for Americans by a German. The fat was in the fire.

As secretary of the American Association, I received a letter from the French saying that, in view of our contacts with Germans, they could not permit us to give a benefit for the French Red Cross. We gave up our benefit plans, but at quiet teas in our homes we passed the hat until we had a suitable gift to forward to the French. We knew who was back of the whole business: our consul asked for information, and a letter from our association informed him of the facts.[4]

Obviously, it had now become impossible to maintain friendly relations with the Germans who remained in Chengtu. Much as they sought to keep up their end of the acquaintance, we had to drop them. I wrote a note to one of the ladies whom I had enjoyed and felt glad to know before this trouble began. She did not reply, and neither did her husband; but another German, a single man, who evidently held great rancor and wished to voice it, wrote an exceedingly nasty note which rankled in my heart for days. How wrong war can be, thus to taint even the contacts of isolated Westerners living on the other side of the globe from the field of combat![5] Now all these matters can be disposed of in a few sentences; at the time they made a vast amount of talk and could create misunderstanding and hard feeling even between friends of the same nationality.

Not all was bad. The attitude of the British consul, which at first was critical toward Americans, grew more friendly as the war progressed and officials of his nation were required to show friendliness to Americans.[6] We had some debate about whether we should follow the example of our homelands in things like "meatless" or "sugarless" days. But there was no shortage where

4. The "instigator" of the anonymous letter and the person "back of the whole business" was the British consul general in Chengtu. Meyrick Hewlett held this post from 1916 to 1922. His book *Forty Years In China* (London: Macmillan & Co., 1943) has much interesting detail about Chengtu and the labyrinthine politics of the day. The theme of the letter was that the friendship of some missionaries (prominently Bob) with a particular military leader or political group could bring retribution on the heads of all missionaries if some other group seized power. The complaint was imaginary. The interests of an organization like the YMCA required that it have the approval (and, if possible, active support) of the governing authorities; and it is clear that the Y under Bob's leadership was consistently successful in gaining this, despite several sharp changes in the warlord governments.

5. Grace might have noted that, except for the British and French consuls, all of the people involved were missionaries preaching the Word of the same God.

6. Grace concedes that Consul General Hewlett became more agreeable, but suggests that it was because he had received instructions to be more friendly to Americans. Be that as it may, my own recollections of the consul general are all favorable. Each year on Empire Day (May 24) we were all invited to his garden party. There was a small circular enclosure heaped with small gifts. Each child had a pole with a line and hook to fish for goodies. If I remember rightly, there was no limit on the number of fish that one might catch.

we were, and any renunciation by us could not possibly assist the war effort. So most of us kept on in our normal way of life, saving all we could for the constant appeals for war funds.

One thing we could do was knit. We Americans did it for the American Expeditionary Force in Siberia. As long as the wool lasted, I knit a sweater a week. These were of the sleeveless sort. After much effort, we managed to get some wool up river. Finally, no more of the heavy sweater wool could be had. So we turned to socks, until that wool also gave out.

I agreed to take on the work of statistical secretary of the West China Missions Advisory Board. This involved sending information forms to all missionaries in the provinces of Kweichow, Yunnan, and Szechwan, tabulating these returns, and then compiling a list with all their names and titles (in English and Chinese) and various other relevant details. It was a job that took time and much attention of a painstaking variety which is rarely appreciated; and there was no pay. After some years at the job I did receive a word of appreciation from someone at the Coast who spoke of our West China statistics as being the best received.

Our children always had pets, and there was a procession of them through these years: dogs, cats, rabbits, monkeys, ponies, a badger, goldfish, canaries, turtles, and various other animals that came our way. Dick wanted a goat. The coolie, thinking of the commission on such a purchase, brought one to the compound. I found it tethered to the fence near the tennis court. Dick knew that I hated the everlasting blatting of these creatures, so he stood by to assure me, "this goat uses its mouth only for eating." The young goat promptly added a vociferous blat to his remark, thereby killing the deal.

During these days I was teaching English to a Chinese businessman older than I. He was a fat, jolly person with a charming manner, a big family, and ambitions of taking a world tour where English would be useful. As long as I knew the family and as often as I heard them speak of various relatives, I was never able to unravel the relationships in their home circle. His first wife had died, leaving a number of grown and adolescent children. The grown sons had families. Also the father had several concubines with children. Then he had married a second time about a dozen years previous to the time of which I write, and this new "real wife" (with the status of a Number One) had already borne him eight children. In addition there were various older relatives, hangers-on and dependents, and a swarm of servants. Certainly, fifty to sixty people lived in the house—which was dirty and poorly kept in spite of the many helpers.

We had known the family for years, but after I began to teach the husband, I found that he was placing considerable trust in me. This resulted in some responsibility which I unwittingly incurred. The husband had to go into hiding. In disturbed times such as we were experiencing in Szechwan, with rival warlords and various military coups changing the rulers of the province, wealthy men were in danger of being seized and squeezed (even tortured!) until their tormentors had extracted every dollar they could wring from them and their family. The Szechwan expression for this was "grabbing a fat pig," and that was the danger that the husband faced.

When the husband left the city, he knew his wife was not well. He told his family that if she did not improve, they were to send for me and do whatever I said. He said nothing to me of this situation. When he told me good-bye, he asked if I would be willing to advise his wife should she need it. Thinking this was a polite way of hinting that I was a woman of discernment, I agreed to do so.

I soon found that my responsibility was heavier than I had ever dreamed. A messenger came to tell me that the wife was ill and wished to see me. I immediately called on her and found her in a bad way; she lacked appetite, was as thin as a thread, and seemed worried and nervous. She would not hear of entering the only missionary hospital for women, or even of going there by sedan chair for an examination. I finally got her to agree that I could bring a foreign doctor to see her at her own home. I accompanied this gentleman (our good friend, Dr. W. R. Morse).

The wife was in bed, where she had been for some time. She was dressed in stiff satin, even wearing a flat satin bandeau-like bonnet, much affected by Chinese ladies in those days. She looked more like a clay figure than a flesh-and-blood woman. Her bed was a mammoth wooden structure enclosed by curtains fastened tightly down on three sides and drawn apart in front. Chinese beds are placed with one side, not the headboard, against a wall, so these drawn curtains were on the front of the bed. At the rear and about two feet higher than the bed there was a long shelf with small drawers below. On the shelf were medicines, food, tea, and a great collection of oddments. In the drawers, some of them half open, were more eatables, rolls of silver dollars, jewels, and a heterogeneous lot of treasured possessions.

At first she did not want to permit the doctor to touch her; after persuasion, this was allowed. Then there was the problem of an abdominal examination. I had to get into the bed, where I sat awkwardly at its foot inside the curtain. A Chinese woman (servant, relative, or what-not) got in at the head of the bed. Finally, with all her clothing on and the curtains partially drawn around the four of us, the doctor was permitted to lay a hand on the patient's well-covered abdomen. After a great deal of talk, the physician assured us all—the room by this time was crowded with people, including several grown-up stepsons—that the wife had anemia and urgently needed hospital care, good food of a suitable kind, rest, and tonics.

I made several visits before I could obtain her consent to this departure from her usual course of life. Finally, a day was set. I sent word to the hospital, where I had prepared the way and spoken for a private room. I went to the house to escort her to the hospital—but she was in bed as usual with all her things about her. She had decided that she could not go. Everything depended on her: she gave out all the money; her hands, weak as they were, controlled every detail of the establishment. She kept insisting that she could not think of leaving. "Yes, you can," said I, "you can leave the housekeeping affairs with your old aunt." She demurred, but I sat down and said that I would stay until she was ready for me to escort her to the hospital.

She was horrified at this and was sure that my children needed me at home, and that it would soon be time for my noon meal. "Don't worry about me," I told her, "I can eat whatever you have here." After I had stayed three hours and eaten a meal, she capitulated. She ordered her sedan chair, changed her clothes, and made ready to leave. I took her to the women's hospital run by the Canadian Methodist Mission. For days she was nervous and ill at ease, and I made several visits to reassure her. For one thing, she hated the comfortable iron hospital bed. It seemed so open and exposed! I asked that the bed be moved into a corner. This was done, but she told me the next day that she had been unable to sleep. In the dead of night, when left alone by the nurse, she had dragged her mattress off onto the floor and slept there! As she expressed it, "I've had eight children, but I've never slept in a bed without sides."

The bathing of her person and the daily cleaning of her room were more trials, and she was greatly irked because no chickens were allowed in the room. She kept telling me, as she told the nurses, that chickens loved to be around under foot and would pick up scraps and keep floors clean. I am glad to say that the wife improved greatly in the hospital. She even became fond of some of the innovations (to her) which she came to know were rules of life there. When I last heard of her, she was a patroness of the institution.

About this time a Chinese friend of Bob's felt, because of a sudden political change, that his life was in great danger. He came to us secretly at night, begging shelter. We kept him on the condition that he remain in our guest room, holding no communication with anyone. Bob then arranged his affairs with another Chinese friend. After forty-eight hours in our home, the man was able to leave at night in the care of his friend, who was a well-known man in the city. A few years later, in happier times, the man who had sought refuge returned from the Coast and came to call. He brought gifts and said that he owed his life to our discretion. Then, before we realized it, he was on his knees to perform the kowtow. Bob quickly stepped to his side and raised him, saying that we did not need such proof of his feeling.

We were saddened in April 1918 by the death of Mother Service. She was eleven years younger than her husband, and we had never thought she might go first. It was hard to realize that death had come so close to us while we were going on as usual about our small daily affairs. No cablegram had been sent to us, even to say that she was ill, so it was a shock to open an ordinary envelope and be confronted with such news. She had always been lovely to me, and I knew her as a person with a deep understanding of life.

29

Our Mountain Home

(1918)

It was wonderful that year to have the bungalow waiting for us. After all the summers spent hither and yon, amid this or that discomfort, it seemed too good to be true to have a place of our own. The mountain, White Deer Summit, stands by itself, a bit in front of the main range. Although its elevation is 6,000 feet, it is actually only a foothill. In one direction, we looked out over the Chengtu plain, 4,000 feet below. In the other, we had a fine panorama of mountain peaks, rising in the far distance to perhaps 20,000 feet. Most of the nearer mountains we named, and climbed, during the summers we spent there. Some day these Szechwan alps will be as popular as European and American mountains.[1]

Szechwan is a land of cloud and vapor. Winds constantly moved cloud-masses around our summit, and often we seemed to be in the center of a vortex of moving cloud. On one side we could see immense, puffy vapor-forms going one way while on the other side of the house the same sort of cloud-masses were moving in the opposite direction. The effects of these heavenly changes made us at times feel that we lived in an unreal world. Beautiful colors at sunset spread all the glories of the sky, not only above us, but frequently at our very feet. And when the soft wetness of clouds lay on our summit we knew ourselves to be wrapped in the same down-like fluff which we could see on clear days lying on the distant peaks.

We never felt the restrictions of overpopulation or possible infection on that clean mountaintop, so the children could run about as American lads play in their own mountains. The two older boys had soon explored the mountain far and near and had a good knowledge of its hidden recesses. They maintained what they called a "scout camp" in the woods and used to

---

1. It has taken a long time, but Grace's prediction may be coming true. The Chinese have recently (1986) started developing large-scale tourist facilities in a nature reserve and scenic area at Jiuzhaigou (Nine Village Gorge) about two hundred miles north of White Deer Summit.

go there with another playmate for tremendous stuffings of fried potatoes and eggs, two things they learned to cook for themselves.[2] They took
the potatoes all pared and boiled, so it was not much work for the frying.
This was done in chicken fat, our commonest form of cooking oil in those
days. Chicken was our only summertime meat, beef and mutton not being
available.[3]

As soon as I reached the mountain, I began the construction of a summerhouse not far from our bungalow, and a laundry and fuel storeroom at the
rear of our lower-level kitchen yard. Later in the summer Bob brought up
some carpenters and started them on a large new veranda off our living
room.[4] This was like an extra room. It stood high off the ground and somewhat overhung the cliff along the outer edge. By making it semicircular, we
did not have to cut down as many trees. We had bamboo sun blinds, a hammock, rattan chairs, and small tables. How many happy hours we spent
there, alone and with friends! The children liked the open rafters, where they
were allowed to climb like young monkeys. The additional space was especially welcome for chicken suppers and such high jinks because we could
take in more friends and be that much the happier. Day and night, and in the
moonlight, the veranda was lovely.

That summer we took a fine trip to Tientai, an 8,000-foot mountain on
the next range. We spent a night at the temple on the summit. The main
work at the temple was preparing soda ash by burning bracken gathered on
the slopes. A big fire of this, all banked with ashes in a particular way, was
kept burning for many days. Lower down on the mountain there was a small
factory where a certain variety of scrub bamboo was made into coarse brown
paper, using this same soda ash. We could hear the workers cutting the bamboo and taking it to chutes down which it was rushed to the steeping vats
below. All this with many shouts and cries.

The views from Tientai (which means Terrace of Heaven) were lovely and
gave us a wider sweep than from our own hill. Nothing exceeds the summer
verdure of these wild mountains. The varying shades of green rest the eyes,
and there are flowers in the glens, marvelous glimpses of land- and cloud-
scapes, and tinkling waterfalls throwing a sudden spray of silver over green

2. Our camp, where we built a simple lean-to in the thickest part of the woods, was a secret
known only to the four members. Nearby was a low spot that was obviously a favorite wallow
for wild pigs. And in the soft earth we thought once that we were seeing the paw mark of a
leopard. Our sketchy ideas of scouting came from the magazine *Boys' Life*.

3. Beef (water buffalo) and mutton (goat) could be found in this part of China only in the
larger towns. Pork, however, was easily available even in the small mountain villages. But we,
and our fellow foreigners, never considered using pork—which to the Chinese *is* "meat"—
except in the rather uncommon form of ham. In eating Chinese food, pork of course could not
be avoided—and we all enjoyed it.

4. The porch can be seen in figure 27. One thing nice about it was that its outer edge put us
above the trees.

bank or rocky cliff. We had no definite schedule but roamed as we pleased. Dick we had left with Mrs. Canright, as he was too young for the climbing, but Ted Canright took his place with us and thus we had three boys for the excursion.

There was some excitement at one wild spot where the road crossed the river. The bridge was merely a series of tree trunks sawed in two lengthwise and laid from boulder to boulder. Iron chains through a hole at one end kept the logs from being swept away by the frequent summer floods, though of course they had to be relaid on their boulders. I was using a light mountain sedan chair and was glad to be carried across such places. But my rear carrier was a big man who was afraid of becoming dizzy, so we had to get someone to take his place on the chair while he trusted his bulk to the strong limbs and steady head of a small load-carrier. The lads also were taken over on the backs of carriers. Generally in such spots there were swinging bridges, but at that particular place the banks were too low.

The cook made a lot of jelly from mountain crab apples that year. It was so delicious that it was hard to save enough for our return to the city. It was especially enjoyed during the winter with our roast goose at holiday time. We always missed real apples in Szechwan, but now they have been introduced there [by the missionaries] and can be bought each year with greater ease.

Bob, as usual, was down in Chengtu most of the summer and came up to us now and then. He was away in late August when we had a visit from a thief. Our bedroom windows all had stout vertical wooden bars. I was not afraid at night but kept a small kerosene lantern lit and turned down very low. By experimenting, I had found that the best draft-free place for this was on the floor under my dressing table. On rainy nights I always put my clothes inside a closet or cupboard, but this particular night was not damp and when I undressed I had laid them on Bob's bed.

In the middle of the night I woke suddenly to a queer little tinkling sound. My bed was in a corner and against the wall. When I opened my eyes they fell at once on a peculiar sight. Some white object, *entirely without legs or feet,* was slowly moving across the room toward the window farthest from me. Of course, without glasses I could not see well, for I am very nearsighted. But I could see enough to make me sure the object itself was not of a terrifying nature. No matter what it was, with one leap I threw off the bedclothes and seized the specter in both hands. It proved to be my corset, and the jingle which had wakened me was the rattle of the hose supporters. As soon as I took hold of it, I realized that there was a long bamboo pole involved. I found myself holding one end while Mr. Robber held the other. He could see me, but I had only a fleeting glimpse of his form outside the window, for I immediately let forth a piercing shriek of "Robbers! come quickly!"

The pilferer dropped his pole in hot haste and tore off into the shrubbery before the servants could come.

There was a guest in the house (Miss Wellwood, familiarly known as Lucy Belle). I called to ask if she missed any of her belongings, Yes, all her underclothing was gone! The children awoke, even Amah came into my room, and there was great talk and excitement. As soon as I heard the man leave, I had thrown open my bedroom door, which gave onto the small front veranda. The first thing that came to my eye there was a snug little white bundle. This proved to be Lucy Belle's underwear. The robber had taken her things first and was at mine when he was stopped. He did get off with a few pieces of mine, but he had been too frightened to remember the other bundle.

The children looked to see if their things were safe, but Amah had put away everything there, so the robber found nothing to tempt him in their room. What most provoked me was that I had a loaded revolver in the chiffonier and should have fired it in the air as soon as the man left. He would at least have known that we had arms. We always had a revolver in such mountain places, and let it be known that we had one, for it acted as a preventative. I do not recall that we used it more than once or twice, and always to fire into the air. However, Bob was a man who felt one should have firearms. He kept a revolver and a shotgun for years in China, never with a thought of using them against Chinese but only to fill a certain need in his mind. He simply considered that people in faraway places should have such things.

That summer we finally received the trunks and boxes that we had had to leave in Chungking. From the summer of 1916 when we had packed the trunks in East Cleveland, Ohio, to the summer of 1918 when they arrived in Chengtu was a long wait. But one box was not received, and to this day has never been found. We could have spared groceries better than that particular case, for it held all the books we had purchased in America plus a number of old ones—including my Bible. We had bought extra books for the children and did not use them in Ohio, telling the youngsters we would have them all fresh to read to them in China. It was a vain hope. All had our names, and often addresses, written in them, so one would think we might have heard of them.

Bob unpacked the trunks in Chengtu before I returned from the mountain. The first one was our newest and best trunk, which held most of the new woolens we had bought in America. The blankets, sheets, and other items were in good condition. Another trunk had been riddled by moths and silver fish. Crib blankets were a sight. Bob lost four good American suits which he had counted on for the coming years. The third trunk, packed with woolens, had evidently been dropped in the river. Everything was ruined, but a few things could be used in spite of their drenching. My winter coat was faded on one side, but it still kept me warm and I used it for some years in that condition.

Perhaps the greatest thrill of these long-delayed boxes was the arrival of a real, honest-to-goodness American cook stove. On October 2, after cooking on a native makeshift stove for twenty-two months, we had a meal prepared on this new range. I took great pride in my kitchen in those days, and no one could find much satisfaction in a dirty, smoky, coke-burning stove of the Szechwan type with its hard-to-manage oven and "fire-eye" holes that were so hard on our foreign saucepans.

That fall we received some Tibetan rugs from the Ogdens. They had been very helpful to us at Tatsienlu in the summer of 1908 but had now moved on and fulfilled their dream of establishing their mission in Batang. The rugs were made by boys and women in their mission, and they needed to sell them to support the work. I had been asked to act as Chengtu agent and agreed out of friendship for these faraway people, thirty days' travel away. The rugs were attractive, and Chengtu people bought quite a number.

Bob and I were sitting quietly by the fire one evening when a note came in from Newton Hayes, Bob's associate in the Y. We supposed it was some local matter and opened it without any special thrill. When we read the words "THE WAR IS OVER" we were greatly excited and could talk of little else for days. The word reached us in Chengtu on November 13.

30

Bob Reaches Forty

(1919)

Since early that year [1918] we had been expecting George and Ruth Helde. We were naturally pleased to have a new couple for the Y, and this addition held a particular joy. On the Pacific crossing to China in 1916, Ruth Tolman had been a favorite among those we met on shipboard. She had married George Helde at language school in Peking. We had expected them in the spring, but the Legation [believing that travel was unsafe] would not permit them to start for the West. They finally reached Chungking early in November and we welcomed them to Chengtu on the twenty-third. Bob rode out about forty *li* to meet them, and we were all excited and pleased.

The very next week was Thanksgiving, and I was full of plans and work. The American community was to have dinner with us. Our house was not adequate, so a large unused room at the Student Y next door was borrowed. We had it thoroughly cleaned and whitewashed, and a carpenter put together a table to fit the crowd. I had only my own linen, dishes, and silver, so things took some arranging. It helped to have the children eat first, and my cheap silver plate that we had for the mountains all came in handy. We made the room lovely with tall feathery bamboos standing around the walls, and the table was cheerful with the bright colors of autumn fruits and chrysanthemums.

At 11:00 o'clock there was a Thanksgiving service at the American Methodist compound. A subscription was taken for Red Cross work with the [American] expedition in Siberia. They had sent us a plea for help, as there was great need among prisoners of war and refugees in the cold weather there. We were on this day able to raise some $750 to send the Red Cross for this work.[1] As soon as the service was over, the Americans began to wander

1. When Grace did not specify, it can be assumed that she was referring to Chinese dollars. The Chinese dollar was usually about half the value of the American dollar, but at this time (1918) it was worth a little more than the American dollar.

along to our house [about fifteen minutes by foot or sedan chair] and very soon drifted over to our improvised dining room.

Of course, other American women helped in preparing food, but all the geese had to be kept hot in our range. By a good deal of careful scheming by our cook, we had hot and attractive food. There were no turkeys in Szechwan, so goose was best for the main dish. The mince and pumpkin pies were excellent, the hot rolls superb, and the coffee extra good. One of the Methodist ladies was responsible for the latter. We had hired a large charcoal stove such as the Chinese use for providing tea at large parties. This was in a small side room and provided as much boiling water and coffee as any emergency could demand. Charcoal braziers warmed the dining room. Thirty-one adults and sixteen children gathered for this celebration.[2]

Early in December the YMCA ended its membership campaign with a total of 1,008 paid members. Bob was much pleased. There were several celebrations that month in honor of the end of the war. We especially enjoyed the large reception by the military governor to celebrate the Allies' victory.[3] The courts of the *yamen* were hung with many red banners; some one told us that over five hundred were used. The Heldes were our guests during this period and we enjoyed taking them about with us.

The end of the year was saddened by the fact that one of the Chinese Y secretaries had to be dismissed for taking a secondary wife, of his own choice, when he already had a wife, chosen by his parents and not to his liking. These situations are very difficult; here the circumstances were particularly hard. If he had sought a divorce openly, the change might have been achieved in the spirit of compromise that the Chinese know so well; but he had used deception, and the whole thing was not pleasant. Bob had much sympathy for him, but under the circumstances he could not remain working in a Christian organization.

In these years mail and telegrams were constantly being delayed by fighting and rumors of fighting.[4] On January 5, 1919, we received fifteen telegrams from the Coast. Most of them were about war relief funds. One told us that the Heldes were on their way. As they had arrived six weeks earlier, they could laugh with us. When the news came of the death of Theodore Roosevelt,

2. In my memory this American occasion has had special significance because we were to be forty-eight—one for each state. Could it be that forty-eight were expected and one was unable to get there?

3. The victory celebration, so far as China was concerned, was to prove an empty one. In the postwar settlement at Versailles, China's allies (including the United States) allowed Japan to take over the German colony of Tsingtao and former German rights in Shantung. Chinese resentment, culminating in the May Fourth Movement (of 1919), was a milestone in turning China away from the Western democracies and toward the Russian model.

4. It was not only fighting that might delay telegrams. In those prewireless days, there was only a copper wire strung across hundreds of bandit-infested miles. Copper was valuable: it could be made into money or brass cartridges.

the Chinese asked us many questions. The seemed to admire "Luo Si-fu" and were always interested in anecdotes about him.

That month I made myself a dress entirely by hand. It was crepe satin of a lovely soft shade of grey. I had a pattern from America. The dress itself was severely plain, almost like a square-necked slip. To wear with it, I had a black velvet tunic, an old-rose fichu affair of georgette, and a lavendar over-dress in the new, long, straight panel effect with silk fringe of the same color at the lower edge. I had sent to a California dressmaker for the tunic and fichu, and Mabelle Yard bought the over-dress for me in America. It really gave me three costumes. High-lacing grey shoes were a perfect match with the crepe satin, and a black velvet hat completed the ensemble.

That winter Bob was talking of a trip for the next summer up into the timber country of our old friend, Yao Bao-san. In 1918 Yao lived some six months on our compound in Chengtu, and many were the tales he told us. Bob wanted to take me and the two older boys to see the wild border country that Yao described in such an interesting way.[5] He had me order khaki riding clothes from Shanghai. To go with the breeches I had short slit skirts, buttoning straight up mid-front and mid-back. There were also khaki Norfolk jackets with pockets, and I made soft pongee shirts. After all these preparations, the trip into the high timber did not materialize that year, but the clothes were fine for White Deer Summit. Khaki was hard to get that year, and a supply that we ordered for the lads' clothes was lost en route on the river. I finally found some locally, but at the price I had to pay it would have been much cheaper to dress them in pure silk of heavy quality.

In January Bob took the two older boys and the Heldes up to White Deer Summit for a few days, and they all enjoyed the snow.[6] I spent the time while they were away trying to get rid of some of my pain. I rested, dozed, and took massage from a friend kind enough to devote time to me, but it seemed that nothing was of much help. Bob came back with an attack of malaria, which usually showed up each winter but usually did not keep him down for more than a day or two. This spell in 1919 was longer than most, and he was in bed a week, making light of his afflictions. After he had an ulcerated tooth pulled, he was soon fit again and at his work as usual.

I was having painful dentistry done that spring and once took small Dick with me to the dentist. When he knew I was suffering, he came to the chair,

5. The country that interested Bob was west of the Min River, north of Kwanhsien. It was somewhat similar to the high country around Tatsienlu, lying along the eastern edge of the Tibetan plateau and populated mainly by Tibetans, with Chinese living as traders in the towns. Along the lower valley slopes there were conifer forests. Yao was in the business of cutting logs and floating them downstream, into the Min, and finally to Chengtu.

6. Snow was a novelty because it was never seen in Chengtu. But Bob had more on his mind than just seeing snow. He passionately loved ice cream and had lived for thirteen years in Chengtu without any. Our mission was to check the loading of an improvised ice house: it was an undertaking that seemed to mystify all the Chinese involved. (To be continued.)

took my hand and kissed it fervently. It amused the dentist, who said he had never seen such a thing from a five-year-old lad.[7] I was busy knitting socks for our men in Siberia. And greatly to my enjoyment, I wrote a paper on "The Sonnet," which I presented before our Fortnightly Club in April.[8] On spare evenings I plugged away at the old mission statistics, which always filled any gap in the routine of daily existence. With teaching and household duties, my time was more than full.

That spring Newton Hayes had a bad time with his eyes. He was living with us, and we both tried to help him as much as possible. He could not use his eyes and had to sit with a dark shade over them, his back to the window. He was able to help me, though, by hearing Jack do his school reading. The text was *The Courtship of Miles Standish;* Jack read it off in good style. We finally had to arrange for Newton to go down river. Among other things, this meant green and red curtains for the inside of his boat to protect against the glare.

There was much illness in the city that spring. One pathetic case was the cook who had worked for fifteen years for the Methodist ladies not far from us. He was working for them as usual up to five days before his death. When taken ill, he stayed in bed at his home just around the corner from the mission. Lulu Golisch had been in to see him several times. He sent word on Tuesday that he was getting better. Then on Wednesday afternoon he got out of his bed and went into the back room of his little place. He arranged two benches (*bandeng*) at a suitable distance from each other. On these he laid two narrow doors (Chinese doors turn on wooden pins and can easily be lifted out of their sockets). He then lay on the doors, composed himself, and asked his sister, who was taking care of his sick wife and himself, to send for Miss Golisch. A neighbor went for Lulu but came back to report that she had gone to the university. He then asked that someone stand on the street to call her in when she passed by on her way home. He told his sister to ask Lulu to look after his two little girls, left some word for his wife about his property, and just lay there and died. When Lulu came home about five that afternoon, they called her in and there he was, all "laid out" by his own hand. He had

---

7. So far as dentistry was concerned, Chengtu was one of the most fortunate cities in inland China. The medical school at the West China Union University had a dental department whose teaching staff included several highly qualified dentists from the Canadian Methodist Mission.

8. The Fortnightly Club can probably best be described as a literary society with broad interests. The evening meetings were held in members' homes and usually involved a potluck supper. Grace's topic was no idle interest: she wrote a good deal of poetry, and the sonnet form was a particular favorite (she liked the challenge that the formula imposed). Other organizations of the foreign community in Chengtu included the University Book Club and the West China Border Research Society, which by this time was publishing a regular journal. Another community effort was a monthly magazine, the *West China Missionary News,* to which Grace was an irregular contributor.

28   *The family in Chengtu about the time of Bob's fortieth birthday, 1919.*

been dead about twenty minutes. The Chinese know a lot about death, and they expect it—even prepare for it—in a way quite unknown to most of us.

Those years Bob carried on a large program of YMCA boys' clubs in the government schools. There were Bible study groups, athletics, English conversation classes, and oratory contests. All this activity took a vast amount of time and energy. The speeches given by the lads in the oratory contests were mostly on old Chinese heroes, and various teachers, both Chinese and foreign, were invited to be the judges. Bob thus became known to many boys of the city. Not long ago on the Coast I met a man who spoke of knowing Bob in one of these clubs. He said Bob was the first foreigner he had ever met, and that he wanted to meet others after meeting him. We never went on the street without seeing some young chaps smiling at us and greeting Bob in a friendly way.

At the end of May Bob was busy with an athletic meet that he had in charge.[9] I asked him what we should do about his fortieth birthday, which the Chinese consider a notable milestone on life's way and which was coming up on the fourth of June. He said he would invite some men guests for tea, so I had better have a good supply of cake and cookies. He had tried to keep the date from the Chinese, fearing they might get up some celebration. I was suspicious, though, when an embroidery man, who called on other business, told me his shop was preparing an embroidered scroll for Hsieh An-tao's birthday. The cook did his best and made heaps of cookies and such things on June 3, leaving cakes to be made on the birthday morning.

The chance never came. The next morning, before we were even up, there was a great clatteration in the *tingzi* in front of the house. The gateman called up that all the Y staff had arrived. It was indeed true! There they were, singing gay matins to awaken Bob. And of course all stomachs were empty. A good hot dish of *mian* (noodles) would have been better than the tea that we had to offer them, and the plates of small cakes and cookies simply vanished before their hungry advances. When their gifts had been received and they had gone, I was appalled. With such a beginning, no one could tell what the day would bring forth. I urged Bob to leave the compound, for if we could tell people he was not at home, surely they would not expect to come in and eat mightily.

When Bob did leave, I went over the situation with the cook. All meals were given the go-by for the day. The great need was for more sweets, cookies, and cakes for the afternoon. The cook was to keep to the kitchen and forgo all other errands; the coolie could run for him; and the Boy and Amah were to fetch and carry. In the meantime I sent a note to my faithful friend Lulu Golisch, asking her if she would play good neighbor and have her cook make some cookies for us. By that afternoon we had a truly formidable array of baked foods in sight. And thus, with the help of friends, we managed to come through the day. Bob received lovely gifts, among them several satin scrolls, colorful and emblazoned with good wishes. Chinese characters are so artistic that they make scrolls of great beauty without any other decoration.

After all the guests had gone, the Boy showed me the few vestiges of cakes and cookies that remained. I could have managed better a second time. But one has only one fortieth birthday![10]

9. The YMCA is usually credited with introducing modern sport competition into China. This included especially Ping-Pong, but also basketball and track and field athletics.

10. My understanding was that it was expected that a male member of a good Confucian family would have become a grandfather by the age of forty. This would ensure that the tablets of his ancestors (and himself) would properly be cared for. We three boys (aged nine to five) tried to keep out of the way but also found the day notable. Each group of well-wishers, all day long, seemed to arrive with firecrackers. Fantastic!

31

Climbing Higher
(1919)

The Round Top bungalow at White Deer Summit was more to our liking than ever that summer, and it took us only a couple of days to be all settled. It meant everything for the lads, who could roam and climb to their hearts' content. Cultivated fields with their unsavory fertilization were far below us: our mountaintop was all wild country.[1] Bob could join us only for long weekends now and then, but his visits were times of the greatest happiness. During cool, damp weather, we would have a coke fire in the living room fireplace. Many evenings we popped corn and sat with no light save that from the luminous coke. We especially loved this black fuel with its glowing, fiery incandescence topped by vivid blue, dancing flames.

Our youngsters came near missing their Fourth of July celebration. Fireworks that had been expected from Chengtu did not arrive. The few simple firecrackers that the cook was able to find at a village market had to suffice. Then about 6:00 P.M. on the Fourth, as I was returning from a stroll, the three boys met me with the exciting news that Lao Liu, Bob's horse coolie, had arrived. He had been delayed by a bad storm on the two-day trip from Chengtu. I hastily sent out a note inviting all the children on the hill (save a few with whooping cough). As soon as supper was finished, we hung "Old Glory" in front of the bungalow, and everything was set for a gay evening. There were a lot of "Shadows of the Moon in a Dish" (whirligigs that rise from a plate, giving off showers of sparks), "Spirit Swords" (fire rockets), "Electric Lights" (which produce a brilliant blue light), and a few other

---

1. The stockaded mountaintop was now becoming less wild. More bungalows were being constructed. A residents' association built community facilities such as tennis courts. We all joined work teams to improve paths, build seats at view points, and so forth. Some of us boys made a little income (figured in coppers) as ball boys at the tennis courts. And I delivered the mail (just for the glory of it).

things such as "Fire Wells." One of these had fifteen fireballs that rose in a series of ever-ascending arcs.

I devoted a good part of the next day to trying out my new fireless cooker. We had brought it from America in 1916, but it did not reach us in time to be used on the mountain until this summer of 1919. I roasted a chicken and made two cakes. In the afternoon I had a few ladies in for tea, and when they arrived I had two tins of baking-powder biscuits all ready to lift from the cooker. Everyone was interested. The hot coke fire in our native kitchen stove was ideal for heating the radiators. Our servants regarded the whole apparatus as some kind of magic. When the steam first puffed from the relief valve on the cooker's lid, Amah was terribly frightened and rushed off to a far corner. "What," she exclaimed, "will this foreign thing do next!"[2]

Chinese guests on the mountain were just as hard to plan for as in the city. One Friday, the head of the *mintuan* (constabulary) in the village at the foot of the mountain sent word that he would call the next day. We expected a short visit for tea, so I had the cook make a very nice cake. On Saturday morning I went out on an errand. When I returned, the guest had arrived— bringing nine retainers. Although the morning had started out bright and beautiful, by twelve noon it was raining pitchforks. A meal, obviously, had to be offered. The servants knuckled right in without a word of direction from me and got up a very good Chinese meal. They had to use their own rice, as we had little on hand. This is where Chinese servants are strong: they regard such emergencies as involving the whole family and do not want to fail in courtesy. With two Chinese guests already staying in the house, there were thirteen men to be fed.

At the end of July the Braces returned from furlough bringing with them a young American, Earl Dome, for the Chengtu Y. Bob brought Earl up to White Deer Summit in August, and he was with us for the rest of the summer, though he sometimes had to be placed with other friends to make room for other guests. During the annual meeting of the White Deer Summit Association we had a regular house party, including our old friends Harry and Lona Openshaw.

Jack celebrated his birthday [in early August] with a big cake, candles, and fifteen hundred firecrackers. I was reading Boswell's *Life of Johnson,* and also George Adam Smith's *Life of Henry Drummond,* along with various light literature.

In August Bob and I took the two older boys and Earl Dome on a trip into the high mountains. It was going to be wild country, with few temples and those mostly broken down, with few priests or available supplies. Before we left, the cook baked a lot of bread and biscuits. We also had some tins of soda

2. After the novelty wore off, I don't recall that the fireless cooker was used very often. Bob was one of the world's great enthusiasts for gadgets. It is a trait that he passed on to his sons.

biscuits. And in some places we could buy cornmeal, which we made into mush and fried for breakfast.

I had a very light mountain sedan chair carried by two men. Three men carried the food supplies, and three more transported our cots and bed rolls. Then there was the Boy, who could cook well enough for our simple needs and was a better traveler than the cook. And finally, even though the horse was left at home, we had the horse coolie, Lao Liu, because he was such a competent and useful man for such adventures. Having these ten Chinese, who had to eat, put a limit on how far we could get into the wilds. Jack walked all the way, along with Bob and Earl, but Bobbie sometimes had a ride on a carrier's back-frame.

We skirted Tientai (which we had climbed the year before) and struck out for Jiufeng (Nine Peaks). We always found a temple to camp in, but they were in all stages of dilapidation. The one where we stayed the first night had merely two caretakers, no priests, and all the idols had been placed in the only large room with a good roof. The next one was a bit better, with three or four priests. By the third night we were in a very good temple, with a lot of priests, at the top of Nine Peaks.

The elevation here was 10,500 feet. We had a suite of three rooms, but life seemed to gravitate to the public fire in the front room of the temple. This was a roofed court with an earth floor and an ever-burning fire of pine logs. Hanging by long soot-laden chains from the rafters was always a huge kettle of boiling water, and perhaps one of steaming brick tea as well. Circling the fire were low benches made from the curved boles of trees. A trunk cut into half made two planks: adding wooden pegs made two very solid benches. Here we sat among the other travelers and pilgrims, priests at leisure, and our own carriers—all on the same level there on the high mountain. I thought of our ancient Anglo-Saxon forebears in their old halls.

The next day Bobbie and I took things easy while the two men and Jack climbed the highest of the Nine Peaks. It was 11,725 feet, and they had magnificent views.

Our next mountain was Yunhua (Cloud Flowers). The approach was wonderful, following a mountain torrent up a steep valley with wild scenery and lovely cascades and waterfalls. One suspension bridge was made of iron rods, about forty inches long, with rings at each end and linked together to form chains. It was a good place to stop for a picnic lunch. We had baked beans, quickly heated on our alcohol stove, while our men regaled themselves on corn pones which they had carried in their sashes.

Our temple that night was dedicated to the Goddess of Mercy but was a wild and desolate ruin. There was no priest, only a half-blind caretaker who could barely see us. Everything was filthy, the roof half gone, only one room in decent repair—and that was open at one end. There was a corn field nearby, and we soon had a campfire boiling fresh ears of field corn still in the milky stage. We made a supper of Campbell's soup, crackers, and corn, sharing the latter with the men.

The next day we arrived at the top (10,300 feet) in time for the men to climb the highest peak, which they were disappointed to find was only 11,300 feet. This temple was in much better condition. We had a fairly good room, and could cook at a central open fire as at Nine Peaks. But what a worried time as I had there!

When we arrived, I found that small Bob could not speak aloud. Croup, I well knew, was in the offing. I never traveled in those days without camphorated oil, squills, and ipecac. I hastened to the road box; to my horror none of the three indispensables was there. I remembered setting them out for packing, but that was little help on our high and remote mountain. But I was not without resource. As soon as we ate, I put the child to bed, rolling him tightly in a woolen blanket. I gave him all the very hot cocoa that he could swallow. Meanwhile the Boy made a batch of porridge, using our home-prepared cracked wheat. With this at the sticky-mush stage, I soon had the child packed in poultices around the neck and chest. They were hot, hotter, and he thought hottest, but I kept at work, scraping off one lot of porridge and replacing the poultices with fresh, hotter porridge until the child was red as any lobster.

I really was in a frenzy to have him so ill with croup at that elevation and when we were having a pleasure jaunt. I even began to think it would be better to be a woman who wanted to sit at home in a giddy summer dress than one to scour off to mountain tops with the men folks. What would I have done had anything gone wrong? One does not need to answer, for it all ended well. Finally, Bobbie began to speak easily. I changed the poultices once again, gave him a potash tablet to suck, and he fell asleep, worn out with my attentions.

At that time we were the only Americans who had made the Cloud Flowers ascent. And, according to the records, I was the first Western woman to climb Cloud Flowers and the eighth foreigner to go up Nine Peaks.[3] Now many have gone up those heights. In the summer season pilgrims come to worship at the shrines, and a few priests will go up from lower temples with food, bedding, and such things to care for the visitors. We were a little too late on that 1919 trip for the pilgrim season.

There was much beauty on these mountain tops. Flowers spread a veritable carpet on flat places and were in every nook and cranny. The eidelweiss

---

3. In view of the important contribution of the stout-legged sedan-chair bearers, perhaps "ascent" would be a better word than "climb" to describe Grace's achievement. The accuracy of these records probably depends on whether those notebooks at the summit temples, in which we and other travelers inscribed our names, had been left there by the first Westerners to arrive.

was particularly fine that year. We had magnificent views of higher mountains—some perhaps as high as 20,000 feet. Often we were overtaken by rain storms and sometimes took refuge in caves or shacks along the way. Once I found a dry place in a cave used by potash burners. They were black with dirt and soot, and seemed to live animal-like lives at their grimy toil. A few torn and dirty pieces of bedding, with rude bowls, chopsticks, and a kettle, appeared to be their only equipment.

Down near the foot of the mountain we failed to make the day's planned stage. A desolate building was our only choice for the night. It turned out to be an old temple, most of which was rented to some rough-looking black-smiths who were working, somewhat mysteriously, at night. We wondered if they supplied weapons to bandits, and when we discovered they were making gun barrels we were sure of it.[4] The only room available for us was also a storeroom for occupied coffins awaiting burial. We four slept in our cots at one end, and Earl laid himself out on a door at the other. His cot and another load had failed to arrive with us, so we loaned him bedding; and for a bed, the door was the best to be had.

The next day we went on to White Water River and its copper smelter. And then up our hill and back to Round Top's hospitality. After these trips the bungalow looked luxurious and oh, so *clean*. To sit at table with dainty linen and one's usual garments felt like entering into a new existence.

We never forgot that trip. It meant croup to me, and the feeling that I had won out. One remembered story, though, concerned our Boy—faithful, conscientious Lao Wu. At the Nine Peaks temple, the only water was in huge storage tubs under the eaves. To get water, one had to stand on a bench, reach over the top, and use a dipper. Sent to get water soon after our arrival, Lao Wu found himself confronted with a massive tub higher than he was. But near the bottom was a wooden bung. A wrench removed the bung, but Lao Wu found himself sent sprawling by a cold stream that hit him in the solar plexus. The priest-custodian of the temple kitchen delivered a thorough and systematic cursing of the ancestors and entire family of the unfortunate principal. Lao Wu looked unhappy thereafter if Nine Peaks were even mentioned.

---

4. My recollection of the weapons making is a little less sinister. There was one busy forge, with a master gunsmith and a couple of apprentices. The master was proud of his skill and happy to have an audience (we were almost certainly the first Westerners he had ever seen). There was some banter, initiated by Bob, about the intended use of the gun they were making. Strictly for hunting, insisted the gunsmith. I was skeptical about its accuracy. "Don't be too sure," said Bob, "Daniel Boone used to shoot squirrels with a gun just about like that."

32

Last Rites for Confucius

(1920)

We were back in the city by late September and soon as busy as ever. Some Chinese friends wanted me to teach them Latin. With teaching the boys at home and teaching at the Y, I reluctantly had to decline.[1] Supplies that we had ordered in April of 1918 reached us on the last day of September in 1919. Our latest arrival, Earl Dome, had to be housed. By cutting a few doors between side rooms in the compound next door (originally the Methodist school and now partly a residence for the Heldes), Bob arranged a very convenient suite. Earl continued to board with us.

The usual Autumn Sacrifice at the Temple of Confucius was to be in early October.[2] The temple was very close to us: it provided the name for our street (Temple of Learning Street). Women were not usually allowed to attend the ceremony, so we had never been. This year Bob obtained permission for us to go (they asked me to dress in dark colors to be less conspicuous).

Ancient custom decreed that these rites take place when the air is most calm and serene; they were usually timed to end just before dawn. We got up about 1:00 A.M., had coffee and a good lunch, and set off in a drizzle. By 2:30 we were at the temple. Then, in good Chinese fashion, there was a wait. The ceremony did not begin until the rain stopped at 4:15, but there were interesting things to watch. A Chinese friend with us was secretary to an official and was able to secure good places for us; also he could explain everything.

The great stone terraces in front of the temple were all decorated for the

---

1. Grace had taught high school Latin for two years between graduation and her marriage.
2. This must have been very nearly the last year that these state ceremonies to honor Confucius were performed. The iconoclastic spirit of the May Fourth Movement was sweeping the country, but the rise of the Kuomintang would soon substitute Sun Yat-sen as a new cult figure to bow to. The Temple of Confucius was one of the few buildings in Chengtu entitled to have imperial-yellow glazed-tile roofs. Within the grounds were some magnificent gingko trees (which were a favorite roost for a great flock of noisy crows).

affair. One of the spectacular aspects was the lighting. Besides many small lanterns, there were two tremendous "heavenly candles" about twenty-five feet high that flanked the middle flight of stone steps up to the main temple hall and were made of bundles of bamboos tied tightly together. The bamboos were very dry and had been well soaked in pitch and oil; they burned with a mighty blaze, giving plenty of light for the scene. The "candles" were as large as good-sized tree trunks; and the smoke, as we found when the breeze veered and blew it our way, was extremely acrid.

The civil governor was the master of ceremonies and must have marched up and down the steps more than a score of times. His permanent station was on the lower level in the center of the large red carpet for the officials. He advanced to the upper level and into the temple building at least seven times during different parts of the ceremony. There was chanting. A strange ancient-style orchestra played most of the time. And every part of the action was announced. This is an important part of every Chinese ceremony or ritual; even at a wedding, for instance, every detail must be announced and then followed out in what seems to us to be a very formal manner.

Most of the ceremony was conducted outside the temple, though the civil governor entered and bowed to the chief tablet (that of Confucius), and the other principal officials did the same to the tablets of the twelve disciples of Confucius. It was odd to see the officials in frock coats and top hats going through the bows and observances of olden times: fortunately, they did not have to perform the prostrations that used to be required. We wished they had been wearing the gorgeously embroidered and colorful robes of imperial days.

After all the bowing and orating were over and the celebrants began to leave, the majordomo gave us permission to go up into the main temple. Here we saw the sacrifices, the ritual utensils, and the old stone musical instruments which hung from a wooden rack. The sacrifices, which had been prepared and put in place before the ceremonies, were on wooden tables and were so arranged that they did not show the marks of having been killed and drawn. The tablet to Confucius was in the center; before it, there was a sheep on the left, a pig on the right, and a huge ox in the center. The sheep and pig carcasses were without hair, but the ox had only the head scraped clean. At the sides were tables for each group of three disciples; on each table was a pig and a sheep.

Shortly before the event, Bob had had the characters "Hua Yang" placed on his calling cards. At that time Chengtu city was divided into two wards, one of them being Hua Yang. After living ten years in a ward, a man was entitled by custom to show his township on his card. It interested Chinese very much that Bob, a foreigner, had wanted to do this. Several people mentioned this to us at these Confucian ceremonies.

Just about this time there was a flurry of activity at the Y to coincide with the civic celebration of the National Day. We all went to a dinner at the city Y on October 8. On that day, 17,500 people visited the building. There were various exhibit rooms, and throngs went in to see charts showing the evils of poor ventilation, bad sanitation, opium smoking, and such things. The visitors were all men and boys. In the evening, crowd after crowd came in to see stereopticon pictures portraying modern developments such as electricity, telephones, good roads, and so forth. There were lectures every fifteen minutes on popular subjects. This went on for days, and each night the Y staff were exhausted.

The Brace family had a lot of illness that fall, but it was a fifty-minute ride by sedan chair to their home.[3] Ruth Helde and I went over as often as possible and tried to help in every way we could. Chair transportation took up so much precious time that one wonders how we carried on as well as we did. All we could do was simply to put ourselves back into the Middle Ages and then settle down to be happy under medieval conditions.

The Methodists had a visit by a party of notables in connection with their mission centenary. Bob was asked to take them to call on some of the officials. It did not matter to Bob that he was already more than normally busy; he always loved to help anyone he could, and he had often helped men from the [West China Union] University in making contacts with officials. We were invited to a tiffin with the American guests under the wonderful old trees in the Methodist compound.[4] Stanley High was one of the men in the party. I was much impressed by a Mrs. Wood, who had short hair and seemed to be fond of it.

We felt the Methodists were lucky to have these visitors, who seemed able to bring them up to date on so many subjects. I wished I could have sat down to talk for hours with people who could read all they wanted from large public libraries and who seemed to be well informed on a thousand and one things. Mrs. Wood's husband came to our gate to meet Bob before some trip they were to take. I had a number of things in mind to ask him. But he would not come in, and stood out there waiting while I was wishing with all my heart that we could *make* him come in for awhile.

This being out of touch was one of the hard things about being so far in the west of China. The journey to us had to be figured, not in miles, but in weeks of travel. The National Committee of the YMCA in Shanghai was sup-

3. It may be recalled that Bert Brace was a member of the Canadian Methodist Mission who had been loaned to the YMCA. His mission connection meant that he was provided a house in the mission's compound, which was in the far corner of the city from where all the other Y people were living. It was in the Canadian Methodist compounds that the Anglo-Saxon community had been concentrated in 1911 (chapter 18).

4. All the American children who grew up in Chengtu will remember the swing and various ropes that hung from one of those "wonderful old trees."

posed to keep in contact with the local Associations. But when trips for their secretaries were planned, Chengtu was left out. It was too much time to give to one Association when so many others, nearer the coast and easier to reach, also had to be visited. It worked both ways: if Chengtu was out of touch with the National Committee, the National Committee also lacked knowledge of our situation and working conditions.

Now, after the strenuous fall, it was decided that Bob should go to a Y conference in Shanghai. He begrudged the time away from his work: in the end, by making all possible haste, he was able to cut his absence to ten days less than three months. He left in a great whirl, working at the Y to the last and signing a thousand membership cards. (The Y had become so popular that cards were being counterfeited: Bob's actual signature was required as proof that the card was bona fide.) He took an empty trunk for all the purchases that friends had beseeched. Travelers to the Coast always *expected* to be so burdened.

He took a small boat to Chungking. The servants had prepared an excellent lay-out of food, and he had paid the boat captain to put on extra rice so they could make fewer stops. He also had extra rowers so the men could work in shifts and thus get at least fourteen hours' travel a day. He took his horse coolie as his only servant (Lao Liu still talks of this marvelous trip and the sights of Shanghai!). And there was a friend. This was an ex-official out of a job and desirous of seeing a bit of the world. To keep his departure quiet, he had stayed at our house the last two days before the departure. He was a YMCA member and a Mohammedan. This had to be considered in preparing the food for Bob. For instance, we used no lard, had the fowls roasted rather than fried, and provided chicken fat for frying.

There were the usual affairs to keep us busy that winter, but everything seemed pointless without Bob. Letters from him were sporadic, and he complained in them of receiving none from me, though I wrote daily. I had taken on some extra teaching. In addition, I was taking a couple of courses with the Extension Division of the University of California, our alma mater at Berkeley. I had wanted a course on the history of the Pacific Basin: they offered none, so I settled on the history of early California. I worked on this for some time but finally faced a serious problem. The course, and especially the assigned thesis topic, required access to a library. I read the texts and then had to give up. In my writing course I was soon vexed with the criticisms. My subject matter was chiefly drawn from China and the affairs of our daily lives. I soon found a most peculiar slant in the mind of whoever corrected my themes. My attitudes, plain descriptions, and characterizations were all questioned; I began to think my critic must be some unfledged youth who knew nothing of alien lands or mentalities beyond his own. So both courses came to naught.

Meantime, Christmas was approaching. Bob was pushing as fast as pos-

sible. He had a swift trip to Hankow on a large British steamer. Then—
because the captain remembered him from 1912—he was able to crowd onto
a tiny ship for the trip to Ichang. But at Ichang the river was so low that no
more steamers were attempting the upper river. Bob had no choice but to
take a small houseboat to Chungking. That ended hopes for a Christmas
reunion.

On New Year's Day, we went on a spur-of-the-moment picnic to the big
temple outside the North Gate. Earl Dome rode Bob's horse, but when we
were outside the city he walked and Jack asked to ride. Things went well
until, suddenly, something frightened the horse. All at once I saw the pony
running wildly, with Jack swaying in the saddle. Just then the horse passed a
man carrying earthen crockets in two baskets with a carrying pole. Jack's leg
caught the rope of one of the baskets, causing it to bang against the horse's
leg. The pony reared straight up, and Jack went off in a pathetic heap in the
dust. It was a dirt road, but with raised stone blocks like stepping-stones
along one side. My heart sank, and all the child's life flashed through my
mind in a second. Then we heard him crying out and knew he was not
killed.[5] Earl gave him first aid, and the doctor saw him when we got back to
the city in the evening. One ear was partially torn loose at the top (by hitting
the corner of a paving stone), but it healed well.

On the same day, coincidentally, we lost our beautiful pointer dog, Scout.[6]
He must have gotten out the front gate when the gateman's attention was
elsewhere. Neighbors let us know that soldiers had him. The servants tried to
get him back but were helpless. After a few days Earl went to the parade
ground near us. He was told that the commandant was out, so asked for the
next in command. After a long delay, an officer came to hear his questions.
This man assured Earl that no foreign dog had been seen. As he escorted
Earl's departure, Earl saw a coolie at the far side of the field leading Scout. He
slapped his leg and let out a cry for the dog. Overjoyed, Scout gave tongue,
tore the leash from the coolie's grasp, and bounded across the field to throw
himself in ecstasy on Earl. There was great rejoicing that evening over the
safe return of "Sigao," as the servants pronounced his name.

When Bob reached Chungking on his return trip from Shanghai, he had
found most of the Yard family there. They were on their return from furlough
and had been delayed there by illness. Then Jim had been called to Peking on
some mission business. Rather than wait any longer for Jim's return, they
decided to make the overland trip to Chengtu with Bob. They reached

5. The family has always insisted that my crying out was in Chinese: "Ai-ya, ai-ya."
6. Scout was a beautiful spotted pointer who had been given to us as a puppy by Mr.
Cavalieri, the Italian gentleman who was the head of the (Chinese) postal service for western
Szechwan. Very few "foreign" dogs had been seen in Chengtu, and they attracted great interest.
It was, appropriately, Mr. Cavalieri who introduced me to philately.

Chengtu on January 16 [1920]. We met them outside the East Gate, and it was a real red-letter day. Bob had brought us all gifts, and we asked hundreds of questions—about things and people at the Coast, shops, happenings, travels.

Mabelle's servants were awaiting her return, and she was soon settled in her house. When her children were in bed in the evenings, she often came down to have dinner with us. Then Jim finally arrived. The big excitement about his return was that he brought a motorcycle. The machine, the like of which had never been seen in Chengtu, caused terror and the wildest excitement. Jim had a good many adventures with his iron steed, but it was never really practical in the old narrow streets crowded with men and animals.[7]

In February Bob took the lads again for a short trip to White Deer Summit.[8] That year Bob was successful in having ice stored there, and several times when the weather got warm in the spring we had some brought to the city by a carrier. As soon as a load arrived, we would make ice cream and invite friends; if there was enough ice, we made more and invited more friends. With one large batch of one hundred pounds of ice, we made twenty-two quarts of ice cream.[9] No easily obtained delicacy could ever have been so enjoyed and appreciated. Luckily, we had our own cows, so we had cream.

In March the Cavalieris of the Post Office gave a never-to-be-forgotten costume party. I made myself a square-necked basque and panniers of rose-flowered cretonne bought on the street. My hair was dressed high and powdered, with a long curl hanging down on one shoulder. I also had a black velvet band around my neck and a couple of black patches on my face. With the help of Chinese friends, Bob appeared in the complete outfit of an "indi-

7. Jim Yard's motorcycle had to be carried, slung between poles, on the backs of men for the ten-day trip from Chungking to Chengtu. It was the first motor vehicle of any kind in Chengtu—and probably in all of Szechwan. Chengtu streets were not only narrow and crowded; they were paved, if at all, with rough sandstone slabs. Finally, Jim was no motor mechanic, and no other was available when, inevitably, it needed fixing. The motorcycle was exciting for the short while that it ran; then it became an exhibit in the YMCA's scientific museum.

8. This trip to White Deer Summit was a sort of milestone for me. I walked all the way on the trip home. This involved a long second-day stage of one hundred *li* (thirty plus miles). Bob did not believe in excessive praise, but he did indicate satisfaction that I would in future be able to "keep up with the men." (I was ten.)

9. Our ability to produce so much ice cream was partly due to the several years that it took to achieve success in storing and preserving ice on the mountain. (The ice was limited in supply: it had to come from the rainwater tubs at the corners of our bungalow. And it was very hard to persuade the frugal caretaker to be profligate enough in using straw and sawdust for insulating.) The first year the plan was made, Bob ordered a two-quart hand-cranked freezer from Montgomery Ward. When it arrived it did not look large enough for our pent-up appetites. A four-quart freezer was then ordered. And the next year it was a six-quart freezer. There were three flavors: vanilla, maple, or fresh peach (the best!). All this took a lot of cranking, but the servants were happy: they got all the brine from the freezers (salt was expensive, and not a drop was lost). Regrettably, Bob never succeeded in having ice last into the summer so that we could have ice cream on the mountain.

gent *Hanlin*," an old Confucian scholar of the highest grade. With black mustache, huge glasses, and a cap with a queue sewed into it, many could not identify him for some time. Madame Bodard, the French consul's wife, was also dressed by Chinese as a Chinese and was superlatively effective.[10]

What I recall as the most pleasure was the planning of costumes out of what we had or could get locally: fixing my own clothes; making a wig for Earl Dome out of raw silk thread, parted, curled, and tied with a black bow; and doing odd and unexpected things for others. We had no "outside amusements" and so had to make what we could, deriving from our own efforts the acme of enjoyment.

On March 18, the anniversary of our engagement, Bob gave me a set of the most exquisite white satin scrolls, each embroidered to represent a season. The card with them said: "In fragrant memory of a day / Long ago and far away." Just after this, I lost the ruby out of my engagement ring. It was there when I dressed, but as I put on my hat to go out calling, I saw it was gone. The servants and all of us spent hours of searching, all to no effect.

For more than two years I had been urging the YWCA to start work in Chengtu. When two American YW secretaries finally arrived, I was disappointed to be unable to meet and entertain them. All that had to be left to Mabelle Yard. I had been in the doctor's hands all that spring, and by the middle of May was down with flu and laryngitis. I had quite a bit of fever and ached all over, and Bob could get no nurse. Finally, one of my good Canadian friends, Kathryn Ross, gave up time from her rest and recreation hours each day to come over to bathe, rub, and fix me up, telling the cook what to prepare for me, and helping in the ways that only a trained nurse knows. For once, I was too ill to manage the house or meals.

I was still weak when June came. The servants aired and sunned the woolens, and Bob helped put them away. He wanted to get me away to the hills. There was a cholera scare in the city, and he pushed up our departure by several days. I was hardly able to get ready before we were off.

10. The son of the French consul, Mr. Bodard, has written at least two books about *his* growing up in Chengtu (Lucien Bodard, *The French Consul*, Knopf, 1977; and *Le Fils du Consul*, Grasset, 1975). His life seems to have been a bit more exotic and exciting than mine, especially his experiences with his amah.

33

To Shanghai with Jack
(1920)

On June 5 we reached Round Top, and it was satisfying indeed to see Bob's "surprise" for me. He had had the whole living room panelled in the clean, prettily grained oak that we had originally used for the ceiling. Sandpapered and polished, it made the room lovely. But in spite of Bob's care, I was not surprised. On the way up the hill, when the way seemed long and I was weary, the Boy tried to divert me by telling how the Master had spent a lot of heart on having the walls of the "big room" covered with wood.[1] (The Boy hoped I would like it because much money had been spent.)

George and Ruth Helde were in a cottage near us, and she was expecting her first child. Two doctors and a trained nurse were also nearby. With the stage thus set, everything seemed ready for the arrival of small Tom Helde, which occurred on June 13. But all the efforts of the doctors, nurse, and those who loved her could not keep her bright presence. A friend staying with us looked after the children so I could give all my time to helping in the emergency. With things looking desperate, I sent a runner to the city for Bob.

Ruth died early on the sixteenth. Bob arrived that afternoon and at once gave attention to the tasks that had to be done: a coffin made, a grave dug. There were carpenters on the hill building new bungalows, so the coffin could be made in a few hours. Dry oak logs that we had left over from our panelling were cut into planks, and it was constructed from them. I chose a beautifully soft and dainty comforter as lining, and we tacked it in place in the casket. Ruth's mother had sent it to her that spring. On the seventeenth there was a little service, and we laid Ruth away, her grave placed near our bungalow in a thicket of shrubbery north of the house.

1. "Spent a lot of heart" is a literal translation of a very common Chinese phrase, *fei xin*, which undoubtedly is exactly what the Boy said.

We had consulted quite a bit about the location, but Bob had forgotten that the property was leased from a temple: the priests should have been consulted. That night, word came from the temple that no woman could be buried on temple land. This seemed the last straw, but Bob found a solution. The Chengtu YMCA had bought some land on the slope of the mountain for a projected camp. A grave site was chosen on the upper part of this land, just outside the west gate of our *zhaizi* wall. The next day, while two friends took George for a long hike, Bob secured enough men to accomplish an arduous task. By nightfall the new grave was covered with ferns and flowers.

Ruth was a lovely person: talented, sweet-natured, helpful. She was to me like a younger sister, and the sudden parting was hard. There were no good-byes. She never even knew she had a son; unconsciousness closed her eyes, and she never saw us again, but slipped away into the Hereafter with no word to anyone.

There were many plans suggested for little Tom, but in the end his father decided to take him to his grandparents in America. In the meantime, Miss Wall, the nurse, would take care of him for the summer.

In late August Bob came up from Chengtu. George and Earl Dome joined us on a trip back to Nine Peaks and the temple that we had visited the year before. The men tried to climb the high mountain behind the Nine Peaks range. They failed to reach the summit but had some thrilling experiences in cold and dampness.[2] The rest of us took short rambles and sat around the fire on the curved benches, listening to talk from pilgrims and others. As arranged, a coolie arrived from White Deer Summit during our stay with fresh bread, rolls, and cookies. It was something that the men thought the food was adequate.

Soon after our return to Round Top we had word by letter of Father Service's death in California.[3] Without either of his parents, Bob felt everything would be greatly changed at home.

We had an excitement while returning from the hills to Chengtu at the end of the summer. We had planned, as usual, to spend a night with Canadian friends in the city of Penghsien. When we reached there, some military row was going on and the city gates were closed. While we were in the street outside the gate, there was a volley of shots. At once the street was empty with not a person in sight. The lads were ahead with their father. Before I knew what was happening, I found myself inside a shop with the board shutters closed. My chair men assured me, "Don't worry; *we* are here and you do not need to fear anything." Still, a woman does feel a bit queer to find herself

2. We got to about 13,000 feet (by Bob's aneroid barometer) but found ourselves blundering about on wet rock in a dense fog that prevented picking a practical route. The Chinese name for the mountain, Big Baldy (Da Guangguang Shan), was very apt.
3. Father Service died on July 5; the letter did not reach his son until the end of August.

in that sort of predicament. Bob finally got all of us—children, loads, men, and wife—into a fairly decent temple outside the city, where we spent the night. The next day we resumed our journey without misadventure.

Soon after our return to Chengtu, we moved into the next-door residence that the Heldes had been occupying. At the same time, the Yards moved into our former house.[4] It was also decided that I would go to the Coast, taking the baby down for George and escorting Jack to the American School in Shanghai. An English girl, recently back from the Chefoo School, would come for lessons with Bobbie and Dick, who would also be under the direct eye of "Aunt Mabelle."

Preparing for my trip, I had the amah change the paper liners in my bureau drawers. As she was doing it, I looked to make sure she had cleaned every corner. There, in a far corner of the lowest drawer, was the ruby from my engagement ring, winking at me as though it had never been a source of anxiety for months. What rejoicing!

There had been some fighting in the province, but by late September the situation looked better for travel. On October 1 our party started for Chungking. We had two small mat-roofed river boats; on one were Harry Openshaw and George Helde, while Dr. Laura Jones, Jack, baby Tom, and I had the other. The two men ate on our boat, so we ran but one kitchen under the skillful management of our old helper, Liu Pei-yun. Several Chinese boats attached themselves to us, either for companionship or for the hope of a sheltering wing.

We reached Suifu early on October 5, and Laura went off with the two men to call on the American Baptists. I told them I would perhaps go ashore in the afternoon, when Laura said she would return to be with the baby. I was getting clean clothes out of boxes when I heard a commotion. There were a couple of soldiers outside, talking to the boatmen. The captains had gone to buy rice, and even my cook was off foraging for eatables. The soldiers said that our boats would have to move at once: there was going to be fighting, and we would be right in the line of fire. I said, "No," and they as earnestly said, "Yes." I replied, "It is impossible for us to move. You can see that. The two boat captains have gone ashore to buy rice and supplies. The

4. Considering that Grace and Bob had lived in this house for thirteen years and had expended much care in planning and improving, it seems surprising that Grace's account is so terse. Both houses, the Heldes' and ours, were rented from the American Methodists, the Yards' mission. The mission was adding staff and needed more housing. With George Helde's leaving and his return uncertain, his house was available. The Yards and Services were the closest of friends (Grace and Mabelle seem to have managed to spend some time together almost daily). So there was enthusiasm on all sides for the Yards to be the Methodists to move to Temple of Learning Street. But they had four children; we, with my imminent departure to boarding school in Shanghai, had only two; and our house was the larger of the two. So it was sensible for us to move to the Helde house and for the Yards to take over ours. It was a move that, under the circumstances, was gladly made.

gentlemen of our party are not here. The boats will have to remain here so these men will know where to find us. You will have to postpone fighting until tomorrow when we will be gone." "But you will be hit by bullets," said they. "No," I insisted, "just wait till *tomorrow* to do your fighting."

The soldiers went away, and we saw and heard no more of them. Nothing was heard or seen of any fighting, either. And we stayed right at that mooring until we left the city early next morning.

I had laid out freshly laundered summer clothes. When Harry arrived back and said I was expected for afternoon tea, I started to change. But Harry would not hear to it. The streets were full of mud and terribly dirty: I had better go as I was. I was wearing one of my khaki mountain outfits with very short skirt, riding breeches, and high brown boots. Taking his advice, I arrived to find my hostess in a flowered chiffon with ruffles and furbelows, and a very elaborate tea party laid in my honor. How dangerous it often is for women to dress for men, not for other women!

It had been a queer day all around, but the climax came next morning at breakfast. Harry had been back in the city during the evening for a Baptist Mission meeting (and had to be lowered by rope over the city wall to rejoin us after the gates were closed). At breakfast he had a great laugh: "You should have heard the remarks about your clothes, Grace." It seemed that the comment was not so much about khaki as the shortness of my skirt. And the fact that it was his advice did not appear to bother him a bit.

Below Luchow we were held up twice by being hailed from the bank. The first time, there were a few shots. These were soldiers wanting to know who we were. The second batch yelled wildly and shot in a more purposeful manner. There was nothing to do but turn in to the shore. We had been warned of bandits in that vicinity and had hidden our valuables (my watch was in the tin of baby food). When we reached shore and saw the ragtag and bobtail group awaiting us, we concluded that our fears were realized.

Harry began to tell the chief that I was the wife of Hsieh An-tao of Chengtu, doing a good deed by taking a motherless infant to Shanghai. He spoke as though the man *must* have been a friend of Hsieh An-tao (Bob). And the man said he was! He even gave us his huge red card bearing his name, Iron Hand, and asked that we take it back with his regards to Hsieh An-tao.[5] Best of all, he waved to us to proceed. But the Chinese boats that had been hoping to slip by in our company were detained—presumably for plunder.

Bob, we learned later, had never heard of Iron Hand. But, since it was an assumed name, it was not impossible that they may have met under other

5. Traditionally, calling cards increased in size with the status of the person. It was not surprising, then, that Iron Hand's card was "huge."

circumstances. Men in China sometimes take to banditry after disappointments or reversals of fortune.

We had to pass another area where robbers were said to be exceedingly
fierce. Fortunately, the river was quite wide, and we held well out from the
shore. Fifteen or twenty shots were fired at us, and we could plainly hear the
yells and threats of the bandits ordering us to draw in. But we feared to tempt
our luck too far, so held our course and did not stop. George was on the boat
with us women and children, while Harry was on the other craft.[6] Late that
afternoon we tied up at Chungking and were welcomed by Dr. McCartney,
who brought fresh bread for our evening meal.

After a few days, George, little Tom, Jack, and I started down river on the
Robert Dollar.[7] The ship was chockablock with Chinese passengers, apparently because of a sudden shift in military power in Szechwan. Many of our
fellow passengers were Chinese gentlemen who seemed to be men of affairs.
Later we learned that several were emissaries of Dr. Sun Yat-sen who had
been sent by him to Chungking to prepare for the removal of the Sun regime
from Canton to Szechwan. This having been frustrated by the recent political
changes, they were in a great fever to leave. One fine-looking gentleman was
much alone and seemed to converse with no one, but he once spoke to me in
fluent English.[8]

Silk-garmented men, with luxurious bedding rolls, lined up for deck pas-

6. There is a bit more to the bandit episode. Since we knew which side of the river the
bandits were on, trunks and baggage had been shifted in the hold under the cabin to make a
protected space for Grace, Laura, and the baby. As soon as the shooting and shouting started,
our boatmen went over the side (the side away from the shots). This surprised and alarmed
George, who felt we should be making all speed to get out of range. He rushed out onto the
foredeck and took an oar; not to be outdone in manliness, I did likewise. (Chinese oars are long
and rather cumbersome; the rower stands erect, facing forward. The effect of our effort on the
speed of the boat could only have been minimal.) As the current gradually took us farther from
the bandits, the boatmen came back aboard and resumed real rowing. Harry thought this was
very funny. He was on the other boat; his boatmen went overboard; and Harry, so he alleged,
napped through it all. Harry—and our boatmen—had had more experience. There were bullet
splashes near us, but George and I could be thankful that the bandits' aim, or ammunition, were
so poor.

7. It is fact, probably forgotten by most, that for many years the Robert Dollar Steamship
Company of San Francisco operated ships on the Upper Yangtze. We always took them if we
could. They were American; and Captain Dollar was a good friend of the YMCA (if my memory
is correct, he gave the money for a Y building in Hankow).

8. Sun Yat-sen's position in Canton was precarious, but the history books do not seem to
mention any plan at this time for Sun Yat-sen to move his base to Szechwan. Since the 1911
Revolution, both North and South had sought to gain support among the various competing
military groups in Szechwan. In late 1920 several Szechwanese generals worked together long
enough to expel the Yunnanese, who had been "guests" for many years. The generals then de-
nounced both North and South, hailed the "federalist" movement then popular in China, and
announced that Szechwan should be governed by Szechwanese (themselves). The Sun Yat-sen
representatives that Grace mentions had probably been dealing with the just-ousted Yunnanese.
Anyone interested in the chaotic history of Szechwan during these years should consult Robert
A. Kapp, *Szechwan and the Chinese Republic: Provincial Militarism and Central Power, 1911–1938*
(New Haven and London: Yale University Press, 1973).

sage until there was no spot without an occupant. The captain saw that the men lay so thick on the deck outside my cabin door that I could not leave my room without stepping on someone and moved me into an officer's cabin on the top deck. This was a fine large room. Of course I had the baby and Jack with me, and we all enjoyed the space and comfort.

We transshipped at Ichang and Hankow and reached Shanghai on October 23. Little Tom was turned over to Mrs. Peter of the Y, who cared for him while his father arranged for the trip to America. Jack went at once to the Shanghai American School, which at that time was in rented buildings on North Szechwan Road. He was late in entering, and so young [eleven], that they would not consent to have him go into high school. This was in spite of the facts that he had completed the Calvert School and I had been teaching him algebra and Latin. So he was obliged to take the eighth grade, and the year was not as stimulating and profitable as it should have been.

In Szechwan, conditions had been so disturbed that we had received no parcel mail for over a year. All my friends wanted shopping done. Earl Dome had become engaged, and I had a long list to buy for them, separately and together. Carriages were still much in use, and I hired one for several days. With Liu Pei-yun to guard my purchases while I was in shops, I made the rounds. It seemed that I finally had enough to start a store. For instance, I bought over eighty pounds of knitting yarn.

But one could not shop in the evenings. Those were given up to friends. They entertained me in what seemed to my Szechwan eyes a very sophisticated manner. My home-made grey crepe satin found favor even in the assemblies of the well-dressed. But I also bought a few things for myself. One of them was a dress of deep old-rose georgette, which was most useful and for years a joy to the eye.

My Shanghai friends never could understand the difficulties of our travel, and I had many a quiet laugh as people told me of their troubles in reaching nearby mountain resorts. They were as serious about their troubles as I was about mine, though a sense of humor helped to lighten mine. Good tailors I envied, and the shops available to my friends on the Coast. But I never even considered being weary of Szechwan and its life and drawbacks. There were always compensations.

One thing that pleased me in Shanghai was visiting the two Szechwan boys who had been sent down by the Fortnightly Club in Chengtu to attend the School for the Blind. About two years earlier I had surveyed conditions of the blind in Chengtu. The paper that I then presented to the Club aroused so much interest that we resolved to work toward establishing a school for the blind in Chengtu. As a first step toward this, our Club had sent two blind boys down to Shanghai in 1919. Whether or not we could eventually set up a school, these trained lads would show the people in Szechwan what could be accomplished for those handicapped by loss of vision. The lads were glad to have a visitor from Szechwan, and I left a money gift for them.

I stayed in Shanghai with a dear friend. She had had some trouble with servants, she told me, but now she was happy that her staff was all right and working well. One afternoon when she was out, I came home about five o'clock. Contrary to custom, the outside screen door was not latched. So, without ringing, I walked in and went to the dining room to get myself a drink of water. As I entered the room, the Boy was in the act of climbing out of the transom above the locked door of my friend's storeroom, which opened off the dining room. He held some tins in the front part of his gown held up like an apron. We looked at each other, and I went up stairs to my room. Almost at once he knocked on my door. Was there anything I wanted? Did I want a bath? Could he fix me tea? And so on—there was nothing he would not be glad to do. The next morning the water came early and hot. Previously, he had grumbled about accommodations for Liu Pei-yun and insisted there was no room for him. Now he was all smiles and kindness to Liu. And I was fairly embarrassed with his attentions.

As my hostess was so happy with her staff, I decided not to repay her kindness by alarming her. But my usual seat at the dining table faced the door to the storeroom. One day as we sat there, I asked her to what it led. She told me, and I asked if she kept it locked. She replied that she certainly did, and I asked if the transom was fastened. She said she thought not, and I remarked that I thought it should be nailed shut. She looked somewhat surprised at the advice—perhaps it was at my interest in her affairs—but said she would follow my suggestion.

All through the weeks of travel, and the busy days of shopping and seeing friends, there had been an undercurrent of sadness. I knew I had to return and leave Jack, who was only eleven and seemed a slip of a lad to be so far from his parents. It was not only the miles, but the difficulties of communication. Letters were often lost, and telegrams delayed. At last I could delay no longer if I was to secure a steamer through the Gorges.

By putting my luggage on a Hankow steamer and then taking the train to catch the ship at Nanking, I could save a day. This gave me the whole of a Saturday with Jack. We made a day of it: tiffin at a restaurant to please him, and dinner with old friends who promised to have an eye on his welfare. He was annoyed because some of the boys at school, with a little knowledge of Latin, had nicknamed him "slave." "Ich dien," I pointed out, was the motto of England's ruling house. Service was a name of which one should be proud. *He* could change the poor connotation the boys had given the name.[9] Soon

---

9. Whatever means Grace had in mind, the means I found most effective on the name question was combat. I could hardly have been intimidating: I was undersized and completely inexperienced in such activity. Fortunately, no upper-grade boys persisted in using the hated name.

after dinner we had to say good-bye, and I turned my face to the West alone.

George Helde took me to the night train for Nanking, and next morning I was waiting on the landing hulk when my steamer pulled in. Liu welcomed me, but I was amazed when I saw my cabin. The bed and every other available space in the room was piled high with parcels of all kinds and sorts. All these things had been sent to the ship by Shanghai people who wished me to carry them to Szechwan friends. Before I could even settle my hand luggage into the room, I had to call in the room boy to help in stowing all this impedimenta. At Hankow, I had to buy a large straw *koré,* and in Ichang we had to descend to the up-river favorite; the ubiquitous huge market basket with a net cover, into which all manner of things can be stuffed—and stuffed. Thus Liu and I finally coped with all the bundles that had come our way.

34

Ten Years for the Chengtu Y
(1921)

When I boarded the ship at Nanking, I found good company. There was a party of Baptists and several Methodists, all bound for Szechwan. My cabin mate was a very pleasant young American nurse, joining the Methodists. At Hankow the head of the Baptist party asked if Liu could help with transshipping their things. Besides personal baggage, they had supplies for their work—in hospitals, schools, and churches. Liu did this but then begged me to excuse him from further work with this gentleman. First, Liu said, they were supposed to have 165 pieces; then he was told the total was 164; a little later it was 166! "This man," in Liu's words, "is a friend, but he is a dangerous man when managing baggage."

At Ichang, the good ship we had hoped to catch had left the day before. The prospect was that we might have to wait a week or more for another good boat. I had no wish to go to the China Inland Mission Home after those long days with my precious little girl there in 1906. Refuge was found with the ladies of the Scotch Mission, who put two hospital beds in an unused study for the nurse and me. With time to spare, I decided to overhaul my luggage, which had been packed in a great hurry. A trunk in which I had placed most of the things bought for Earl Dome's bride was full of cockroaches!

It was an old trunk—the hinges were loose—and it had been down in the ship's hold. Such a time as Liu and I had with large basins of boiling water for scalding and drowning.

After many trips to shipping offices, there seemed little hope of passage on any of the better ships. The water was too low to permit them any more trips through the Gorges. Then it was a scramble to get on any boat that would attempt the trip. Finally, a dozen or so of us foreigners left Ichang on November 12 aboard the old *Mei Shun*. She was a miserable ship. The captain, who did not care for women passengers and made no bones about saying so, told me that she "had sewing machines for engines." But I had no mind to try another houseboat trip and would take any steamer that went.

The captain was a Lett or a Finn, I forget which, and had a wife, or perhaps a companion, with him, but she could not speak English. The ship was tiny, and was crammed with passengers, freight, and luggage. There were only three cabins and one lavatory; about half a dozen men slept on tables and seats in the small saloon. This, the only public room, was so small that the cook had to serve three sittings for every meal. The galley was certainly no larger than six by six, but we had fine meals from a cook trained in the "American manner." He even produced delicious golden-baked biscuits as flaky as one's heart could desire, and his hot cakes made us all eager for breakfast.

On such a small ship in falling water, the rapids were formidable. The whole boat shook at the throb of our engines under forced draft, and the captain's temper was decidedly on edge. Slowly we would crawl up a channel and have a try at its passage, only to slip back as though no machinery was forcing us upward. Nature was simply too much for that old ship. Then lines would have to be put out; there would be a vast amount of yelling; and hundreds of men would bend to the task of helping us up the stream. We passengers tried to keep off the narrow deck and out of the way. At Wild Rapid our ship had to try four times. Twice cables snapped, and we fell back in considerable danger. But the captain knew how to handle this ship in such an emergency. He kept her nose straight, and we escaped the rocks always lying in wait. At New Rapid it was the same story. Just as we were struggling up, pulling ourselves by cable and winch, the palatial *Loong Mow* steamed past us, carrying the Baptist party we had left behind in Ichang. My companion, the nurse, ran out to wave a towel to our friends, and the captain bellowed: "All you —— —— missionaries keep off the deck!"

Shots were fired at us near the city of Kweichowfu, which had been looted by soldiers from Kweichow Province the night before we reached there. We were obliged to stay there for a day until the citizens would open their city gates; we needed coal, and they were at first too demoralized to do any business. Ninety *li* below Chungking we passed the *Mei Tan* beached after running onto rocks.[1] The USS *Monocacy* was standing by, and we took her doctor up to Chungking.

On November 19 I was safe in Chungking, at the Davidson's once again and glad to be by a cozy fire. Irene Hutchison of the [English] Friends' Mis-

---

1. The *Mei Tan,* as those familiar with the river would know, was a ship of the Standard Oil Company (*Mei* was the first character in the company's Chinese name: it was also the character for America). American oil companies in those days did not go in for flags of convenience: there were no Panamanian or Liberian gunboats on the Yangtze to give aid and fend off looters.

sion had just arrived on her return from home leave, and we decided to travel together. Fighting had closed the "Big Road" to Chengtu for over a year. One party had recently tried it, so we waited to hear how it had fared. Bob wrote that I should not travel without a foreign man in the party. The news, finally, was favorable, and I set out for Chengtu and home on November 26. It was my forty-first birthday.

There were five in our party: Mr. and Mrs. Starrett and my ship companion, the American nurse, all for the Methodist Mission; and Irene and I. The Starretts had been in China, but could not speak Mandarin. The nurse was entirely new, just out from America. My Chinese was not very abundant, but Irene could act as our spokesman. And I had Liu, on whom we depended largely for the management of the journey. Irene had a constant stream of visitors at villages and towns through which we passed. Word of her coming seemed to precede us, and her old pupils came bearing gifts, so that her sedan chair was hung with squawking hens and slabs of ham all the way to Chengtu. The Starretts proved easy companions and, having lived on the Coast, knew something of China. The nurse, however, was fresh and green to all the ways of the Orient. We were afforded a good deal of amusement by some of her reactions—to rats and other friendly inn neighbors, for instance. But she took it all good-naturedly and endured our laughter with serenity.

Now that travel has changed so much, it is interesting to look back and see what we had to arrange and expect on this trip. All bedding, food, and luggage had to be carried by men. On this trip we had sixty-seven coolies. I handled all the accounts. In Chungking a $200 payment was made to the *hong* (company) which contracted for the men. I wrote ahead to the Methodist Mission in Tzechow [six days from Chungking] for another $200 to be ready when we arrived there. At Chengtu we had a final settlement. The sixty-seven carriers came to $670; inn money, food, tips to military escorts, and all extras brought the expenses of the ten-day overland trip, for five foreigners, to a total of $825 in Chinese currency.

In Chengtu it was a great satisfaction that my purchases pleased the friends who had entrusted me with their requests. The children were well, and it was wonderful to be back with Bob and the two at home, but I could not forget the empty feeling left by Jack's absence. I was so busy getting back into the routine of teaching, unpacking, and settling that I did not even go into my kitchen for four days after I arrived.

My special care had been spent on things for Earl's bride, and I was indeed thankful that she liked everything. The engagement and wedding rings had been next to my heart on the whole journey, and I was most thankful when I could deliver them. Our YMCA wedding came off on Christmas afternoon in the home of the Braces and was very beautiful. Earl had been living since autumn in a small foreign-style house in the Manchu City. After the ceremony, they went there. We had our own Christmas dinner that evening, with the Yards and the two YW secretaries as our guests.

On the last night of 1920 I sat up to see the New Year in. Our house guest was a geology professor from Oberlin College named Hubbard. Bob was kept late at the Y, so we visited while we waited for him. Professor Hubbard and I talked of many things. He urged me to think seriously of sending at least one son to Oberlin. I told him there was very little chance of it.[2]

Soon after the new year, the Hodgkins returned to China and visited Chengtu for the tenth anniversary of the YMCA. The Chengtu Y had actually opened on December 23, 1910, but the tenth anniversary celebration was postponed to January 10, 1921, so that Dr. Hodgkin could be present. It was almost eleven years since the Hodgkins had returned to England. Their hosts, the Davidsons, had a tea for their old Chengtu friends. Out of a foreign community of over one hundred and seventy adults, fewer than twenty had been there for eleven years.

During the last part of their stay, the Hodgkins were our guests. A touching incident occurred when they left for their return to England. Our gardener had worked for them before he came to us. When they arrived to stay with us, I put this man in charge of their room. He was to get their baths, keep a fire going in their fireplace, and generally look after their needs. He did so, and very acceptably. When they left, Henry made a gift to the servants and then told us he wanted to leave a special present for Lao Chen. But it was not accepted. Lao Chen said it was through them that he had gotten a place with us; that they had always been kind to him; and that he could take no gift. He quoted Scripture: "Silver and gold have I not, but such as I have I give unto you." He wanted his loving service to them to be a gift. Henry, a wise man, accepted it.

Our usual round seemed very busy during that period. The YMCA was seething with life. Classes, lectures, and activities both at and away from the building absorbed Bob so that he spent his entire days there, eating noon meals in Chinese restaurants wherever he found himself. A group of Chinese friends had formed a mixed organization for social contacts. It was a new idea for men and women to meet together this way. There were about twenty Chinese married couples. Bob and I were the first foreigners invited to join. Later the Yards and the two YW secretaries became members. The latter were

2. The point to the Oberlin story is that one of Grace's sons (namely, I) did go there. But it was none of Bob and Grace's doing. It was always taken for granted, as the son of two fervent Californians, that I would go to Berkeley. A prefreshman experience of summer session at Berkeley convinced me that I would prefer a smaller school—such as Oberlin, where friends were going. Grace and Bob, by cable from Shanghai, characteristically said that the choice was for me to make—but it was a blow. Young Bob did go to UC, but Dick chose Pomona. Moving from a small high school in China to a big place like the Berkeley campus was not easy.

the only unmarried folk in the group. The fortnightly meetings were pleasant with games and tea. Now and then we had a meal together. Children came with their parents in true Chinese style. We were also active in an Anglo-Saxon League that had been organized during the war. And there were other irons in the fire. When we looked back on our early days of 1906 and 1907, it seemed in 1921 that we were living in a continual whirl.

There was a serious famine in North China in 1921. The Red Cross organized a bazaar to raise money for relief. The YMCA loaned space in its building, and both Bob and I were involved. One activity was a large room with ten or twelve tables for serving tea and cakes in the foreign manner. Behind this was a smaller room where I served fancier refreshments, including coffee, which at that time was new to the Chinese and therefore seemed more luxurious. I took over a carpet, curtains, large mirrors, dishes, table linen, and table silver. There were two small tables with a total of eight seats.

I served the guests myself, and my costume was an old black satin dress, a tiny black velvet hat, and a black silk coat which the Chinese seemed to consider elegant. Some women came, but wealthy men were my best patrons. One day I was happy to serve the governor, and also to sell him a large cake. I think many of the men were intrigued to see a foreign lady serving food this way. Word had gone out that no spitting was allowed. In those days it was quite normal in Chinese homes, though spittoons were coming into use in a way that was not pleasing to most of us. My coffee shop took in slightly more than two hundred dollars.

Many other foreigners worked hard for the bazaar. One of the most popular was Jim Yard in shabby clothes and blackface makeup. As none of the Chinese had ever seen a real Negro, he was always followed by a fascinated crowd who strained to hear his patter—promoting the need for charity. The military band was there to play. A native theatrical troupe gave its services. There were jugglers and other entertainment. Every afternoon at four a musical program was put on by foreigners. And of course there were lectures and pictures about the famine. It was all very *lao ray*.[3]

The entrance gate was a difficult spot, and Bob spent much of his time there. Many silk- and satin-garbed women with several children and amahs would try to push in on one ticket, never seeming to show any shame in hoping to beat down the gatekeeper in such a way. We took in over $3,500 but had hoped for $5,000. The old theater manager who took refreshment daily in my tearoom blamed the weather. He may have been right: the weather was unseasonably cold, and we even had a snow flurry one day.

To most of us, the bazaar had seemed a success. Foreigners and Chinese

3. *Lao ray* is the Szechwan version of *je nao,* which might be translated as "bustling with noise and excitement." (The characters are the same, but the Szechwanese reverse them and change the initial *n* to *l*.)

had cooperated at every point. A good end had been served in a pleasant way. But not everyone agreed. Some missionaries were very angry at the YMCA for allowing Chinese actors to appear in the building! One foreigner even told Bob that he would take the matter to the British consul and have the Y forbidden to have actors there again! This was rather a joke, the Y being a purely Chinese organization not in any way under the British consul. The man who complained so bitterly was a British Baptist. The man who arranged for the actors to appear was an American Baptist. The YMCA had nothing to do with securing the troupe. So we just had a good laugh.

35

Farewell to Chengtu

(1921)

For more than two years there had been discussion about opening YMCA work in Chungking. A group of Chinese there had asked for an Association to be organized, and the YMCA's National Committee in Shanghai had agreed that it would be carried out. Bob was the man who was spoken of to undertake this; and Bob, who loved pioneering, was much interested. Personally, I had always been intrigued by Chungking, the vitality of life in its crowded streets, and its rivers and hills. Selfishly, now that Jack was at school in Shanghai, there would be an advantage in being nearer the Coast. But our lives had become closely linked to Chengtu. Bob knew so many Chinese and had such wide interests. I was devoted to many friends, both Chinese and foreign. And then there was the bungalow at White Deer Summit: we would not be able to use it if we moved.

Other things entered into our thinking. Our home leave was due in 1922. It had been planned that I would take the children to Europe in 1921, having a year there before Bob came along to take us on to America. Bob, however, would not agree to take on the Chungking assignment unless he could have two years there before leaving for home leave. He felt that the task would require that much time in order to establish an organization of permanence and value. This meant that there could be no home leave until late 1923 or even 1924. Frankly, I wanted the European year. My plans had all been made with Miss Wellwood, a dear friend, and I hated to give them up. Also, I was not well. And I did not believe in always deferring furloughs.

Bob felt that duty always should come first. His devotion to the interests of the Y was ever the determining factor with him. In January 1920 I gave up plans for the European travel and told him that I agreed to the Chungking move if that seemed best. It was expected that we would move to Chungking sometime in 1921.

But early in 1921 it developed that there was some opposition to organizing a Y in Chungking. This was not from Chinese, but from some of our foreign missionary friends. At least two missions were attempting to carry on programs in Chungking that were somewhat similar to the Y. At first they had indicated a friendly attitude. Then they began to fear that they would be overshadowed if the Y came in. To them, the YMCA had a national and international background, which meant influence and prestige. It would soon succeed in attracting strong local support. And this would tend to weaken their own sectarian efforts.

One foreign gentleman, we heard, expressed the view: "That man Service is a whirlwind and if he gets down here, he'll soon have the Y booming." Bob had always emphasized that the role of the Y in relation to the missions was to be "ready to help the Church in every way possible." At first, the facts were hard to believe. When we were forced to realize that the opposition was real, we withdrew our offer to go to Chungking. Our Chengtu friends hoped that we would remain there. And some of my friends congratulated me on escaping the Chungking climate.[1]

The National Committee, though, decided to proceed with the plan to organize a Y in Chungking. And they wanted us to go there to do it. We would have a last summer at White Deer Summit and then move to Chungking. Our time suddenly was short; when spring ended, our life in Chengtu would also in effect come to an end. We decided to try to host the various organizations to which we belonged.

When the Fortnightly Club met at our home I presented a paper on George Bernard Shaw that I had been working on for two years. The subject was printed on our program as "G.B.S." Thinking only of my initials, one of the club members was heard to remark, "Well, I *am* surprised that Mrs. Service would give a whole evening about herself!" Meeting with our old friends of the Social Club gave us a new joy in those contacts. Bob was to speak at the university commencement. He tried so hard to prevent me from attending that I was determined to go. He spoke well and I was proud of him. His subject was "Laying down one's life in service for others."[2] He talked with the students, not at them.

Jack arrived from Shanghai with George Helde on June 25. It was a joy to have the lad home again. He seemed well, thin but with a good appetite for home food. George also looked well, and we were glad to have him back in West China. He had brought clothes ordered for Bob in Shanghai, and some purchased for me in New York. He also brought a movie projector for the Y, and a generator to make it work.

1. The Chungking climate is infamous: damp and foggy in winter, hot and muggy in summer. The Chinese refer to it as one of the "three furnaces." High hills, especially on the south bank of the Yangtze, block most breezes.
2. Most of the talks that I heard Bob give usually brought in the theme of "service."

EX-LIBRIS

R.R. & GRACE B. SERVICE

29   *Bob and Grace's bookplate, drawn by Ferry Shaffer about 1923. The mountain in the center is White Deer Summit. The knob on the left of the summit is Round Top. The small pagoda, below Round Top and in the center, is the pagoda at Fengtu near which Virginia died in 1906. The structure at the lower right is the ornate gate of the first Y building in Chengtu (mentioned in chapter 15). The Chinese characters below it are Chengtu and Grace's Chinese name. The building at the lower left is the YMCA at Chungking. The characters below it are Chungking and Bob's Chinese name. The characters on both structures are Qing Nian Hui (Youth Association), the usual Chinese name of the YMCA.*

Now we could leave for the bungalow at Round Top. All that summer my mind was constantly on our departure. The bungalow meant a great deal to all of us. The children loved it, but children can change allegiances easily. To Bob and me it meant home, *our own rooftree.* Practically every path on the mountain's summit had been planned or worked on by Bob. He used to love to cut away underbrush and clear new trails to points where surprising new vistas could be enjoyed. I had built a summerhouse with rustic seats and so

Bob thought to place rustic seats here and there on his paths. We loved the whole hill, and it was a wrench to think of leaving.[3]

The Y had stipulated that Bob was to have a real vacation that summer. He planned a mountain trip as his grand finale. It was the expedition he had thought of for years, but never felt he could take the time away from the Y to attempt. It would go beyond our nearby mountains, follow an old opium smugglers' trail across the main divide into the Min River valley, and reach Yao Bao-san's lumber country.[4] They would cross wild high country, far from towns or temples, so had to be equipped for camping.

The party—Bob, Jack, George Helde, and Dr. Reginald Morse—set off at the end of July. I had made sleeping bags for Bob and Jack with wadding of silk floss and tried (not very successfully) to make them waterproof. We also prepared food to last them for a week, and a load of supplies was sent to meet them at Weichow after they had crossed Big Ridge. One thing I prepared for them was two five-gallon cans of zwieback. They had two cameras, two fine compasses, a new aneroid barometer which George had just brought from America, hypsometers, thermometers, and what not. Dr. Morse was planning to take head measurements. He was interested in "cranial index" research, and looked forward to working in unstudied territory. Bob had fourteen cheap watches for possible use in barter.

There were ten carriers. They had lighter than normal loads (none over

3. After Grace and Bob left Chengtu, they had a bookplate made, which Grace used, I think, until her death. The central feature of the bookplate is the mountain White Deer Summit with Round Top clearly shown. See figure 29.

4. The Opium Wars established, among other things, that the Chinese government could not prohibit the import of opium. The principal importer (shipping opium grown in India) was Great Britain. The official British attitude was that China could not rightfully limit imports while freely permitting opium to be grown within China. In 1907 an Imperial edict ordered that opium growing in China be eliminated within three years. It was astonishing, for a dynasty generally considered to be tottering and no longer effective, that this herculanean task was largely achieved. After confirming the facts by on-the-spot investigation, the British stopped the export of opium from India. An account of this can be found in Sir Alexander Hosie, *On the Trail of the Opium Poppy* (Boston: Small Maynard, 1915?).

One area where growing was not completely stopped was the Tibetan border country, where Chinese control was very light. This would include the tributary valleys of the Min River above Kwanhsien. To evade inspection at Kwanhsien, trails like ours were used to smuggle opium out to the Chengtu plain. The anti-opium measures continued to be enforced during the first years of the Republic. But as the warlords took over, the situation was reversed. Far from being prohibited, opium planting was encouraged. Everyone, and especially the generals, was able to make money from it. With opium freely planted everywhere, there was no longer any need for smuggling. When we made our trip in 1921, our trail had probably not been used for six or seven years. The area where timber was being cut by Yao Bao-san (see chapter 30, note 5) was west of Weichow and the Min River near Lifan and Tsakulao (Zagunao). This borderland area had been visited more than twenty years before us by an intrepid Victorian lady, Isabella Bird. Her astonishing account, *The Yangtze Valley and Beyond,* has recently been republished in paperback (London: Virago Press, 1985). Miss Bird has vivid descriptions of traveling through the Yangtze Gorges by junk and overland by sedan chair. For the Lifan-Tsakulao area, see her chapters 29–34.

fifty pounds), and and each man carried extra clothing and a supply of food (mostly dry corn cakes). There was a headman for the carriers, two servants, and the essential guide, who claimed personal knowledge of the smugglers' trail. The carriers were all fine, strong fellows and looked fit for anything as they stood about laughing with Bob before the departure. Bob's idea was always to have the men in good humor before setting off on any journey.

It was well that the whole caravan had been carefully planned. The trip proved even more strenuous than they had anticipated. They had to cross two high divides, often camping in what the Chinese call "cliff nests" (nooks under overhanging crags). After the heights, they had to negotiate a tortuous gorge where heavy rains forced them to build several bridges. Their food, and that of the carriers, was exhausted before they reached Weichow, the first town. Jack celebrated his twelfth birthday on the trip, and wrote an account that was printed in our small local monthly, *West China Missionary News*. After Bob's death, fourteen years later, Dr. Morse wrote in the same magazine about Bob and the way he proved his sterling qualities on that mountain expedition.[5]

We left White Deer Summit earlier than usual that year. We had to prepare for our departure from Chengtu, and Jack had to be started on his way back to school in Shanghai. Adding to the problems, Dick was in and out of bed with an undiagnosed fever. Our last Chengtu days were more than full, with constant Chinese callers, engagements for this and that farewell meal, packing, and the thousand and one things that are more difficult in a land of medieval communications.

On September 2 there was a large farewell for Bob at the YMCA, with gifts, photographs, and speeches. The next day I fixed Dick up and left him with amah while I went to a tiffin in our honor. After tiffin I rushed home to see Dick and to dress for the farewell reception being given by the Braces and Domes. But when I reached our house, I found Chinese callers who had been awaiting me for three and a half hours! I felt I had to spend a few moments with them. When I arrived late at the reception, several asked me what could possibly have kept me so that I was late to a party being given in *my* honor!

5. Very briefly, the smugglers' trail was overgrown and in places had disappeared, so the guide repeatedly got lost. The Da Liangzi (Big Ridge) that we had to cross was higher than we anticipated (about 15,000 feet). That would not have been so bad if, in heavy fog and above the timber line, the guide had not followed a wrong line of ducks (small piles of rocks to indicate a trail). This lost us most of a day—at high elevation, in bitter cold and wet, with all of us (and especially the load carriers) poorly equipped for these conditions. When we finally found and crossed the pass, night was coming on and it was vital that we get down to timberline where we could find firewood and some shelter. In the darkness, one of the carriers (whose load had been taken by others) straggled and could not be found. Searchers found him, dead of exposure, in the morning. Bob felt responsible and took it very hard. When we returned, he made provision—considered generous by the Chinese—for the man's family.

This lawn reception was a lovely affair, and it happened to be on the same grounds as the reception to welcome our Chengtu arrival in the spring of 1906.

On September 6, 1921, we left Temple of Learning Street at eleven in the morning, got on our boat, and dropped down a mile or so below the East Gate to a teahouse at the Thunder God Temple. Here some thirty YMCA friends, all Chinese save George Helde, Earl Dome, and Bert Brace, had gathered to share a farewell meal in our honor. Immediately afterward we returned to our boat and were off. Long and imposing strings of firecrackers set off by our devoted friends signalled the departure. While we had been eating ashore, Amah had made my bed. As soon as we came inside the boat from waving farewells, I undressed and retired, utterly weary. I had been miserable for a week, but could not give up.

Since we were transporting our household and all our possessions, we had four mat-roofed boats (*wuban*) for the trip to Chungking. A Chinese Y secretary, Mr. Yuan, traveled with us; and with him was a young Chinese student bound for Shanghai. There were also four servants, two dogs, and two canaries. The horse coolie took the two ponies by land.[6]

6. With hindsight, it seems that this departure from Chengtu was a watershed in Bob's life. In the fifteen years since he had arrived there in 1906, Chengtu had become his field of accomplishment in a way that was remarkable for a foreigner. Unknowing, he passed, at the age of forty-two, the apex of his career.

PART FIVE

CHUNGKING

36

Starting in Chungking

(1921–22)

The down-river journey was uneventful, and on September 11 we were in Chungking. Two days later Bob and I took Jack and the Chinese student across the river to a Dollar steamer to start them on the long trip to Shanghai. We had friends in both Ichang and Hankow who could help them in changing steamers. Jack had some qualms about escorting a much older youth. He was the son of one of Bob's Chengtu friends, on his way to enter St. John's University in Shanghai. As the young man had never been to the Coast or traveled alone, the father had asked if he could send him with Jack. So Jack, only a high school freshman, had a college student in his care! He even turned his money over to Jack so it could be locked in a foreign trunk.[1]

In Chungking we wanted to rent a certain foreign-style house which was available and could have been occupied with very little renovation. However, the International Committee [in New York] would not approve the rent of Chinese $125 a month. We were told such rents were not paid, but the Committee evidently overlooked the rates in some other cities, such as Hankow. So we had to take the only other residence that was for rent. For this we paid $75 a month, but nearly $1,000 had to be spent to put it in livable condition. It was a small compound, on three levels (common in Chungking, where everything is built on hillsides), and located on Grazing Cow Lane. Bob tackled the place with his usual optimism. I was horrified at the many large windows, ugly in size and framing, and got off an order to Shanghai for curtain material. It would take several months to get the place in shape.

In the meantime we rented a bungalow belonging to the McCartneys. This

---

1. The important consideration was not so much "the foreign trunk" as that the boy was in very crowded dormitory accommodations where security of valuables was a problem. The only way for me to communicate with my charge was for me to go below: he could not come topside to the first-class (foreign) space on the breezy upper deck.

was on the crest of the hills across the river from the city, in a grove of large pine trees—which gave it the name of Pine Lodge. The house was pleasant, but had some odd features. The two lads loved the dumbwaiter from the basement kitchen to the large living-dining room. This spacious room and its adjacent hall had no doors connecting them to any other part of the house, and to reach our bedroom we had to go outdoors and even off the veranda.

One of the many strange things about this house was the way our landlord's wife kept sending up for furniture from it. We had rented the place "as is" and already had found much less than we had expected. One day her coolie came for the only decent mirror. This was the straw that broke the camel's back. I sent him back to tell his master and mistress that if they wanted us to move, we would do so; but I would not allow anything more to be taken from the house. He went dejectedly away, but never came again to bother us.[2]

Dick was still not well. We found there was a mission doctor who was a child specialist. She ordered no lessons, and plenty of time on the hills among the pines. As soon as the horse coolie arrived from Chengtu with the ponies, the two lads had great fun on the hill paths.[3] Young Bob, though, had to do his lessons every morning.

The foreign community in Chungking was much more heterogeneous, and more scattered, than in Chengtu. Being a treaty port, there were representatives of foreign business firms. In addition, there were the personnel of gunboats of several foreign nations, and some of the commanding officers might have their families living ashore. And there were more consuls than in Chengtu, including an American consul. Most of the missionaries lived in the city or on the city side of the river. Most of the business people lived across from the city on the south bank of the river. I soon began to have callers, who came in spite of the considerable trip to our hilltop. City friends had to cross the river by sampan[4] and then climb the hill. One fortnight there was only one afternoon without callers. Everyone was hungry and thirsty when they arrived, so the servants were busy with sandwiches and tea.

2. By this time, Dr. McCartney had left the mission. He was running a drug and general store. His wife was acquiring and renting summer bungalows on the hills. It has always been assumed that he is Somerset Maugham's "Dr. Macalister" in the story by that name in *On a Chinese Screen* (New York: Doran, 1922). When I served in Chungking during World War II, Dr. McCartney's widow was still very much present. With the moving of China's capital to Chungking, there had been a great influx of foreign diplomatic, military, and other war-related personnel. Her bungalows on the hills had now become a bonanza (and not just for summer occupancy).

3. Grace speaks of both horses and ponies. They are the same. The Szechwan horse is a rather runty breed, but it is still a horse.

4. A sampan is any small Chinese boat. The name, *sanban* in Mandarin, means three planks and refers to the width of the flat-bottomed hull. The larger boats used for travel between Chengtu and Chungking were *wuban*, meaning five planks.

At Chungking the Yangtze makes several turns, and the ranges of hills across the river cut off the summer breezes from the city. Soft-coal cooking fires, both summer and winter, make the air smoky. When this smoke haze unites with river mist, there is formed a blanket of cloud which acts like a greenhouse. The air is close and stuffy and much dirtier than in Chengtu. The summers are very bad, and the foreigners have to go to the hills.[5]

In early October telegraph communications with the Coast were broken, and we heard that ships were detained for a while by fighting in and around Ichang. We finally had a letter from Jack posted in Ichang, so we knew he had reached there safely. He said the "Dollar" was fired upon on her way down. We had repeatedly urged Jack both to wire and write us when he reached Shanghai. Although he had left Chungking on September 14, we did not hear of his arrival at the Coast for over a month. We then received a letter one day and a telegram the next. Both had been sent from Shanghai on the same day! He had had a somewhat exciting trip, and in Ichang was on a steamer in port when there was some fighting involving troops of Wu Pei-fu. When the shooting commenced during the night, the captain had the foreign passengers (whose cabins were on the upper deck) called to come to his cabin, which was shielded by steel plates. Through an oversight, Jack was not called and lay asleep in his cabin while bullets flew thick and fast and the ship was struck many times. The next morning the ship's officers were astonished to see this twelve-year-old boy emerge from his cabin for breakfast.[6] Fortunately, I did not learn of this until Jack had been safe for some time in Shanghai.

That fall, under Bob's impetus, the board of directors for a Chungking YMCA was formed and began functioning. Part of a very large and fine guild

5. From Chengtu it had been at least two days travel to the hills: in Chungking they were just across the Yangtze. But instead of being 6,000 feet high (like White Deer Summit), the Chungking hills were not much more than 1,000 feet above the city. Still, they got one above the fog and smog and high enough to catch some breeze.

6. Grace's account is not quite accurate: I was not asleep. But I didn't know that the captain's cabin was swathed in boiler plate; and I thought that remaining horizontal was the best position to assume. General Wu Pei-fu had become something of a super-warlord with his principal base in Hupeh, the province just east of Szechwan. The Szechwan warlords had traditionally stayed at home: there was a lot of turf to fight over there, and always the need to compete with greedy intruders from the poorer provinces of Yunnan and Kweichow. But in 1921 Wu Pei-fu began to intrigue to establish alliances that could gain him a foothold in Szechwan. This annoyed the Szechwan generals sufficiently that several of them forgot their usual squabbles long enough to form a joint expedition against Wu. This was to coordinate with a simultaneous attack on Wu by the warlord in Hunan, the province to Wu's south. In the skirmish in which I was "involved," the Szechwan forces held the city of Ichang. During the night some Wu Pei-fu troops, on commandeered Chinese-owned steamers, anchored offshore and bombarded the city. It was probably not by chance that these attacking forces positioned themselves so that the foreign ships along the Ichang waterfront served them as a protective screen. This ended the Szechwan expedition; they evacuated Ichang (looting the banks and main businesses as they left) and returned to their usual domestic squabbles.

hall had been secured for a place in which to start the Association.[7] Early in December the Y moved into this place, pushing out soldiery who had been in unauthorized occupation for many months. General Yang Sen had a notice posted on the door that the building had become headquarters for the YMCA and that no one was to molest them in their use of it. It was a fine stroke of business for the guild to rent to the Y, as the building had been treated badly by the military. The location and building were excellent for Y work, and Bob had many congratulations for having secured so fine a place. We succeeded in establishing friendly relations with everyone, even with the two Britishers who had opposed the coming of the Y, and ourselves in particular. We understood their zeal and concern for their own organizations, and tried to see their point of view. Bob's idea of the Y was that it should supplement other lines of Christian work, not run as competition.[8]

In November, Hugo Sandor, a Hungarian, was assigned to Chungking by the American-Oriental Bank of Shanghai. He used to come to our house often. At Christmas we had him and Arba Heald, an American from the same bank, with us at Pine Lodge. We all had a good time in snappy cold weather, with some sunshine to gladden our hearts.[9]

As 1922 began, we were more and more impatient to move into the house in the city. There was much work to be done. One thing we had learned was that people referred to it as "the house with the awful mantels." We had the over-mantels removed, leaving plain shelves. We found enough tiles for simple fireplace facings. All the walls were scraped and painted buff. Three doors (those leading out from the front hall to living room, dining room, and study) were scrapped. They were terribly chewed (evidently by giant rats!) and were also poorly made. These were replaced by attractive new doors, chiefly of glass set in small panes. These brought light into the hall and improved all three rooms. All the woodwork was scraped and painted white. Screens and outside wood work were done in green.

The kitchen was thoroughly renovated, rat-proofed, and screened. The

7. The guild hall that the Y was able to get the use of was a *huiguan,* which is a club of fellow provincials in an alien province. In this case, it was the Kiangsi guild.

8. Apparently, the Y in Chungking was able to organize itself in less than four months (Bob had arrived in early September), whereas organization took more than four years (1906 to 1910) in Chengtu. Certainly some preliminary spadework had been done, but it seems likely that the most important factor was that leaders of the Chinese community in Chungking knew about the popularity and success of the Y in their neighboring city.

9. Hugo Sandor had been an officer in the Austro-Hungarian army in World War I. Captured by the Russians, he escaped from prisoner-of-war camp during the Russian Revolution, managed to cross Siberia, and reached Shanghai. His English became perfect, and he had been employed by a local American bank in Shanghai to help staff their newly opened Chungking branch. When Bob and Grace met him, he was unmarried, in his early thirties, handsome, cultured, with a dash of élan and continental gallantry. Grace had just reached forty-two. I think he provided a stimulus to her, both as an intellectual and as a woman, that she had not found in the more limited, missionary society of Chengtu. Their warm friendship (which certainly was never more than that) was lasting and important to Grace.

massive sand filters were arranged in tiers. In them the Yangtze water had to be strained through gravel, sand, and finally charcoal. A new door from the kitchen into the ironing room gave much better ventilation to both rooms, and also made it possible for the flatirons to be heated on the kitchen range. The cook had a fire anyway, so this plan was more economical than the usual practice of having a charcoal fire simply for iron heating. We moved into the city at the end of January 1922, and it took quite some time to get everything in running order.

About this time I attended an interesting social event. It was an elaborate tiffin party given at the home of a British friend by the wife of a Chinese military official. She had begged the British lady to "help her to entertain" in this manner. Every resource of my friend's home had been placed at the disposal of the Chinese hostess, who was to foot all the expenses. The long table was beautifully decorated and appointed. A delicious Western meal was served. Twenty sat down at the table, three or four foreigners and fifteen or more Chinese. The British lady had "spent much heart" and intimated to me that once was enough for her to undertake such entertainment.

Imagine our amazement during the meal when one of the Chinese guests (Mrs. A) began to praise the meal and the arrangements, and to ask the Chinese hostess (Mrs. B) how she was able to entertain in this way in a British home. Hearing that it had been arranged through the kindness of the British lady (Mrs. C) with Mrs. B paying the cost, Mrs. A promptly said (in Chinese, of course), "That is very good. I enjoy foreign food and like the Western ways of entertaining. I have known Mrs. C a long time and am sure she will be as willing to let me entertain here as she has been for Mrs. B—that's true, isn't it, Mrs. C? Well then, please all come here as *my* guests next Tuesday." Poor Mrs. C was struck dumb and could foresee a long succession of parties to upset her already busy existence. She finally rallied to tell Mrs. A that she was sorry but she already had other engagements for Tuesday. But Mrs. A was not to be done out of her tiffin party and announced in a loud voice, "It cannot be on Tuesday, but Thursday will do. So everybody come on Thursday." In an aside to Mrs. C she remarked, "Don't let it bother you at all. Today is fine. On Thursday we can have the very same things to eat." As we left, Mrs. A urgently begged me to be on hand for "her" party.

I had not intended to go, but a note from Mrs. C urged me to come. The tiffin went off as planned, and practically all the same guests were present. No doubt the pride of the Chinese hostess was satisfied. Perhaps there was a desire to keep up with a social rival in some intrigue of the hour. Real Chinese ladies have a genuineness of breeding which would prevent such presumption. Unfortunately, among the plural wives of warlords, one may find anything but the refinements of culture.

Soon after these tiffin parties, a wife of a general sent word to me that she had heard that Westerners knew how to knit very cleverly. She also knew that I had children and had done knitting for them. Now she was about to have a child and would be very happy if I would be so good as to knit a complete outfit for it, as she intended to dress it in foreign-style clothes. I am sorry that my kindness did not extend this far. Anyway, the baby was to be born in hot weather, so would not suffer much if it lacked the knit bootees, cap, coat, and panties she specifically mentioned.

Small Bob celebrated our moving into the city by falling over one of the dogs while playing in the yard. He tore ligaments in his heel, and had to be put in bed with his leg in splints. It gave him a great deal of pain. Often he begged me not to come into the room, saying the floor shook, the bed shook, and everything shook until it hurt him. But he enjoyed his many make-believe games, and the servants were his willing slaves to bring things to him and find ways to amuse him.[10]

It took me some time to repay all my city calls, foreign and Chinese. I extended my list to include the Seventh-Day Adventist ladies, also a French woman who was the wife of a businessman. Although they had been in Chungking over a year, the Seventh-Day Adventist ladies knew almost no one among the more than a hundred and fifty foreigners in the city. There was a considerable feeling against their church by other missionaries because of their proselytizing habits.[11] They knew of me, as I had a calling acquaintance with ladies of their mission in Chengtu. The French lady had few friends and was delighted to see me, albeit that we were obliged to converse through her French-speaking Boy.

The Seventh-Day Adventists had gone to call on the lady at one Chungking mission compound. While their sedan chairs were being put down in the court, a gentleman member of that mission, seeing the initials SDA on the bearers' coats, came out and told the ladies he thought they had better not come in to call. In the States many people of all denominations go to the Battle Creek Sanatorium and other SDA facilities, and we do not expect anyone to refuse civilities to people of that faith. Later in the spring I had a tea especially for the Seventh-Day Adventist ladies and invited a few chosen spirits, who were happy to meet them and have tea in their company. We had a jolly time and broke down a barrier or two.

10. Among the three of us boys, Bob was the one who spent most time with the servants. He was interested in their work about the house and enjoyed talking with them. One result was that he excelled us in spoken Chinese.

11. The unfortunate Seventh-Day Adventists were unpopular for several reasons. They refused to respect missionary territorial agreements. Their insistence on a different Sabbath was believed to be more confusing to potential Chinese converts than the less-conspicuous doctrinal differences between, say, Methodists and Baptists. Because tithing was successful among their church members in America, their missions were relatively well supported. This led to accusations that they sometimes lured Chinese staff away from other missions by offering higher pay. To many, they were "sheep stealers."

That spring we became acquainted with some of the officers on the two American gunboats in port, the *Palos* and the *Monocacy*. When the captain of the *Palos* was visiting us, he said that he had not been in a real home for over four months. He later entertained us royally in return. Having heard of Bob's fondness for ice cream, there was a large freezer of a delicious caramel flavor—of which we all had more than one dish.

There were several German ladies in the city, so I struck up an acquaintance with them. They were lonely and had no contacts with either the British or the French. I got on very well with an engineer's wife who could speak a little English, and I enjoyed her clever remarks. Frau Fischer, whose husband was in the consulate, gave us great pleasure with her beautiful voice.

All spring we had a succession of house guests. Every now and then the two children had to be moved into our bedroom so that we could have the use of two guest rooms. Among the guests were the Owen Robertses of New York, who were particularly interested in our Tibetan things.[12] Mr. Roberts talked Bob out of a pair of long telescoping horns. We had a pair of these eight-foot-long horns hanging in our front hall. They were brass and copper, polished until they shone. One Chungking lady was intrigued by them and asked what they were. "Lama horns from Tibet," was my answer, and she soliloquized, "Indeed! Fancy an animal having horns like that!"

Our faithful old laundry boy, Lao Wu, was ill for a month and we missed him sorely. Noticing that he looked poorly that spring, I had asked him several times how he was. He always said he was well. But finally Amah told me that he could not sit down. Lao Wu feared to tell me because he dreaded foreign hospitals and was sure that I would send him to one. That is just what I did. The doctors found that he had a terrible case of piles and needed an immediate operation and rest. I went to see him in hospital while he was lying there still on liquid diet. He was quite upset to have me standing by his bed without him being on his own feet. He came back a bit thinner but feeling well, and his ideas of hospitals were somewhat changed.

12. Some years later, Owen Roberts became an associate justice of the United States Supreme Court.

37

River City

(1922)

In Chungking there was one constant interest, the Big River. The difference between high and low water levels could be as much as one hundred feet. We soon learned to regulate life by the river's rise or fall. It was most exciting when the summer floods came. The stream rose day by day, sometimes hour by hour. At the city gates the steps became fewer and fewer.

From the veranda of our city house we looked down on the river. The children watched a row of sharp rocks near the opposite shore. In winter they stood out as small islands. In spring they became covered. And in summer they produced a bad rapid where many boats met disaster. The sandbank island above the city, now used during the winter as an airplane landing field, became covered by the swirling flood. Then the winter homes of thousands who lived in frail shelters clinging to the cliffs below the city walls had to be taken down. They were like swallows' nests but less enduring. The swift-moving mass of the river's sweep around the city was always impressive; in high water it was awesome. Daily in high water, the river took its toll in life; I saw many boats sunk and lives lost there.

Life in Chungking was quite different from life in Chengtu. The Chungking streets were dirty, but I have heard doctors say that Chungking is better off for sanitation than most Chinese cities. Its location on a steep hill of solid rock means that heavy rain (of which there is plenty) flushes away all the refuse and sewage.

Both cities had busy streets, with open shop fronts and all kinds of crafts and manufacture being carried on. But in Chungking there was the added work of the great river commerce. Near the riverbank were huge godowns,[1] of hides, bristles, Chinese herbs, tung oil, and all the other many exports.

---

1. A godown is a warehouse. It comes from a Malay word, *gedang*. For some reason, no one in the Far East would think of saying "warehouse."

There, too, were piles of cotton yarn, cloth from spinning mills at the Coast, and all sorts of foreign goods. The steps were congested with laboring coolies struggling under large bales, or working in groups to move large containers with poles and ropes. Often our ears were filled by their singsong chants to keep in step as they labored. The junkmen, too, had their own chanteys while they rowed in unison as their long junks came sweeping down on the current.[2]

There is a push to Chungking affairs, a surge in the seething life on its rock, an urge in ordinary affairs which shows the virility and force of the Szechwanese. Some have said they lack the polish of the men of the Coast. They may not have the suavity of the south. But—when they keep away from opium—they are vigorous, stalwart, and democratic. And in Chungking they show it.

There was also, as I have mentioned, an active and diverse foreign community. One of its activities was a small Community Church. This needed renovation and new seats. Bob and I helped with an ambitious auction and tea. It was a novelty that appealed to many who were tired of appeals for money. There were many unusual contributions of things to be auctioned. And we had a record crowd for the event. A British businessman proved to be an excellent auctioneer. Friend bid against friend. A bachelor found himself with a sewing machine. General Yang Sen bought a sofa cushion with the embroidered names of most of the foreign community.[3] A few Tibetan things that Bob had donated went like hot cakes. Bob himself won a freezer of ice cream from the *Palos*. The sale was a huge success and netted $1,000, besides providing fun and a get-together such as the community had seldom seen.

The military situation was very unsettled that year and there were frequent troop movements. One result was that it became very hard to get chair carriers when we needed them. Many men had been seized and forced into serving as load bearers for the military. Those who had not been impressed did not want to run the risk of appearing on the street. We finally had to adopt the practice of the consulates and foreign firms: employ our own full-time carriers and outfit them with uniforms. My tailor produced attractive outfits with red triangles and the letters Y.M.C.A.[4]

2. Grace was interested in collecting and transcribing these songs and chanteys. So far as I know, she didn't have much success. There was, of course, nothing like a tape recorder in those days.
3. Yang Sen was probably the most flamboyant of the Szechwan militarists. He cultivated a reputation for modern attitudes, tried to stamp out footbinding and gambling, widened streets, and supported education and athletics. His ambitions were often greater than his means; he was unable to follow through on most of his progressive plans; and by 1927 he was losing out to General Liu Hsiang, who became the Szechwan Number One. It was Yang's wife (or one of his wives—his "modern" ideas did not include strict monogamy) who initiated the tiffin-giving in the home of Grace's British friend.
4. The point, of course, was that the soldiery knew that there would be complications if they impressed even chair bearers of foreigners, which shows that extraterritoriality could reach

Mr. Edgar, our old friend from Tatsienlu, spent some time in Chungking that spring. He was a man with a thousand interests, who could talk well and with authority on many topics. Beyond his righteous zeal in God's work, he had broad knowledge of ethnology, geography, philology, Asia, and his native Australia. Instead of despairing at the isolation of his life on the remote Tibetan border, he made sure that his environment, and his books, enlarged his mind and vision. I owe much to this man, whose knowledge was profound and whose humor was penetrating and kindly.

That year the Dragon Boat Festival, in May, was unusually good. There were more than twenty boats, some with as many as forty-six rowers. Each boat represented a *matou* and had been training for weeks.[5] Most of the decorative care was in the dragon heads on the bows of the long, narrow craft. These were gaily painted in reds, blues, and greens, with beards that reached the water, long white fangs, lolling crimson tongues, horns, scales, and all the other accoutrements of dragonhood. Each crew had its own distinctive, colorful uniforms. Each boat had a coxswain, a man to beat a great drum, and many banners. Thousands of people lined the shores, cheering the rival craft. All this went on in the Small River (the Kialing). The swifter waters of the Yangtze were too turbulent and dangerous. I was content with seeing a practice a few days earlier from the safe (and close) vantage of the Dollar Company launch.

The actual day of the races was very hot. The servants all rose early and ate a huge meal to fortify themselves for a day of sightseeing. Amah topped this off by drinking a bowl of molasses. She said afterward that this had been diluted with some hot water. Evidently it was a potent draught! In the middle of the morning she was taken violently ill. She took a lot of Chinese medicine. I tried to help by giving an emetic. She called a Chinese doctor and ate more drugs, but nothing eased her suffering. She lay howling on her bed in her small room which, by the peculiar arrangement of our house, was over our front vestibule. Thus she was very close to the street, and it sounded to passers-by as though someone was being murdered just inside our gate. Bob came to take the children to see the boat races and told me we simply could *not* have such a screeching going on in our place. Apart from Amah's obvious suffering, it would not do to have such a commotion attracting the attention of people in the street. His verdict was that dealing with it was a woman's job. It was not that he shirked responsibility, but he felt this was essentially an occasion for my offices.

---

rather far. Grace was certainly the only YMCA wife riding in a sedan chair with liveried bearers.

5. A *matou* on the rivers in Szechwan is a riverbank area where boats moor or discharge cargo, a landing place. It may also be a jetty or wharf.

Finally, after Lao Wu, the laundry coolie who had lived through his own hospital experience, and Lao Chen, the faithful gardener she had known for years, had talked to her for a long time, she consented to go to the Methodist Women's Hospital. Then no chair men could be found to carry her—everybody was hanging over the city wall to watch the races. Finally, late in the afternoon, we were ready to move her. She was still groaning heart-rendingly, but was too weak to talk. I managed to raise her to a sitting position. Lao Chen sat on his haunches beside her bed; we put her arms around his neck and he held them fast. We helped him rise, and he staggered down the stairs with her on his back. There we laid her on a light bamboo couch, and the chair men carried her off to the hospital with an urgent note.

The hospital folk told me later that it was cholera morbus, and that they were obliged to use the stomach pump before she had any relief. She lay weak as a rag for days; had to have enemas and finally worm medicine; and at last came home a sadder, and I hoped, a wiser woman. Many a time later did I hear her discoursing on the "stomach machine."

The American navy's new admiral paid a visit to Chungking that spring and brought his wife, who I found charming.[6] When we entertained them at tiffin, she was fascinated by my table decorations. These were particularly nice Chinese hair ornaments of wired gardenias and jasmine buds, the flowers set off by silver beads. A Danish engineer friend had happened that morning to meet a flower seller with a tray of these fragile creations. He bought all the peddler had and had them sent to me, fresh and lovely, just in time to become my impromptu table ornament. When my guest left, I gave them all to her, but their fragrance lives on in my mind!

There was an important mission conference in Shanghai that year. We heard reports of it that were interesting for their diversity as well as their content. Several told of the spirit of unity, of how wise it was that the Chinese should want their own indigenous church without the denominational differences of Western churches, and of progress being made along these lines. Later we heard from the "minority side." A man spoke with bated breath of the dangers confronting us, of how we must expect serious splits in the church in China, of painful events ahead. Bob and I talked long about these matters. He was constantly saying how glad he was to be in inter-

6. The admiral was Rear Admiral W. H. G. Bullard, who had just assumed command of the United States Navy's Yangtze Patrol and was taking his wife on his initial tour of inspection. In 1922 the Yangtze Patrol was six or seven ships with a combined tonnage of less than 3,000 tons. The admiral's flagship, USS *Isabel* (950 tons), was unable to navigate the Gorges, so the admiral and his wife had to arrive by a passenger ship of the Robert Dollar line. The strange and surprising saga of the U.S. Navy on the Yangtze is well told by Kemp Tolley in *Yangtze Patrol* (Annapolis: Naval Institute Press, 1971).

denominational work, such as the YMCA, where there was no need to preach any "ism."

About this time it came to our ears that a certain group was praying for us because we read the books of Harry Emerson Fosdick, and also because these books were distributed by the YMCA Publication Department and could be obtained through our Chungking Y. A few missionaries were much opposed to the liberalism of Dr. Fosdick and prayed that the curses of Heaven might fall on him and his books, and those who spread his doctrines.[7]

All that spring I was miserable and found the heat very trying. We had rented a Friends' Mission bungalow, but moving in was delayed by repairs. The agent of the Dollar Company had a company bungalow on the first range which he seldom visited. We were glad to accept his invitation to use it for several weeks. Jack, traveling alone from Shanghai, arrived while we were there in late June.

The American community gave a big sports event and picnic on the Fourth of July. We were able to use the playing field of the Friends' Mission Boys School on the first range. The entire foreign community was invited. Bob and I were both on the committee, and the American gunboats helped by providing baked beans and ice cream. After supper there was a program in the school auditorium. A British businessman loaned a generator so there could be movies; an American businessman did some sleight-of-hand; and there were other entertainments. Everyone had a good time, and we decided that 135 must have attended. This was quite a record for Chungking. We kept one Seventh-Day Adventist couple for the night, and Mrs. McCartney took the other couple, so they were not left out. We had eleven people sleeping with us that night.[8]

The next day we moved to the Friends' bungalow that we had rented on the second range. That made the sixth house we had lived in within a year. I was tired out. White Deer Summit was often in our minds, but we tried not to speak of its cool breezes. This bungalow had four rooms, nicely arranged. There were verandas, and a special corner had been built out to the cliff's edge for view and any breeze there might be. The site was known as Killing Cow Flat, which seemed a bit odd because in Chungking city we lived on Grazing Cow Lane.

---

7. Dr. Fosdick, 1878–1969, was a Baptist minister who became a professor of theology at Union Theological Seminary and then pastor of the Riverside Church in New York. He became internationally known as a Modernist leader and spokesman in the Fundamentalist controversies of the 1920s.

8. It was dangerous and usually impossible to cross the Yangtze at night by sampan. When people living in the city were invited to dinner or an evening engagement on the South Bank, the host normally had to arrange accommodations for the night. When Bob and Grace were spending the summer on the hills, there were few weekends without overnight guests.

The Y was considering another couple for the Y in Chungking. We had been corresponding with them and trying to be helpful. They finally sent word in August that they would not be coming west: the climate and lack of school facilities did not please them.

While we were at the hills Bob went to the city daily, and it was a long, hard trip. Our sturdy chair men who carried Bob expected to be drenched daily, so the frequent rains did not disturb them. They wore only two garments. If the weather was dry, these would be soaked with perspiration; if it rained, they would also be wet. We provided hats for sun and for rain, and they wore whichever was appropriate. He usually had lunch at the tiffin club that had been started by the American-Oriental Bank, and often was not home until after eight in the evening. The Y was going quite nicely by that time, and the rooms at the guild building were attractive and useful. Bob was constantly enlarging his circle of Chinese friends. The general commanding our resident troops had seen and admired Bob's silk shirts, so that summer I superintended the making of several for this gentleman.

We shared a tennis court in a shady dell some two hundred feet below the bungalow. Twice a month I poured tea. Everything had to be carried down from the house. Several times we had sudden downpours and, no matter how we rushed, everything got soaked. I had a samovar for boiling water, and that helped, because some days it seemed as though I poured hundreds of cups of tea.

Some of our rains that summer were truly subtropical. One evening, British friends near us planned a large supper party. They had invited fifty people. The lanterns were hung, decorations up, tables set on the terraces, and an elaborate dinner ready. About 6:30 a terrific storm came up. The cloud effects were such as I have never seen before or since. I had been out calling, and the chair men came running to get me home to escape the storm. Bob had come home early to dress. Just as he was getting into the tub, a window above it was shattered by the force of the wind, and a shower of broken glass fell over and about him. We lived too near to have a good excuse, but even in my chair I got well soaked getting there. Counting the hosts, only twelve made it to the party. Without refrigeration, there was no way to save most of the food. Some of the nearby villagers must have eaten well that night.

There were many fine trees on the Friends' property where we were living. The largest were pines, but we also had laurel, holly, bamboo, banana, tung oil, blue gum, and more whose names I did not know. From those tall pines around our bungalow there was an incessant soft murmur of the upper branches whose susurrant harmony never ceased, day or night. How often I lay listening to that delightful sound, as though the hissing of the sea surge had been captured far inland by those aromatic branches! Those trees were friends of our summer life in Chungking.

Unfortunately, the hard storms that year took a toll. But much worse happened during the troubles of 1927. The Friends' bungalows, including this one, and their girls' school nearby were all destroyed, and every one of our beautiful trees cut down.[9]

9. From 1924 to 1927 the Kuomintang and the Chinese Communist Party worked together in the First United Front. In the name of nationalism, there was a broad campaign against "imperialism," which was often interpreted (by the more radical elements) to include missionary work. Most missionaries were evacuated from Szechwan, and there was some destruction of mission properties. Many missionaries blamed the Communists, but they also used to refer to Chiang Kai-shek, until he turned against the Communists at Shanghai in April 1927, as "the Red general." There will be more on this later.

38

Young Bob to Shanghai
(1923)

During that year I had seen that small Bob was not going forward with his lessons in the best way for his development. He was not happy working alone, and would be better off doing classroom work with others of his own age. He was then eleven, the age at which Jack had gone to Shanghai, and it seemed wise to send him, also. But whereas Jack was pleased to go away, Bob was not at all eager; indeed, he was anxious *not* to go. To send a boy of that age away from home for ten months is hard; when he has to be pushed out of the home, it is even more difficult for the mother's heart. The only way seemed for me to go to the Coast with the two boys, planning to stay there until Bob felt somewhat at home in his new surroundings. So this trip was in mind during that summer on the hills.

In August there was fighting on the river around Wanhsien. The foreign steamers refused to transport Chinese troops. The angry and frustrated soldiers sometimes subjected the steamers to heavy gunfire. Our American gunboat, the *Palos,* went down to Wanhsien, but could not prevent ships from being fired on at other points on the river. On one recent trip the *Alice Dollar* had received more than three thousand hits; more than four hundred went through the foreign cabins! The passengers were in the captain's cabin and bridge, which were protected by steel plates. Miraculously, the only casualty was the captain, and he had only a nick on the chin from a spent bullet. I was glad that I would be with the two lads. No matter what the dangers, it would be better than sitting at home with no word as to their welfare.

It was still very hot, but the time came to move to the city. We were expecting the whole Yard family to stay with us. They were moving from Chengtu to Shanghai, and the two lads and I would travel with them. We and our goods reached the Chungking city house on a Tuesday. That midnight we had a telegram saying the Yards would arrive on Thursday. So we had Wednesday to accomplish a thousand errands, clean house, and get clothing—mine and that of the two lads—ready for our imminent departure. I told Amah that we would leave the making of guest room beds and such items until early Thursday; we agreed to rise at 5:30 to have plenty of time.

On Wednesday afternoon, like a bolt from a clear sky, there came a note from Jim: "Will arrive at your house in about five minutes." I just had time to slip into a clean dress as they came in the gate. The Boy immediately put on tea. While we were having it, the amah and coolie made beds and arranged their rooms, so all was well. Everyone was excited, and we forgot how tired we were in our joy over their safe arrival. Though hailed by bandits six times, they had never stopped and reached Chungking in excellent traveling time.[1]

Originally, I had thought I would take Dick to the Coast with me. Later we changed that and he was left in Chungking. He would sleep at home, spend the day at the McCurdys' house, and return home in time for dinner with his father. Mrs. McCurdy would give him his lessons.[2]

The heat, excitement, and rush of preparations were too much for me. My ankles and knees were painful and began to swell with rheumatic fever. The doctor told me to get out of town as quickly as I could. The last day in Chungking was torture; severe pain, six guests, packing to finish, and orders from the doctor to keep off my feet. We went to the *Alice Dollar* on the afternoon of September 1. I was thankful to hobble aboard and lie on a deck chair.

The *Alice* was still full of bullet holes from her recent experience, but we got through quite well. In Hankow, the lads and I had to wait two days for the next ship. I rested and saw the doctor, and the delay did me good. As usual, I had brought along some reading material; this time it was *Social Psychology,* by E. A. Ross,[3] and Keynes's *Economic Consequences of the Peace.* After our brief Hankow interlude, we had a pleasant trip to Shanghai. But when we arrived, on September 12, we found ourselves in the midst of a raging typhoon. Our ship did not even venture up to a hulk but tied up to buoys out in the Whangpoo.[4] There was nothing for it but to take a tiny, eggshell sampan to reach the shore.

It was always exciting to visit Shanghai. I stayed with good Y friends near

1. Wind and weather may have helped the Yards to arrive earlier than expected. Probably more important was high water: generally speaking, the higher the water, the faster the current.

2. Mr. McCurdy was a pastor of the American Methodist Mission. He and his wife were probably Bob and Grace's closest friends among the American missionary community. Their closest British missionary friends were Hetty and Warburton Davidson of the Friends' Mission (see chapters 6 and 7).

3. E. A. Ross, it will be recalled, had stayed with Bob and Grace in Chengtu in 1910 (chapter 16).

4. Because of the great fluctuation of water levels at most river ports, steamers tie up to large floating structures, known as hulks, that are usually connected to the shore by some sort of bridge.

the American School. The boys were soon settled in school. I was able to see a good deal of them, particularly of Bob, and of Mabelle Yard, who was getting her family settled in an apartment. Bob had told me to stay on the Coast until young Bob was willing for me to return to Chungking. The lad finally admitted that he liked school "well enough, but not as well as home." I told him I was pleased to hear that; I certainly hoped no son of mine would ever like any school as well as his own home! When I asked if he thought it would be all right for me to return to his father and Dick, he hesitated but at last said, "I suppose so." Within a few days I began to make preparations for the long trip west.

I left Shanghai on October 24. When I arrived on the ship in the late evening, it was discovered that, though my ticket was in perfect order, no space had been reserved for me. And none was available; a British theatrical troupe (The Powder Puffs) on their way to Hankow had filled most of the cabins. The Number One Boy [steward] insisted that I would have to leave the ship. Finally, we discovered that a married couple was getting off at Nanking; if I could find a place to sleep for the first two nights, I could have their cabin. More investigation found that there was a missionary lady with a baby in a two-berth cabin. They were in bed and asleep, but when I explained my situation she kindly rearranged her child and possessions so I could share the cabin. All this time, the two lads and a friend who had brought us down to the ship were standing by. In the exigencies of the occasion, I had little time for last words with small Bob. He behaved well and agreed to do his best.

I had gone to the Coast with one trunk, one suitcase, and one small handbag. With all my purchases, mostly for others, I returned with three trunks, three suitcases, one bag, seven boxes, and various bundles. In Hankow I secured the help of the Christian and Missionary Alliance baggage coolie to transfer my luggage to the Ichang steamer. I had to descend with him into the bowels of the ship and check the fifteen pieces there. He took these and my hand-luggage to the Ichang steamer. I went along and saw everything placed there in a proper way, dry and safe. After this I returned to the city and took a room for the day at the Christian and Missionary Alliance Home. Here I had a good rest, shampooed and bathed, and read nine long letters from Bob, totalling sixty-two pages of his small, fine hand!

Throughout all this trip I was suffering from rheumatism, with swollen ankles and much pain. The weather on the upper river was lovely, but always the air was damp. In Ichang I had a pleasant time with my friends the Windhams of the Dollar Company and got off for Chungking by the *Robert Dollar*. My friends told me I ought to be going in the opposite direction with that rheumatism. At Wild Rapid the ship had a hard struggle. The paint was burned off our smokestack as our engines labored in vain to conquer the swift current. Finally, a hawser had to be put out, and the steam winch helped us up.

On November 7, I was back in Chungking. Bob and Dick were on hand to meet me in the early morning. Lao Wu, our laundry man who had been so ill that spring, had been ill again on the day before my arrival. Bob had sent him to the hospital. When he was being carried out our gate, he asked Amah to tell me that he would be back in a few days to do our laundry. On the way to meet me, Bob had stopped at the hospital to inquire about Wu. He was told that Wu had died that very morning.

We all missed him, for he had a warm and cheerful personality. He expected life to be full of labor, and he was grateful to work in a place where he was sure of pay and a roof over his head. Every month he had sent money to his mother for her food. Bob felt that he must continue this help to the old woman, and did so for years as long as she lived. Amah said about Wu, "He had a good home, got money every month, was able to help his old mother, went to hospital with bills paid when he was ill, was buried in a good coffin in a suitable manner. What more could one want? I hope I am so fortunate."

That year some forty Americans got together for Thanksgiving dinner at the American-Oriental Bank's tiffin club. The ladies furnished the dessert— mince and pumpkin pies with cheese—with candy, nuts, and coffee.

It was hard to prepare for a joyous Christmas with two sons away from home. Hugo Sandor and Ferry Shaffer,[5] our young Hungarian friends, stayed with us over the holiday; and Mr. Spiker[6] and the McCurdys came for Christmas dinner. Bob had the cutest gifts for us: figures, seven or eight inches tall, cleverly made of dough. Each was appropriate to the recipient: for Mr. Spiker there was a Chinese official in full regalia; for Dick, a student; for me, a Chinese lady. With each figure Bob had written a clever verse. In addition to these jokes, there were other gifts from Bob. He was always keen on a thorough-going Christmas and could always think of longed-for things

5. Ferry Shaffer was a Hungarian engineer-architect who had been a friend of Hugo Sandor's since they escaped together from a Russian prisoner-of-war camp. He was employed at this time in Szechwan to survey a motor road to be built from Chungking to Chengtu. He became a close friend of Grace and Bob's and was the artist for their bookplate (see chapter 35, note 3).

One day in Yenan in 1944, Chou En-lai remarked that an enemy alien being detained by the local authorities claimed to know me, and handed me a rough piece of paper with the name Ferry Shaffer. Non-Axis in sympathy, Ferry had a good job, so had stayed on in Shanghai under Japanese occupation. By 1944 it seemed a good time to leave. As an "ally," he was able to wangle a travel pass to visit Taiyuan, the Japanese-held capital of Shansi Province. Once there, he went for a walk in the nearby hills until he encountered Eighth Route Army guerrillas, who did not know what to do with this eagerly friendly enemy alien and so passed him along until he finally reached Yenan. The Communists were relieved that I could vouch for him, and I arranged his travel on our Dixie Mission plane to Chungking and on to the United States.

6. Mr. Spiker (Clarence J.) was the American consul. He was still unmarried and a very literate, worldly, and agreeable person. After the war in 1946, Dick was assigned to the American consulate in Tsingtao and found himself working for Consul General Spiker.

which delighted the whole family. One interesting gift was a large box containing four dozen chocolate bars. It was marked "To R.R.S. from S." Three of our guests had surnames beginning with S. After all had disclaimed it, we discovered that Bob had given it to himself. It was nice that, once in awhile, he did think of himself.

There was a strike at the post office. Salaries had been raised, but the higher grades of employees got a larger percentage increase than the lower grades. The junior clerks struck, and the mail was left unsorted. After some time without letters, I called on the postmaster and he allowed me to enter the sorting room. There I had a fine time and came home triumphant with a huge bundle of mail for us and other bundles for our near neighbors, the China Inland Mission and Mr. Knipe of the Tract Society.

Life was burdensome to me those times because I seemed to do nothing but take medicine, and only by it could I keep going. I was taking calomel and salts twice a week, and stuffing down soda plus fifteen grains of sodium salicylate each day. Still, on one of the last days of the old year, I took my turn at serving tea for the American "gobs" off the two gunboats. This was in the lower part of the little Union Church and followed a concert of Christmas music. I took three immense cakes, lots of cookies, and cheese biscuits. Everything melted before the frontal attack of the sailors. On the way home, my Boy remarked: "Chinese can eat, but, *ai ya,* those Americans!"

We celebrated New Year across the street with Mr. Knipe and, in Scots fashion, partook of his famous old gander, who had been fattened for eighteen months and had been lord of his compound. Another holiday festivity was the bachelors' costume party, where I received a prize. It was the same homemade outfit that I had worn several years earlier at a party in Chengtu.

In January [1923] Dick started to attend the small Canadian school for foreign children. As the distance was considerable, the streets dirty, and the noon hour short, he had his tiffins with one of the Canadian Mission families. There were only twelve pupils in three classes. Dick was in the second class, but did advanced third-grade work, probably what we would have called fourth grade. After so many years with children at home for daily lessons it was odd to find myself alone every morning. Bob never came home at noon, and the house seemed very quiet with no child at table with me.

Each child has his own separate and special bond with his parents, but it seems to me that the youngest, when he leaves, is the most missed. Others have gone before; the youngest remains and is cherished for that fact. When *he* goes, the full force of inevitable change comes to the parent and the break is hard. So often one hears an American parent rejoice that the children are away most of the day at school; I never had that feeling, and now, as I look back, I am glad that I didn't. To me, a home without youth lacks something. But, after all, I was relieved not to have to spend my mornings teaching Dick.

The days seemed long when it was dark and rainy. But I still had my classes at the Y, and I was still statistician for the West China Missions Advisory Board. So I managed to keep busy.

In January that year we helped Chinese friends to start a social club, somewhat after the plan of the similar organization that we had belonged to in Chengtu. Married couples formed the membership, and the intent was to foster social contacts of a modern nature.

We missed our old laundry coolie, Lao Wu, very much. As he had always been the peacemaker among our servants, his absence soon showed. In January we had to let our Boy leave. He had been with us for thirteen months, and was the only servant from the Chungking area—the others had come with us from Chengtu. He had always had a bad temper, and Wu had had many a fuss to settle in the servants' quarters. After Wu died, things had gone from bad to worse. Finally, the other servants simply would not work with the Boy.

As far as his work went, he was very good, for he had been well trained while he was with us. He had come green from the country and he left with expert knowledge. He was quick and neat, kept the dining room spotless, cleaned silver incessantly, washed windows with speed and understanding, and was so useful that he left a big gap in the smoothness of the household routine.

When he left, he told the other servants that he was going to get a job with some businessman—"High wages, little work!" Unfortunately, this was only too true. Missionaries might be looked down upon by some, but no business person disdained a servant who had been well trained by a conscientious missionary. At that time there were forty-six bachelors in the Chungking business community. Jobs with them were apparently the ambition of every Chungking servant.

And there was more than good pay. Not working for a woman with a sharp eye meant less work. Our Boy had told the other servants that I could see dirt where he could not. I considered that a compliment.

39

Treaty Port Life

(1923)

Early in 1923 we had word that our furlough had been approved. It was to be the whole year of 1924. We planned to start it by traveling to America via Europe.

When Bob had deferred his furlough and gone to open the Y in Chungking in 1921, the National Committee in Shanghai had agreed that from January 1922 two foreign secretaries would be in the city. Now, in 1923, Bob was still alone. The Y work had been started in an encouraging way, and crowds were coming to the building. But the local Y was understaffed and Bob was working too hard. His doctor had already warned him that he must have a rest. He drank milk as ordered, and faithfully took the medicines prescribed—almost the only time I ever knew him to keep to such a regime. But he insisted that he would never be a man to ask favors from the Committee. He would do his job.

One of his duties was to train young Chinese to be secretaries. As part of their course, I was teaching a class in economics. I have never had a more interesting and appreciative class. They would linger after class to bring up all sorts of subjects brought forth in their study. I had been reading a good deal along these lines for many years; summarizing it for a course was as instructive to me as I hope it was for them.

February of 1923 was largely taken up, for me, by a house guest, Kathryn Ross, who was a surgical nurse at the Canadian Mission hospital in Chengtu. Chinese New Year is a relatively slack time for hospitals; Chinese want to be home, even if they are ill. So Kathryn decided to take a month of vacation then, instead of during the summer. She was a good friend of ours from our Chengtu days; and of course it is possible that word had reached Chengtu of our forty-six bachelors. She was pretty, attractive and good-natured, sang and played the piano, rode, danced, and was a charming guest.

The zeal shown by the bachelors in entertaining her was interesting to watch. They enjoyed themselves, and we all had a good time, for in those days there were still such things as chaperons, perhaps especially for a young missionary lady. I doubt if any one month in Chungking had ever seen so many festivities, gay parties, and happy excursions. Between the launches belonging to the oil companies, various navies, and trading companies we never seemed to lack speedy river transport. And there was other transportation as well; one swain insisted on walking beside her sedan chair up all the uneven stone steps and crooked lanes to our house. The tough old chair men at least shortened his trip by speeding up their pace and swinging around the turns with extra gusto.[1]

The Yangtze was unusually low that spring: at the end of March the river level was two feet below zero. That meant a delay in the opening of shipping. April brought a rapid change. By the sixteenth the river was up to fourteen feet. On April 18 three of the biggest steamers arrived in port, all on the same day and all of them coming straight through from Shanghai. The *Robert Dollar* was the first one in, then the *Loong Mow,* and later the *Mei Ren*.[2] With their arrival, communication with the Coast was greatly improved, and our lives were not so dependent on the vagaries of the river.

However, life in Chungking had other causes for concern. The military had been squeezing the people very hard. Taxes were being levied in advance. Merchants were being forced to pay all sorts of special impositions. It was surprising to see how much was demanded and how long the citizens endured this kind of brigandage. Perhaps the worst of these military brigands was a freebooter named Chou Hsi-cheng from the neighboring province of Kweichow who had established himself near Chungking. General Yang Sen, who was in control in Chungking, began to talk of the need to "clean up Szechwan" [i.e., push out General Chou]. General Chou accused General Yang of planning to "sell out" Szechwan to General Wu Pei-fu. Preparations for combat began. These involved troop movements, and those always made people nervous. If you have contributed to one band of ruffians, some contact has been established. Who knows what to expect from a new gang? And departing troops are prone to loot.

The city was full of rumors that "soldiers might make trouble at night." The city gates were closed earlier. Load carriers were impressed in great numbers to provide military transport. This affected our water supply, which had to be carried up from the river. Instead of paying 40 cash for a man's load

1. It was always my impression that Grace promoted the visit by Kathryn Ross in the hope of finding a nice wife for her friend Hugo Sandor. Hugo ended up, some years later, marrying a Hungarian lady—whose relations with Grace were never especially close.
2. It may be noted that the "winning" steamer was American. A British ship was second.

(two large pailfuls), we had to pay 300 cash or more—and even then some-times could not get enough to do our laundry.

On April 4 there were reports of fighting a few miles down river. The next morning there was heavy gunfire that seemed close by. There had been many soldiers on the street that morning, and Bob escorted Dick to school. In the afternoon Bob came home to see how things were in the upper part of the city where we lived. The shooting, we had learned, was across the Kialing River—between Chungking and Kiangpei, the town on the Kialing's north bank. I went with Bob to the American consulate to see if there was any late news. While we were there, the firing became much worse. And there was no certainty about what was actually happening.

Our consul thought it would have a good effect if the American navy ships could send a landing party ashore. So he went off, accompanied by Bob and Hugo Sandor, to try to get in contact with the gunboats—which were an-chored on the other side of the Yangtze.[3] The gunboat commanders agreed and sent twenty men. Bob and Hugo then escorted them to various strategic places: two at Dr. McCartney's store, four at the American-Oriental Bank, eight at the American Methodist Mission, and six at the consulate. I got ready to take in some of the Methodist women if they wanted to come to us for the night. Their mission compound was in an exposed position on the side of the city just across from Kiangpei, where the firing was coming from. When they learned they would have a navy guard, they decided to stay with their stuff.

There were several cannon shots during the evening, and rifle fire con-tinued through the night. But on the whole things were not very bad. The next morning Dick went with his father to the consulate. He and the horse coolie soon came back with the exciting news that Yang Sen's flag was still flying over the military headquarters and the worse was probably over.[4] The rival faction had been driven off. But, as has been too often the way since 1911, the defeated ones only withdrew to plot a comeback, to the future spoliation and sorrow of the citizens.

About the middle of April, the gunboat *Palos* went up river to Luchow to free some Standard Oil junks being held by bandits. While we had a letup in the almost continual fighting which had surrounded us, we learned that Chengtu was having a bad time. But that was a different war from ours.

3. As a Hungarian, Hugo Sandor had no claim to protection by the U.S. Navy. Austria-Hungary and Germany had lost their extraterritorial rights in China when they lost World War I. But he was representing an American company, the American-Oriental Bank.

4. The military headquarters were on the highest point of the city on a hill that looked down on the Yangtze and Kialing rivers. During World War II it was Chungking's air defense headquarters. The only reliable communication with the branch air raid headquarters was vi-sual. When the air raid signals, hung from a tower on the hill, were changed, the subheadquar-ters could see and do likewise. Now it is a very pleasant public park.

As the formal opening of the Y was scheduled for early May, our Chinese Y secretary thought I should end my class for the staff members early in April so that they would be free for extra work at the Association. However, they were keenly interested in our lessons on economics and begged me to continue. I did so until the end of April and thoroughly enjoyed the class sessions.

On Saturday, May 5, amid tremendous enthusiasm and the Chinese decorations and éclat so loved by the Szechwanese, the Chungking YMCA was formally opened. The building, which was part of an extensive provincial guild hall, had been renovated and remodeled to adapt it for Y use. One feature was a restaurant serving both Chinese and foreign food. And there were some dormitory rooms. These proved to be a popular adjunct, and more rooms were subsequently added. There was a basketball court on one side and bathing facilities on the same level. Everything was fresh, attractive, and in running order.

Of course, regular Y work had been going on for many months, but the Chinese prefer to delay an "opening" until an organization is more than started. It should be in a position to show what it is for and how it operates. General Yang Sen and the American consul were two of the speakers. Thousands visited the establishment; the secretaries were busy for days with extra crowds at movies and lectures, besides all those who came merely to "look see."

Early in May I was happy to have finished my laborious annual job of preparing the statistics of the Protestant missions in West China. Just before sending the material off to the press, I was informed by the West China Missions Advisory Board—whose statistician I was—that it did not wish me to include any records concerning the Seventh-Day Adventists. Their figures had been included the year before [1922], and this had caused discussion and trouble. Now the Board had ruled that they were to be omitted.

I had no sympathy with this instruction. It was true that the Advisory Board felt that it should have been consulted by the Seventh-Day Adventists before they started work in Szechwan. But once they were in the province and carrying on work there, it hardly seemed right to omit their statistics if we meant our public statements that we were reporting on Protestant mission activities. I was going on furlough and giving up the statistician post. But I was embarrassed by having to be the one to inform the Seventh-Day Adventists of the Board's decision.

About this time we heard of a young American missionary who did not like us. At first we were given to understand that he was opposed to the ideals of the YMCA. Then it developed that he was annoyed because we paid our cook eight dollars a month. He was afraid we would cause a rise in wages! Missionaries in China often paid less than a decent living wage, either because they wanted to be able to keep more servants, or did not want to upset "local custom." But the comparison that they made with what Chinese paid their servants was misleading. Chinese give their servants a small wage in money, but they feed them, clothe them, and provide many other perquisites more adapted to their use than anything that foreigners have to bestow.

June was quiet as far as warfare went. I was not well, but there seemed no way to avoid the committee for the Fourth of July. I tried to do most of the committee work by letter, for people lived far apart and the weather was exceedingly hot.[5] The gunboats lifted much of the burden of food by baking lots of beans. They also fried many chickens. By packing the sizzling pieces in large baskets lined with oiled paper, they got the meat to us piping hot just in time for the supper. Our menu also included sandwiches, salads, ice cream, cakes, soda water, coffee, and tea. I added some things as the time drew near; it was well that I did, for we later found that at least one hundred and eighty had eaten. Considering that there were only ten American families, we thought that the Americans did pretty well. Of course, we *did* have the two gunboats. Their help was of the greatest value in many ways. For instance, we did not have to worry about drinking water, because they could supply all the distilled water we needed.

The sports program pleased both adults and children. But the movies scheduled for the evening had to be abandoned. The coolie bringing the portable generator apparently got lost. There were fireworks, however, that partially filled the gap in the program. The sailors seemed to have a good time, and it was fine to have so many people of different nationalities picnicking and competing in sports together. No Germans came and no French. But we had Swedes, Russians, Hungarians, Letts, and plenty of British, with a fine feeling throughout the gathering.[6] We rented dishes, and I personally had seen them washed and scalded, so I knew there was no danger of illness from that source.

Hugo Sandor's Tibetan bear cub added a good deal to the fun. This animal had delighted our children, so he was taken to the picnic that other children might also enjoy him. In preparation for his public appearance on the Fourth, our lads had tried to give him a bath. Such spitting, fussing, and

5. The committee work was done by letter because there were no telephones. But it would have taken much too long to send them through the post office. So notes (called chits) were hand-delivered by a coolie. If he was told to wait for a reply, you might have an answer within a couple of hours. "Coolie" was a word used by foreigners for laborers and for the underservants in a household. Because the work involved was usually physical (and often for little pay), an explanation has become popular that the word comes from the Chinese for "bitter strength" (*kuli*). Actually, it is derived from a Tamil word, *kuli*, for wages.

6. Admittedly, it was a foreign gathering for a foreign holiday, but one might think that the international goodwill would have been heightened by the inclusion of at least a few Chinese.

snarling![7] When we set out for the picnic on the Fourth, there was the problem of carrying the bearlet. There was a compartment under the seat of my sedan chair that seemed to be suitable. The door of the compartment opened forward just behind my legs as I sat in the chair. We tied the rattan door tightly, but in no time the cub had chewed through the twine and was struggling to be free. I could only prevent this by holding the door shut with my hands and feet. I never want to share a chair with a bear cub again, no matter how small he may be.

We had moved to the hills at the end of June. The Friends' had had some repairs done, and an extension had been added to the veranda where we had the best view. The main drawback was that there were no screens; our evenings had to be spent in a smoky haze from burning punk to keep the mosquitoes away. One new improvement was a small refrigerator.[8] This meant cool drinks, and now and then a dessert like Jell-O, greatly appreciated in our terribly hot season.

Bob went to the city six, and sometimes seven, days a week. It was a long trip. He left home at seven in the morning, and it was usually after eight in the evening when he returned. He had had no vacation in 1922 and seemed to me to be run down. After I had talked a good deal about this, he finally agreed to take Saturdays off during July and August, and a Wednesday now and then. But he had more of a vacation than he had planned.

---

7. The bath was a fiasco and we abandoned the attempt. When we came back a short while later, the bear was sitting in the pail, happily splashing himself like a baby. He was a Himalayan bear, about like an American black bear except for a V-shaped white blaze on his chest. Hugo had bought him on the street in Chungking. He eventually became too large for a pet and was given to the (rather dreary) zoo in Shanghai's Jessfield Park.

8. The refrigerator was like a miracle; it was run by a small kerosene flame. In our hot summer weather, it could not produce much ice. But, as Grace says, we had cool drinks and delicious Jell-O (for which I still have a special fondness).

40

A Near Thing

(1923)

By the middle of July, soldiers were everywhere on the hills, and trouble was in the air. In fact, we were in the midst of war. Chungking was besieged by an erstwhile robber chief who used to be an ally of General Yang Sen. Now he had turned traitor and was taking advantage of General Yang's absence.[1] His forces occupied the south bank of the Yangtze ("our side," with its hills and summer bungalows), and began to fire cannons at the city across the river. The two American gunboats were normally anchored on the south bank. Now the *Monocacy* was moved over to the city side to be closer in case of need.

The firing across the river was not very alarming. But ferry boats on the river seemed to be attractive targets. Bob (and many others) had to cross the river daily by sampan. The *Palos*, on the south bank, started sending a motor launch over to the *Monocacy*, on the city side, going over at nine and coming back at four in the afternoon. The opposing forces promised not to fire on this launch, but no Chinese were to be transported.

The army defending the city had detained most of the Chinese river craft on their side of the river. Even if boats had been available, the river was quite high, and any attack across it would have been difficult. Chou, the robber chief, looted what there was on the South Bank (particularly the Mint) and sent the plunder south toward his Kweichow home. The reports were that he had brought three hundred mule loads of opium with him from Kweichow to finance this incursion. Perhaps the same mules hauled the plunder home. After about ten days of this stalemate, our besiegers departed silently one night. Everything soon resumed its normal aspect and routine.

1. This was the same General Chou Hsi-cheng who, in April, had tried to attack Chungking from across the Kialing River. In Szechwan warlord politics, Yang Sen was one of the big boys. Chou Hsi-cheng was small fry. There was a struggle going on for control of Chengtu; this would be of major concern to Yang Sen and probably accounted for his absence from Chungking.

In fact, things became normal enough for there to be a controversy over movies. There were still no movie theaters in Chungking, and movies were a great novelty. One of the British businessmen on the South Bank had a large house and a small electric generator. The Y had a portable projector and films selected and circulated by the National Committee of the Y. The businessman would supply the electricity and the veranda; Bob would supply the projector and film; and the foreigners on the South Bank were invited to a free weekly movie.

We soon learned that some of our Fundamentalist neighbors were grieved that missionaries attended such shows. That "so-called missionaries" (the Y) should sponsor the films was even worse. Papers and declarations concerning the showing of films were circulated. I suppose that many of these people told their Chinese Christians not to have anything to do with the YMCA. Bob avoided argument and would only smile; the Fundamentalists, he thought, put doctrine above love.

That summer was torrid, and there was very little rain. Wells dried up, and very few green vegetables could be bought. We got on mostly with potatoes and large onions. Our lads refreshed themselves by going to a neighbor's swimming pool, a mile or so along our range of hills.[2] Young Bob rejoiced in earning seven dollars one afternoon. His father had promised five dollars to each boy as soon as he could swim the length of the pool, and I had added two dollars for the *first* to accomplish this feat. Jack could swim the width, but Bob was the first to accomplish the longer distance.

About the middle of August there were rumors that Chou Hsi-cheng was coming back. He had disturbed us twice already, in April and July, and had soon departed; no one seemed especially alarmed.

When we were at our tennis court on the afternoon of August 20 a number of soldiers appeared. They seemed to be looking around the area and investigating the several paths through and around the Friends' Mission property, which was quite large (about sixteen acres). This did not seem too strange. We were close to one of the important passes across our range of hills. The main road through the pass ran along the north edge of the property. Having soldiers about was quite common that summer. We asked the men what army they belonged to. They were General Deng Hsi-hou's men. And he was (at that time) an ally of General Yang Sen, and so an enemy of Chou Hsi-cheng.

That evening Bob returned late from the city. He reached the house at about nine. We finished supper, and the lads went to bed. I was reading from the Shanghai paper the account of a recent incident at Ichang in which the

---

2. The swimming pool was somewhat less than the usual American version. It depended on fresh water diverted from a small stream. When the stream dried up, the pool suffered.

Alice Dollar had been fired on. Suddenly there was much yelling and rifle fire—close by.[3]

I ran into the bedrooms at the front of the house to tell the boys to lie still in their beds. The walls of the house were brick, the windows rather high, and the beds low. Bob and Dick were in the room at the left of the small front hall; Jack and a friend were in the bedroom on the right. The attack was coming up the hill, toward the back of the house; the safest place seemed to be the front. Of course, we put out all lights. We could hear our servants calling out that this was the house of foreigners, that there were no soldiers present. Still the shots and shouting came nearer and nearer. Bob and I were standing in the corner of the left bedroom, near its door into the hall, and thus very close to the front entrance of the house. Suddenly, we could hear men talking and the sound of their feet as they ran up the brick steps to our front door.

Bob caught my arm and said, "I must speak to those men before something happens." I think he really felt more fear for our servants than ourselves: their lath and plaster walls gave them little protection compared with our brick. The front entrance of the bungalow was a double door. The top half of both sections was glass. The right-hand door stood open, the left-hand one was closed. As Bob stepped into the hall, he was just inside the closed, glass-paned door. At that instant there was the shattering report of a rifle, the sound of splintering glass, and yells from soldiers. I was only a few feet away, but no sound came from Bob. I stepped at once into the long, narrow hall. Moonlight streamed through the front door and I could see soldiers on the veranda. In the gloom of the hall I saw Bob bent over double at the far end, away from the door. He was holding his head in his hands.

I rushed to him and asked if he had been hit. He told me to keep away: he was injured, but *must* speak to the soldiers. With this, he brushed past me and went to the door. He told the men that we were foreigners, and asked to whom they belonged. One man, perhaps the man who had fired the shot, spoke up and said they were Chou Hsi-cheng's men. Bob had met this general in Chungking, so he told the men he knew their commander and was sure that General Chou did not want foreigners to be molested in this way. "You might have killed me," said Bob, "You had better go away now for we have no soldiers around this place." "All right, all right," said they, and moved down the steps and slowly off the premises.

3. Grace's mention of "yelling" hardly seems adequate. This was an attack, not just on our house, but against a range of hills. It involved a force of hundreds, perhaps several thousands, of men. The Chinese have always believed that sound effects have an important place in military tactics. In this case, there seemed to be hordes of men, advancing up the hill toward us in the dark, all hoarsely shouting, "*Sha! Sha!*" (Kill, Kill). So far as we boys were concerned it was a very effective tactic: it was the most frightening sound I have heard in my life. It was, apparently, also militarily effective. Any defenders there may have been on our hilltop very quickly decamped.

I ran to Bob and asked him where he was hurt. Then I saw him groping at the wall of the hall. He was saying, "My eyes, my eyes." "Well," I said, "surely you weren't hit by the bullet or you couldn't be going around as you do." But his remark frightened me. We went into our bedroom and I called to Amah to bring a lamp. As soon as Bob sensed the light coming near, he cried out that he could not have it. Even a tiny hand-lamp was too much. We had to fetch a candle before I could get a real view of his eyes. In spite of pain, he tried with his own fingers to pull up the eyelids so I could look. Amah, the cook, and I all stood there, and all we could see was blood covering both eyeballs. His forehead was cut; his hands and handkerchief were covered with blood. The servants and I exchanged glances: nothing was said. Amah told me later that my face was "like a dead woman's"—fortunately Bob could not see it. I felt an awful despair; but I knew I *must do something*.

It was out of the question to send for aid; soldiers still ran riot all over the hills, and the doctor was forty-five minutes away. It was clear that Bob's only injury was to his eyes, and that probably by small bits of shattered glass. Boiling water was at hand. With the cook's help, I soon sterilized our eyecup and made boracic solution, cooling it with cold drinking water—thanks to our new refrigerator. With eyecup and abundant boracic solution we washed the eyeballs thoroughly. As it proved later, very good treatment this was. The doctor told me that I had cleared out any glass particles that might possibly have remained within the lids.

After this, Bob lay on his bed fully dressed (neither one of us undressed that night). We lacked ice for cold compresses, so I used hot ones to take away soreness. I think Bob felt he must have lost the sight of one eye. He told me he could bear it if I could! I tried to cheer him. The servants wanted to show their sympathy and concern, and it was hard to keep them out of the bedroom. They asked if they could stay the rest of the night in the living room. I gave permission, so they all brought their sleeping mats and lay there on the floor, the chair men and all. Doors were all left open, so I had them on one side; on another side was the lads' room, and there lay Amah on her mat between the two younger boys. I did not sleep a wink, and could hear the men servants discussing the whole affair in low voices during the night. "If our teacher (Bob) was a man like some of the foreigners, who would care? But he is always kind to everyone. It is a great pity our teacher should be injured when he was quiet in his own house." And so on and on.

That night will live forever in my memory. I learned the value of reticence and discipline. What Bob and I both feared, we did not put into words. The knowledge lay between us; each tried to save the other. We could still hear the soldiers all over the hills, yelling and shooting until it sounded like Bedlam. But the moonlight made it almost light as day. It shone into the living room on the men lying there, and into our bedroom on our beds where we lay. I threw myself on mine between fixing compresses for Bob. There was the fragrance of pines on which rain had fallen that day, a scent of flowers, a freshness of the night breeze. The dogs whimpered and lay under our beds. They were never allowed in the house, but that night we took pity on them. In the far distance we could hear faint sounds of soldiers, sudden bursts of gunfire, and echoes of turmoil rolling across the hills from range to range. Amah called out to me now and then, telling me that the children slept, or asking what she could do to help.

The chair men had said that as soon as there was light and the soldiers were gone, they would carry Bob to the doctor. At dawn, we got him off in his sedan chair, with a bath towel around his head to keep out the light. The head chair man carried a note to Mr. Spiker, our consul, who lived near the doctor. The chair man was to tell the consul's Boy to waken his master and deliver the note at once. Thus it was delivered before six. Mr. Spiker got up at once and went over to the doctor's. The relief was tremendous when it was found that Bob's eyes were safe. The right eyeball, closest to the bullet's path, was badly cut and always carried scars; but the vision was not impaired. He had had a most fortunate escape.

The rifle had been fired from the hip. The bullet had gone upward, through the glass, close past Bob's head, through the frame of the door into the bedroom, and finally imbedded itself in a comforter folded on a cupboard shelf in the lads' bedroom. When we measured it carefully, it seemed that the bullet missed him by an inch or less. Bob always said that he felt it pass his temple!

A few days later, Chou Hsi-cheng sent an officer to call on Bob and to find out how badly he was hurt. Mr. Spiker came at the same time. We held a thread from the bullet hole in the glass to the hole in the door frame, showing the officer the tiny space in which Bob's head was when the bullet passed. He looked and could make only one remark, "Ai-ya, ai-ya!" General Chou expressed regrets and offered to pay any hospital bill. There was none, so he paid nothing.[4]

Although I have referred to this man as a robber—and that is what he was called in Chungking in those days—he was highly thought of in Kweichow Province. A few years ago I heard of his death there, and learned that he was considered a benefactor in the city of Kweiyang, the provincial capital.

4. General Chou was probably happy to express regrets, and genuinely happy that Bob was not more seriously injured. His soldiers on the spot, however, could not—under the circumstances—be entirely blamed. There had been opposing forces on the hill (the soldiers scouting about the tennis court that afternoon). When the attack started, the men on the hill may have fired some shots (we were confused at the beginning about the direction from which the firing was coming). If there had been shots from the defenders (visible as flashes in the dark), they might well have come from the grove of trees on the crest of the hill, just above our bungalow. The attackers were strangers to the area; there was no way for them to know—or for us to indicate—that the house was occupied by foreigners.

I understand that there has been a statue to his memory erected there by friends.[5]

The very morning after Bob's injury, when it was still none too safe to be going around freely, the news of his trouble flew all over our hills. It was an illustration of how news travels in China.[6] In some mysterious way it soon became known even to those at considerable distances. Notes began to come in as soon as he returned from the doctor's. By afternoon, when the fighting had cleared away from our neighborhood, men came to call, and more messages rolled in. Everyone rejoiced with us that his vision was going to be saved.

Still Bob suffered a great deal. He had to remain in a dark room for days, and his eyes had to be bathed and treated every two hours. In hot weather this was trying, but our joy that his eyes were saved carried us through these minor discomforts. The shock of the whole affair, however, seemed to have done something to me. I could not sleep more than an hour at a time, and felt on the edge of a catastrophe during most of the daylight hours. At night we felt more restless. The fighting cut us off from the city for eight days, so Bob would have had to take a vacation anyway. During these days there was always the sound of gunfire. One day, five sailors on the *Palos* were injured by splinters from steel plates being hit by bullets. Shipping was at a standstill. When it resumed, foreign ships were fired on whenever they moved—the military hated them because they refused to transport troops.

The urgent thing now was to get the boys off to their school in Shanghai. Dick had not been very well that spring. Life was so tense in Chungking that we decided to send him to Shanghai with the two older boys. He was only nine, too young to go to the American school as a boarder. However, the Yards—our old Chengtu friends, now in Shanghai—urged us to send him down, saying that they had room and would gladly keep him that fall. As we were to go on home leave in January 1924, Bob had already planned for me to leave early and spend the month of December in Shanghai with Mabelle. This meant that it would be only three months until I would be there with Dick. So we got the three lads ready to leave for the Coast with Hugo Sandor. Small Bob gave us some excitement for two days as he ran a temperature after being bitten by a snake. He also had a headache, but had no other bad

5. When I retraced the Long March with the Salisburys in 1984, we stopped in a county town named Tungtze in northern Kweichow. It was a pleasant place. After the local historian had told us about the Red Army stopping there, we asked him what else the town was famous for. "For fighting men," he said; "the town is known as the home of generals." Pressed for names, he came up with some early ones and then mentioned Chou Hsi-cheng. "Ah, yes," I said, "my father knew him." I think Grace's story of a statue of the general in Kweiyang can be treated with some reserve. If there was such a statue, it was certainly paid for by the general. And it certainly does not still stand.

6. Today this phenomenon is known as the "bamboo wireless"; in those preradio days it was the "bamboo telegraph."

effects. Around us, things were happening every day, and we were anxious to get them away.

On Sunday afternoon, as we sat on our veranda trying to keep cool, we heard awful screams. A man accused, our servants told us, of being a spy had been seized by soldiers at the pass below our house. He had been hung up in a tree, feet first, and was being beaten with slender split bamboos. Of course the lads wanted to go at once to see what was happening. I told them not to go, but they found a spot where they could look down and see what was going on.[7] I said over and over to Bob, "If we can only get the children away before another storm breaks!"

Everything was packed for the three lads. We left for the city on the afternoon of September 3 and put them on the *Robert Dollar,* scheduled to sail the next morning.

---

7. For us boys the adjustment to military conditions may not have been as difficult as Grace assumed. We found enough material lying about to start an ammunition collection. At first this showed the remarkable diversity in caliber and bullet characteristics of bush league warlord armament. Then, when we found that we could disassemble live ammunition, we put together quite a display of different types of explosives. (The family had recently had its periodic series of typhoid inoculations: the small bottles were just fine for powder samples.)

One day the three of us boys encountered a group of soldiers. For some reason which I cannot now imagine, we had our Daisy air rifle, ordered from Montgomery Ward. The interest of the soldiers was immediate. A foreign rifle! It must be something special! When their acquisitiveness became transparent, my quick-thinking brother Bob whispered, "Shoot me." So I did, aiming at his chest from about fifteen paces. He was wearing a heavy khaki shirt, which the BB did not penetrate. The soldiers had no more interest in the air rifle, and we all parted amicably.

41

Grace Leaves Szechwan
(1923)

We wanted to stay with our three lads as long as possible that evening. So we had planned to spend the night at our house in the city. And Bob had obtained a special permit from the garrison commander allowing us to enter the city after the usual time of gate closing. Hugo Sandor, with his bear cub, arrived at the ship soon after us. Our consul, Mr. Spiker, was also there. We knew the officers on the *Dollar,* and they invited us to remain on board for the night. We had just refused when along came our head chair man to tell us that an attack was threatened and the military had already closed the city gates. Bob gave him our permit, but he soon returned with the word that no permit would suffice because no gate would be opened for anyone. So two of the boys slept on the sofas in their cabins that night to give us beds. We all sat up until nearly twelve talking and having a pleasant time.

We were up with the dawn and were off the ship by five. We told the lads good-bye as they stood on deck in their pyjamas. Dick was game and never shed a tear. It was all a great adventure to him, and he was delighted to be traveling with a real bear. While we were still standing on the steep stone steps leading up from the hulk, I said to Bob that no matter what happened to me, at least the boys were safely out of trouble. Then we turned to get into our sedan chairs and approached the city gate. Outside the gate, and blocking the way, was a mob of soldiers. We finally realized that they had come across the river in the night, running away from Chou Hsi-cheng! Why the gate was not opened for them we could not understand, for they were the allies of those inside. It soon became clear that the gate was not going to be opened for us, either.

There was nothing to do but try the next gate. With us were Mr. Spiker and the Dollar Company agent, Mr. Fleming. Again we found a mob of soldiers and crowds of people. Between Bob's permit from the garrison commander and Mr. Spiker's card as American consul, the guards at the gate finally agreed to let us through. What a scene ensued! Hundreds pressed from all sides, all hoping to push in with us. Many got between our chair poles. Others crouched like dogs beneath the chairs, hoping to slip through unseen. One huge fat fellow with a tremendous paunch and wearing nothing but flapping cotton pants got between the poles of my chair and shouted to the world that he belonged to me. The crowd laughed, and the guards dragged him out ignominiously.

At last, with our chairs and bearers, we were inside the wall and on our way to the home of Mr. Fleming, who had kindly invited us for breakfast. Having prepared for one man, the cook was surprised to see three guests arrive with him. Soon after seven, we were sitting down to our meal—but not in peace. There had been heavy firing for some time. It was obvious that war was in progress again, and that we would not be returning to the hills that day.

Our kitchen equipment and servants were all at the house on the hill. The Canadian ladies lived near the Y, and they had moved back to the city a few days before to prepare for their school's opening. Fortunately, they could take us in. But our summer clothes were also at the bungalow, and even our bathtubs were there. I had only one dress and, in the heat, certainly needed a clean one every day. This meant washing my dress every evening.

Between this washing, the excitement of our situation, and the intense heat, I could feel that an attack of rheumatism was coming on. To try to head it off, I began heavy dosages of medicine. Every day Bob went to the Y. He should not have been going, but he was restless and felt he should be near the Y staff. Like everyone else, they were nervous and apprehensive. During the days, there was almost constant firing; at night it kept up sporadically. On several days it sounded as though there was cannon fire in the hills in the direction of our bungalow. We could imagine the state of mind of our servants, alone so long without news from us. It was well into September and they had not yet been paid for August.

We were having our own troubles. Bob had a bad attack of asthma and puffed terribly at night. I slept poorly anyway, and worse than usual with the shooting and Bob's labored breathing. During the day I went with Bob to the Y because his eyes still gave him trouble and he could not read. He could really do little except sit in a dark corner and talk to those who came to him, but he seemed to be a great comfort to his associates. The Y was hit by bullets, and so was the house where we were staying, but the chief damage was to roof tiles.

After eight days we were finally able to cross the river and get back to the bungalow. I am sure I never spent a longer eight days in all my life. Fighting at the pass near our bungalow had been very fierce and many were killed.

The fighting had gone on night and day and must have terrified the servants. Indeed, the cook reported that during one spell they had lain flat on the floor of our living room for thirty-six hours, not even daring to get up to cook or eat food. They may have lain on our beds, too, but more likely under them. We told them we intended to move into the city at once—no one ever saw any house servants work with greater zeal. One would have thought that the walls of Chungking were those of Heaven itself! In two days we and all our belongings were again in the city house.

Bob's eyes were not doing as well as at first, and the prescribed drops kept him from being able to read. I continued to go to the Y with him and wrote dozens of notes and letters for him while he sat talking in dark corners. Sometimes I wondered if I should not have bundled him off to the Coast with the three lads. Several weeks after the event we heard from the National Committee in Shanghai. They hoped Bob had a good doctor and was getting well. No word came about anyone to take up his work. He began to wonder a bit about that, it being twenty months past the time that he had been promised an assistant.

Though Bob could not read, he could do packing. He started on this because he had made up his mind that he would get me out of Chungking. I was miserable and my nerves were decidedly jittery. He kept telling me in those days that I had given up too much, and that he was afraid my health had suffered more than he should have permitted. The military situation was poor and no one could tell what might happen. Our house was being hit by bullets every day or so. We had moved into the west bedroom (which had been the boys') because our room had large windows facing toward the hills. From them we could see the flashes of gunfire every night. But even in the west room I slept poorly and roused at nearly every volley. Bob began to be afraid I would have a breakdown and said he would *make* me leave. I did not want to leave, but we finally agreed that I would go when he could read.

In the midst of all these unusual affairs, Mr. Spiker had to be operated on for appendicitis. We went to the hospital to act as "family."[1] In plain view from the hospital windows, active war was being waged on the opposite bank of the Yangtze, close to our gunboat anchorage. It was a wonder that patients could improve amid such surroundings. But in those days we had no airplanes and bombs. That was something to be thankful for—though we did not know it at the time.

In the midst of packing at our house, the wives of General Yang Sen, who had taken a house close to us, sent word that they wished to call. (This was

---

1. Consul Spiker was not only a bachelor, he was the solitary American on the staff of the consulate. It may seem surprising to those familiar with today's generous staffing patterns that a consulate could actually function with only one American. George Kennan has suggested that American Foreign Service establishments may even have been more efficient in the lean old days.

the proper old-style Chinese etiquette.) I replied that I was sorry that I could not receive guests because I was leaving soon and already packing. Twice they repeated this desire, and twice I sent word that I was not receiving calls. I even told my servants to tell them I was ill, for I really was too ill and nervous to start entertaining Chinese ladies, or anyone else. Also I felt that these ladies might ask embarrassing questions regarding coming to our house in case of danger. I told Bob I was sure there was something behind their urgency in wanting to call.

At the end of September there was a long-drawn-out battle about a mile and a quarter, as the crow flies, from our house. We could watch it all from our windows and it was much too close for comfort. Fortunately, we had plenty to do. I helped Bob at the Y, and such time as we had at home was spent in packing. It rained almost every day, and this had delayed such jobs as blanket washing, which I wanted done before packing them.

In the midst of all this, we learned that one of our good Chinese friends was being held by Chou Hsi-cheng as a spy. He was a peaceable merchant, and they were probably holding him to squeeze money out of his family. On the strength of the injury to his eyes, Bob asked the general to release this man. Later, Bob had the consolation of knowing that his trouble had brought safety to one man who had been in imminent danger of losing his life. Some new American YWCA secretaries arrived from Shanghai en route to Chengtu, but I did not try to have them stay with us. We were too far in our packing, and they would be safer in a less exposed location.

Thus passed the days. When we met friends all the talk was of warfare and this or that item of news. We felt caught in an endless whirl of narrow escapes, bullets spattering on walls, and such items. Mrs. McCartney, sitting at her desk in their flat, was endangered by a bullet which passed over the desk and close to her head. Early in October our neighbor, Mr. Hick of the China Inland Mission, was at the McCartneys'. He asked about this narrow escape. The doctor insisted on escorting him upstairs to see the actual spot of his wife's close call. As they stood there near the window talking of bullets, one hit Mr. Hick in the neck. He cried out that he had been hit, and put his hand up to a wound on one side of his neck. The doctor was beside him, could see the wound, and was astonished that Mr. Hick was still able to stand and to talk. While the mystified doctor looked at the wound, Mr. Hick complained of a lump on the opposite side by his ear. The doctor examined it and finally cut a small slit in the skin. Out popped the bullet!

This was our prize war story, and we all congratulated Mr. Hick on his unusual escape. After his experience, we all felt satisfied to *hear* of bullets, and did not feel it imperative to *see* where they had passed. Meanwhile, the war continued into October.

Shanghai friends had written to ask that we help an American woman tourist who would arrive in Chungking by the *Robert Dollar*. The first day that I went down to the Dollar Company hulk, the ship had been delayed. On the second trip, I learned that the tourist had turned back without braving the last stretch of her journey.

The American gunboat *Palos* was tied up there at the Dollar hulk, but that did not prevent volleys from being fired in that direction every little while. Bullets would spatter on the stone steps leading up from the water. When we wanted to go or come from the hulk, we waited until a volley had been fired, then hustled to negotiate the steps before another volley. The second day I went down, the captain of the *Palos* invited me for tea, and I was there when the *Dollar* arrived. I went on board at once, but then there was a lot of firing. After a long wait, I managed to get up the steps to where my chair men waited in an angle of the massive city wall. The Scotch engineer of the *Dollar* had offered to escort me up those dangerous steps, but then he would have had to make the return trip to his ship.[2] I preferred to have him watch me from its deck. In case I was hit, he promised to carry me to the *Palos* for medical attention.

So in those days we joked our way around, using the lower streets of the city, keeping behind walls, and playing safe as much as possible. However, there was a rhythm in the Chinese shooting. For weeks that autumn soldiers shot from the city gate nearest our house at fifteen-minute intervals both day and night. The volleys were immediately returned by their enemies across the Yangtze. Later, when I saw the elaborate electric signs in cities like New York and Chicago, their recurrent cycles suggested nothing but fighting to me. Even the periodic flash of a channel buoy or lighthouse is, to me, associated with gunfire.

Years later, someone was talking to me about cowardly missionaries being scared out of their stations by fighting and such things. I was asked if I had ever left a place because of warfare. I said I had not—but later this Chungking episode came to my mind. It is true that I *did* leave; but eighteen strenuous years in Szechwan, our experiences of the summer, and our imminent furlough all had something to do with my going. Anyway, Bob felt the urge to speed me on my way. Throughout those days, he frequently said that he had asked too much of me, and that he could not be satisfied until I was out of the city. And I, in turn, reminded him that it was he who bore on his eyeballs the scars of the fighting.

We were cheered by letters from the boys, safe in Shanghai. Hugo Sandor had looked after them well and they had had a wonderful trip. The small bear, "Teddy," had been a great addition to the party.

On October 13 I packed the last things, leaving the house arranged so that

2. Every engineer that I ever met on a Yangtze or China Coast ship was a Scot.

the servants could care for Bob easily. I sold my piano that day, so felt I was ready to leave. On the afternoon of the fourteenth, Bob took me down to the *Alice Dollar*. He stayed for dinner and all night. The next morning there was a fog, so we could not sail until it cleared about half past nine. Then Bob left me. I hated terribly to go and leave him, but he insisted, and I myself was afraid that I was going to be ill. I had even asked the doctor about my heart. He had said that it was not normal, but he thought that I would be all right after I got away from our tense atmosphere.

The trip down the river was not particularly eventful. Soldiers fired on us a good deal. Our American navy guards had orders not to shoot unless our ship was hit. And despite the shooting, we were not hit. So the waiting men, with machine guns ready for the command, did not return the fire. Once, though, we were fired on by bandits; then our machine guns did answer. At several places, we passengers were called behind the armor plates around the bridge. But it was a peaceful trip for those days.[3]

I was on my way to Peking, so the lads in Shanghai did not expect me. However, it seemed best to go by way of Shanghai so that I could leave my trunks there and attend to other matters. I was to arrange our travel to Europe for early in January of 1924. And I was to lay before the YMCA National Committee the urgent need for a man to relieve Bob. There was now a larger, more active Y in Chungking than in Chengtu, which had been opened so much longer. In Chengtu there were several foreign secretaries, and a larger, better-trained Chinese staff. In Chungking, Bob alone was handling a growing Association with a much smaller and less-experienced staff. To save the work he had done, someone *must* be sent to take his place.

After a fine visit with the boys, and an exceedingly hectic week of usual Shanghai affairs, I got away on my trip to the northern capital.[4] A big laugh as I was departing was caused by a letter from my mother. Writing as a careful American woman, she counseled me apropos Bob's eye injury, "I hope this experience will be a lesson to teach you all to keep out of the range of gunfire." As we had all been in our house when the incident occurred, and Bob was even within the building when shot at, we certainly were amused by such advice.

In my letters home there was much of our China experience that I never succeeded in "getting across." Perhaps Mother lacked the imagination to en-

3. On the day that Grace reached Ichang, the war in Chungking ended. General Yang Sen conceded defeat; General Chou and his confederates took over. Because of Yang's alliance with General Wu Pei-fu, it was considered a victory for the Szechwanese (though Chou Hsi-cheng was from Kweichow). But Chou did not last long, and the Szechwanese kept outsiders away until Chiang Kai-shek and his Central Government army arrived in 1935 to chase the Communist Red Army.

4. "Northern capital" is, of course, the literal translation of Peking—or, more phonetically, Beijing.

ter into any foreign situation. She was ardent for mission work, but wanted to hear of it without touching on unpleasant topics, so that she could experience it vicariously in the abstract rather than the concrete. She certainly read and re-read my letters, which were directed to her and for which she assumed the role of family interpreter. But everything was so thoroughly colored by her own opinions that any deviation from what she expected was not to her liking.

And so, for me, the Szechwan chapter ended. Had I known when I left that we were not to live again in the West, my departure would have been much sadder. The province had been our first Chinese home, and we loved it and its people with a persistent affection. Our small daughter lay in the cemetery there in Chungking. Our hearts were held by the many friends in the province. Also, we had three Szechwan-born sons. And recollections of many happy days.

PART SIX

SHANGHAI

42

A Time of Reckoning
(1923–24)

It was the last day of October when I started north. I traveled by the Blue Express, the same train that had been held up that spring by bandits, who took off a large number of passengers. All these trains had military guards. Later I heard a woman who had been on the same train with me explaining to friends how there had been special guards when *she* went north. I stopped off in Shantung and went up Tai Shan, one of China's sacred mountains. My only companions were the excellent Mohammedan chair bearers who make this trip their specialty, but I was very happy and enjoyed the day immensely.

I had looked forward for many years to visiting Peking. I stayed in the hospitable home of the Robert Gaileys of the Y, and spent most of my time in sightseeing. I did things in a leisurely way, and had a private ricksha to take me about. But in spite of these precautions, one day I was ill; I kept feeling faint and my heart was bothersome. We called a doctor and he said, "heart over-strain." I must rest. Then our old friend, Dr. Morse of Chengtu, arrived in Peking for his own medical problem. He thought I should have a thorough examination and made an appointment for me with the heart specialist at the Rockefeller hospital, usually known as the P.U.M.C.[1]

During the examination I was told that I must enter the hospital at once. A dinner was being given for me that evening by an old Chinese friend of Nanking days, and I could not well be absent. The doctor finally agreed, if I would stay only a short time at the dinner and enter the hospital early the next morning. I followed his instructions, and the next morning saw me ensconced in a hospital room. Here I spent a month.

1. Our family has many reasons to be grateful to the Peking Union Medical College (P.U.M.C.). Grace was there in 1923, Dick was treated for tuberculosis in 1936, our son Bob was born there in 1937, and my wife, Caroline, has been helped with bronchitis (the modern Peking complaint) as recently as 1984. Of course, it is now the Capital Hospital, but the taxi driver still uses the old abbreviated Chinese name, *xiehe*.

As soon as I "let go" in the hospital, I was like a wreck and, contrary to my usual nature, shed quarts of tears. The Austrian doctor in charge of that section of the hospital used to sit by my bed and stroke my hand, asking me where I suffered. I could not lie down, and lay there propped on a mound of pillows while the tears ran down my cheeks. Friends were thoughtful, and I had constant messages and gifts.[2] Legation friends supplied me with books, but life seemed hardly worth living. I had written Bob that I was going in "for a rest"; only Shanghai and Peking friends knew I was ill—and even I, myself, did not know how sick I was.

As soon as I could have visitors, I was much diverted by a Chinese of the Salt Gabelle, whom I had known as a young man in Chengtu where I used to teach him English.[3] He told the nurses he was my pupil and faithfully came to the hospital every day to see me. The nurses all became very friendly when they found I could speak Mandarin, even though it was the Szechwan brand. My friend was also visiting in the north and told me much of interest concerning his doings, the places he visited, and the things he was buying for gifts to those at home. In the Chinese way, gift selection was an important part of his journey; he even brought some of these presents to show me.

Doctors are often wary about telling patients of their ailments. They gave me no name for my illness; it was only later that I learned it. I had written Mabelle Yard and a few other friends in Shanghai that I was miserable, but Bob knew little of the truth. The heart specialist insisted on rest. I took little medicine, was not allowed to walk, had plenty of heart tests, and had X-rays of teeth and such things. Finally my kind Austrian doctor told me I would not be able to go to America by way of Europe. This upset me a good deal. I had assumed that after the hospital interlude I would be getting up and going about as usual. To relinquish such long-cherished and somewhat hard-earned plans seemed very hard to face, alone as I was in Peking.[4] I had to write to the shipping office to cancel the reservations, and also to Bob in Chungking.

I already knew what Bob's reaction would be: if we could not start for America as planned, he would choose to stay on in Chungking and help the new man get used to the work at the Y. But I still expected that we would soon be going to America by way of the Pacific.

2. Grace, as would be expected, kept up her diary without a break. One of the visitors she noted was John Hersey's mother (also named Grace). Mr. Hersey's *The Call* (New York: Knopf, 1985) describes YMCA life in a different part of China—the north. The principal legation friends were UC classmate Julean Arnold and his wife (see chapter 3).
3. Salt Gabelle was the usual foreign way of referring to the government's Salt Administration. All through Chinese history, a tax on salt has been an important revenue of the state. In 1913 the credit rating of the new republic was not high. In order to secure a large foreign loan, China had to agree to place the collection of this tax under foreign administration. "Gabelle" was a tax levied on salt in France before the French Revolution.
4. Grace never was able to realize her dream of visiting Europe.

Although the doctors wanted me to stay longer in Peking, I was determined to be with the lads in Shanghai for Christmas. I was allowed to travel with a YW secretary who was going south, and had to promise that I would put myself in the hands of a physician as soon as I reached Shanghai. I did call a doctor the day after my arrival. He told me at once that I would have to spend eighteen hours a day in bed for the next six months.[5] This was blow upon blow. If it had not been for the Yards, I do not know what I would have done. The lads and I were there for Christmas together.

When our Y friends in Shanghai heard the word "endocarditis" and saw how ill I had been, they began to tell me that Bob would be down very soon. They entirely failed to understand our attitude. I prided myself on never interfering with any appointment or work of my husband. I would never send for him. If there were to be such a call, I expected it to be from the National Committee. The Committee, however, assumed that I would write urging him to come to the Coast. In the meantime, no full report of the seriousness of my condition reached him. I had the Yards' guest room with a private bath, and Dick was in a small study across the hall.

The year 1923 closed on a somewhat somber note. Though not athletic, I had always been very active. I rode and walked, though perhaps not as much as some. I had given up tennis because of my eyes. Now to be laid aside with severe physical restrictions for the future was devastating. I could not accustom myself to it; and I knew how disastrous it would seem to Bob. This was the truly unexpected. I thought of how I had been able to help Bob when his eye was injured, and felt that now I had failed him in my health. I was distressed that I would not be able to do as much for my family as I had done before. I knew I was going through a period of depression, but I tried to win back confidence and hope.

Life for Bob in Chungking had been having some different complications. Yang Sen and his forces started to retreat from Chungking the day after I had left that city. As is common in Chinese sieges, a gate was left uncontested for the retiring army. But Yang Sen's wives, who lived near us and had been so eager to call upon me that autumn, knew they might fare badly in a flight, and they rushed to our house in short order when the rout began. Indeed, inside of half an hour after the capturing troops entered the city, the former home of the Yang ladies had been thoroughly looted. Our faithful Lao Liu, the horse coolie, rushed to the Y to tell Bob.

When Bob reached the house, he found three or four wives with female relatives and servants of both sexes. The party was more than twenty in all. They had no interest in the upper part of the house. Fortunately, our ground

---

5. Grace did spend a great deal of time in bed or resting, but her diary for this period indicates that she found many needs to bend the doctor's eighteen-hour admonition.

floor was almost like a basement. Bob arranged several rooms for them there and also gave them the living room and study on the first floor.[6]

Bob often laughed about this experience. He had interesting talks with several of the wives' mothers. In 1927 Bob was in Hankow during a very tense period. One day an old Chinese dame in a ricksha waved, called, and made her puller stop. She was one of those mothers. She cried out with pleasure: "This is indeed good fortune to meet Hsieh An-tao. He helped us in Chungking four years ago and will help us again." The women were trying to get to Shanghai. Bob was able to send a Chinese to assist them.

When I learned in December 1923 that we would have to give up the trip through Europe, I was still in the hospital and could not conveniently send a telegram. I asked Mr. Gailey to send one for me. Bob knew I was in the hospital; when the telegram arrived and he saw the word Peking, he was afraid to open it. He took it home with him and kept it several hours before tearing it open. The change in travel plans was not the bad news he had feared! He then sat down and wrote me a beautiful letter telling me of his apprehension, and of his relief. He could not visualize me as anything but my old self. His letter took several weeks to reach me but was a great comfort.

Bob's replacement finally arrived in late January. Bob left at once and joined me in Shanghai in early February. I think he was surprised that I had been so ill. Actually, I have to thank him for sending me away from Chungking when he did. Had I remained, I might not be alive now.

Now that we were together, the next problem was our furlough. Because travel would be difficult for me, and I would not be able to keep house when we arrived in America, we decided to remain in Shanghai until the end of the boys' school year. The YMCA residences in Shanghai were impractical for me because the way they were planned required much climbing of steps and stairs. Jim and Mabelle Yard had a large ground-floor apartment. We were glad to accept their invitation to stay on with them.

Bob did some local work for the Y that spring and attended the annual YMCA conference in Hangchow. His Tibetan collection, which he had been accumulating for fifteen or more years, attracted attention and comment. He spoke about it at the American Women's Club.[7] I amused myself during those

6. I believe that Yang Sen's harem stayed in our house for about two weeks and then left Chungking on a safe-conduct pass. However inconsiderate of human life the warlord generals might be where their peasant soldiers were concerned, they were usually considerate—and even chivalrous—when the lives of their rivals and their rivals' families were involved. Perhaps the kaleidoscopic nature of warlord politics reminded them that today's winner might well be to-morrow's loser.

7. I think this was the origin of a Tibetan collection that Bob loaned to the museum at Shanghai Baptist College. The college was several miles below Shanghai on the Whangpoo River. During the Japanese attack on Shanghai in 1937, it was occupied by the Japanese army. Bob's Tibetan collection, and most of the contents of the museum, disappeared. The Japanese

months in bed by compiling an anthology of Chinese poetry. It necessitated much reading, but I had plenty of time. And it was interesting to have some objective as I read.[8]

---

agreed to pay the insured value, but that was lamentably low. Apparently, when Bob placed it there and was asked about its value, he had merely estimated his own cost of procuring the articles in West China. Financial affairs were not Bob's forte.

8. The anthology was of English translations of Chinese poems. And that was the problem. Grace had a good working command of spoken Chinese, but she could not read. The nature of poetry, and the lack of any relationship between Chinese and English, mean that there can be as many different translations of a Chinese poem as there are translators. Which translation was Grace to take as "best"? It was a project that Grace would work on for a time and then put aside. Finally, in the late 1930s after Bob's death, she completed her manuscript. Her friend Pearl Buck suggested that she send it to John Day, the publishing firm that Mrs. Buck's husband was associated with. But their answer was negative. Grace's diary does not indicate that she tried anywhere else.

43

Unsettling Furlough
(1924–25)

We sailed from Shanghai on June 12, on a ship going to Seattle. When Y people returned from the field, the International Committee required them to have a medical check-up. Because of my health problems, we expected this to have special priority. But we assumed that it could wait until we reached California, where we would be staying with Bob's family. Unexpectedly, a telegram from the Committee insisted that we have the medical examinations before we left Seattle. The examinations were thorough and took several days—while we all had to stay in a Seattle hotel. The doctors were not pleased with my history or condition and thought I should not return to the Orient. It seemed hard to convince them that life for a housewife and mother might be easier in China where she could have all the servants that were needed. Still, we were both fairly optimistic and hoped for great improvement after I reached California.

The International Committee had told us that we would be living in Berkeley that year. As soon as we arrived, we started looking for a furnished house to rent. With three growing boys, it was not easy to find a suitable one. At last we advertised. This produced an attractive place on Spruce Street, not far from two of Bob's sisters.[1] That settled, I went south to spend three weeks with my parents. Bob took the boys to the old Service family ranch near Ceres, and then, with two of his elder brothers and two older cousins, on a fishing and camping trip to Tuolumne Meadows.[2]

1. There were eleven siblings in Bob's family; eight reached adulthood, married, and had an average of three children apiece. His two married sisters near us in Berkeley had a total of seven, close in age to us boys. It was a great getting-acquainted of cousins.
2. Toulumne Meadows was very different in 1924: narrow, unpaved, one-way roads; no specified campgrounds; not many people. My uncles went every year and always camped at the same spot on the bank of the Merced River. One of the uncles had an open touring car called the Apperson Jackrabbit. It was misnamed. First, a short circuit caused a minor fire under the seat. Then we broke an axle. I have been back to the Meadows many times, but that first time was the best.

30 *Seeing the family off on the ship at Shanghai in 1924. The four Yard girls and the three Service boys. The NOW famous Molly is hiding under the bushel at the right.*

We all returned to Berkeley in August and settled into the Spruce Street house in time for the three boys to start school—in three separate public schools. The house was comfortable, with a spacious redwood-panelled living room and fine views of San Francisco Bay. We were also pleased to have a fireplace. But there had been a disastrous fire in Berkeley the year before, and the neighborhood was very nervous. As soon as we lit a blaze in our grate, the phone would ring: "Do you know that sparks are coming out of your chimney?" We had little joy out of that fireplace.[3]

Bob at once started to learn how to drive. As soon as he had a drivers' license, he bought our first car, a second-hand, 1922 Studebaker with a "California top." This made a touring car into a semi-sedan by adding sliding glass side windows. We enjoyed the car exceedingly, and soon felt the greatest confidence in Bob's driving.[4]

Bob also started to take some work at the University, but there were so many interruptions that he was unable to complete any course. For one thing, he was asked to give many talks. For instance, on one day he talked to the Lions Club at noon and the University YMCA in the evening.[5] The next day he addressed the University Meeting, and we had lunch with the acting

3. There was another disappointment related to the fire hazard. I was astonished, coming from rainy Szechwan, to find that Berkeley has no rain from May to October—and watering the many flowers and shrubs surrounding the house was my assigned responsibility. In China, of course, we had a gardener.

4. Grace, a non-driver, was being kind. I expect it is not easy to learn to drive at forty-five. But we all loved the car (Walnut Creek was a favorite, almost weekly, "drive in the country").

5. Bob's name was kept alive on the Berkeley campus because the University YMCA (Stiles Hall) considered him its "representative in China" and staged an annual "Roy Service Day" to raise funds for his partial support.

31 *The family in Berkeley, 1924. The picture was memorable to Jack because he had just persuaded Bob to let him don his first long pants.*

president of the University. That same afternoon he talked to a women's meeting at St. Marks Episcopal Church. In the midst of this he had to go east to bring a Chinese friend, the president of the Chungking Y, across the continent. The friend, who spoke no English, had expected to travel via Europe with us. When our European plans were canceled, we arranged for him to travel with some Canadian friends. But they could bring him only as far as Toronto.

When we set up housekeeping, I tried to get on without help. This soon proved impracticable. The doctor told me to stay in bed in the mornings until nine or later, and I was not to do any kind of hard work. After several part-time arrangements did not work out, we got a maid. This pretty well solved the household problem.

In November Bob had to go to Southern California to make some speeches. Mrs. Strite, an old friend of the Service family, agreed to stay with the three lads, so I was able to go with Bob. We were back by Thanksgiving for a wonderful gathering of more than thirty members of the Service clan at Ceres. It was a jollification such as the Services well know how to manage. There were two mammoth turkeys and plenty to go with them. Singing and games ended the day.

Our own Christmas-present opening was in the morning around my bed. For weeks and even months Bob had been encouraging the three boys to hope for an electric train. The lads had each secured catalogues, and there had been hot debates over relative merits. As our gifts were opened on my bed, the parcels disclosed no trace of any train. When the air showed tension and disappointment, Bob remarked that there had been a lot of gifts *on* the bed, perhaps there was something *under* it. Immediately there were dives for the floor, followed by shouts and various signs of pleasure. It was the brand they had deemed the best, with extra track and equipment. That night there was a tree at the home of Bob's sister Irene, and our children had their only chance to share the fun of Christmas with cousins.[6] A few days later we were off to Asilomar, where a YMCA conference was to be held.

When we had rented the Berkeley house, it was with the understanding from the International Committee that we were to be there for the whole school year. At the end of 1924 we had word from the Committee that we were to move to New York early in January. This seemed an impossible feat to me. We were all nicely settled; to uproot the three boys from their school work when all were so well established and happy seemed unreasonable. Also, we feared that the doctors might not permit my return to China. If so, Bob would have to face a job hunt for Y work in America, and that would probably mean more moving. So we felt it best not to move the family at this time. As soon as we returned from Asilomar, Bob started off alone to New York.

After a few weeks, I had word from Bob that I had to go east and should make some arrangement for leaving the boys. Fortunately, Mrs. Strite was able to come again. Then my doctor would not let me travel alone! Finally, Bob came west to get me. On February 27 we left for Chicago, where Bob was to spend about four weeks. This gave me a chance to visit my relatives in Iowa.

Then we were off to New York. Here I found that arrangements had been made for me to enter a sanatorium in New Jersey. This was a place that took only "hearts, Bright's disease, and diabetes." We were pleasantly surprised to find a University of California classmate as head physician and manager.[7] He very generously arranged a large double room for me so that Bob could stay with me (he was able to commute from there to the Y offices in New York City). I was on a very rigid salt-free diet, with minimum fat and sugar. But the primary objective was tonsilectomy.

Because I had imbedded tonsils, they had not been entirely removed in 1916, and both had become infected. In Peking, Seattle, and later in Califor-

6. It was Irene's collection of teacups that Grace had accidentally ruined in 1905 (chapter 2).
7. The doctor was Fred W. Allen, UC 1902.

nia I had been told that they must come out; but no one was anxious to operate. Now, finally, with the most skillful anesthetist, with a clever throat specialist, and with our doctor friend (out of personal interest) in the operating room, I had the operation. I returned to the sanatorium for ten days and, at the end of April, was pronounced fit to return to China—but *not* to Szechwan. The doctors would not consent to my living where I would need to go to the mountains in the summer. And the Coast was thought to be better for me than the interior.

There had, of course, been consultation between the International Committee in New York and the National Committee in Shanghai. The National Committee had work for Bob on the Coast, and he would also be used for regular trips to the YMCAs on the Yangtze and in Szechwan. Bob felt that this would be in many ways an ideal arrangement. One of the chief problems in Szechwan had been isolation and the lack of two-way contact with the National Committee in remote Shanghai. If he were to be based in Shanghai and travel back and forth, he felt that this would be solved. On the day before we were to leave the sanatorium, he returned from the city full of happiness and thoroughly pleased with what he called a "surprise" for me. It was the news that our passage for China had been booked for August 22 on the *President Pierce*.

I knew the whole situation had been very difficult for Bob. He felt I had had too strenuous a life in China, and that it might be his duty to remain in America. He had been offered several Y positions in the States, but he always said to me that he had no place in America. He had given his life to China; he belonged to the China work. And, as the International Committee had stood behind us, so we must stand by the Committee. He did not speak of his ability to speak Chinese, or of his many friends there in China. He could not bear to give up in his forties the work to which he had turned his hand and heart when he was in his twenties. I agreed, and was as rejoiced as he to be able to return to the country and the associations so dear to both of us.

Practically all the thrill and excitement of near-normal American existence for me during that year in America was condensed into six marvelous days of May when we stayed at the Hotel Commodore in New York, saw old friends, shopped, went to theaters, entertained our niece Lynda Goodsell from Wellesley,[8] and stored up numerous memories that are still a source of happiness. We had a visit with relatives in Chattanooga, and two days with my parents in Southern California. In no time, we were back in Berkeley.

In the midst of "last things," Bob had his teeth pulled. We were closely scanning the newspapers those days for accounts of the "Shanghai Incident"

8. Lynda was the eldest child of Bob's sister Lulu (see chapter 2, note 2). She had grown up in Turkey and would return there as a missionary.

32   *Bob and Grace on their furlough travel to the East Coast, early 1925. They look as if they knew that their return to China had been approved.*

of May 30, when foreign police in Shanghai had shot into a crowd of students and other sympathizers staging a demonstration in support of strikers in a foreign-owned textile factory.[9] Jack graduated from Berkeley High School in early June. He was still only fifteen and would return with us to China to work for awhile before going to college.

By mid-June we were with four other Service families camping together in Yosemite Valley. We had rented equipment; the others had their own. There were continual hikes, swims, and other good times. As soon as the men were back from any activity, a table of bridge would be started. If four players could not be found (very seldom), Bob and his elder brother Bert would sit down to cribbage, at which they were persistent foes.[10]

9. The May Thirtieth Incident in Shanghai was seized upon by the Kuomintang and Communists, then in a united front, to galvanize the country against foreign imperialism. It was a milestone toward the Kuomintang's victory in 1927. For a time, the situation in Shanghai looked very uncertain, and Grace and Bob were scanning the news in the fear that their return might be affected. It will be recalled that their arrival in 1905 was also during a period of disturbance.

10. Bob and all his family loved almost all games, and especially cards. This posed a problem for Bob in China. Missionaries were opposed to gambling. Chinese assumed that anyone playing with ordinary cards was gambling. So most missionaries avoided games with conventional cards. Our family went through a long, gradual transition. First, games with special cards: for instance, Old Maid and Rook; then Five Hundred; and finally bridge (auction and then con-

I rode on some of the excursions and picnics, but soon began to feel badly. It did not seem to be my heart. Bert's wife and I had gone into the Valley by train to avoid the elevation of the old road by Big Oak Flat (in 1925 there was no river-level motor road through El Portal). Finally, a day before we had planned to break camp, I had to leave. After I had spent a day in bed at Ceres, Bob arrived with our car and the boys and took me on to Berkeley. They drove me immediately to the hospital. I had an infected gallbladder, and a boil on a leg, and felt sicker and crosser than I can remember having felt before or since. For awhile I could eat nothing, and odors nauseated me. When they finally told me I would *have* to eat, the only thing I could think of that might be palatable was Chinese tea, which was not much of a food. Bob got some from a Chinese vegetable dealer. Gradually I added a dry cracker, a bit of toast, a taste of this or that—until eventually I was pronounced fit to leave the hospital.

All this time Bob was greatly worried. It was already July, and we were to sail for China in August. I wanted no guests at the hospital as I was actually too cross to talk—when that happens a woman *does* feel ill. But of course Bob came, usually twice a day; and always he asked whether the doctor had said anything about our return to China. I was thankful I did not have to report anything. The doctor knew our plans, and he never spoke of them at all. Neither did we.

Bob and the boys had moved into an apartment on Ashby Avenue, and our maid from the Spruce Street house came back to help out. As soon as I could travel, I went south by train (the doctor would not let me go by car). Bob and the boys joined me at Long Beach, where we took an apartment for a couple of weeks and visited with my parents. By August 10 we were back in Berkeley and busy with all the bustle of packing and last errands.

There was a great send-off by friends and relatives when we boarded ship on August 22 and started back to China.

---

tract). After we went back to China in 1925, bridge was the order of the day. Grace was a good sport about all this. She lacked the Service zest for competition. She avoided "ladies' bridge." But she was willing to please Bob and her sons.

44

Settling in Shanghai

(1925–26)

We had a pleasant voyage across the Pacific. There were various parties and the usual athletic contests.[1] Bob got out some of his Chinese hangings for the "Arabian Nights" entertainment and, dressed as a Chinese gentleman, took the prize for "most handsome man." In Honolulu we hired a car and had a wonderful day. With swims both at Haleiwa and Waikiki, the boys were very happy. Our only regret that evening was that we so soon had to throw our leis in the bay.

By mid-September we were among friends in Shanghai. Bob left in early October for his first trip to west China on his new regional assignment. After he left we moved into a rented house at the end of Avenue Joffre.[2] With the younger boys at school and Bob away, Jack was my mainstay for the move. He did well until he developed a sinus infection and had to go to the hospital. When he was well again, he started working as an apprentice draughtsman at the architectural office of the YMCA. Several residences and Y buildings were being built around the country, and plans were being drawn for a new Foreign YMCA in Shanghai. Bob got home on December 24, just in time for the holidays. So ended 1925.

The new year started out to be a busy one. Bob was away in the West for three months in the spring and early summer. And I began to become active in a new way. I felt set free in Shanghai. After the long years when I had taught in the YMCA and at home, I was now entirely without that employ-

1. My chief interest was in the table tennis tournament, which was won by Edwin O. Reischauer, later my Oberlin classmate and American ambassador to Japan. I was runner-up.

2. The house we rented was in the same compound where Grace had been staying with the Yards in the spring of 1924. The Yards, however, had left China only a couple of months before we arrived back in Shanghai. Jim sympathized with the Chinese desire for more significant participation in the policy and administration of the Christian church in China. The mission considered him too radical and he was not returned to China. Mabelle continued to be Grace's boon companion—through a copious correspondence.

ment. In America I had seen many of my friends doing much in club activities; but I had never had a chance to do such things myself. Some years previously, I had become a member of the China National Committee of the YWCA. But living where I did, I had no opportunity to attend meetings or take any active part in its work. Now, in Shanghai, I became active on the Committee. I also joined several other organizations, among them the American Women's Club and the Association of American University Women.

Late in 1926 I became the chairman of the "Foreign Finance Committee" of the YWCA. This had charge of the allowances, living arrangements, and financial emergencies concerning the foreign secretaries loaned by various foreign YW organizations to the China National Committee. I continued as chairman for some years until the need for the committee's services were ended by a change in allowances and the decision to dispose of the YWCA residences.

When my mother heard that I had taken on this work, she was rejoiced and wrote that she was so glad that I was doing some missionary work at last! Nothing that I had done in Szechwan—keeping house amid difficulties, teaching, looking after children, entertaining many Chinese and foreign guests, doing everything possible to assist my husband's work—none of this seemed to her to come under the heading of "missionary work." I think she was probably embarrassed and bothered in her mind as to my worth or accomplishments. Certainly, she did not consider that work done by a non-denominational organization, such as the YMCA, had the true stamp of the missionary. As far as I can judge from what she said to me at different times, I remained an enigma to her as long as she lived. That I was satisfied without definite contact with a "Mission Board" was something she could not understand.

When we were in Szechwan, I once asked her to help educate a small lad (the son of our gateman), and she replied, "What good would it do? You are not connected with the work of the Church Board." She was an ardent Presbyterian, but in Szechwan that denomination had no missionary work; obviously, therefore, our work there was beyond the pale. She never helped financially in any way with the myriad benevolences crying at our door; to her, money for missions should go through the Presbyterian Board. No matter what causes I might espouse, nothing could move her from the rock of her sectarianism. I often wonder what my attitude would be if I had a daughter living in and trying to be helpful in a country like China. But I could never have the attitude of Mother's generation; I have seen too much in too many places, and I do not bow down in special reverence to any denomination. I want to be a Christian, and that suffices me.

We spent that summer in Tsingtao, on the Shantung coast. Bob was with us for his vacation, and Jack joined us for a short stay before going to sightsee in Peking. We were out at Iltis Huk, some three miles beyond the city, and loved the quiet around the bungalows and the beautiful beaches. Bob took a trip to Chefoo with a Shanghai friend. There was still no real motor road connecting the two cities; this was the first time the trip had been done by car. I led a very quiet existence and was glad to rest after Shanghai's rapid pace.

My chief excitement was a weekly jaunt to the excellent market in the city. On one occasion I took a carriage, and in 1926 that meant an old vehicle of the victoria type. In color it was bright canary with a rusty black top. The driver was a man of ancient mien, clothed in flapping blue and black garments and wearing a tall, peaked straw hat. Under his feet he had a large sack of fodder for the two steeds; he could pick up a snack here or there, but they could not. After my visit to the market we added to the boot two live fowls of a somewhat disputative disposition, and two very large market baskets full to the brim with garden truck and fruit. Out of one of these stuck a tall beer bottle full of molasses, for thus did we buy that comestible. In our part of the vehicle we had groceries and a fish, a roast of beef, a roll of flypaper, and miscellaneous articles. Dick reported that a lot of people stared at us, but that did not worry me at all. We always enjoyed these market excursions but left other buying for the cook.

The autumn in Shanghai was occupied with a succession of house guests and the usual full program of city life. We became acquainted with more Chinese and several Japanese. I had Portuguese and German friends. Every acquaintance broadened one's horizons. And there were always unexpected happenings to swell the daily program and add tension to life.

One thing happened to me that autumn that I can never forget. A certain wealthy New York gentleman and his wife had been in Shanghai, staying at a hotel. We had met them several times. The annual YWCA funds campaign was in progress, and I was much concerned for its success. I knew this couple were interested in such activities, so I asked them for a subscription. I was surprised at the amount they gave. Indeed, they expressed themselves as delighted to help us and immediately invited us to dine with them the next day!

The mere idea of asking for money frightens some women. But all those organizations working to help people in need, and without finances of their own, depend on some one to raise money. I would never prefer such a task, but I have never shirked a part in the effort. I have collected funds for Red Cross campaigns, for churches, and for Christian Associations. But never did I meet such a warm reception, when a simple request for a worthy cause brought a generous check, a delightful dinner, and a most enjoyable evening.

There was a sad note late in the year: Jack, now seventeen, was preparing to go back to America for college. We planned for him to go by way of India and Europe. He was to travel through Europe with the Heldes.[3] But as they did not want as long a stay in India, Jack was to go ahead of them on an earlier boat and they would catch up with him at Colombo. On December 6 we saw Jack off on a German ship. Half an hour later, Bob left on an unexpected trip to Hong Kong with Dr. David Yui, the head of the YMCA National Committee. Later that same day a cable from the International Committee in New York instructed the Heldes to return to America immediately via the Pacific. And Jack was already happily on his way.

Bob's ship was a fast one; he would be in Hong Kong before Jack. I cabled them both: they could discuss the matter and work out a solution. Bob cabled back: could I find any other couple or party to which Jack could attach himself? Several days of inquiries were unsuccessful. On the fifth day there was another cable from Bob. He had seen Jack off for Manila; the decision whether he should go on or come back to Shanghai was left to me: Jack would do whatever I said. There were dinner guests that evening, and I felt easier in my mind than I had for some days. Possibilities and probabilities chased around and around in my head all night. I remembered myself at seventeen, and knew Jack would be terribly disappointed if he had to return to Shanghai. It would be almost as if I told everyone that I did not trust him to travel alone. He had already started off to go alone through the Malay States and India. If he could do those alone, why not Europe? The next morning I cabled Manila, telling him to go on. As it happened, he managed exceedingly well. YMCA people in India helped. In Italy, he met by chance two University of California classmates of Bob's and mine.[4] Letters to friends from West China who had returned to England smoothed his way around Britain. I felt justified in my reliance on his judgment.[5]

All during 1926 there had been much tension in China. The North and the South were at odds. Within a year of Sun Yat-sen's death in 1925, the Southern government had come under the control of the Left Wing, which was allied with the Russians and advised by Borodin.[6] Chiang Kai-shek,

3. It will be recalled that George Helde's wife had died in childbirth at White Deer Summit in 1920 (chapter 33). He had now remarried, and his young son was with them.
4. The classmates were Mary Irene Morrin and Katherine F. Smith, both UC 1902. They took me in tow through Italy. In Ravello we found ourselves staying in the same small hotel with Monroe E. Deutsch, vice-president and provost of the University of California—and also a 1902 classmate of Grace and Bob's.
5. Grace's diary entry about this telegram to me has the brief phrase "Hugo helped me." So perhaps Mr. Sandor deserves at least part of my thanks for a fine trip. Perhaps, also, Grace—long thwarted in her own hopes to visit Europe—had some vicarious pleasure in giving me the go-ahead. Grace's diary is a succinct listing of each day's events, weather, letters received and written, books read, meetings attended, who won the evening card game, and so forth. But it is clear, from this instance and others, that in Bob's absences it was to Hugo Sandor that Grace turned for help and advice.
6. Michael Borodin had spent many years in the United States, as had Sun Yat-sen. This made it possible for the two men to dispense with interpreters and to use English in planning China's revolution. While Borodin was orchestrating the campaign against missionary imperi-

though not entirely under Russian control, was leading the Northern Expedition against Peking. There was continual unrest and fighting throughout the Yangtze Valley. The fall of 1926 saw many foreigners concentrating in Shanghai. Consular officials, alarmed by unrest, antiforeign strikes, rioting, and fighting here and there, would not permit travel to the interior. Many missionaries were being urged to take early home leave; people returning from home leave were being held at the Coast, hoping for a time of less uncertainty. Our house was full of guests all that winter.

Early in 1927 the Left Wing set up a National Government at Wuhan (the three cities of Hankow, Wuchang, and Hanyang), and Chinese took over the British Concessions in Hankow and Kiukiang. Many foreigners were told to leave the interior. Their arrival added to the large numbers already in Shanghai. Many people from Szechwan were among them, and we did all we could to help. A British bank turned over a large old-fashioned residence for use as a hostel. It gave shelter to a number of our Canadian friends, but they needed furniture and other necessities. I took over a lot of curtains.

About the middle of February a British steamer arrived from Hankow with one hundred and fifty refugees from the West. The whole ship had been taken over for this purpose, including the space below decks that was normally occupied by Chinese coolie-class travelers. We were in the big crowd meeting the boat because we expected two girls [women] from the American Methodists. We found them at last in the bowels of the ship, where they had certainly traveled "hard."

After they reached our house, the first thing they mentioned was a bath. "Oh, yes," I said, showing them their bathroom across the hall. "This is for your use and no one will be sharing it with you. Here are towels and everything, so make yourselves at home." A little later I saw them floating about the hall and one murmured, "We were thinking of taking baths." "Certainly," I agreed, "I hope you have everything." She looked uncertain. I went on about my own affairs, and still later they again mentioned bathing. So I said, "Well, why doesn't one of you start in on a bath?" "But the hot water?" said one of them. I looked puzzled. "There is plenty," said I, "just turn on the tap." They shrieked and began to laugh. "We haven't seen a real American bathroom for such ages. . . . You know how in Szechwan we always have to get the coolie to carry in hot water. . . . Oh, Mrs. Service, what *do* you think of us!"

The Southern forces came into the Shanghai area in March. They took over most of the Chinese-controlled areas around the foreign settlements without incident. North of the city some Northern troops made an attempt

---

alism, his wife and two Chicago-raised sons were living with an American missionary family in Shanghai while the boys attended the mission-dominated Shanghai American School. They were, of course, using a name other than Borodin.

to fight and then tried to flee, with their arms, into the International Settlement. They were kept out by the Shanghai Volunteer Corps and other available units, but this involved considerable shooting. With the inflamed anti-foreign sentiment of the time, Southern agitators tried to distort this defensive action. The situation was very tense for about thirty-six hours. There was talk of a general strike by the servants of foreigners, but nothing came of it. Indeed, our servants appeared to be exceedingly happy to be right with us in a foreign house. The Boy lugged in some boxes belonging to his father, as he believed our house to be a place of safety.

One day I was in the city, walking along Nanking Road a few blocks from the Bund. Usually the street is crowded with vehicles and pedestrians. Suddenly I noticed that the street was empty. At the same moment a lady spoke from the recess of a shop entrance and asked where I was going. "Why, I'm on my way to the silk shop," I said. "You had better wait awhile," was her response. "A bomb was just thrown from the roof of a building in the next block." It was surprising how quickly I found myself inside that shop with a crowd of other passers-by.

Bob's idea was that if there was any trouble, I would be found close by. He said he always missed such things, but I reminded him of the bullet affair in Chungking. Each one usually has a share of danger, known or unknown.

45

Tense Times

(1927)

The interplay of politics, ambition, and envy, together with a desire to see the discredit of the new Nationalist leader, Chiang Kai-shek—all these elements fused to produce the Nanking Incident of March 24, 1927, in which several foreigners were killed by Southern troops.[1] Two days later I was at a meeting of the YWCA National Committee. I shall never forget the dismay and concern shown by its Chinese members. We were all faced with most alarming news as to the temper and actions of the soldiery there in Nanking. The Chinese were anxious to know the foreign attitude to the new National Government and wondered if we would be leaving China.[2] Our discussion settled nothing, but it showed us the sadness of our Chinese friends over the situation.

The Nanking Incident set off alarms around the world, but especially in Shanghai. If this attack on foreigners by Chinese troops was a forerunner of things to come, the situation could be very grave. The concern of our Chinese friends that we might be leaving China did not, at the time, seem so far-fetched.

In Shanghai the foreign military forces enforced a strict curfew.[3] Barbed-wire barricades were set up at key points. There were constant military patrols throughout the International Settlement and the French Concession. The city was divided into sectors. The national group in each area had in-

1. Not much is known for certain about the background and motivation of the "Nanking Incident." Grace was accepting the later Kuomintang explanation—that the attack was Communist-inspired, intended to provoke trouble with the foreign Powers and embarrass Chiang Kai-shek.

2. The "new National Government" was not the Left Wing "National Government" already in business in Wuhan, but the Right Wing "National Government" just then being established in Nanking by Chiang Kai-shek. The Wuhan government collapsed a few months later.

3. Besides the naval forces normally in the area, all the principal Powers had sent military units to defend Shanghai. The American unit was the Fourth Marine Regiment. There was also the Shanghai Volunteer Corps, a sort of home guard organized by nationality. Finally, there was a very sizable police force. In the International Settlement the police had British officers and a large contingent of Sikhs.

structions for emergencies. Bob was responsible for notifying a list of Americans in our neighborhood. We kept a couple of small trunks packed, and suitcases stood ready in the upper hall. Many organizations, including the American Women's Club, opened relief headquarters. The American Community Church housed fifty people, members of the Augustana Synod Mission. These people were mostly of Scandinavian stock from Nebraska; they had been living in Honan and had suffered much hardship and loss. The gymnasium of the Navy YMCA became a women's dormitory with rows of cots; men had rooms on the upper floors; and the restaurant did a tremendous business.

Early in April I was in the North Hongkew section to pick up my supply of matzoth, the Jewish unleavened bread (I lived on a salt-free diet from 1925 to 1929 and ate no regular bread). While I was there a big sign was erected at the street corner by the Jewish shop I was in: "No traffic permitted north of this point." In the YWCA we were thankful that our Foreign Finance Committee had not renewed leases on houses occupied by our people on North Szechwan Road Extended. All but one or two of our secretaries had already moved south of Range Road.[4]

Bob and I were having tea one day at the Astor House Hotel. There was a sudden excitement at the Soviet consulate building, just across the street, as members of the Shanghai Volunteer Corps surrounded the building. This was a few days after the Chinese Government had raided the Soviet embassy in Peking. We heard that the Red officials burned masses of papers before clearing out. It was said that a thousand foreigners left Shanghai in one week, and all that spring outgoing ships were crowded. The tension seemed greater during the second week of April than during the first. After that, things gradually became less tense.

A friend with an invalid husband decided to take him to America. She offered us her large and attractive house. The move would save rent for the YMCA, and it was a better house for hot weather than the one we had been living in. We accepted the offer. Several days before we planned to move, the National Committee received a telegram from the Hankow Y asking specifically for Bob to go there. We did not know just what the emergency was, but Bob felt obliged to go. I was terribly upset, but a couple of house guests from Szechwan promised to help me through the move. When Bob's ship for Hankow entered the Yangtze it had to wait for a naval escort; just when we needed his help in the moving, he was sitting idle on shipboard only a few

4. The area on North Szechwan Road Extended that Grace refers to is precisely the sector, beyond the boundary of the International Settlement, that Bob and Grace found to be of dubious safety in 1905 (chapter 3 and its note 2). Grace was the head of the committee making the decision.

miles away. It took him over six days to reach Hankow—the normal time was three. Bob returned home in late May, but went back and spent most of that summer in Hankow while the American secretary from that city, who was not well, took a holiday with his family in our new Shanghai house.

At a meeting of the American Women's Club in May there was a heated discussion about the suggestion of some of our members that we cable a conference in the United States of the General Federation of Women's Clubs to ask for its aid in securing protection for American women in China. I took part for the first time in club debate when I opposed this suggestion from the floor of the meeting.

In mid-June the lads and I went to Tsingtao. The big excitement of the summer for us was the building of a sailboat, centerboard and all, by young Bob, then sixteen. He had sent to America for patterns and had been working for some time in Shanghai on the small pieces. At Iltis Huk we had a two-story house with a large open veranda on the second floor. This was given over to the carpentry. Young Bob bought American lumber from the Dollar Company and was soon deep in construction work. By strenuous efforts he completed *Flying Cloud* just before we left at the end of the season.

The Chinese military forces in Tsingtao went into a state of extreme alert in early July.[5] Things were very tense for a couple of days: lots of soldiers around, machine guns at main intersections, and plenty of talk and rumors. After several days I was almost without money, and we had almost no food save potatoes. Rickshas were unavailable. Any pullers not already impressed by the military were in hiding. I was glad to get a ride into the city with some friends.[6] I carried a small American flag with me.

After a trip to the Y, where I secured money, and a purchasing time at the market, I went to the garage to hire a car. Cars, it seemed, had either been taken by the military or put into hiding. If I could supply a flag and would wait some time, a conveyance might be found. At last, I was off in a large open car with the top put back in the favorite beach fashion. There I sat all alone, surrounded by my purchases; a fish, two chickens, and the usual greens and fruits added color to the picture. I told the driver where we lived, and sat back in peace. When he took me into strange territory, I found that he was a stranger and had never heard of Iltis Huk. I was able to direct him and we got home safely, but much delayed.

That summer I went to the Tsingtao Barber Shop and Beauty Parlor where

5. After Chiang Kai-shek took Nanking and Shanghai in the spring of 1927, the Northern warlords joined together to oppose Chiang's expected northward advance. The Northern forces actually drove south to the Yangtze in August. Tsingtao was experiencing ripples of this activity.

6. Grace had no car in Tsingtao because there was no way of transporting the car that she had in Shanghai. In Shanghai, her car—with a chauffeur—was indispensable. Without it she could never have kept up the pace of her social, organizational, and club activities. Not many women in the missionary community had this mobility.

André, with a few snips of his long shears, cut off my long hair.[7] The coil looked very pathetic and made me think of our queueless friends in Chengtu in 1911. I was so distraught that I left my extra-good hairpins on his table, and went home with my new short locks blowing in the stiff sea breeze. It had taken me a long time to come to the point of the shears. My men had opposed it; but as soon as they saw me, they approved. So did I, and since then I have never even considered long hair. There is a vast relief in the absence of pins and fussing; and with "Irish hair" like mine, I do not need permanents, combs, or pins to give me the freedom and effect that suits my taste.

One evening soon after Bob's arrival in late August, Dick was absent when supper was ready. I supposed he was at a neighbor's, so after a wait we started dinner. Suddenly, the Boy came in to say that Dick's clothes were on his bed. He must be in the ocean. It was then fully dark. Dick was thirteen, thin and slender. Bob told me not to leave the house. He rushed off with flashlights to the beach, young Bob and his friend spending the summer with us going along. Our Canadian guest, a young woman from Peking, hurried around to the neighbors making inquiries. I spent some of the longest minutes of my life before I heard the welcome call from Bob. They had found the young chap watching some fishermen hauling in their nets on the beach. He had not realized how late it had grown.

Back in Shanghai in September things had settled down to more peaceful ways. There was the same old rush carrying us along in its usual way. The annual dinner of the American Women's Club was at the Hotel Majestic, and I was seated by Admiral Bristol.[8] It was a big thrill for me to respond to one of the toasts. I had occasion to remember it because Madame H. H. Kung thanked me for the toast when we met at the wedding of her sister, Mei-ling Soong, to General Chiang Kai-shek.

The Chiang-Soong wedding was in the same Hotel Majestic ballroom and was an interesting ceremony. What we saw in the hotel was the public ceremony; the religious one had already been performed privately at the home of the bride's mother. At the Majestic there were between eight hundred and a thousand guests. The flowers and decorations were lavish. The bright lights were intensified by reflectors to facilitate the movie cameras. The refreshments were varied and delicious. But the changing, beautiful scene in that incomparable Majestic ballroom will always be mingled in my memory with a friend's urgency to have some sausage rolls like those being passed at a

7. André was certainly a White Russian. Thousands of these refugees from the Russian Revolution managed to cross Siberia and find a rather desperate haven in Manchuria and along the China coast. Generally speaking, they had to compete with Chinese for a livelihood. Hairdressing and beauty care was one occupation in which they did very well. Dressmaking was another. Grace thought very highly of Lily, her Russian dressmaker in Shanghai.

8. Admiral Mark Bristol was commander of the U.S. Asiatic Fleet (of which the Yangtze Patrol was a unit).

nearby table. We were close to the bride and saw her dress and veil. Each of us had a slice of the wedding cake. The whole event was a kaleidoscope of beauty, color, and light. I took my piece of wedding cake home and divided it so that each person in the household might have a taste, including the servants—who were much pleased. The newly-weds set up an establishment in a house two doors from us, and we often saw their dark blue Packard in our neighborhood.[9]

There was still some risk in travel, but Bob left again for Szechwan in mid-October. We heard from him at Hankow and at Ichang, and then there was a silence. Finally, on November 11, I received some letters that had been posted at Wanhsien. This was a relief because it meant that he had passed that portion of the river where there was most danger, both from the river itself and the troops and bandits ashore. He wrote that the steamer had been guarded by two hundred soldiers at the first night's anchorage above Ichang. In spite of this, some bandits got aboard and demanded $1,000 but were finally bought off for $100. It would seem that bandits and guards may not have been complete strangers. The ship was fired on several times, but they got through safely. And Bob was glad that no woman had been along.

The Hankow Y wanted Bob to be posted there permanently, but it was decided that we should remain in Shanghai. Bob was willing to go wherever he might be sent, though he still felt that his greatest contribution could be made through his knowledge of and friendships in Szechwan and his ability to provide a link between the two Szechwan Associations and the National Committee.[10] That was his main objective. Neither Association wanted to give him up, and in both cities he was in urgent demand for all their money-raising campaigns. The mails were very irregular that winter. Though Bob and I wrote constantly, there were often long gaps between mails. This made things harder for us, as there was still considerable anxiety in the air.

9. Despite the Kuomintang support of the campaign against foreign settlements and the unequal treaties, the Chiangs were not the only high officials who saw no anomaly in their choosing to reside in the French Concession at Shanghai. Nanking, the capital, was about two hundred miles away.

10. As a membership organization with varied and innovative activities, the YMCA relied heavily on regular conferences involving Chinese and foreign staff drawn from both the central, coordinating organization (the National Committee) and the local Associations. The motives were to "recharge batteries," introduce new programs, exchange experience, and enable the center to identify and assist in meeting local needs. The long travel time from Shanghai (as Grace has pointed out) deprived the Szechwan YMCAs of the benefit of these conferences, and meant that the National Committee (rather conspicuously) often lacked understanding of the situation and needs of the Szechwan Associations. Bob's assignment as regional secretary was an attempt to remedy this situation: since they could not come to Shanghai, he would go there on a regular basis as a representative of the National Committee. It seemed to work out that he made two extended trips a year (in the spring and fall), which involved his being away from Shanghai about seven months of the year. The suggested move to Hankow might seem to make sense, since it would put him six hundred miles closer to Szechwan; but, by removing him from direct contact for several months each year with the National Committee in Shanghai, it would reduce his ability to provide the linkage that was the purpose of his regional assignment.

46

Committee Woman

(1928–29)

It was a quiet holiday season at the end of 1927. Bob did not get home until mid-January 1928, and he left again three weeks later for Hankow, where he stayed until May.

I worked very hard that spring in the YWCA financial campaign. A friend and I made scores of calls and we were fairly successful. We met a number of rebuffs, a little rudeness, and once in awhile genuine opposition. It was often tiresome waiting to see the higher-ups in company offices, and we sometimes had to repeat our calls several times before seeing the person we sought.[1] One such series of calls was repaid by the most courteous treatment and fifty dollars in crisp, new bills—a great encouragement to us. As the YWCA at this time operated the only employment agency in Shanghai for stenographers, we did not feel that we had to offer any apology for asking businessmen to help this kind of essential welfare work.

Our worst experience that year was with a real dyed-in-the-wool Fundamentalist. Previously, she had been much interested in the YWCA, but now she told us that she was no longer interested. She would not give a cent, because during Lent we had had some talks at the YW by a faculty member of the Shanghai Baptist College. This man was a fine, forceful speaker, a person of breadth and vision. But to her, "his doctrine was broad enough to take in the very Devil." She kept saying this and that about the YW's "objectionable doctrine," so I took her up on that. My friend and I both insisted that the Christian Associations [YMCA and YWCA] taught *no doctrine;* all such teaching was left to the churches. We tried only to put on a program of Christian helpfulness in which men and women of all denominations could

1. Grace's companion on the fund-raising rounds was Gerry Fitch, whose husband, George, was in the YMCA. H. H. Kung was easier to see, but gave them only twenty dollars. T. V. Soong was hard to see, but gave them fifty dollars.

meet, drawn together by the love of Christ and a desire to further a Christian order of life. She became very fussed and finally declared emphatically that it was better for the Chinese—or anyone—to die in entire ignorance of the gospel than for them to listen to the preaching of a man like our Baptist.

There is nothing in the world that tells one more about human nature than fund-raising. I had my initiation during the Great War, and my education has continued with every such task that I have undertaken since then. One man—I omit his emphatic phrases—said to me: "Don't come to me for money for women! They are after me the whole time for it. My mother wants me to help her; my sisters have the same idea. My wife spends more every year; my daughters are already large enough to come to me for money. I don't get any peace at all; women are after me every day asking for money, money, money. I don't care how people and causes get their support, but I know I have my hands full with my own women and I cannot help any others by so much as a cent." Poor man, I felt great sympathy for him.

A visitor that spring was a woman who made herself out to be a friend of my sister-in-law in the Near East.[2] I had never met her before, and later discovered that she had used my name to my sister-in-law, who entertained her because she thought the woman was *my* friend. She was a person who wanted only the best; when I took her shopping, she looked through linens worth about eight hundred dollars and finally spent about eight. Her clothes were rather gay, with flying ribbons and furbelows. When I appeared ready for church on Sunday morning, she let out a great laugh and thought me very amusing. I hope I can see a joke, but I was rather at a loss to understand her levity until she said, "Well, I never! Do you know you look just like San Francisco in your tailored suit, your smart shoes, and plain hat." This was a true compliment. Few have pleased me as much.

The boys were very busy in school. Young Bob was the student manager and enjoyed the position, which carried some responsibility. We all looked forward to the summer: Tsingtao, the boat, and the outboard motor. Bob had promised that if the boat was finished and was a good job, he would buy an outboard motor for it. We had this in Tsingtao in 1928 and the lads greatly enjoyed it. Young Bob also made surfboards, so this was added to other vacation sports.

That spring, after a great deal of discussion, we had bought a residence lot in the French Concession, hoping to build there within the year. We were working on house plans and were getting help from Ferry Shaffer, our Hungarian architect friend. During the summer we learned that the International Committee did not approve of our building a residence. This was a great

2. The sister-in-law was Bob's sister, Lulu Goodsell, in Turkey.

disappointment to all of us, and especially to Bob, whose dream of building had grown through the years. We were willing to promise that we would move from Shanghai if the need should arise, but that did not suffice.[3] Other Y men had built homes in China, and at first Bob thought he would build, whether or no. But we finally laid the plans aside. Bob told me that he had given himself entirely to the Y; he had never consciously gone against the desires of the International Committee; and he felt it best not to do so in this case.

The upshot was that Bob abandoned a cherished plan, sold the property, invested his money in other ways—and lost it in Shanghai's financial crash in the spring of 1935. Then, when his money was gone, he regretted bitterly that he had not built as he wished. We would at least have had the house.[4]

That autumn Bob was off on a strenuous trip into Shansi. He traveled by private car from Taiyuan to Sian and saw a lot of country new to him.[5] He reached home in Shanghai just before Christmas. The year 1928 had held both joy and disappointment for us.

For the past year I had been one of the representatives of the American

3. The rationale for the YMCA rule was that owning real estate in the foreign city of one's assignment might limit one's transferability in case that was desired. The American Foreign Service has a similar but broader rule.

4. One rigid taboo in our family was that finances were never discussed in front of the children. There is much in this sector that we sons have never known. Many years later, Grace told me that Bob had never received more than US$3,000 a year from the YMCA. But we had a bit more to spend than many of our missionary friends (examples: the motor car, my trip to Europe, and some of the mountain equipment Bob bought), so it was no secret that Bob had some outside income. This may have started earlier, but after Bob's father died in 1920, the ranch lands were divided and Bob received his share (one-eighth).

Besides improving our comfort, Bob used this income for good works: some extra-budget items for the local Y, school aid, help to Chinese friends in difficulty, and so on. He also started a commitment which, I am sure, grew in size and duration far beyond Bob's anticipation. When we left Chengtu in 1921, our cook, Liu Pei-yun, who had been our trusted and devoted servant since 1908, decided that he wanted to better himself by going into business. The Chengtu YMCA was about to start construction of a new building; the West China Union University was expanding and new buildings were being built; the city of Chengtu was growing and modernizing; there seemed, therefore, to be a good market for lumber. Nearby supplies were inadequate, but there were forests up the Min River in the "Tribes Country," which we had visited in the summer of 1921 and where Bob's friend Yao Bao-san was already cutting trees. Liu decided to go into the lumber business, and Bob—we assume—agreed to provide some funds to help him get started. Perhaps several things were in Bob's mind. He would be helping a deserving and capable man. He would be helping the YMCA and Union University in construction costs by ensuring that Liu gave them preferential prices. He would maintain contact with this area, which fascinated him, and develop a source of Tibetan religious and household articles (which he collected enthusiastically as long as he lived). And, finally, he would certainly recoup his investment and probably gain a generous profit. Alas, for reasons I did not know and Grace—if she knew—never divulged, things did not go as Bob expected. Instead of receiving a profit, he had to put more and more money into the enterprise.

Grace also mentions losses in the Shanghai financial crash of 1935. Those will best be discussed at that point in Grace's story.

5. This trip to the YMCAs in China's Northwest would seem to indicate that his regional work in Szechwan had been considered useful.

Association of University Women on the Joint Committee of Women's Organizations. At the Joint Committee election at the end of 1928, I was chosen to be its chairman for the coming year.[6] This position took up a great deal of my time throughout 1929. I found the responsibilities engrossing, and I deeply appreciated a growing acquaintance with outstanding women of other nationalities. Like every other group, the organization had its problems; but we tried to stick to our goal of exerting an influence for the welfare of the city.

When I was approached about taking this chairmanship, I told the nominating committee that they should consider any possible implications of my belonging to the "missionary group." If it would be a hindrance to the organization, I did not want to accept. To many people in Asian port cities the word "missionary" is like a red rag to a bull. On river steamers I have had women sit at the same table and refuse to converse with me simply because I was classed as a missionary: nationality, education, family, or general appearance are nothing to these critics. I always had the effrontery to think I was about on a level with many that I met; sometimes I felt I might be able to classify people as well as did those who blithely consigned missionaries to the outer limbo of existence. The Joint Committee did not consider my affiliations a hindrance.

I was still a member of the YWCA National Committee and had my own special YW committee, the Foreign Reference Committee. This carried some of the responsibilities of what had been the Foreign Finance Committee. As each month rolled around, I found that I had many committees and such engagements to take up my time.[7]

My parents had not been well, and I wanted to see Jack, who was finishing his sophomore year at Oberlin. I decided, in April, that I would go to America for the summer. My trip was financed by Bob, and the Y had nothing to do with it. Young Bob finished high school in early June. We sailed a few days after his Commencement, on a ship which carried many of our friends. Young Bob visited California relatives and entered the University of Califor-

6. I suppose it can be said that Grace, as chairman of the Joint Committee of Women's Organizations, had become the top club woman of Shanghai's large and diverse foreign community (although there was one Chinese organization—the Shanghai Women's Club—that was a member of the Joint Committee). It was just over three years since Grace had returned from America in 1925 and begun to be active. Not bad, one might say, for a woman whose health was deemed to be so frail that the doctors in America did not want her to return to China at all.

7. Grace omits a great deal. In addition to leadership roles in the Joint Committee and the National Committee of the YWCA, she was active in the American Association of University Women, the American Women's Club, the Daughters of the American Revolution, and a Pan-Pacific Tiffin Club. She also was writing book reviews (usually at least one a week) for the *China Weekly Review,* published by her friend John B. Powell. And because the Yards in America were having a difficult time, she was buying quantities of Chinese needlework goods for Mabelle to sell. Grace's diaries indicate that she usually tried to sleep late in the morning; but she was normally up before tiffin, and then it was all "go," often until after midnight.

33   *Grace in her active Shanghai days—probably during her year (1929) as chairman of the Joint Committee of Women's Organizations.*

nia at Berkeley that August. I visited my parents in Southern California and relatives in several states.

Jack was working at a boys' camp in Michigan. As soon as his season ended, he met me in Chicago. I got off my train from the west early one morning and found him waiting, having reached the city a couple of hours ahead of me. I had not seen my oldest son for more than two and a half years, and was proud of the tall, lithe, sunburned young chap who replaced the stripling of seventeen that I had parted with in Shanghai.[8] He went with me on several visits, and I had a week with him in Oberlin where I saw his surroundings and met his friends.

Then back to California I hurried. After farewells there—it was very hard to leave young Bob behind—I was off by train to catch my ship in Vancouver. In the sleeper I had some conversation with a lady who seemed familiar. Later, we met again on shipboard and I learned that she was Dr. Aurelia Rhinehart, the president of Mills College, whom I had met years before when I was a student at Berkeley.

An especially interesting group of my fellow passengers was en route to Japan to attend a conference of the Institute of Pacific Relations. However, sad for me, they were all in first class, and I was in second (this gave me more to use for gifts to take back with me). The rules governing contacts between classes were being rigidly applied. A friend invited me to dine in first class; I had gotten out my evening clothes and was about to dress when he came to my cabin to tell me, in embarrassment, that he was not allowed to entertain me. I then attempted to entertain him and a few others: such a thing, the steward assured me, could not be.

I did have a number of old friends in second class, and I made at least one new one—a young Japanese woman returning from school in England. She had been in another cabin, but her cabin-mate made some fuss about the assignment. I told the steward I had no objection to having her with me. She was a quiet, pleasant roommate.

In our social hall, I played cards almost every evening with three English missionaries, ladies traveling alone like myself. There were several Fundamentalist ladies aboard and they looked askance at us. One of them asked me one day if I was saved. After her opening, we went on to have many conversations. I found I had spent many more years in China than she, and that I knew far more of Chinese life and problems. She had no interest in the YM or YW; most Shanghai church work she considered futile; and of welfare organizations she wanted no part. All that mattered to her was "the evangel" as interpreted by her rigidly narrow sectarianism.

I could not find that she read anything. I was finishing a re-reading of *The Brothers Karamazov,* and had Clive Bell's *Civilization.* She would have none of them and even refused *Man's Social Destiny* by Ellwood. A travel-wise New York friend had sent a large parcel of current magazines to the ship, with the instructions that it was to be delivered to me on the fifth day out. I pressed some of these on the Fundamentalist, but she was not interested. Despite her

---

8. Also waiting on the platform to meet Grace was Mabelle. They had not seen each other for more than five years. Indeed, to meet and stay with the Yards was the reason we met in Chicago: Jim had become university chaplain at Northwestern University in Evanston.

concern for my salvation, she was not interested half as much in me as I was interested in her!

Back in Shanghai, I threw all my energies, renewed by the sea voyage, into the affairs of the Joint Committee. For some years there had been talk of staging a large international pageant. The expense, lack of a trained director, and other difficulties loomed large. Now, the China National Committee of the YWCA underwrote the production, and the National Board of the YWCA in America loaned us a director of skill and experience. The Joint Committee undertook the work. Numerous committees were busy for weeks. And the last days were full of errands, rehearsals, unexpected emergencies, sudden changes, and the thousand and one details that go into the staging of such a production.

There is a famous phrase in the Confucian classics: "Within the four seas, all men are brothers." We named our pageant "Within the Four Seas." We advertised and advertised. There was a gorgeous poster, but it offended our White Russian friends because, in drawing the national flags, the artist had included the emblem of Soviet Russia. There were three performances. At the first, the hall was not full. Attendance was better at the second. And for the matinee on the third day, we had a packed house. The effect was cumulative; if we could have had one or two more performances, we would surely have had big crowds—and ended up with a profit.

Our director told us that it was to be expected that we would not at once reap the full benefit of our efforts, that they would appear as time passed. Certainly we benefited by learning to work together. Never can those dancing, lively groups of Scandinavians, Hungarians, Russians, and many others in colorful costumes fade entirely from our minds. At the end, when our tots from all countries in their varied national garb mingled joyfully on the stage with a message of Peace and Brotherhood, we did catch a glimpse of idealism that at the time seemed almost tangible. The Japanese children were so darling. Perhaps if we had a world ruled by children there really would be an end of war!

But all this was work. I look back on that week as the most hectic of my career as housekeeper, helpmeet, and committee woman. Immediately after the last pageant performance, Bob started west again. Meanwhile, I welcomed old Y friends, Will and Mary Lockwood, who were to spend a couple of months with Dick and me.[9]

9. The Lockwoods, it may be recalled, welcomed Bob and Grace to China in 1905; and it was with Mary that Grace shared a shaking bed on her first night in China (chapter 3).

47

Storm Brewing

(1930-31)

With Bob away, the family gathering for Christmas that year was reduced to Dick and me. In Szechwan, Bob had an infected hand. Typically, I heard about it, not from Bob, but from a friend in Shanghai who had received a letter from a friend in Chengtu. When I learned the identity of the Chengtu friend, I stopped worrying. He was famous as an inveterate purveyor of bad news. Time proved that I was right, and Bob came home safely soon after the new year of 1930 had begun.

At the end of January I had a tiffin for members of my college fraternity; a dozen of us celebrated Founders' Day of Kappa Alpha Theta with as good a lunch as my Boy could produce. The next month I had the flu and was laid up in bed for some days. Then, one day, I hemmed three towels, read over three hundred pages, wrote a long letter and two book reviews, played Parcheesi with Dick, and had some bedside visitors. So I felt that I might as well get up.

In April I had a terrible fall on our stairs. Fortunately, I was wearing my heavy fur coat. After resting a few moments, I went on to a Chinese meal with some YW secretaries. When I got to the restaurant I began to feel faint, and even hot tea did not help. So I crept down the stairs and went home in our car. A friend came to spend the night, and the doctor came and ordered bed rest. For days I lay flat as a flounder, cross and suffering. Dick did everything he could for me. Bob was away again, for he had taken Dr. and Mrs. David Yui to Szechwan. This was the first time that a general secretary of the YMCA National Committee had visited Szechwan. Bob had encouraged and arranged their trip, so it was right that he accompany them.

When I was just able to get about from my injury, I had a telephone call one morning from a man in the business office of the American Methodist Mission. He had received a telegram from Chengtu asking him to pay for a piano which I was to purchase and send west by a man in the Baptist Mission. Then I discovered that the man was leaving Shanghai the next day.

And, in true Shanghai fashion, it was pouring rain. I had to find someone to go with me to hear the tone of the instrument, and then it had to be re-tuned to international pitch. Finally, there were the details of packing, customs clearance, insurance, and obtaining the bill of lading so that it could accompany the piano. My next outside task was to purchase two thousand dollars worth of lingerie for friends in America who wanted to sell it at a hospital benefit. It was rather fun spending such a sum of money so delightfully.

We had arranged to rent a house at Tsingtao for the month of August. In mid-July, with our steamer tickets bought, we had a wire from the owners that it would not be convenient for them to let us have the house. It had been a very hot summer in Shanghai, and we were greatly disappointed. Furthermore, we had to forfeit money on our steamer tickets. The owners were upset that we felt they should pay us that amount, but they did send a check. It was too late to make other plans, so we stayed on in Shanghai. I had recently been elected corresponding secretary of the American Women's Club. That included editing the club yearbook. So most of the hot days of our holiday month, which Bob had expected to spend with Dick and me in Tsingtao, were devoted to typing lists of names and all the other details of publication.

With autumn, Bob was away again, and we had a succession of house guests. In November some of us went to the airfield to meet an English aviatrix, The Honorable Mrs. Bruce, who was making a record-breaking trip, all alone in an open cockpit plane, from London to Tokyo. I found it difficult to imagine such a long flight in so tiny a plane—it was so small that she almost seemed to be riding on the back of some large bird. We women of the Joint Committee entertained her at tiffin. I had expected to find her eager for publicity and excitement; she turned out to be a person of poise, character, and courage, who acted as though she had not done anything unusual.

On his trip to Szechwan, Bob had taken Professor Robertson of the YMCA Lecture Bureau.[1] It was possible, by that time, to travel between Chungking and Chengtu by motor vehicle.[2] Because Professor Robertson had a good deal of equipment, they were traveling by truck. While Bob was standing in the back of the truck trying to improve the placement of some of the boxes, an apprentice driver suddenly let in the clutch, causing the truck suddenly to lurch forward. Bob fell backward out of the truck and landed flat on his back. He had a great deal of pain. When he could be examined by doctors in Chengtu, they decided that he had probably cracked a couple of ribs.

Christmas was shadowed by tragedy. The chairman of the YMCA Na-

1. This was C. H. Robertson, who had become famous for the originality and dramatic clarity of his popular lectures on science. He was, I expect, one of the models for John Hersey's composite central figure in *The Call*.

2. The road surveyed about 1922 by our Hungarian friend, Ferry Shaffer, had finally been completed (chapter 38, note 5).

tional Committee, Mr. S. C. Chu, was kidnapped as he was leaving his home on the morning of the twenty-third. He had a bodyguard, and numerous shots were fired.[3] It was known that Mr. Chu was wounded. On Christmas Eve he was found, close to death, on a remote street. Although he was rushed to a hospital, it was impossible to save his life.

The funeral, on the last day of 1930, was like no other that I have ever seen. Hundreds of people were there. The large Chinese coffin was in the middle of the large hall. Mr. Chu's body, laid out on a light bamboo cot and covered with a gorgeous red satin embroidered pall, was carried down the stairs into the room. In life, he was a tall, striking-looking man with clear-cut features. In death, his face was like one carved of ivory. The body was placed in the coffin and packed around with small rolls of aromatic herbs. The casket was then sealed with ceremony. Then came the service, conducted according to the Christian procedure, but affecting beyond the ordinary.

The manner of his going, the sadness of knowing that so good a man had been struck down in a craven way while he had been going about his own affairs, the feeling of insecurity that seemed to gather about our thoughts of life, cast a spell on every person in that assembly. Chinese gentlemen in middle life, older people, youths, all had the look of inarticulate suffering that we seldom see in mass expression.

Early in 1931 the question of home leave appeared on the horizon. Normally, we would be due that spring. But, by this time, money was tight: Bob felt that we should offer to remain in China another year.[4] I was not much in favor of this: Jack was graduating from Oberlin, and Dick was due to go to America to start college. In addition, I was tired of our always being the ones whose furlough was postponed for some reasons connected with the welfare of our organization. It was twenty-six years that spring since we had been appointed to China. We had had only two home leaves, and my health had never been really robust. However, it was decided that we would remain in China.

The next thing to give us pause was the sale of the house that we rented. The new owners wanted a much higher rent, beyond what we could ask the Y to pay in hard times. With Dick soon to be leaving, and Bob away so much

3. Even the police of the foreign areas of Shanghai were unable to stop these occasional kidnappings for ransom of wealthy Chinese or members of their families. Employment as bodyguards was one line of work in which White Russians were favored.

4. Writing so soon after the event, Grace apparently considered it unnecessary to explain why "money was tight" in 1931. The Great Depression had started in late 1929; in 1931 the American economy was still sinking. At a time when there was a much greater need for their services, organizations dependent on contributions, like the YMCA, were struggling for their own survival. The International Committee of the YMCA had little endowment or direct income of its own; for its foreign work, it was largely dependent on funds raised by the local associations. In a time of stringency, it was the contribution to distant foreign work that got cut. The reduction in the income of the YMCA International Committee was drastic.

of the time, I felt that the thing was for us to move into an apartment. We found an attractive four-room place at one of the most convenient and fascinating street corners in Shanghai.[5] Because of the multiple intersections, the building was shaped like a flatiron, and our apartment was on the seventh floor in the nose of the flatiron.

We settled in happily, and Dick was thrilled with a secondhand motorcycle, which ate up the distance to his school each morning. One good servant was all we needed, and I reveled in a super-clean electric range and other modern equipment. Our servant was a coolie-boy, not a cook-boy, and I planned to do much of the cooking myself. The Boy was so careful of the kitchen that each night before he left, he washed the white-tiled floor on hands and knees, backing himself out of the apartment—thus leaving his realm spotless.

But it was not a restful year. Soon after we moved, word came from New York that some of the Y men were to be "demobilized" (I never could bear having that word applied to religious work!). Bob actually received one of these letters. Incredibly, an office blunder sent it to him after the New York office had already decided that he was to be kept on in China. Only the prompt despatch of a cable to the Shanghai office saved Bob the deepest sorrow. I would not minimize by one iota the devotion of every man who had served, or was serving, the YMCA in China, but I doubt if any of them was as deeply affected as Bob by thoughts of change. For one thing, he had been a longer time with the Y than any of the other men involved. And his work was truly his life.

That spring was a terrible one for him. Night after night he lay awake. When Dick was out, he walked the floor—up and down, up and down, through the length of the hall, into the bedroom, and around to the living room again—until I feared that we would have complaints from those living below. Sometimes he walked on the roof. I tried a thousand things to divert him and to change his feeling about the shame that he felt. "It is no shame to lose a position when there is no money to pay employees," I said. But he always countered that the Y was a brotherhood; he had given his life to the work; he knew only China: what could he do in America.

Although Bob stayed, the nearness of his own calamity, and the fact that many of his friends were dropped, oppressed him in a way that even I found hard to understand. His whole life had been shaken. He begged me not to tell our sons of the letter.[6] He was still devoted to the Chinese Y organization,

5. They were in the Denis Apartments where Bubbling Well Road was joined by Burkhill, Carter, and Yates roads. But these roads cannot be found in Shanghai today: all the names have been changed.
6. Grace respected his wishes. But the fact that we boys had no inkling of the true situation, and of the danger Bob was in, increased the shock when the final blow fell.

but I was amazed at the depth of his feeling about the broader situation. He had used his own money freely for the work. When the new Y building was put up in Chengtu, he gave the gymnasium. Many secretaries owed their training to his financial assistance. Few people knew of these benefactions, and he preferred to give in that quiet way. But he had relied upon the Retirement Fund for his old age. It was a terrible blow that his future income was jeopardized and his whole life threatened.

He talked over every detail of his past life, asking me where he had failed. I assured him that there was no implication of failure. The unintended slight caused him such poignant suffering that, in the end, I wished that what had happened could have been anything else. I felt almost sorry that he had ever gone to China under the Y. But I well knew that the other mission boards had also had to retrench, and that many good and worthy men and women were facing the same problems that had brought him such heart searching.

In the midst of all this, Bob made up his mind to go to America at his own expense. He would see Jack graduate; advise young Bob, who seemed to be unhappy at Berkeley; and welcome Dick when he arrived. Almost as soon as this decision was made, a cable informed us that young Bob was already on the ocean on his way to Shanghai. Having sent him no travel money, we were interested, when he arrived, in how he had financed his trip. Very calmly, he said that he had simply drawn his own funds from his bank account. Young Bob was a hard worker who always delighted to stand on his own in financial matters. He was not satisfied with college life and wanted our permission to go into aviation. I longed to keep him in China, but our own existence seemed uncertain, and we knew of no immediate opening for him. We gave our consent to the aviation venture. But, back in California, he changed his plans again and entered the College of Commerce at UC. His father gave up his intended trip to America.

Our next parting was with Dick, who left soon after his high school graduation. He had arranged to help a family of American friends from Shanghai drive across the American continent.[7] He saw a lot of his own

---

Grace used the word "demobilized." As I recall, the International Committee of the YMCA sought to make a virtue out of necessity. Its public statement was that it was carrying out what had always been its stated intent: to develop Chinese leadership and then turn the work over to it. This was a policy which Bob had always approved and supported. The issue, to him, was different. When he signed on for international work with the YMCA, John R. Mott and the leaders of the Student Volunteer Movement had asked him to make a life commitment. Bob had gladly given it, but he thought the commitment to be reciprocal.

7. The family that Dick helped drive across America was that of Richard M. Vanderburgh, director of the Mission Photo Bureau in Shanghai and perennial scoutmaster of the Shanghai troop of the Boy Scouts of America. His imagination, enthusiasm, and patience were almost beyond belief. He brought all three of us boys up through the classes of scout craft. If I were nominating people for heaven, he would be in the front rank.

country, visited Washington, D.C., and returned to California by bus.[8] That September he entered Pomona College.

It had been hard to see the other boys go, but to lose Dick was a calamity. As long as we had him, we felt that we were not bereft. It is a difficult thing to have to part from children during their most formative years; and at the time that Richard left us, we needed all the solace we could get from our own. But, by Bob's choice, Dick left without knowing the circumstances which had oppressed us so for the past several months.

We continued on as usual. Bob went to Szechwan again that autumn. I was occupied with the various activities that would have filled my life to overflowing had I permitted it. I had to hold back constantly because of the doctor's orders.[9] In September the Japanese had gone into Manchuria and, ignoring the League of Nations, had speedily set up their puppet empire of Manchukuo. Some of our friends among the Japanese club women in Shanghai were pressured into a rather amusing effort to propagandize us about the "kind" intentions of the Japanese.

Bob reached home on December 23 just in time for Christmas. Then we were surprised by a cable from New York telling us to leave for furlough as soon as possible. We had a hectic month. We were fortunate in selling our lease (and the Austrian doctor who bought it considered himself fortunate). Then we had to pack. And Bob, as always, had a long list of commissions and orders from his recent trip. As the time for the ship sailing came close, the tension with the Japanese in Shanghai increased each day. On the day we sailed, in late January [1932], Chinese friends seeing us off said they felt certain that serious trouble would begin within a few days.

8. Dick also stopped in Oberlin for our first reunion in five years.
9. Despite the doctor's orders, Grace became an active member, at about this time, of the Shanghai Short Story Club. One reduction in her activities was to resign from the Daughters of the American Revolution; but it was disagreement with some of its policies, rather than the doctor's wishes, that motivated her.

48

The Blow Falls

(1932–34)

Our Chinese friends' fears were right. By the time we reached Kobe, the Japanese had launched their attack of January 28, 1932, on the Chinese-controlled areas of Shanghai close to the International Settlement.[1] In mid-ocean we had a radiogram from Dick in California, asking if his father was on the ship. Knowing his dad's wanting to be on hand to help in all Szechwanese catastrophes, he feared that he would not have left China at such a critical hour! It was good to cable back that we were both on board.

Distressing as the news from Shanghai was, we had an important reason for feeling relief and joy. Just before we left Shanghai, we had received word from the YMCA of Scranton, Pennsylvania, that Bob's support had been taken on by that Association and would be continued until his sixtieth year, the retirement age for all Y secretaries.[2] And we had confirmation of this from the International Committee in New York. Nothing else at that time could have put such thankfulness into his heart. Over and over, he related to me the feeling that he had for the Y.

His remarks to me were painful to hear. He reminded me that he had no

1. After the Japanese seizure of Manchuria in September 1931 there had been much anti-Japanese agitation in China. The Japanese government tried to hold the Chinese government responsible for not doing better at controlling these expressions of popular feeling. After several rather minor anti-Japanese incidents in the Chinese areas of Shanghai, the Japanese decided on punitive measures. The gallant, though unsuccessful, defense by General Tsai Ting-kai's Nineteenth Route Army proved that Chinese soldiers, well led, could fight—and won China much international sympathy.

2. A younger Y secretary in Shanghai was one of the first men affected by the Depression-caused reduction in force. Returning to America at a relatively early stage, he became general secretary of the YMCA in Scranton. He had been a close friend and admirer of Bob's. Perceiving, probably more clearly than Bob and Grace, the trend of events in America and their probable effects on the Y's foreign-work budget, he thought he could save Bob by persuading his board of directors to guarantee the funding of Bob's salary.

34 *Bob in Berkeley in the spring of 1933 just before returning to China with his Y future, he thought, assured.*

ambition save to work with the Y. Late furloughs meant nothing to him; he was pleased that he had never taken time out for any long illness save the one that laid him low when he first arrived in Szechwan. He had never asked for special treatment. As a general secretary, he was willing for the other members of the staff to make summer plans and leave him to carry the burden of the less desirable months. He asked for nothing except a chance to work in China for the Y.

We were on furlough in the United States for the rest of 1932. Bob returned to China in March of 1933; I did not go back until that September. During all that time we moved around a good deal and had no settled home. Bob spent most of his time in visiting YMCAs, giving talks—and helping the International Committee raise money for its foreign work. We went first to Berkeley, where young Bob was at the university. It was good to see him and to meet his fiancée, Esta Fowle, and her parents, who lived nearby. For much of the spring, I was in Southern California, near Dick and my parents. Bob and I motored east in August. We traveled via the Redwood Highway, the Columbia River, Yellowstone National Park, and the Black Hills (Bob was eager to see Borglum's gigantic carvings on Mount Rushmore). This gave us the opportunity to visit many relatives and friends in various states. In the Chicago area I stayed (several times) with Jim and Mabelle Yard, and visited my many relatives in Independence, Iowa. Bob filled a large number of speaking engagements. Because we were in the East, we missed Bob and Esta's wedding in September.

For Christmas we were in Brookline, Massachusetts, with the Goodsells, the family of Bob's sister Lulu. From there we went to New York. Next was a heart-warming week in Scranton. We stayed with our Y friends from Shanghai. Bob talked at Rotary and other organizations, and we were made to feel that we had enthusiastic support. Our next stop was Washington, D.C. We were there, in January 1933, when Jack passed the oral examination for the State Department's Foreign Service. We also had the pleasure of meeting Colonel and Mrs. E. H. Schulz and their daughter Caroline, whom Jack was hoping to marry.

From there our car took us down through the Carolinas, with stops to visit relatives and friends. We went on to Florida, met Jack in New Orleans, and drove to the West Coast. Bob had planned this trip carefully and was very eager to take it. I hesitated to go with him for fear that I would get too tired and spoil his pleasure. He was most thoughtful and made the stages short enough for me to enjoy them. Bob loved driving and felt boundless happiness in conducting this tour around the States.

Back in California, the next order of business was to get Bob and Jack off for China. Although Jack had passed the entrance examination for the Foreign Service, he had learned that—because of the Depression and reduced appropriations—no appointments to the career service would be made for some time. He therefore decided to go to China and seek a clerical position in one of the consulates there.[3] Just before they were due to leave, in March

3. The plan was successful. In June 1933 I was appointed clerk at the consulate in Kunming (then still often called Yunnanfu) in southwest China.

1933, our newly inaugurated President Roosevelt declared a bank holiday. This meant that it was a scratch to secure enough ready cash so that they could attend to necessary shopping before they left.[4]

I did not go back to China with them. During the spring I was in Claremont, where Dick and I had a small house and enjoyed life together. The summer we spent in Berkeley, and there I was joined in September by Caroline Schulz, who went to China with me to marry Jack. When I was ready to leave, my Berkeley doctor thought I should not return to China at all. I finally got his permission by using the old argument that life in China was physically less work for the foreign housewife. Caroline and I shared a cabin on the ship and arrived in Shanghai at the end of September. Getting married might seem enough excitement for one year, but on arrival in Shanghai Caroline had to have an operation for appendicitis. The most practical plan for the young people to get together was for Jack to meet her in the French Indochina port of Haiphong and for them to be married there.[5] But it turned out that there were many obstacles to the marriage of nonresident aliens in a French colony. Bob spent days and days, with the help of an American lawyer friend, in getting the French officials to unwind the endless red tape involved.

The Y wanted Bob to become the regional secretary for Shantung. He felt that he had to leave Shanghai before Caroline was ready to start south to meet Jack. So he went ahead, and I followed as soon as I had seen Caroline off on a ship for Haiphong. I had a terrible time leaving Shanghai, on November 4, because my ship was not at the wharf where I had been told it would be—but across the Whangpoo River at a dock in Pootung. I, and my friends seeing me off, found out just in time to hire a motor launch to catch the boat.

Shantung was an entirely new venture for us. We had spent several summer months at Iltis Huk, the beach resort just outside Tsingtao. But our contacts were all with the summer holiday crowd, most of them—like us—from Shanghai. The Y wanted a man for regional work there. And they held out hopes to Bob that he still might now and then be able to go west. It seemed that some of the people in New York could not understand how Bob could function adequately as a regional secretary for Szechwan while living, not within his region, but far away in Shanghai. Of course an important part of his work was to provide a continuing link between Shanghai and Szechwan. But these matters were not always clear to offices halfway around the world.

4. The most important item of the "necessary shopping" was to pay for our steamship tickets (checks were not being accepted). One of Bob's elder brothers, who was a jeweler in Berkeley, was able, finally, to help us.

5. It was a three-day trip by train from Haiphong to Kunming—not to be thought of, in those days, for a young unwed couple to make alone.

When we first went to China we had resolved never to stick at any appointment. Now the Y wanted a regional man in Shantung, and we were glad to go.[6]

The first plan had been for us to go to Tsinan and occupy a YMCA residence there. But Bob had been traveling all through his region since he had reached China that April. He had concluded that he was needed more as a resident of Tsingtao. Incidentally, it would also be better for me to be there in the summers. He was glad, therefore, when his appointment was altered and we were told to go to Tsingtao. We were eagerly looking forward to having our home set up there.

In Tsingtao we were welcomed by the Chinese staff of the Y. Within a month we had found a house, unpacked our goods, and settled in quite nicely. There was a lovely view of the hills and sea from our windows. The only drawback was that I felt the cold of the floors, but Bob did not feel that we should incur the additional cost of renting a house with a furnace. He wanted to keep our rent lower than the amount brought in by the rental of the Y house in Tsinan. Most of the time we were comfortable with a stove-like heater which substituted for a furnace.

Christmas passed. In January 1934 Bob went to Shanghai to attend a Y conference. He wrote me that more men were being dropped by the New York office, but we had had a letter saying that we were to be kept on. My health was not good that winter, and my new Tsingtao doctor (a German) had ordered me to spend one day a week in bed. On January 29 I was in bed when a packet of letters arrived. I opened Bob's first. He had been "demobilized." This seemed an especially cruel blow; but I did not know then how cruel it was.

It was a broken-hearted letter. He asked me what to do. He was lacking a few months of being fifty-five. He knew there was no hope of a post in Y work in America, where even young men were being let go because of lack of funds. Should we stay in China, or what could we do? I sent word back at once that he should remain in Shanghai and try to secure some work there. I knew he could never carry it through to go home from his beloved China after being "turned off," as he phrased it.

His reputation and his friendships were more valuable than Bob realized. Within a few days, he was approached by friends on the staff of the China International Famine Relief Commission (CIFRC). The Commission wished to open an office in Shanghai to raise money from Chinese for its annual budget and reserves. Bob had always been successful at persuading Chinese to contribute to the Y, so they thought he would be a good man for this position. He came back to Tsingtao on February 11. A few hours before he was

---

6. A regional secretary was being assigned to Shantung because the several YMCAs there were by this time without a single American secretary.

due, a telegram had arrived, telling him to come right on to Peking as he was wanted there at the headquarters of the CIFRC for a conference. When I saw him and realized how bravely he was keeping up under this new change, it almost broke me up completely. I felt that I could not bear to let him go off alone. When I told him that I wanted to go with him, he agreed.

Two days later we both left for Peking. On the train, Bob made a remark that has come back to me many times since: "I thought I had given you certainty when I brought you to China. Now I know I have nothing of that kind to offer you." His heart seemed crushed by the turn things had taken. I kept telling him that it was not his fault, that these things were not of the fault of any individual, but of the times and of the Depression. He never could view these matters as I did. We looked for some letter of explanation from the New York office: none came. Later, we heard from Scranton that our support was still being carried by the Association there: this only made the wound in Bob's heart the deeper. All we could do was to try to forget; but after so many years it is not an easy thing to change one's life plan. And I knew the blow was largely my fault because my health had not permitted us to remain in Szechwan.

We spent a fortnight in Peking and then came back to Tsingtao. The new work meant that we must return to Shanghai. In many ways I welcomed that. We started to pack the very day that we arrived back. Tsingtao women had been most cordial, and I was just beginning to entertain some of them when everything had to be canceled for the trip to Peking. Now it was all haste for departure.

In Shanghai we rented a small furnished flat while we hunted a more permanent location. Caroline, Jack's wife from Kunming, was with us that summer. When a suitable apartment was found, she helped me move and get settled. It was a modern building, and we enjoyed its comforts and excellent location. Soon we had swung back into the busy life of Shanghai again.[7] Bob found his work agreeable and challenging. He was touched by the friendliness of all his old companions.[8] A young Chinese friend who had worked with Bob in the Y decided to leave the Y in order to join him in the Famine Relief Commission.[9]

7. Grace was soon asked to let her name be put up for president of the American Women's Club. She declined. She did go on the executive committee of the Joint Committee of Women's Organizations, but resigned after a few months. She was having more trouble, again, with her health. And she no longer had a car.

8. They were still a part of the, by then very much reduced, YMCA community. Bob kept up his regular participation in the weekly Y prayer meetings—which also served as a social gathering.

9. Grace was referring to Mr. C. H. Lowe (Lou Chuan-hua). After many adversities, Mr. Lowe ended his working career as librarian of Chinese books at the University of California at Santa Cruz.

But as the months passed I realized more and more how deeply Bob had been hurt by the fact that he had never had any letter of explanation as to his "demobilization." In the summer of 1934, he had letters from the YMCA at the University of California, where they still considered him their China representative, asking why he had not sent them his usual Y letter. He was obliged to write and inform them that he was no longer under the Y in China. The fact that he, not the New York office, was the one to impart this news to his university association was hard for him to take. He never, no matter how much one could say, seemed to get away from the belief that he must have been considered unworthy.[10]

10. One of the most unhappy aspects of a situation like that of the Y in China was Who stays? Who gets fired? Only a small nucleus could be retained. Those kept on tended to be either top executives or men with a strong public personality. Bob no longer had an executive position. And he was not really a public person. He worked most effectively with small groups and always avoided the center of the stage (in group photographs he would always be found in the back row or at one side). He excelled in personal contacts, in patient, nonconfrontational leadership. These were qualities that the Chinese he worked with valued highly; but the decision was made in New York. It was not, then, a matter of being "unworthy," but rather that his quiet, self-effacing work-style was not what the New York administrators of the Y felt was needed at the time.

What then of Grace's belief that he would not have been terminated if her health had permitted them to remain in Szechwan? There is no way of knowing; but my guess is that Grace may have been right. If Bob had been able to stay in Szechwan, he would have been on his home ground as the founder and kingpin of the two active, well-established Associations in Chengtu and Chungking. His prestige and friendships would have been important considerations. But he had gradually been moved away from Szechwan and direct involvement there. The local Associations had gotten along in early days without a regional secretary; the position, then, could be seen as nonessential. Living so far from his region made it also appear—in New York—that it could be dispensed with. The final step that weakened his position was for him to be cut off entirely from Szechwan and sent away to a wholly new region, Shantung, where he had no roots and no local support.

49

Bob Leaves Us
(1935)

In November 1934 young Bob and his wife, Esta, came from America and stayed with us. I had a bad time with ulcerated teeth that winter. Six had to be extracted, and I was laid up in bed a good deal. As soon as I was able to be around, I noticed that Bob was losing flesh and did not seem in his accustomed good health. We all thought that he was not well. As usual, he made light of it; but he did tell us that he had been to the doctor. We attended to his diet and tried to do all we could for him. In July young Bob and Esta went to Macao, where Bob had work with an engineering construction company building a new waterworks. Almost as soon as they left, we welcomed Dick, who had just graduated from Pomona.

That spring two events occurred which should have affected Bob more than they did. One of the men from the New York headquarters of the International Committee was in Shanghai and told Bob that his separation from the Y would not be long. It was the intention of the Committee to take him back. One would have thought that this would be great good news to Bob. He was glad, because he felt he was irrevocably bound to the Chinese Y. Also, he hoped to regain his retirement benefits. But now he was doubtful about the administration of the Retirement Fund, which he felt was being administered in the interest of the New York office rather than to protect the interests of the employees. He was approaching fifty-six and should be working for the Y if he was going to be able to receive a pension. He could receive no assurances whether he would continue to be eligible. But he believed that some such arrangement must be within the power of the International Committee, if it wished to do so.[1]

---

1. Grace was writing soon after the events, while the wounds were still fresh. To her, the important fact was that the Y had "fired" Bob. The situation, I think, was a bit more complicated.
   The original decision to terminate Bob (in January 1934) was taken in New York. It may have

Bob was humble, but he felt that he had done a man's work in the Y. He said many times to me that he could not bear to think of any other man suffering as he had because of the financial effects of the Depression. Now, he did not want to work with the organization of his long allegiance any longer than was absolutely necessary. And he told me that if he was taken back, he planned to ask for retirement at the earliest possible moment. In his mind, he was still a secretary in good standing, and his budget for foreign work was still being raised by the Scranton Association. He had been dismissed by cable for no reason save that the International Committee wished to use his salary and allowances elsewhere. When he protested against this treatment, he was told by the New York office that he had nothing to say in the matter.[2] The result of all this, he said, was that he could never be at peace again in the Y. He stood for a higher idealism than he had found in the organization.

The other event of moment to our family was a financial crash in Shanghai, which carried away all our savings for our years in China. This made strangely little impression on Bob.[3] I never heard him rail against his losses,

---

been influenced in part by the impression Bob made during his home leave in 1932–33. What the International Committee wanted at the time was a strong, effective speaker to help their failing efforts to raise funds. This was not Bob's forte. No matter how strongly he believed in the cause, he was not very good at convincing strange American audiences that they should give money to Y work in China when their own needs at home were so close and so apparent.

After the termination became known in China, there was a critical reaction there. Bob was well known (in China, if not in New York), and he was a senior secretary with almost thirty years of service. After Bob had joined the Famine Relief Commission, the executives of the Y in China persuaded New York to accept a different formula. It was decided that Bob had "been granted a two years' leave of absence for special service in establishing and directing the Shanghai Office of the China International Famine Relief Commission." The general assumption, however, was that the two-year term might be longer—depending on whether the financial situation of the International Committee improved. And there were legal and technical uncertainties about how this "loaned out" status might affect Bob's rights in the YMCA retirement fund.

2. "Nothing to say in the matter" probably refers to the fact that the central organization had to have the final word in important personnel decisions. If enough local Associations adopted individual secretaries and demanded that they be retained, the International Committee would lose effective control over its program and personnel.

3. Grace's brevity about the Shanghai financial crash may have been because the events were recent. But it was probably also a particularly painful subject to dwell on.

Shanghai's prosperity during and just after World War I encouraged a local American businessman, Frank J. Raven, to organize the American-Oriental Bank. Mr. Raven married the daughter of a well-known American missionary family. He was active in the American community church and supported the appropriate good causes. His small, friendly bank was glad to have the (usually small) accounts of missionaries. They responded eagerly. Many of them put their money in the American-Oriental Bank, and some of the business agents of various missions entrusted it with their missions' operating funds. Through the 1920s business tended to be good in Shanghai. Mr. Raven's bank grew, and he started several affiliated enterprises: realty, finance, and investments.

Soon after Grace and Bob moved to Chungking in 1921, Mr. Raven visited Chungking to establish a branch of his bank. He was a fellow Californian (UC 1899). Bob and Grace became friendly with him and with several of the men who came to work for the bank in Chungking. An especially warm friendship was formed, as we know, between Grace and Hugo Sandor. Later, in Shanghai, Grace was a close friend of Mrs. Raven's. It was natural for Bob and Grace to bank

or blame any persons concerned. He blamed his own judgment, which he had always said was not that of a businessman; his interests had been elsewhere, and he had left investments to those who managed them. He did frequently say that he had made a mistake in not building a house in Shanghai as he had wanted to do. And he often mentioned that because of these losses, it was, all the more, "a time when he should have been in the Y" (because the Y would have provided some security for old age).

In July he was taking half days off in lieu of a vacation. Having worked for the Famine Relief Commission only about fifteen months, he felt that he could not take a full vacation. He went to his office every morning and came home many afternoons. At home he did not do much but sit about. Looking back now, I can see that he felt more ill than he acknowledged.

In early July there was the good news of the birth, in Kunming, of our granddaughter Virginia. Bob spoke frequently of how happy he was to have another little Virginia in the family and of how he wanted to see the child. It was not until he had to go to bed in August that he gave way at all. He was worried about the work in his office and sent Dick down as a volunteer to try to help out. Day by day, in spite of the doctors, his strength declined. The doctors came often. Other doctors were brought in for consultation. Everything possible was done.

Our Y friends were so used to knowing Bob as a strong, athletic man that they could not believe he would not recover. But I knew that the spring of

---

with the Raven bank. And Bob, who did not pretend to be a businessman but trusted his friends, invested his outside income (from the ranch land he had inherited from his father) in stock and other offerings of the Raven companies.

By 1933 Shanghai was feeling some effects of, but seemed to be weathering, the worldwide depression. Then it suffered a totally unexpected blow. The political clout of two American senators from Nevada strong-armed the Congress into passing the Silver Purchase Act, and President Roosevelt into signing it (he needed the senators' support for New Deal legislation). The benefit to the few remaining silver producers in Nevada was minor (there was no hope of reviving the boom days of the Comstock Lode). But the effect in countries, principally China, on a silver standard was catastrophic. By greatly raising the price of silver, it caused sudden deflation, credit contraction, and severe slump. China was quickly forced to give up her historic silver standard.

This blow, on top of the depression, was too much for many Shanghai enterprises. The American-Oriental Bank, and the affiliated Raven companies, failed and went into bankruptcy. Depositors in the bank eventually received about one-third on their deposits, but the investments were all lost. Unfortunately, it was later found that in the attempt to save the companies there had been some legal improprieties. Thus, as Grace says, she and Bob lost all their savings. (Caroline and I also had our checking account in the American-Oriental Bank. Fortunately, it was small.)

But the situation for Bob was even more bleak. To finance the lumber business and other enterprises of Liu Pei-yun (see chapter 46, note 4), Bob had borrowed money from a Chinese bank. By 1935 this debt amounted to about five times Bob's annual salary—and was growing at one percent a month. So Bob was worse than penniless. Knowing none of these details at the time, I had been much surprised, before Bob's illness, to receive a letter asking if I could loan him a thousand dollars. He offered no explanation, but I knew the situation must indeed be dire—and was glad I had the money to send.

There was no blame or responsibility ascribed to Hugo. That friendship continued.

his life was broken. When the doctors told me that he could not live, I took the news as I knew he would want me to take it.[4] There was no time those days for tears. We cared constantly for our sick man at home. He knew that he was often in a half-coma and asked that visitors not be taken in to see him. There were continual callers; some old friends, especially Chinese, were surprised and disappointed at not being able to see and visit with him.

The Y men in Shanghai made a vigorous effort to have Bob reinstated in full standing so that medical costs could be paid, and so that I would receive a pension. Papers were signed, but he was skeptical of their effect. He told me not to expect anything from it all, but I always assured him that he was "back in the Y." Actually, we were assured that pension rights would be restored as of October 1 of that year.[5]

We kept ourselves busy in this way for the last few weeks. The doctors had asked me not to tell him that he could not live. Bob, I believe, thought that, because of my health, the doctors had not told me of his true condition. Neither of us, therefore, ever spoke of death. Finally, on September 11, I sent a telegram to Jack at Kunming. When I told Bob, he said at once, "I shall not see him. It takes too long for him to come." But the next day I was able to tell him, "Jack is flying and will soon be here." As it happened, he arrived that very day, even sooner than we had thought possible.[6] Jack was a great comfort to his father, and a support for me. In a few days Bob arrived from Macao. I was indeed fortunate to have my three sons with me in those hard days.

Friends constantly sent flowers to Bob, and he was always pleased and surprised. Many times he said that he had never sent flowers when people were ill: why should anyone send them to him? He was anxious to have thanks sent; I made it my business those days to answer every note and inquiry that came. Finally the letters began to come from those far away, and it was hard to read them—but such things have to be done. I was glad that I could occupy my mind in such ways, for life seemed to be closing around me. When we had talked, long before, of old age or death, Bob had always assured me that he would be with me to care for me. I think he assumed, since I had been far from well at various times, that I would surely go first.

4. The doctor's diagnosis was "cirrhosis of the liver," but he told Grace that Bob's case could be considered "similar to cancer."

5. As I understand it, when the leaders of the China Y learned that Bob was dying, they asked the International Committee in New York to return him to active duty (he was technically on a leave of absence). This was to clarify Grace's pension situation. The best that New York felt able to arrange was October 1. Many of the men in Shanghai helped in these endeavors, especially Eugene Barnett.

6. The quick flight was possible because a plane of the China National Aviation Corporation was in Kunming to check out terrain and facilities in preparation for opening regular service. The plane was just preparing to return to Shanghai and they gave me a lift. My first impression when I saw Bob was the surprised realization that this inveterate competitor had given up and had no wish to go on living.

All I could say was that I wanted to go with him. Death, after all, is not the hardest thing; life can easily be far more difficult.

There is no need to recount the anguish of days in watching the slow starvation of a loved one. Little by little, his strength failed. When he could no longer shave, he apologized to me. When he could no longer bathe, he was unhappy. He hated being a trouble to anyone, but he did want to stay in his own home. The doctors agreed to this, and I am glad that the presence of the three sons made it possible. With them and two excellent man-servants, we were fixed for nurses and helpers.

Bob slipped away in a deep coma one Sunday evening, somewhat as our little Virginia had gone. I had hoped that he would rouse and know us at the last, but there was no sign of that—simply a deeper sleep and then the ceasing of his breath. The date was September 29, 1935.[7]

Years before, we had talked of death and I knew his wishes. He desired no funeral. We arranged only a small memorial service, held by the kindness of the Chinese YMCA in their new building in the French Concession. Brief remarks were made by several old friends from different circles of his associates: Szechwan, the YMCA, California, the Masons, and the Famine Relief Commission. His body was cremated and left in the undertaker's vault until I would be able to carry the ashes to our grave in Chungking.

The tributes that poured in to me were heartfelt and touching. In his quiet way Bob had influenced many people. His lovely spirit made itself known in a myriad of kindly acts, often unknown save to the recipients. Szechwan friends arranged memorials there, and I later received a bound volume of the addresses. One friend wrote of Bob as "your splendid, energetic, vital husband." Those words seemed well chosen. Another, a Canadian who had known us when we first went to West China, wrote: "We express our gratitude for his friendship and the stimulus of his stirring and courageous life. It was a great thing to have known him in those early years when, so full of vigor, laughter, goodwill, and great aims, he had all Chengtu from lowly coolie to highest officials for his friends, and when he, as no other, helped to set high standards for rulers and people." One of his Chinese associates spoke of him as one who had Chinese characteristics. This referred to his tolerance and willingness to see another's position. Often he felt that compromise was better than arbitrary action.

---

7. Bob died thirty hours before he would have been returned to active duty—and Grace made eligible for a pension. Some time later, the International Committee, through the active efforts of Mr. Barnett, did approve a pension for Grace, but smaller than she would have received had Bob lived to October 1 (my recollection is that it was US$50 per month).

50

Starting Anew
(1935–37)

There were a thousand things to attend to. One of the first was to find a smaller and more affordable apartment. This was quickly done, and Jack was able to help me move before he left for the long trip back to Kunming. While he was in Shanghai, Jack had received his long-awaited appointment to the career Foreign Service. He was assigned to the embassy in Peking to study Chinese. Bob had already gone back to his job in Macao. The next event was that Dick, who was staying with me in Shanghai, received an appointment as clerk at the American consulate at Foochow.

One November day Caroline arrived and laid my sweet little granddaughter in my arms. She and the baby had been able to come by air, and it seemed like a miracle to hear of the speed and safety of their trip.[1] Jack came the long way, by Haiphong and Hong Kong, to bring their luggage and household goods. He arrived in a few days, and they were off to Peking by train. Dick soon left for Foochow, and I was alone in the apartment over Christmas.

These very hard weeks after Bob's death seemed harder than I could have endured without my friends. I was still worried over my finances. If Bob had lived into October, I would have been eligible for a pension. As it was, I was not to receive anything. There were also some complications about the New York office's handling of some of the insurance matters. Mr. Robert E. Lewis

---

1. Air service—by the Chinese company in which Pan-American was a partner—had just been extended to Kunming. The first day's flight was from Kunming to Chungking in a Ford trimotor. Caroline and the baby stayed overnight with the McCurdys, old friends of Grace and Bob's Chungking days. The second day was from Chungking to Hankow in a four-passenger Loening amphibian (Caroline remembers that one of the plane doors was tied shut with string). The plane actually flew through the gorges. For the third day's flight to Shanghai, the plane was a Stinson.

gave me a great deal of help, and progress was made in solving some of these problems.[2]

In Foochow Dick had a pleasant apartment and asked me to join him. I hurried my departure from Shanghai in late December when I learned that Dick had pneumonia. By the time I reached him, just after New Year of 1936, he was recovering from the pneumonia but had new symptoms which finally required an emergency operation for appendicitis. While I was on my way to his hospital, I was thrown from a ricksha when the puller lost control going down a hill. So when Dick was being operated on, we were lying in separate hospitals. Fortunately, I had no serious injury. But the operation to remove Dick's appendix revealed that he had intestinal tuberculosis.

The doctors said that Dick would have to stop work so that he could have complete rest for at least six months or a year. And they urged that this rest be in a better climate than hot and damp Foochow. But how and where were we to go! Travel cost and medical and living expenses in America would be a problem. Jack and Caroline had a comfortable house in Peking, and the Peking Union Medical College was the best in China—and perhaps as good as could be found anywhere. They offered us a friendly roof. We stayed several days in Shanghai with Eugene and Bertha Barnett, who had already been like brother and sister during Bob's illness and death.

Jack came and helped us travel to Peking by train. After a month at the P.U.M.C. hospital, Dick had made good progress, and the doctors urged us to find a way for him to live in the hills outside Peking. Jack found a very suitable house at Patachu in the Western Hills, about ten miles outside the city. He sublet his city house, bought a car, and found that one of his Chinese teachers was willing to make the trip from the city each day by bus.[3] So we all—five, including the baby, Virginia—spent six delightful months looking off our hillside terrace onto a peaceful countryside—which only a year later was to be the scene of the hostilities that started the 1937 Sino-Japanese War. We had a capable Chinese male nurse for Dick, who cooperated so well with his treatment that he gained sixty pounds.

At the end of the six months, the P.U.M.C. doctors were pleased with Dick's recovery. He was to continue rest, but it was agreed that we could move back into the city (welcome news because it was now October and the

2. Mr. Lewis was one of the two Y secretaries who met Grace and Bob when they arrived at Shanghai in 1905. Even though Bob did not qualify for a pension, his widow did receive several death-benefit payments from the YMCA. In addition there was Y group insurance and several personal insurance policies. The Chinese bank, which over many years had already received interest payments exceeding the original loan, accepted a final lump sum payment of about one half the outstanding debt. The balance of the insurance and other funds was put into a ten-year annuity for Grace. She outlived that term, but by that time she had a modest inheritance from her father.

3. It was Grace who paid for the car. When we left Peking, the car was sold for what it cost, and Grace received her money back.

hill bungalow was not built for Peking's cold winters). When I had settled Dick with Jack and Caroline in the city, I felt that I was finally free to carry out one important unfinished mission: to take Bob's ashes back to Chungking.

From Peking I traveled by train to Shanghai, and then by steamer up the old familiar route to Chungking. When I arrived there, Chinese friends wanted to have a ceremonious laying away of the ashes. I knew that Bob would not have approved. I did not even wish to set a time very long ahead, since the weather was apt to be wet, and nothing is more dismal than to gather around a grave in the rain. One bright day I told the few Chinese and foreign friends who were to go with me that we would meet at the grave of our little Virginia at three that afternoon.

One friend at the mission near the cemetery had had a considerable layer of earth taken off the grave, which is enclosed by a stone coping. Another old friend from the Canadian Mission had unsealed the casket containing the ashes. I sat on the stone coping and poured the ashes slowly onto the earth. The ashes were beautiful, silvery grey, tangible rather than impalpable. With my bare hands I spread them about on the brown loam. The fresh earth from the grave lay there ready to be put back. But the men of our group carried the first layer in their hands and laid it over the ashes until none could be seen. I said a few words trying to express how deeply my husband loved Szechwan and its people, and how, when I first stood by that grave, we had no friends in the province. The Canadian friend offered a short and beautiful prayer, and the American friend spoke to the Chinese of our feeling regarding cremation—which they do not favor.[4] The waiting attendant soon replaced all the earth on the mound. By the kindness of a friend, we left a sheaf of bright chrysanthemums to cheer the bareness of the newly turned sod.

I had done what Bob desired, and I was thankful that strength had been given me to do it. A new stone, with the two names of Virginia and Bob, was soon set up. I like to think that now the grave lies among friends. As long as friends remain there, someone will care for the spot.[5]

After a pleasant stay in Chungking, I flew on to Chengtu. Here I spent

4. Since the establishment of the People's Republic, the official policy has been to encourage cremation—in order to reduce the use of valuable farm land for graves. Many Chinese, however, still prefer burial.

5. When Grace lay ill, shortly before her death, she charged me to place her ashes with Bob's in the Chungking grave. At that time, in 1954, there was no way for Americans to travel to China. We carried the ashes with us for sixteen years. In 1970 Nixon—who in McCarthy days had been loud in his attacks on State Department men for the "loss of China"—was president. There seemed even less hope of carrying out her wish. Our son Bob and I scattered her ashes on a high and distant peak in California's Sierra Nevada. As Grace would have liked, it was a spot with a magnificent view. The very next year, thanks to the same President Nixon, the door to China was opened for Americans, and I was able to return to Chungking. But there would have been no point in having the ashes with me. After foreigners had to leave China in 1949, there had been no one to "care for the spot." The grave and cemetery had disappeared (see chapter 6, note 3).

more than two months and met scores of old friends. It was especially good to renew contacts with Chinese we had known but not seen for many years. One day I visited our old Chinese house, which we had remodeled so many years before. It had since been sold to Chinese owners and had now reverted to being a wholly Chinese establishment.

There were many good changes in Chengtu. The West China Union University, whose beginnings we had watched, was inspiring with its busy students, many of them women, and its progressive and well-planned curricula. Electricity, roads, motor cars, and radios were common, though Chengtu as yet is not quite as far along as Chungking in adapting these new things to its needs.[6]

Because unusually low water on the Yangtze had stopped ship traffic between Chungking and Ichang, I stayed in Chengtu until late February of 1937. The flight from Chungking to Chengtu had been exciting because we accomplished in one hour what used to take ten days of strenuous travel by sedan chair. We had flown low, so all the details of the earth below were constantly and clearly visible. The pilot—the same who had flown Jack from Kunming to Shanghai in 1935—kept me informed about what we were seeing. There was too much of interest for me to sit back and relax in my comfortable seat.

On the return trip from Chengtu to Chungking, I enjoyed the new and magnificent thrill of entering an ethereal realm. We flew mostly above clouds and into the eye of the morning. Surely, as we flew above the earth's cloud covering, John on Patmos never saw more of the glories of Heaven than lay near us to the south. We beheld huge turrets and towers of creamy clouds massed where they caught the brightness of the rising sun. Opalescent colors lit the snowy peaks as the golden light poured through the vast spaces of Heaven, while below lay a fleecy cloud mantle covering everything mundane. Just as I began to wonder how we could find our port or even make a landing, our pilot guided the plane down through a rift in the clouds. We were above the Yangtze only a few miles from Chungking.

Low water kept me in Chungking much longer than I had planned. I did not reach Shanghai until early May. Then I went on by rail to Peking, stopping for a few days in Nanking—which I had not visited since we lived there briefly in 1912. Finally, it was a joy to be back in Peking with Jack's family and Dick, and to be able to welcome the precious little grandson, a new Bob Service, who had been born in February while I was in Chengtu.

6. Grace's diary mentions another change in Chengtu: rickshas had replaced sedan chairs. One effect was to make it much easier for Grace to get around and visit her old friends.

Epilogue

When one looks back over life, the effect is far different from what one imagined it would be when looking forward from one's youth. The idealism of the twenties gives way to sober realities, until in the fifties one begins to think back over the happenings of the past, viewing them in a new light. This is especially true when death has come into the circle of our lighted hearth and taken away the central figure.

Knowing my husband's love for and devotion to the Y, I had encouraged him to remain in it. My health was the stumbling block on which his career broke. I knew he should have stayed in West China, but I could not live there. I became the unconscious cause of all his sorrows of heart during his last years. It takes time and many sleepless nights to erase even a part of the thoughts that arise after such a trial of the spirit.

My husband never failed me. In our long association, friendship and marriage, joy and sorrow, he was in every sense a lovely companion. And he taught me the self-discipline that I needed. What I am I owe to him. I am not at all pious, but I do think that discipline has had a definite part in my life. Without it I could not have carried on during many tight places in Szechwan. I lacked much of it when we lost the small daughter. Later, I had more, and was able to brave the houseboat trip up the Yangtze without my husband and with the two small children. It helped me endure separation. It stilled complaints. It made me strive to be worthy of my husband. It kept my nerves steady when Bob's eyes were injured. It made it possible for me to pass through the deep sadness of his death without a tear or a breakdown.

On the Western Hills, outside Peking, I began to write these pages in 1936. They were laid aside when I traveled to Szechwan in the fall of that year. Now in Claremont, California, near the snows of Old Baldy, I am bringing them to a close. There was a burden laid on my heart to write this story, for I knew my husband desired it. And the writing has cleared my feeling and given me a long look into the past. "The only use for a past is to get a future out of it."

Now I feel that I can turn my thoughts back to China again. I am still the woman my husband loved: interested in people, happy with books, fond of clothes and a good time, looking forward—not back. Fortunately, I have three sons, so there is much to brighten the future. And a confidence rises within me that I have known the worst that life can bring me. Perhaps I am wrong, but time alone can tell.

Editor's Epilogue

Grace returned briefly to America in August 1937 to escape the Japanese war on China. But, as usual, she did not escape all the shooting; her ship from North China landed her on the Bund at Shanghai on August 13, 1937, shortly before the Chinese bomb fell that killed hundreds of people at the Bund and Nanking Road. In 1938 Dick was vice-consul at the American consulate in Tsingtao. Grace returned to China and lived with him until he married Helen Gardes in August 1940. That November the State Department, concerned over developing tension with Japan, ordered the families and dependents of government personnel to return to America.

Grace went to Claremont, California. Here in Pilgrim Place, a retirement community for missionaries and Christian workers, she had a small cottage built to her plan, and settled down to a quiet life, with friends nearby, an enormous correspondence to maintain, the stimulus of a college town, and easy access to beloved books. She had learned to cope with high blood pressure and angina.

In July 1954 she suffered a severe stroke. We three sons assembled (from California, Belgium, and New York) and, as we had for our father nineteen years before, watched and cared for her around the clock. When the last son arrived, she had told the doctor (a good friend) that he was to do nothing more to prolong her life. But she was stronger than she thought: she made a partial recovery. We sons ended our vigil and had to leave. There followed several minor strokes, and then, on October 24, 1954, a final one, so sudden that none of us could reach her.

She had, however, told us, after the first stroke, of all that she wished to have done. In a box close to her desk were a large number of envelopes which she wished mailed as soon as possible after her death. They contained a poem, handsomely printed and individually signed in her firm and vigorous hand. My recollection is that there were about three hundred and fifty, to go to many countries around the world—but none, sadly, to the mainland of China.

A whisper stirred old pine-trees,
A fleeting shadow swept a wall,
Light foot-steps climbed a mountain,
A scent of honey over all . . .
Long echoes filled a river canyon,
A glacier moved its inch today.
Did you, by chance, look out the window,
Or did a lady pass your way?
Today's the day appointed!
So while the world rolls smoothly on,
I've slipped away to Bob, my husband,
No one should grieve that I am gone.

Members of the Service Family

Robert Roy Service = Grace Josephine Boggs
(Bob)   (Grace)

b. June 4, 1879   b. Nov. 26, 1879
Weston, Mich.   Independence, Iowa
m. June 30, 1904
Independence, Iowa
d. Sept. 29, 1935   d. Oct. 24, 1954
Shanghai, China   Claremont, Calif.

Virginia

b. Aug. 26, 1905
Berkeley, Calif.
d. Mar. 4, 1906
Fengtu, China

John Stewart = Caroline Edward Schulz
(Jack)   (Caroline)

b. Aug. 3, 1909
Chengtu, China
m. Nov. 9 and 13, 1933

Robert Kennedy = Esta Jane Fowle
(Young Bob)   (Esta)

b. May 8, 1911
Chengtu, China
m. Sept. 15, 1932
d. May 28, 1964
Chester, Calif.

Richard Montgomery = Helen Margaret Gardes
(Dick)   (Helen)

b. Apr. 21, 1914
Chengtu, China
m. Aug. 24, 1940

Glossary

amah	from Portuguese *ama;* the word used by foreigners in China for the Chinese nurses of their children
bandeng	a narrow wooden bench
baozi	a small ball of chopped meat and vegetables folded in a thin sheet of dough and usually steamed
beizi	a wooden frame for carrying loads on one's back
bund	a causeway or embankment, usually along a river front
catty	a weight called *jin* in China, approximately one and one-third pounds avoirdupois
chit	(1) a note or letter; (2) an I.O.U.
compound	a walled enclosure within which foreigners reside
cumshaw	a gratuity, tip, present
dzo	a hybrid between a yak and a domestic cow
fengshui	the art of adapting the residences of the living to harmonize with the cosmic currents of the local environment
gai	street; the Szechwan pronunciation of *jie*
godown	a warehouse
guanxi	relationship, personal connections (usually implying those that can be turned to one's personal advantage)
hsien	an administrative district subordinate to a province and usually translated as county
kang	In Szechwan, a wooden couch or divan; in north China, a flue-heated sleeping platform of brick
koré	the Japanese name for a large, telescoping rattan hamper
li	an approximate measure of distance, usually about one-third of a mile
mafu	a horse coolie, groom

matou	a place where boats tie up or discharge cargo; a boat landing or jetty
miao	a temple, shrine
peng	mat shed or awning; the mat roof on a boat
pugai	a quilt or comforter of wadded cotton; the usual Chinese bedding
sampan	any small Chinese boat
squeeze	the commission taken by Chinese servants on purchases for their employers
sze	a Buddhist monastery
tael	a word from Hindi used by foreigners in China for an ounce (Chinese, *liang*) of silver.
tiffin	the midday meal, lunch
tingzi	a pavilion, an open-sided structure
tusi	a hereditary headman or chief used by the Chinese for governing ethnic minority groups in west China
wang	a king; a hereditary leader of an ethnic minority used by the Chinese for indirect rule of his people (usually more important than a *tusi*)
wuban	a Chinese boat or junk of intermediate size, commonly used on Yangtze tributaries such as the Min
yamen	the residence, official and private, of a magistrate or any high official; any important government office
yuan	dollar (the word means "round"); the monetary unit of China
zhaizi	a walled or stockaded mountain stronghold

Designer:	Barbara Jellow
Compositor:	G & S Typesetters, Inc.
Text:	10/13 Berkeley Book
Display:	Berkeley Book
Printer:	Maple-Vail Book Mfg. Group
Binder:	Maple-Vail Book Mfg. Group

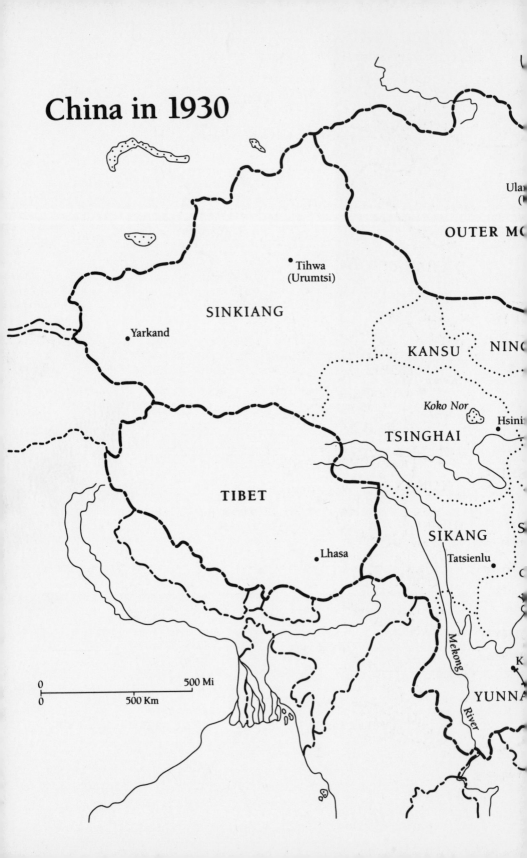

China in 1930

Tihwa
(Urumtsi)

Yarkand

SINKIANG

KANSU

NING

Koko Nor

Hsini

TSINGHAI

OUTER MO

Ula
(

TIBET

Lhasa

SIKANG

Tatsienlu

Mekong

River

YUNNA

K

S

C

0 ——————— 500 Mi
0 ——————— 500 Km